# COLLINS PHOTOGRAPHIC KEY TO THE TREES
## OF BRITAIN AND NORTHERN EUROPE

# A Guide to Identification by Leaves and Needles

# COLLINS PHOTOGRAPHIC KEY TO THE TREES
## OF BRITAIN AND NORTHERN EUROPE

# A Guide to Identification by Leaves and Needles

**Jean-Denis Godet**

Translated by Clive King and Helen M. Stevenson

Additional material by Alan Mitchell

Collins
8 Grafton Street, London W.1

First published in Great Britain in 1988 by
William Collins Sons & Co. Ltd
London · Glasgow · Sydney · Auckland · Toronto · Johannesburg

Typeset by Ace Filmsetting Ltd, Frome, Somerset
Printed and bound in Belgium by Brepols Fabrieken N.V., Turnhout

To My Mother

# Contents

# Foreword

My first book, 'Trees of Europe in Four Seasons', demonstrates the wide variety of important trees in Central Europe. My next two books, the pocket guides to 'Buds and Twigs' and 'Flowers', were identification guides to indigenous and introduced species of trees and shrubs from autumn through to early summer. This, my fourth book, is a guide for the summer season. As with the other two pocket guides, particular attention is paid to the introduction. In the second section, the most important species are described, in each of the four seasons, and an indication is given of their significance in and influence on our culture.

For the purposes of identification, only those features are described which are visible to the naked eye or with the use of a good magnifying glass. To ensure that the fine details do not cause the reader to lose sight of the general picture of the tree, a short description of the tree in question is highlighted against a grey background in the 'key' section.

In the main section of the book, 260 species and varieties are described in detail with full colour illustration. An English and a Latin index at the end of the book allow the user to locate references to species known by name.

I should like to thank, for all their guidance and stimulation over the one and a half years during which I wrote this book, all the staff at the Botanic Gardens in Basel, Bern, Geneva, St Gallen and Zurich. I hope this book will be a reliable guide and a good companion to all who use it and that it will play its part in preventing the beauty and variety of our trees from being forgotten, for they play a vital role in the formation of our countryside's character.

Bern, December 1986                                                      Jean-Denis Godet

# 1. Introduction

## 1.1. Preface

In order to identify a tree or shrub during the summertime, when flowers and fruits are often absent, it is only the leaves which are of any practical value. It is important to describe these with precision at the beginning so that mistakes may be avoided at a later stage. With this in mind, only those characters have been used here which can be seen with the naked eye or with the aid of a good lens.

## 1.2. Structure of leaves

### 1.2.1. Leaf-forms and age of leaves

A leaf consists of a flat, usually green blade (lamina) and often a shaft-like stalk (Fig. 1–3). The point where the leaf is attached to the shoot is called the leaf-base, and in some species this may be enlarged.

In Butcher's Broom (*Ruscus aculeatus*) the typical leaf-blade is absent, but in its place is a flattened, leaf-like lateral shoot known as a cladode (Fig. 5). At the base of the cladode are modified leaves, reduced to small scales. Flowers arise from a point on the upper surface of the cladode, in the axil of a small, scale-like bract (Fig. 6).

Where the leaves are without stalks (sessile) the base of the blade is attached directly to the shoot (Fig. 4).

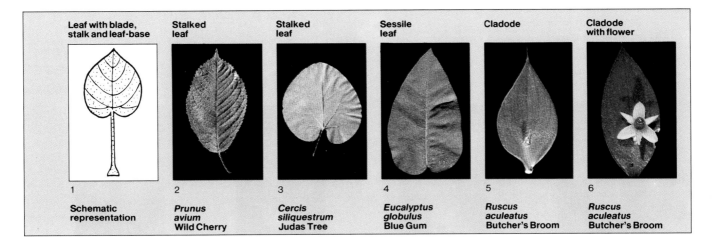

| Leaf with blade, stalk and leaf-base | Stalked leaf | Stalked leaf | Sessile leaf | Cladode | Cladode with flower |
|---|---|---|---|---|---|
| 1 | 2 | 3 | 4 | 5 | 6 |
| Schematic representation | *Prunus avium* Wild Cherry | *Cercis siliquestrum* Judas Tree | *Eucalyptus globulus* Blue Gum | *Ruscus aculeatus* Butcher's Broom | *Ruscus aculeatus* Butcher's Broom |

**Three kinds of leaves may be found on the shoot:**

| 1. Scale leaves | Simple leaves which, in woody plants, are usually found only as coverings for the winter buds. |
|---|---|
| 2. Foliage leaves | Most of the leaves on a shoot are of this kind. |
| 3. Bracts | Simple leaves, situated above the foliage leaves, especially frequent in the floral region. Since they are often coloured, they frequently resemble petals. |

**The life-span of a leaf can vary considerably:**

| One year | Leaves are green in the summer, and are shed at the end of the first foliage period. |
|---|---|
| Winter-green | Old leaves are only shed when the new ones appear. |
| Two years | Leaves are shed at the end of the second foliage period. |
| Evergreen | These leaves remain throughout several periods of growth, and as they do not all fall off at the same time, the tree or shrub appears evergreen. |

## 1.2.2. Shape of the leaf-blade

### Oblong leaf-blades

In oblong leaf-blades the ends may be obtuse or acute (Fig. 7–10):

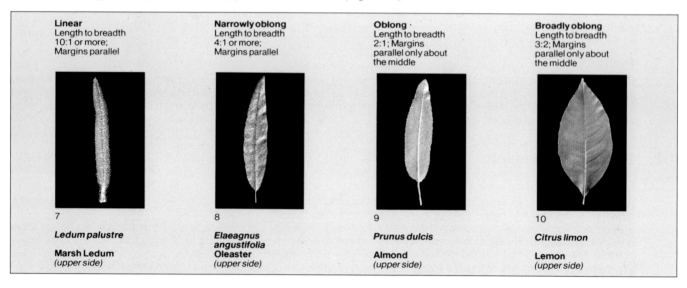

**Linear**
Length to breadth 10:1 or more; Margins parallel

**Narrowly oblong**
Length to breadth 4:1 or more; Margins parallel

**Oblong ·**
Length to breadth 2:1; Margins parallel only about the middle

**Broadly oblong**
Length to breadth 3:2; Margins parallel only about the middle

7

*Ledum palustre*
**Marsh Ledum**
*(upper side)*

8

*Elaeagnus angustifolia*
Oleaster
*(upper side)*

9

*Prunus dulcis*
Almond
*(upper side)*

10

*Citrus limon*
Lemon
*(upper side)*

### Lanceolate leaf-blades

The greatest breadth is always below the middle of the blade. The base is usually rounded and the tip usually pointed (Fig. 11–14):

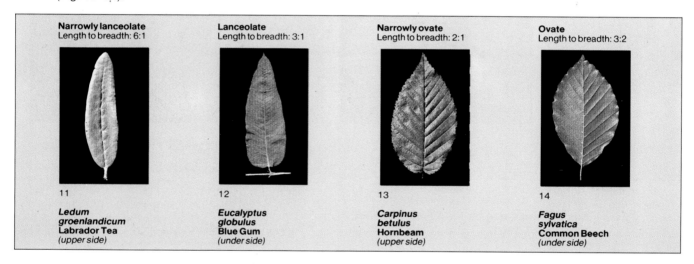

**Narrowly lanceolate**
Length to breadth: 6:1

**Lanceolate**
Length to breadth: 3:1

**Narrowly ovate**
Length to breadth: 2:1

**Ovate**
Length to breadth: 3:2

11

*Ledum groenlandicum*
Labrador Tea
*(upper side)*

12

*Eucalyptus globulus*
Blue Gum
*(under side)*

13

*Carpinus betulus*
Hornbeam
*(upper side)*

14

*Fagus sylvatica*
Common Beech
*(under side)*

### Elliptic and orbicular leaf-blades

The greatest breadth is always at the middle of the blade. The ends are usually pointed (Fig. 15–18):

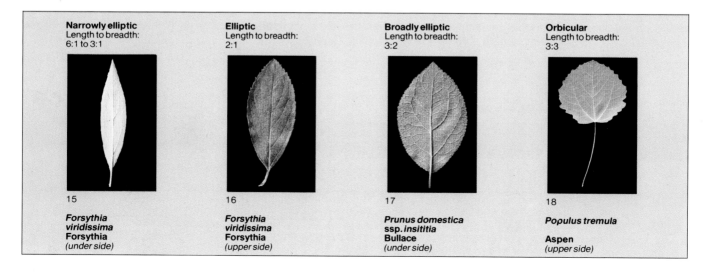

**Narrowly elliptic**
Length to breadth: 6:1 to 3:1

**Elliptic**
Length to breadth: 2:1

**Broadly elliptic**
Length to breadth: 3:2

**Orbicular**
Length to breadth: 3:3

15

*Forsythia viridissima*
Forsythia
*(under side)*

16

*Forsythia viridissima*
Forsythia
*(upper side)*

17

*Prunus domestica ssp. insititia*
Bullace
*(under side)*

18

*Populus tremula*
Aspen
*(upper side)*

## Obovate leaf-blades

The greatest breadth is above the middle of the blade. The base is usually pointed, but the tip is rounded (Fig. 19–22):

**Narrowly oblanceolate**
Length to breadth: 3:1

19

*Myrica gale*
**Bog Myrtle**
*(upper side)*

**Narrowly obovate**
Length to breadth: 2:1

20

*Salix aurita*
**Eared Willow**
*(under side)*

**Obovate**
Length to breadth: 3:2

21

*Salix caprea*
**Goat Willow**
*(upper side)*

**Broadly obovate**
Length to breadth: 6:5

22

*Alnus glutinosa*
**Common Alder**
*(upper side)*

## Other kinds of leaf-blades

**Heart-shaped**

23

*Tilia cordata*
**Small-leaved Lime**
*(upper side)*

**Quadrangular**

24

*Liriodendron tulipifera*
**Tulip Tree**
*(upper side)*

**Triangular**

25

*Populus nigra*
**Black Poplar**
*(upper side)*

**Kidney-shaped**

26

*Cercis siliquastrum*
**Judas Tree**
*(upper side)*

### 1.2.3. Venation (veining)

**Parallel-veined leaves***

The numerous, equally strongly formed veins run parallel or in a curve from the base of the blade to its tip. There is no prominent midrib. This kind of venation is found mainly in monocotyledonous plants (Fig. 27).

* The example shown is of a cladode.

27

*Ruscus aculeatus*
**Butcher's Broom**

**Net-veined leaves (pinnately veined)**

A characteristic feature of the leaves of most dicotyledonous plants is the prominent midrib, from which lateral veins run to the leaf-margin. These are connected to each other by smaller veins forming a close network (Fig. 28–40).

28

*Salix caprea*
**Goat Willow**
*(under side)*

**Net-veined leaves**

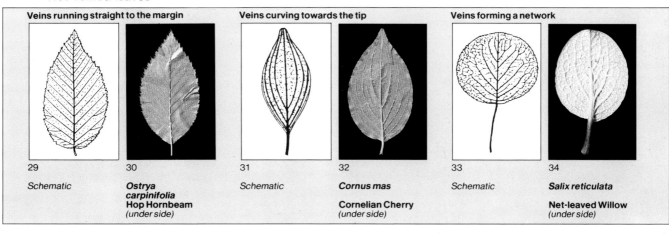

**Veins running straight to the margin**

29

*Schematic*

30

*Ostrya carpinifolia*
**Hop Hornbeam**
*(under side)*

**Veins curving towards the tip**

31

*Schematic*

32

*Cornus mas*
**Cornelian Cherry**
*(under side)*

**Veins forming a network**

33

*Schematic*

34

*Salix reticulata*
**Net-leaved Willow**
*(under side)*

Veins curving towards the margin | Veins palmately arranged | Veins unequally pinnate

35 Schematic

36 **Rhamnus alpinus Alpine Buckthorn** (under side)

37 Schematic

38 **Acer pseudoplatanus Sycamore** (under side)

39 Schematic

40 **Populus x canadensis Hybrid Black Poplar** (under side)

Digitate or palmate venation represents a modification of pinnate venation. It occurs when several prominent lateral veins radiate from the base of the leaf-blade like the fingers of a hand (Fig. 37, 38).

## 1.2.4. Margin of the leaf-blade (leaf-margin)

The margin of the leaf (or leaflet in the case of compound leaves) may be entire or it may be indented in various ways as follows (Fig. 41–56):

**Entire**
The margin has no indentations and is completely smooth.

41 *Magnolia x soulangeana* Magnolia

**Serrate**
The sharp teeth resemble those of a saw, and usually point towards the tip of the leaf.

42 *Sambucus racemosa* Red-berried Elder

**Crenate-serrate**
The teeth also point forward, but have curved edges and are bluntly pointed.

43 *Populus trichocarpa* Western Balsam Poplar

**Doubly serrate**
The large teeth are themselves toothed; all the teeth are sharply pointed.

44 *Betula pendula* Silver Birch

**Doubly serrate and dentate**
The indentations (sinuses) between the large and small pointed teeth may be narrow or broad

45 *Sorbus mougeotii* Mougeot's Whitebeam

**Dentate**
Between the sharply pointed teeth are shallow or rounded sinuses

46 *Vitis vinifera* Grape-vine

**Sinuately dentate**
Between the sharply pointed (and here glandular) teeth are rounded sinuses

47 *Salix fragilis* Crack Willow

**Sinuate**
Both the teeth and sinuses are rounded

48 *Populus tremula* Aspen

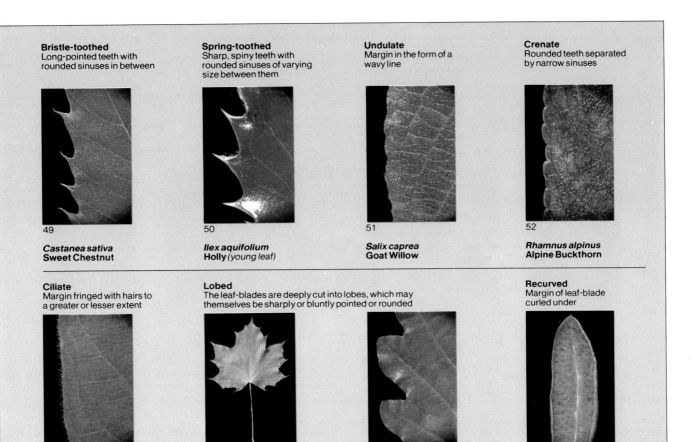

**Bristle-toothed**
Long-pointed teeth with rounded sinuses in between

49

*Castanea sativa*
**Sweet Chestnut**

**Spring-toothed**
Sharp, spiny teeth with rounded sinuses of varying size between them

50

*Ilex aquifolium*
**Holly** (young leaf)

**Undulate**
Margin in the form of a wavy line

51

*Salix caprea*
**Goat Willow**

**Crenate**
Rounded teeth separated by narrow sinuses

52

*Rhamnus alpinus*
**Alpine Buckthorn**

**Ciliate**
Margin fringed with hairs to a greater or lesser extent

53

*Lonicera alpigena*
**Alpine Honeysuckle**

**Lobed**
The leaf-blades are deeply cut into lobes, which may themselves be sharply or bluntly pointed or rounded

54

*Acer platanoides*
**Norway Maple**

55

*Quercus pubescens*
**Downy Oak**

**Recurved**
Margin of leaf-blade curled under

56

*Ledum palustre*
**Marsh Ledum**

## 1.2.5. Apex of blade (= tip of leaf)

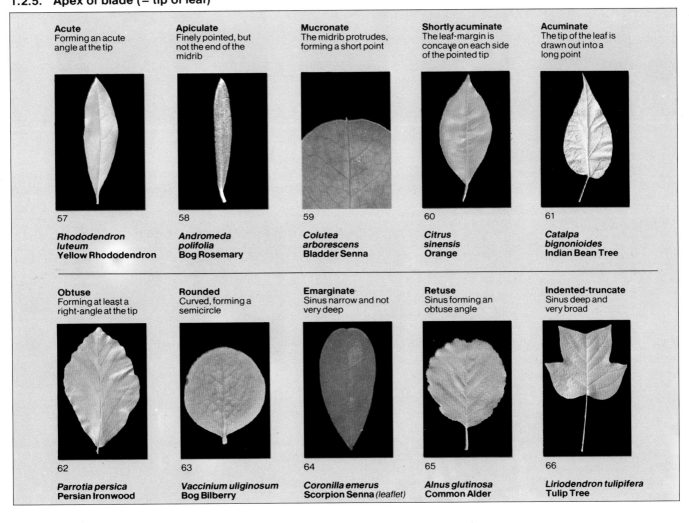

**Acute**
Forming an acute angle at the tip

57

*Rhododendron luteum*
**Yellow Rhododendron**

**Apiculate**
Finely pointed, but not the end of the midrib

58

*Andromeda polifolia*
**Bog Rosemary**

**Mucronate**
The midrib protrudes, forming a short point

59

*Colutea arborescens*
**Bladder Senna**

**Shortly acuminate**
The leaf-margin is concave on each side of the pointed tip

60

*Citrus sinensis*
**Orange**

**Acuminate**
The tip of the leaf is drawn out into a long point

61

*Catalpa bignonioides*
**Indian Bean Tree**

**Obtuse**
Forming at least a right-angle at the tip

62

*Parrotia persica*
**Persian Ironwood**

**Rounded**
Curved, forming a semicircle

63

*Vaccinium uliginosum*
**Bog Bilberry**

**Emarginate**
Sinus narrow and not very deep

64

*Coronilla emerus*
**Scorpion Senna** (leaflet)

**Retuse**
Sinus forming an obtuse angle

65

*Alnus glutinosa*
**Common Alder**

**Indented-truncate**
Sinus deep and very broad

66

*Liriodendron tulipifera*
**Tulip Tree**

## 1.2.6. Base of blade

In stalked leaves the base of the blade is immediately above the leaf-stalk. In sessile leaves it forms the lower end of the leaf and is joined directly to the shoot. It can be formed in the following ways (Fig. 67–76):

**Cuneate (wedge-shaped)**
Leaf-margins straight, forming an acute angle at the base

67

*Prunus domestica*
Plum

**Obtuse**
Leaf-margins forming a right angle or an obtuse angle at the base

68

*Populus nigra var. italica*
Lombardy Poplar

**Truncate**
Appearing as if cut off at right-angles to the midrib

69

*Populus alba*
White Poplar

**Rounded**
Leaf-margins of the 2 halves of the blade forming a semicircle

70

*Prunus lusitanica*
Portugal Laurel

**Asymmetrical**
The 2 halves of the blade unequal in size

71

*Ulmus laevis*
Fluttering Elm

**Oblique**
One side of the blade extends further down than the other, though both are about the same size

72

*Tilia cordata*
Small-leaved Lime

**Heart-shaped**
Semicircular at the base with a deep sinus

73

*Tilia cordata*
Small-leaved Lime

**Auriculate**
Each half of the blade is extended at the base into a small lobe

74

*Quercus robur*
Common Oak

**Connate**
The leaves lying opposite each other are joined together

75

*Lonicera caprifolium*
Perfoliate Honeysuckle

**Decurrent**
(in needles)
The lower part of the leaf is prolonged down the shoot

76

*Taxus baccata*
Yew

## 1.2.7. Leaf-stalk (petiole)

Between the leaf-base and the blade is the leaf-stalk, a cross-section of which may be circular or laterally compressed. It may sometimes also be grooved. If its formation is suppressed the leaves are described as sessile.

## 1.2.8. Leaf-base

The leaf-base is the part of the leaf that is joined to the shoot. In sessile leaves it is the base of the blade, while in stalked leaves it is the lower part of the leaf-stalk.

In many species of plants the leaf-base is not clearly distinguished from the leaf-stalk. There may be only a slight broadening at the base (Fig. 77) or even none at all. By contrast, plants in the Rosaceae and other families develop large stipules which last throughout the entire life of the leaves (Fig. 78). In the

77

*Lonicera caerulea*
Blue Honeysuckle

78

*Rosa canina*
Dog Rose

79

*Robinia pseudoacacia*
False Acacia

case of the Hornbeam, Hazel, Lime, Poplar, amongst others, they quickly fall and are therefore of no use as a character in identification. In the Robinia the stipules are converted into spines (Fig. 79).

### 1.2.9. Hairiness of leaves

Both shoots and leaves may be hairy. They may be described as sparsely hairy, slightly hairy, densely hairy, silky, felted, or woolly according to the degree of hairiness. Often only certain parts of an organ have hairs, as for example the veins of a leaf, the axils of the veins (axillary tufts) or one of the surfaces. It is not uncommon for these hairs to disappear during the growth period.

### 1.2.10. Form of leaves

Leaves may be classified as simple (undivided) or compound (Fig. 80-92):

#### Simple leaves

The leaf-stalk bears only a single blade. If it is absent, the base of the blade is joined directly on to the shoot. The following forms can be distinguished according to the depth of the sinuses between the lobes:

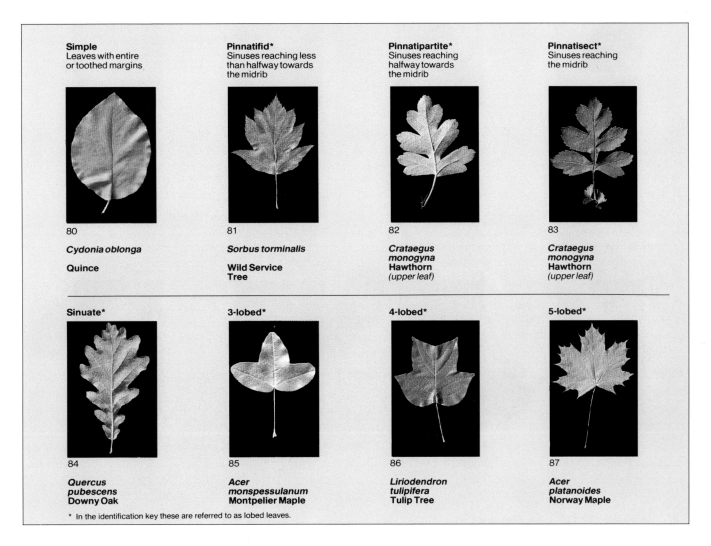

**Simple**
Leaves with entire or toothed margins

80

*Cydonia oblonga*

Quince

**Pinnatifid\***
Sinuses reaching less than halfway towards the midrib

81

*Sorbus torminalis*

Wild Service Tree

**Pinnatipartite\***
Sinuses reaching halfway towards the midrib

82

*Crataegus monogyna*
Hawthorn
(upper leaf)

**Pinnatisect\***
Sinuses reaching the midrib

83

*Crataegus monogyna*
Hawthorn
(upper leaf)

**Sinuate\***

84

*Quercus pubescens*
Downy Oak

**3-lobed\***

85

*Acer monspessulanum*
Montpelier Maple

**4-lobed\***

86

*Liriodendron tulipifera*
Tulip Tree

**5-lobed\***

87

*Acer platanoides*
Norway Maple

\* In the identification key these are referred to as lobed leaves.

#### Compound Leaves:

Each leaf is composed of 2 or more blades (leaflets) attached to a common axis – the leaf-stalk:

**Imparipinnate**

88

*Robinia pseudoacacia*
False Acacia

**Paripinnate**

89

*Ceratonia siliqua*
Carob

**Trifoliate**

90

*Laburnum anagyroides*
Laburnum

**Trifoliate** stalked terminal leaflet

91

*Acer griseum*
Paper-bark
Maple

**Palmate**

92

*Aesculus hippocastanum*
Horse Chestnut

### 1.2.11. Heterophylly

In certain trees and shrubs leaves on the same plant may have a different shape according to their position on the shoot. If the leaves at the same level are different in size, the condition is known as anisophylly (Fig. 93–100):

**Example 1: Sycamore**
Cotyledons, juvenile and adult leaves show a difference in shape.

**Example 2: Common Ash**

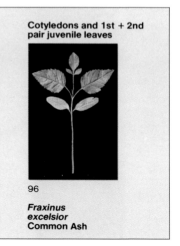

Cotyledons and 1st pair of juvenile leaves

93

*Acer pseudoplatanus* Sycamore

1st and 2nd pair of juvenile leaves

94

*Acer pseudoplatanus* Sycamore

Adult leaf

95

*Acer pseudoplatanus* Sycamore

Cotyledons and 1st + 2nd pair juvenile leaves

96

*Fraxinus excelsior* Common Ash

**Example 3: Blue Gum**
The juvenile leaves are very different from the adult leaves.

**Example 4: Mulberry**
Adult leaves can show considerable variation in the shape of the leaf-blade.

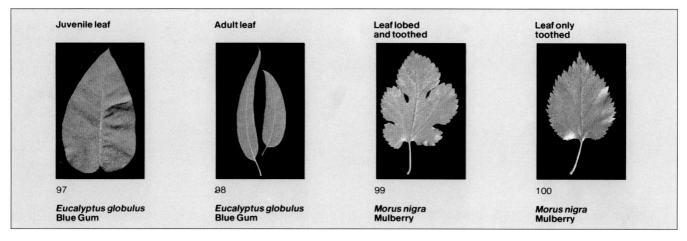

Juvenile leaf

97

*Eucalyptus globulus* Blue Gum

Adult leaf

98

*Eucalyptus globulus* Blue Gum

Leaf lobed and toothed

99

*Morus nigra* Mulberry

Leaf only toothed

100

*Morus nigra* Mulberry

### 1.3. Arrangement of leaves on the shoot

Leaves may be arranged on the shoot in the following ways (Fig. 101–112):

**Alternate**
Leaves arranged alternately on the shoot

**In 2 rows**
Leaves arranged alternately or opposite on the shoot, but with their blades lying in the same plane

**Fascicled**
Several or many leaves clustered at each node

101
*Schematic*

102
**Prunus avium** Wild Cherry

103
*Schematic*

104
**Fagus sylvatica** Common Beech

105
*Schematic*

106
**Crataegus** Hawthorn

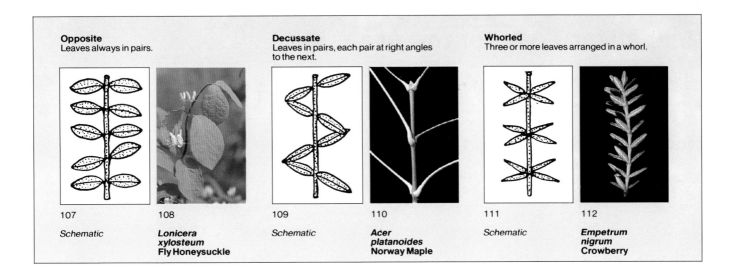

**Opposite**
Leaves always in pairs.

**Decussate**
Leaves in pairs, each pair at right angles to the next.

**Whorled**
Three or more leaves arranged in a whorl.

107

*Schematic*

108

***Lonicera
xylosteum*
Fly Honeysuckle**

109

*Schematic*

110

***Acer
platanoides*
Norway Maple**

111

*Schematic*

112

***Empetrum
nigrum*
Crowberry**

## 1.4. Structure of needle-like leaves

Leaves of conifers differ considerably in their external and internal structure from those of deciduous trees. In addition to flat leaves with an upper and an under side, there are needles which are triangular, square or circular in cross-section. Most needles are evergreen, stout, and xeromorphic. Some exceptions with deciduous needles mentioned in this book are Larches, Swamp Cypress and Dawn Redwood.

The scale-like or needle-like leaves may be in a spiral, opposite, whorled or imbricate (overlapping) arrangement.

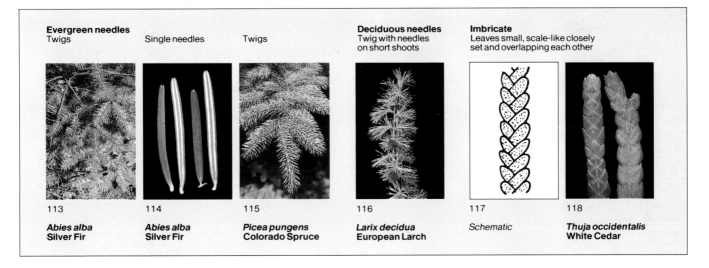

**Evergreen needles**
Twigs

Single needles

Twigs

**Deciduous needles**
Twig with needles on short shoots

**Imbricate**
Leaves small, scale-like closely set and overlapping each other

113

***Abies alba*
Silver Fir**

114

***Abies alba*
Silver Fir**

115

***Picea pungens*
Colorado Spruce**

116

***Larix decidua*
European Larch**

117

*Schematic*

118

***Thuja occidentalis*
White Cedar**

## 1.5. Fan-shaped leaves with forked veins

The Maidenhair Tree (Fig. 119–122) is the sole surviving representative of the genus *Ginkgo*, which appeared in an abundance of forms from the Triassic to the Cretaceous period and had a world-wide distribution. It was cultivated in China and Japan, and in this way was protected from extinction. Nowadays it is planted throughout the world in gardens and parks. From a seedling with two cotyledons the Ginkgo grows into a branched, deciduous tree up to 40m high.

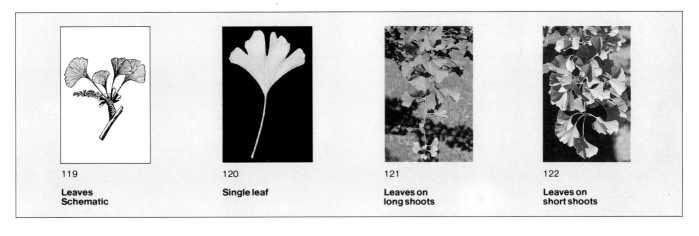

119

**Leaves
Schematic**

120

**Single leaf**

121

**Leaves on
long shoots**

122

**Leaves on
short shoots**

# 2. Familiar Trees of the Area

## Norway Maple

*Acer platanoides* L.

Erable plane
Spitzahorn

Pages 85, 150, 151

The Norway Maple is a medium-sized tree, growing to a height of 20-30m. Its trunk is slim and straight, with a diameter of 1m. Its crown is domed, densely leaved, and, in the case of free-standing trees, becomes increasingly spherical with age. Its growth is very similar to that of the oak, but its twigs are glabrous, shiny brown, thinner and attenuate and, when damaged, emit a white, milky juice. This juice is only soluble in ether or pure alcohol, is highly acidic, and is easily dyed. It grows much more rapidly than the Sycamore Maple (Scots Plane), but does not reach such a great height. Even at their oldest (and the Norway Maple may live for up to 200 years), the two species of maple are easily distinguishable.

Inside the brown-black, longitudinally cracked, non-scaly bark, which is sometimes used for tanning, is to be found a yellow to pinky white, fairly hard, elastic, resistant, finely grained, sticky, easily split wood, which will preserve well only under dry conditions. One cubic metre of seasoned, chopped wood weighs 500-650kg. Because it has a marked tendency to snap and warp, it should be dried with particular care. There is also a risk, as with all other woods, of fading. It is easily and securely held together by glue, nails and pins, and is generally held to be a good joinery timber.

It is only durable, however, if kept dry. As it is not inclined to contract or warp, it is very suitable for making veneers for knives, light-coloured living room and bedroom furniture, chairs, tables, kitchen utensils, table tops and musical instruments. It sharpens well to a point, so can be used for skewers, but it in inferior to the wood of the Sycamore, which is preferred for all kitchen tools used for food.

Its buds are usually dark red to reddish brown, and smooth. Many-flowered panicles appear in April or May, a few days before, or at the same time as the leaves unfurl. The flowers may be male, female, or hybrid. All flowers have five independent greenish yellow sepals, 3-5mm in length, and five greenish yellow, roughly ovate, independent petals, 5-6mm in length. All eight anthers are smaller than the petals and lie on the outer edge of the disc.

The ovary consists of two fused carpels and develops into a schizocarp with two separate achene. The achene are flat, about 4cm long, each with very slightly curved husks, projecting more or less horizontally. They are glabrous on the inside and heavily veined.

The trees only begin to flower after 15-20 years. The Norway Maple is an excellent source of food for the Honey Bee, as it yields large quantities of flower and leaf honey.

At the end of the stalk, which may be up to 15cm long, lies the blade, which is 10-20cm long, and the same again wide. It is orbicular, reniform, or broadly ovate in outline, with 3-5, or 7 dentate lobes.

In contrast to the dark green glabrous superior surface, the inferior surface is pale green, with tufts of hair at the vein axils.

The leaves are golden yellow to scarlet in autumn and are arranged in opposing pairs along the branch.

The Norway Maple favours deep, wet to damp, calcareous soil, and thrives in humid conditions. It is, however, less demanding of light, warmth and nutrients than the Sycamore Maple. It is also less susceptible to the risks posed by long-term flooding.

It is at its best when growing not alongside the Sycamore Maple but amongst mixed lime woodland, where oaks, limes and elms predominate. Today such woods are to be found in only a few places, for example in the mountains of Southern France and in Alpine valleys, such as the Rhone. It predominates only occasionally, in patches, in the Turinmeister mixed lime woodland. Otherwise it is found interspersed amongst beech woods. It is dispersed throughout most of Europe, from the mountains of Northern Spain and the Pyrenees, through France, southern Belgium, Germany, Denmark, Norway, Sweden, Central Finland, spreading eastwards right up to the Urals. The species has been planted in the USA.

The Norway Maple was introduced to Britain in the seventeenth century. The first reference to it is in the list made in 1683 by Sutherland of plants he had moved from Holyrood Palace to reform the Royal Botanic Garden of Edinburgh. It is likely that at the time this list was compiled, Sutherland's tree was already some 20 years old.

This species is indigenous to hilly and mountainous regions. However, it has been planted very widely throughout the British Isles in gardens and parks, and also occasionally in shelterbelts and small woods – rarely as a forest tree. It has been freely used in the Salisbury Plain chalklands for landscaping and sheltering purposes. It grows equally well in the high rainfall areas of western Scotland and in the dry East Anglian brecklands. In fact, few large gardens or city parks are without it.

Thanks to its modest requirement of light, and its ability to put out shoots, it is well suited to existence within, as well as on the edge of mixed woodland of European Ash and Sycamore Maple. The rapid decomposition of its leaves encourages biological activity.

According to folklore, the maple offers protection against witches. For this reason, in Hinterpommern, it is the custom to decorate doors and inner walls with maple wood. In Mecklenberg, plugs of maple wood were driven into walls and doorsteps as a safeguard against witches.

123 Norway Maple in spring

124 Erect, many-flowered panicles

125 Male flowers, with 5 sepals and petals, 8 anthers and a disc

126 Cross-section through a male flower

127 Norway Maple in summer

128 10–20cm long, lobed leaves, arranged in opposing pairs

129 Superior leaf surface, dark green and glabrous

130 Inferior leaf surface, pale green at first, with tufts of hair in vein axils

131 Norway Maple in autumn

132 Fruit clusters

133 Schizocarp with two separate achenes

134 - Whitish, often slightly pinkish, elastic, resistant wood

135 Norway Maple in winter

136 Broad-ovoid, pointed, terminal buds dominating the side buds

137 Narrow-ovoid, lateral, wine-red, terminal buds

138 Straight, cylinder-shaped trunk with longtitudinally cracked, dark brown bark

# Sycamore

*Acer pseudoplatanus* L.

**Erable de montagne, Erable sycomore
Berg Ahorn**

Pages 87, 154, 155

In pastureland at alpine and sub-alpine levels, where the ground is wet to slightly damp, and rich in nutrients, the Sycamore develops a huge crown, which broadens out with age. In woodlands, where it grows more upwards than outwards, its slim, straight trunk bears its first branches quite a long way up its length. In mixed woodland, together with the Mountain Ash, it reaches a maximum height of 40m.

This species of maple, which, together with the Norway Spruce and the Mountain Ash, frequently occurs on the edges of a wood, is usually planted in the hill zone. They are also found in avenues, parks and forests.

The Sycamore spreads rapidly on fertile, damp soils and its seedlings arise in dense masses, soon shading out shrubs and flowers in woodland. It is extraordinarily robust in conditions too severe for most trees. It dominates in central parks of industrial cities because it could prosper when sooty fogs were frequent. It is planted for shelter on high, exposed farmlands on chalk and limestone hills and succeeds there better than any other broadleaf tree. Although its natural range is nowhere near the sea, it stands up against the salty sea-winds along our west coasts where all native trees are deformed and low.

The bark, which, on young trees, is light brown, later develops flat plates, which tend to taper at the bottom. When they eventually drop away, they expose fairly smooth indentations of reddish brown colour. As a result of this process, the trunk become multi-coloured. The trunk of an old tree will have developed a very patchy, light and dark brown patterned bark. The maximum age of a Sycamore is around 500 years. The Sycamore can yield a naturally white, top-quality wood. In order to achieve this, the bark must be removed shortly after the winter felling and the wood immediately sawn up. Immediately after this the planks are brushed clean of sawdust and stacked upright. As a result of the air movement through them the wood is evenly and gently dried. If it is necessary for the wood to be dried artificially, this should be done as soon as possible, to avoid splitting and discolouration.

Sycamore wood is thick, shiny, has no colouration, contracting only slightly, dries extremely well, and, if it is done carefully, to a dazzling white shade. One cubic metre of cut, naturally dried wood weighs 650–750kg.

It is easy to work, polish, carve, and particularly to stain. Thanks to these excellent properties it is highly valued for making furniture and veneers. Kitchen equipment, billiard cases, table tops, parquet floors and parts for musical instruments are made from this wood. In its peculiarly gnarled form, as so-called tone- or resonance wood, it is much beloved of violin makers.

The timber itself has little resistance to weather conditions. For this reason it is not very suitable as a building material. Its light-coloured medullary rays appear in cross-section as bright, shiny lines and lengthways as dark patches or stripes. The timber was used for the rollers in wool mills and grown for this purpose in Yorkshire.

Shortly before the tree blossoms, out of large, green, opposite buds, emerge the five-lobed leaves. In summer they grow up to 15–30cm long and 10–16cm across. The individual lobes are coarsely dentate, or notched, each separated from the next by a pointed sinus. In autumn they turn a golden yellow colour.

Once the leaves have appeared, dangling, grape-shaped racemes, 5–15cm long, emerge out of the many separate buds.

The five or so petals and sepals are 2–6mm long. Each of them is independent, and is at first hairy on the inner surface and glabrous on the outer. Around the inside edge of the receptacle lie 8 stamens, which can be up to 2 or 3 times the length of the petals. The superior ovary is covered with long hairs and consists of 2 fused carpels. Once flowering has finished they form two small bumps, which, during the development of the fruit, grow into large seed-wings.

The fruits – schizocarps, each with two separate achenes – are constructed in such a way that when they fall they spin earthwards with a sort of propeller-like flight. This increases the time it takes for them to reach the ground, and depending on the air currents which take them up, they are often carried quite some distance from the parent tree.

The Trojan horse (Troy: the town celebrated by Homer on the north-west point of Asia Minor) was fashioned out of maple, although not out of Sycamore Maple. The story goes that Epios, on the advice of Odysseus, and with the aid of the goddess Athena, built a wooden horse. Inside the horse the Greeks hid a troop of hand-picked heroes. The enormous wooden beast was then left standing outside the gates of Troy and the army sailed away. Heedless of the warnings of Laakoon and Cassandra, the Trojans tore down a portion of the walls and brought the horse inside the city. Typically for that age, they were convinced that this animal, being visible for miles around, would make their city sovereign over all of Asia Minor and Europe.

Under cover of night, the Greek army returned. The heroes emerged from the horse and after a short battle the town which hitherto had been unconquerable was completely destroyed.

The strong and powerful wood was greatly prized not only in the heathen age, but also by Christians in the Middle Ages. If a large tree was to be felled, it was done so bare-headed and on bended knee with votive offerings and invocations.

In certain parts of Europe the Sycamore is considered a safeguard against evil spirits. Plugs of maple wood, driven into walls and doorsteps, will ward off witches. To the same end, branches of Sycamore are piled up against doors and windows. This is also thought to act as a safeguard against lightning.

In Scotland, the Sycamore was occasionally used as the 'Dool Tree', the tree from which those unfortunates who fell foul of the laird were hanged. This would be a large tree with branches suitable for the task, and near the castle. One such tree still stands at Blairquhan in Ayrshire.

The celebrated Martyrs' Tree at Tolpuddle is a Sycamore, measuring 18m by 183cm. To this day the cost of maintaining it is met by the Trade Union Congress.

This species was unable to spread to England after the Ice Ages because it did not grow on the lowlands near the French end of the land-bridge. It has been suggested that it was brought by the Romans, but this is rather unlikely. The first trees were probably planted in Scotland after 1500. One near Edinburgh is reputed to date from the Reformation, which spanned many years around 1550.

139  Sycamore in spring

140  Dangling racemes with male and female flowers

141  Older bisexual flowers with young schizocarp; wilting stigmae

142  Older bisexual flowers with young schizocarp; stigmae and styles no longer present

143  Sycamore in summer

144  8–20cm long, lobed leaves, arranged in opposite pairs

145  Superior leaf surface, dark green and glabrous

146  Inferior leaf surface, bluish green, villous at first, later glabrous

147  Sycamore in autumn

148  Fruit clusters

149  Schizocarp with two separate achenes

150  Well-treated wood, dazzling white, compact, hard

151  Sycamore in winter

152  Newly formed stigma on pointed-ovoid terminal bud dominating side buds

153  Pointed-ovoid, often projecting yellow-green to green side buds

154  Crumbly grey bark flaking away; bare patches usually brown

23

# Horse Chestnut

*Aesculus hippocastanum* L.

Marronier d'Inde
Gemeine Rosskastanie

Pages 81, 144, 145

The Horse Chestnut grows to a maximum height of 30–35m. Its trunk is usually short, strong, woody and always has a spiral grain to the right. Its crown is broad and dome shaped, with gnarled branches and abundant foliage. Its thick leaf coverage affords a good deal of shade.

It is grown throughout the British Isles and has long been the traditional tree of village greens and rectory gardens. It occurs at woodland edges only near habitation from which it has escaped. It is frequent as a large specimen in grazed parklands and in avenues there, as well as in town and city parks. It grows equally well in all parts given good soil. Some of the biggest and finest trees are: Hurstbourne Priors Church, Hants., 36m × 213cm; West Dean House, Sussex, 26m × 197cm; The Rectory, Much Hadham, Herts., 37m × 181cm; Castle Ashby, Northants., planted 1762, 31m × 171cm, with widely layered branches; Preston House, Midlothian, 26m × 186cm; and Grays House, Dundee, 36m × 140cm.

The bark of the young tree is light grey or greyish brown and smooth. Later this turns to dark grey bark, with coarse, cracked plates. The new, young shoots are very strong, almost a finger thick, very long, light brownish in colour, with pale lenticels.

The underlying wood is nothing if not colourful – whitish yellow to pale pink, fine, soft, supple, easily chopped, with a dull sheen. One cubic metre of seasoned wood weighs 500–600kg. It is easy to handle, to carve, and chisel. Since it stains easily, it should be dried very soon after felling. Once dry, it warps and distorts very little, and is therefore excellent for making furniture. It is used for carving, and for making clogs, kitchen equipment, toys and pianos.

In April or May, palmate leaves, which will eventually grow to 10–30cm in length, emerge from very sticky, shiny red-brown buds. The stalks are long and grooved. The 5–7 leaflets are long-obovate, being at their widest in the outer third, abruptly acuminate, 8–20cm long, and irregularly serrate.

Once the bud-scales have fallen off, the erect, many-flowered panicles start to grow. They reach a length of up to 30cm and a width of 8–12cm and produce mostly bi-sexual flowers. The bell-shaped calyx has 5 lobes. The white, ovate petals, of which there are usually 4 or 5, are 10–15mm long, and curl back at the edges.

The nectaries are found in the heart-shaped base. They are yellow to begin with, turning red after pollination by the bee. The superior ovary consists of two fused carpels.

Once the stigma has been pollinated by insects and the ovules fertilised, the fruit capsules appear, each up to 6cm thick, with flexible spines. Inside the green husk lie 1–3 shiny, brownish red horse chestnuts.

The outer rind contains *saponin*, the fluorescing glucoid aesculin, tannic acid, resin, fatty oil and starch. Aesculin is able to intercept ultra-violet rays and is therefore used in sun-shields for the skin. The chestnuts themselves contain a large amount of starch, fatty oil and, above all, *saponin*.

The extract from chestnut bark strengthens the veins and accelerates the blood flow, thus preventing blood-blockages. The use of this extract is also advocated for the treatment of varicose veins (blood blockages, haemorrhoids, abscesses on the tibia). Before the Ice Age, the Horse Chestnut was indigenous throughout central Europe, and, retreating in the face of the ice, found its only refuge in a very small area of the Balkan peninsula.

The area of main concentration is centred around southern Albania, northern and central Greece, either side of the Pindus Mountains, where it is found in the lower pine zone, as well as in the mixed deciduous woodland of Epitus and at sea level.

In this region it is found together with the Common Alder, the Common Walnut, the European Ash and the Norway Maple, all trees which prefer damp soil.

A second, but important area of distribution is in Northern Bulgaria, on the north side of the Little Balkan, to the south of the town of Preslav. Whereas most Greek locations are in mountainous areas, the Bulgarian *refugium* is distinctly lower lying. Where at first the Horse Chestnut occurred only in isolated patches in wild-flower and mixed-woodland habitats above 380m, it is now dominant here, although it nevertheless abruptly yields to the Common Beech at 500m. In spite of the dense leaf canopy, there is still a good deal of undergrowth and a varied herbaceous layer.

Two main factors militated against a return to the original areas of indigenous growth. Firstly, the weight of the fruit, and secondly the extensive dry regions lying between the tree's refuge areas and central Europe, in which the Horse Chestnut is unable to compete with other species.

In 1557 the Turks introduced the Horse Chestnut to Constantinople. In 1569 it reached Italy, 1625, France and 1629, England. It did not arrive in America until the mid-nineteenth century. Many people take exception to its abundant shedding of leaves and fruit in the autumn. But what a delight it is for children to go collecting conkers. This alone should provide sufficient reason for planting the Horse Chestnut. When it is planted on the edge of a wood, though, it needs the protection of the forester as the Red Deer uses it to scratch against and the stag for rubbing the velvet from its antlers.

155  Horse Chestnut in spring

156  20–30cm long racemes, erect or projecting at an angle

157  Individual racemes; nectary yellow at first, red later

158  Two flowers; flowers often become monosexual as they mature

159  Horse Chestnut in summer

160  Leaves 10–30cm long, with 5 or 7 leaflets

161  Superior leaf surface, dark green and glabrous

162  Inferior leaf surface, pale bluish green at first, with brownish tufts in the vein axils

163  Horse Chestnut in autumn

164  Inside the prickly, green case lie 2 or 3 horse chestnuts

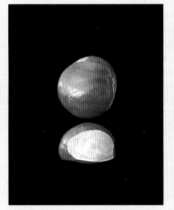

165  Shiny red-brown horse chestnuts

166  Consistently coloured whitish yellow, very fine, soft wood

167  Horse Chestnut in winter

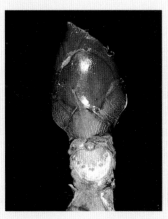

168  Broad-spherical, sticky, terminal bud

169  Pointed-ovoid side buds in opposing pairs

170  Fairly short trunk; dark brown to black bark, cracked into thin plates

25

# Common Alder

*Alnus glutinosa* (L.) Gaertn.

Aune glutineux
Schwarzerle, Roterle

Pages 13, 15, 108, 188, 189

After the first year, during which the process of growth is very slow, rapid and hearty growth takes place until around the twentieth year. But the Common Alder's fine, sparsely leaved, broadly conic crown does not develop until after some 4–5 years of growth, formed out of the narrow trunk, which grows right up to the treetop, and almost horizontal, outward-stretching branches.

If it is to reach its maximum height of 30m and maximum age of 120 years, the Common Alder needs soil which is high in humus content and rich in nutrients, deep and water-logged, or at least with a constantly available water supply; it also requires a good deal of light and moist atmosphere. Acidic, marshy or calcareous soils are not really suited to the Common Alder. However, the alder does have nodules on its roots, where nutrifying bacteria live. It can therefore grow well on very poor soils so long as they are damp, and will enrich them by its leaf-fall. The roots grow into the open water beside which the tree is so often found, as dense masses of hard, dark red cords which hold the bank firm against spates and the wash of passing boats. It coppices well and sprouts from a stump can, with the big root system of the former tree supplying them, grow 2m in a year. It grows along spring-lines in oak woods and in damp hollows or on wet slopes in high rainfall areas, away from the waterside. One in an oak wood in Kent is among the biggest few in Britain, 31m × 126cm and the biggest trunk, 170cm in diameter, is on a hillside in Wester Ross.

No alder shows any autumn colour beyond the normal dark green, then the black of decay. The seeds attract flocks of Redpolls and Siskins, often mixed, and some Goldfinches, all through the winter.

Of all the alders this is the one most often found in hilly regions, along the banks of streams and rivers, in damp marshy woods and riverside woodlands. It is frequently employed in the afforestation of wastelands. In the Alps it is found up to a height of 1300m above sea level. As the tree very readily puts out shoots, it is also planted in lower woodlands.

The young bark is greenish or greyish brown, soon turning to dark grey-brown, cracked into square plates. Underneath is to be found the light, soft, pale reddish yellow, fairly firm, non-supple but rarely splitting wood. One cubic metre of seasoned wood weighs 550kg.

The wood makes a poor firewood but one of the best charcoals, which was formerly prized for gunpowder-making. It was also the wood for making soles of clogs because it not only holds nails well near its edge, but once dried, the wood is highly durable in alternating wet and dry conditions. It was therefore also used for small timbers in canal and bridge works.

As it is very low in fat content it is easy to stain. This often used to lead to its being used as a substitute for precious woods, particularly mahogany. It keeps well underwater and, under such conditions, turns black and hardens over the years. Because of this particular property it used to be used for building ships and water-taps.

Above the leaf buds are found the female cones, which remain bare throughout the winter, and the male 'catkins'. The tree flowers in February or March, that is, long before it comes into leaf. The female flowers come in the form of inflorescences of 2–8 many-flowered, 1–2cm long, greyish green, stalked cones, arranged side by side, like grapes, or ears of corn on a hairless stem.

The male flowers, consisting of 4 stamens and 2 outer and 2 inner perigynous leaves, are found in groups of three behind the 2 small inner and 2 larger outer sprout-leaves and the axil of a bract.

By autumn the female inflorescences have developed into brown cones. The small brown nuts, consisting of a flat seed and a narrow opaque wing, fall in late autumn and winter. The cone remains on the tree long after this. It is often used for handicrafts or decoration.

After the flowering season, broad, obovate to roundish, sticky, emarginate and dentate leaves emerge out of the characteristically stalked, purplish-brown, long, alternate buds. They are 4–10cm long, and at the base of the blade they usually narrow inwards, forming a wedge shape. On their inferior surface, in the vein-axils, are whitish to rust-coloured tufts of hair.

Because the Common Alder grows on the edge of moors, and on the banks of insect-infested ponds, it should not surprise us that, particularly in centuries gone by, it was associated with evil spirits, the devil and witches. It was said that witches used alder wood to summon up storms.

The alder features in Greek mythology on a number of occasions. It is said to have grown in Kalypos's cave, as well as in that of the nymph loved by Odysseus, who detained him for 7 years. Only on the order of the gods did she release him. According to Virgil, the Heliades – the sisters of Phaeton – were changed into alders by Zeus. In Homer's Odyssey, the island of death, 'Aia', is skirted with alders belonging to the sorceress Circe. Alders also play a role in the business of fertility potions, because of their early flowering blooms.

Time after time, in Northern European folk legend, various afflictions are cast out and absorbed by the alder; for example, fever, toothache, and warts. Alders and ashes play a special role in rural superstition. During the sowing seasons, on Good Friday, people place tiny pieces of alder in their mouths, or receive the sacrament through a ring woven out of alder. This is supposed to keep sparrows away from the fields. Mice and moles are shooed away by placing chips of alder wood in all four corners of the field or barn on Good Friday.

171 Common Alder in spring

172 Male catkins, 3–12cm long, drooping; female flowers in small cones

173 Stalked, female inflorescences (= cones)

174 3 male flowers on a bract

175 Common Alder in summer

176 4–10cm long leaves arranged alternately

177 Superior leaf surface, mid- to dark green and glabrous

178 Inferior leaf surface, light green, with whitish to rust coloured tufts in the vein axils

179 Common Alder in autumn

180 7 cone-shaped fruits

181 Nuts, each with a flat seed and opaque wing

182 Yellow-white wood; discolours to yellow-red to dark red when exposed to light or air

183 Common Alder in winter

184 Narrow side buds, each stalked with 2 visible scales

185 Young bark, grey-brown to greenish brown

186 Dark brown, cracked bark on old trees, flaking away in vertical plates

# Silver Birch

***Betula pendula*** Roth, *Betula verrucosa*    **Bouleau verruqueux**
**Hängebirke, Weissbirke**    **Pages 108, 188, 189**

The Silver Birch is a graceful and charming tree which grows to a height of 20–30m. Its trunk is slender and supple, reaching a maximum diameter of 40–60cm. Its crown is at first narrow, conic, and pointed, eventually assuming a rounded, dome-like or irregular shape.

The rate of growth slows down once the tree reaches the age of 20 years. Growth in height ceases altogether after 50–60 years. It is not unusual to find birch trees over 100 years old. It used to be very common to find brooms made from their long, dangling twigs. On the lower part of the trunk the bark is bulging, cracked, dark brown to black and has small white patch-marks. Between the white patches lie large, gnarled, deeply cracked, black, diamond-shaped patches. The rest of the trunk and the branches have a smooth, silvery white to yellowish, shiny outer rind, overlain by separate grey-white cross-strips. The bark is structured in two layers. It is from the originally snow-white strips which peel off horizontally that we derive birch tar and, by a process of distillation, birch oil. The tar forms the basis of a good conserving agent for leather and wood, and is often used to make car polish. The inner part of the bark, because of its high tannin content, is often used as a tanning agent, particularly in northern European countries. The whole bark, which is almost totally waterproof, is also used as an underlay for doormats, roof coverings and balconies. Even today, many roofs in Scandinavia are covered with birch bark and sealed with a layer of tar. The North American Indians used to construct lightweight canoes and wigwams from birch bark.

Boreholes, 2–5cm deep, are made in older trees in April. Birch juice pours out of these holes and ferments to make a foamy drink known as birch wine. In 4 days, 50 tree trunks with a diameter of 40–50cm would yield around 175kg of birch juice. This alcoholic birch water was known to Albertus Magnus as early as 1240 BC.

Underneath the bark is a slightly shiny, supple, sticky wood, which is extremely difficult to chop and is a yellowish white shade, turning reddish near the medulla. It is quite difficult to distinguish the heartwood from the sapwood. One cubic metre of seasoned wood weighs 600–700kg. It must be dried slowly. There is a danger, during drying, of discolouration and the formation of irregular patches. As this wood cannot support a great deal of weight it is not very good for use in building. It is, however, popular for use in making bobbins, reels, trays, bowls, boxes and tool-handles. It is also commonly used to make plywood. Because it contains ethereal oil, birchwood oil burns well and produces a rapid heat. It is therefore a popular firewood.

Birches begin to flower after 20–30 years. Birches bear both male and female flowers. Male catkins appear in autumn at the tips of many branches. Between March and May they increase gradually in size until, several days after the leaves emerge, they are up to 10cm long. They are long and cylindrical in shape, hang downwards, but have no stalk. The female catkins are also formed in autumn and are preserved in buds until the first growth movements. They are cylindrical, stalked, 2–4cm long, covered in tiny flowers and bright green. During the flowering season they are mostly erect and project outwards; once the flowers fade they start to droop.

In very early autumn the fruit cones are already a brownish colour. The protective fruit scales enclose the light brown nuts, with their propeller-like attachments. After the fall these are carried large distances by the autumn wind.

The Silver Birch was a very early colonist in Britain but was preceded a little by the White or Downy Birch. This has no hanging shoots but a crown of confused shoots and its bark has horizontal bands and patches of grey speckling. It ranges north into Orkney and the Shetlands, beyond the Silver Birch, but is also found all over the country on damper sites, often among Silver Birch, which keeps more to drier places like sandy heaths. In the Highlands, the glens have Silver Birch along the steep, often rocky, well-drained hillsides and White Birch along the bogs and ditchsides of the valley bottom. Both will grow on clays and are in many town and city parks.

The birches coppice well and seedlings grow fast, as a pioneer species needing rapidly to overtop competitors.

Placenames derived from birch are numerous: Birchington, Kent; Bartley, Hampshire; Berkhampstead, Buckinghamshire; Much Birch, Herefordshire; Berkeley, Gloucestershire; Birkenhead, Cheshire; Birks Bridge, Lancashire; Birkhill House, Fife; and Birkhall, Aberdeenshire.

187   Silver Birch in spring

188   Dangling male catkins; female catkins erect or projecting

189   Erect female inflorescence

190   Section of a female inflorescence with yellow stigmae

191   Silver Birch in summer

192   3–7cm long leaves, arranged alternately

193   Superior leaf surface, dark green and glabrous

194   Inferior leaf surface, pale grey-green and glabrous

195   Silver Birch in autumn

196   Brown, long-stalked, fruit cones, up to 3cm long

197   Fruit scales enclosing small nuts, each with a transparent fruit wing

198   Yellowish white to reddish, fairly soft, elastic wood

199   Silver Birch in winter

200   Side buds and hibernating male catkins

201   (left) Young and (middle and right) older side buds

202   Young bark, white, smooth, peeling away in thin, horizontal strips

# Common Beech

*Fagus sylvatica* L.

Hêtre
Buche, Rotbuche

Pages 101, 178, 179

On this medium to large tree, branching starts very close to the ground where the tree stands in the open, and relatively high up the trunk where it stands in the forest. It has a straight, nearly cylindrical trunk, which reaches a height of 25–30m over a period of 120 years. The crown is narrow in young trees, but broadens out with age into a vaulted dome. Beeches over 300 years old grow as tall as 45m, with a diameter of 1.5m.

Woodland beeches have a heavily foliaged crown, which allows only a small amount of light to pass through. For this reason only very early-leafing and shade-bearing trees are able to flourish in beech forests, which are usually very dark.

The bark is grey-green, later turning to ash grey, and even in old age remains thin, smooth and silver-grey. It is rare for the beech to develop ridged bark. If trees which have grown up in a forest are abruptly transplanted into open spaces, or if a tree in a wood is suddenly exposed, the bark can suffer 'sunburn'. If the bark is over-exposed in this way it may loosen and the vascular cambium is likely to dry up.

The beech is a mature wood tree. The heartwood is differentiated from the sapwood only by its hardness and firmness, not by its colour.

The diffuse-porous wood is whitish grey to reddish yellow in colour, tough though not very supple, but even so, pretty strong, heavy (one cubic metre of seasoned wood weighs between 650kg and 800kg), contracts significantly, is resistant to pressure and preserves excellently under water.

The steaming process gives it its well-known reddish hue, but also has the disadvantage of inducing a certain amount of cracking, contracting and warping. If the drying process is carefully and slowly carried out these problems can for the most part be minimised.

The medullary rays are broad and well-spaced. The pores are not visible to the naked eye; on the other hand, the growth zones can be recognised as annual rings in the end-of-season wood, which has noticeably few pores.

If the wood is stored in damp conditions it will soon be attacked by insects and fungi.

It is easy to work, handle, stain and polish.

In the Chiltern Hills in Buckinghamshire, the trade of 'bodging' was plied until as recently as the 1950s. The bodger would fell a beech tree, saw and hew it into pieces which could be transformed on the spot into chair legs with the use of a hand-made lathe.

It is used particularly for cabinet-making and carpentry, for making chairs, tables, kitchen equipment, toys, staircases, work benches, school desks, plywood and railway sleepers (which will last for up to 40 years), for veneering, trimming and edging. It can also be processed to make plywood boards and compressed wood.

Because it produces a high degree of heat it is also very popular as a firewood. Recently it has been widely cultivated for the production of cellulose and the manufacture of artificial fibres. The quality of the wood starts to deteriorate once a 'false' heartwood starts to develop. At the same time as the leaves start to appear in May, flower buds also appear, supporting female and male inflorescences. The female ones are spherical, stalked, more or less erect, and always have two flowers. These are contained inside a slightly prickly fruitcase, the cupule, which is covered in scales at the base. The male inflorescences are also round, supported by 3–5cm-long stalks, bearing many flowers and covered in villous hairs. Each of the flowers has a 5–7 part perigone and 6–15 anthers, which protrude from the hairy flower case.

In the autumn each of the 20–25mm long fruits contains 2 reddish brown seeds, usually triangular in section, and rich in oil. These 'beech-nuts' fall from their cases until well into the autumn and are then collected and eaten by coal-tits, chaffinches, bramblings and wood-pigeons. If these animals leave nuts lying on the ground instead of eating them they contribute considerably to the propagation of the beech.

A heavy 'mast year' usually follows a hot summer in the previous year.

The buds are up to 2cm long, spike-shaped, reddish brown and pointed. They stand erect, are scaly and alternate. In May they put out stalked leaves. The blades are 5–10cm in length, elliptic or ovate in outline, very slightly cuspidate, with an entire margin tapering or rounded at the base. When young they bear soft hairs and have wavy margins.

Common Beeches favour alkaline, damp, loose, well-ventilated soil and a relatively humid atmosphere. They will avoid low-lying ground, where the soil may be water-logged. As beeches are very sensitive to winter cold, late frosts, drought and heat, they do not occur in regions with a 'continental' climate, in the far north or in hot areas with low precipitation. As well as in central Europe, where they are particularly common on plains and at mid-altitude, they are also found in the southern parts of the Scandinavian peninsula, in England, in the higher regions of Italy and at the tip of Greece. The Common Beech is widespread throughout most of the central band of Switzerland and in many valleys on the northern side of the Alps. Here it can occur as high as 1500m above sea level.

Although the Common or European Beech was not indigenous to Ancient Greece, Theophrastus refers to it by the name of 'oxya'. Roman writers knew it as 'fagus'. Macrobius Theodosius compliments the tree in noting that its wood is especially good for making sacrificial urns. The Gauls used the ashes of the beech to make soap.

As a late-comer crossing the land-bridge across the chalk ridge from France, the beech did not progress very far as a native tree, reaching probably the Usk Valley in South Wales and perhaps to the Pennines but not into Scotland. It is, however, well suited to the climate there and is planted everywhere, in extensive shelterbelts in the Southern Uplands and as a roadside and parkland tree in the Highland glens. Many of the biggest beeches are in Scotland, the tallest, 46m tall, on the Perthshire–Angus border and the biggest good bole, 220cm diameter, in Inverness-shire, and many nearly as big, especially in the Lothians.

Although traditionally a tree of the chalk hilltops, which seem so dry, the beech is a thirsty tree and thrives there only because it roots powerfully into the fissures in chalk and reaches the water which this rock holds so abundantly. It is also perfectly at home on sands and clays where the surface soils are quite acid and where foxgloves and rhododendrons may grow. Beech pollards well and many of the old woods like Burnham Beeches were pollarded to grow smallwood beyond the reach of browsing deer.

Numerous place-names are derived from 'beech', for example: Bookham, Surrey; Boxted, Essex; and Long Buckby.

203 Common Beech in spring

204 Male inflorescences with long stalks and many flowers; female inflorescences stalked, more spherical

205 Male inflorescences with numerous flowers

206 Female inflorescences (from above); stigma lobes yellowish green and curved

207 Common Beech in summer

208 5–10cm long leaves, alternately arranged

209 Superior leaf surface, shiny, dark green, glabrous at first

210 Inferior leaf surface, pale blue-green, with tufts in the vein axils

211 Common Beech in autumn

212 Young fruits with soft brown barbs

213 Seeds, triangular, red-brown, with high oil content

214 Yellowish red hard wood

215 Common Beech in winter

216 Very long, spindle-shaped terminal and side buds

217 Softly barbed fruit cases and spindle-shaped side buds

218 Long, straight, cylinder-shaped trunk; grey-silver bark, smooth and thin

# Common Ash

*Fraxinus excelsior* L.

Frêne commun
Gemeine Esche

Pages 78, 138, 139

The ash is one of the taller of the indigenous trees, usually growing to a height of around 40m. The crown of younger trees is very open with ascending branches. In older trees it is ovoid or spherical, being broadest at the summit.

It shoots upwards at a remarkable rate until its 50th year. Once over a hundred years old it ceases to increase in height, whilst continuing to expand outwards. Old trees can be up to 1m in diameter. Where the environment is favourable, it can live for 200 to 300 years. The greenish-coloured outer bark is smooth for the first 30 years. Thereafter it develops longitudinal ridges and furrows, forming a lattice-like pattern, turning grey to brown-black with age.

In many museums are to be found lances, spears and javelins, all made from highly pliable, long-fibred, non-brittle, extremely supple and hard ash wood. This would explain why as early as the Middle Ages the ash was frequently planted near to towns.

Inside the light-coloured, wide, tough and very useful sapwood is to be found the heartwood. This darkens considerably with age, has large pores set in rings, is very strong, with long, straight fibres, and very pliable.

One cubic metre of naturally dried, cut wood weighs 700–780kg. It usually dries fairly successfully. If it is to be artificially dried, it is advisable not to hurry the process, otherwise the wood will crack.

The wood is commonly used for making tool handles, wheels, skis, gymnasium equipment, hockey sticks, furniture, table tops and wooden floors. As it stains well, it is often used by cabinet makers. A distinction is made between chalk, water, wood and garden ashes. The chalk ash grows on dry, stony slopes, has fibres, is brittle and consequently of little practical use. The garden ash yields the hardest, firmest wood.

Ashes first flower and fruit at some point between their 30th and 40th years. The many-flowered panicles emerge in April, before the leaves, out of spherical, slightly pointed, black side-buds, which project somewhat from the twig. The flowers have neither petals nor sepals, are wind-dispersed and either bisexual or single-sex. The male flowers consist of 2 or 3 anthers, whose pollen sacks are originally violet-red. Female flowers have an ovary. a two-lobed style and 2 spatula-shaped staminodes (sterile anthers). The anthers do not open until 2 to 4 days after the styles have matured. This feature is designed to preclude the possibility of self-pollination. The closed fruits are gathered together in overhanging clusters. They are elongated, slightly twisted, and, in the early stages, green in colour. They only begin to turn brown towards the end of autumn. They may become detached from the panicle at any time up to the early spring.

Inside the oblanceolate, flat, elongated fruit-wing, or 'key', lies an elongated, pointed nut. Once the tree has flowered, the large, pinnately compound leaves appear. The individual pinnate leaflets are oblong to ovate, 3–12cm long, acuminate, irregularly serrate, with woolly hairs along the veins on the inferior surface of the leaf. The leaves are arranged in opposite pairs along the twig.

The ash is only able to develop its magnificent crown when it grows in deep, fairly damp, mineral-rich soil in a place where it will not experience late frosts, and where the atmosphere is not too warm or humid. It grows less successfully on completely dry slopes with a thin soil layer and a deficient supply of ground water. It is most frequently found on river banks, in meadow and valley woodland, with rich ground-level vegetation, and in mixed deciduous woodland between the hilly and montane zones.

The ash requires a lot of light – about the same amount as the oak.

When the tree is grown commercially it is often planted in narrow passes, to encourage it to grow to maximum height.

The manuscript of Edda, written in the second half of the 13th century, contains references to a large number of gods and heroes. This is just about the only piece of evidence we have on which to base our notions concerning the religious beliefs of the Teutons. Here we can read of the mythological ash, 'Yggdrasil', whose roots were anchored in the abyss of the underworld, and watered by the streams of wisdom and fate; its trunk was supported by the earth, and its crown touched the arc of heaven. Mythical animals lived in the tree and fulfilled particular roles which contributed to the successful perpetuation of life on earth. And each day the gods would come over the bridge of the rainbow and hold court under its shade.

Earlier still, ash wood was considered efficacious when applied to fresh flesh wounds. The leaf sap was used as an antidote to snake bites and the distillation of young shoots produced an excellent cure for earache and unsteady hands.

Many Slavic people believe that snakes are afraid of the constantly shifting shadow of the ash tree. A traveller should therefore be able to rest at ease under its generous shade.

English place-names derived from 'ash' include: Ascot, Berkshire; Ashton, Northamptonshire and other counties; Ashton-under-Lyne, Lancashire.

219　Ash in spring

220　Erect panicles with bisexual flowers

221　Wilted bisexual flowers with young fruits

222　Part of an all-male panicle

223　Ash in summer

224　20–30cm long leaves, in opposite pairs, usually pinnate

225　Superior leaf surface, dark green, glabrous

226　Inferior leaf surface, light green with red-brown hairs along the veins

227　Ash in autumn

228　Numerous fruits clustered in overhanging panicles

229　Narrow, dark brown seed, enclosed by flight organ

230　Heartwood turning brownish with age

231　Ash in winter

232　Pyramid-shaped, black, terminal buds, larger than roundish side buds

233　Black side buds with leaf stigma

234　Older bark, grey, pitted with 'plaitted' grooves

33

# Common Walnut

*Juglans regia* L.

Noyer
Gemeiner Walnussbaum

Pages 76, 136, 137

The Common Walnut is a sturdy, well-proportioned tree. Growing singly it has an open, roundish crown and is well endowed with foliage. Its maximum height is 30m, diameter 1.5m, and it can live for up to 400 years. Given the right habitat it can grow to 15–20m by the time it is between 60 and 90 years old.

It thrives best in loose, porous, deep soil which is rich in nutrients, and in the gentle climate of the wine-growing regions. Particularly fine examples may be found in hollows on sheltered valley bottoms and gently sloping hillsides.

The young Common Walnut has a smooth, ash grey to grey-brown outer rind. With age this changes into a deeply fissured, grey bark.

Within the white to grey-white sapwood, which can be very wide in young trees, lies a grey to dark brown, heavy, fairly hard, tough and not very pliable heartwood. Its pith is shot through with dark stripes.

The increasing demand for walnut wood can easily be explained. Seasoned wood is very durable and has a beautiful colour, which contributes to its increasing rarity. The colour and the structure of the wood can vary a great deal according to climate, habitat and composition of the soil. Thus it is possible to distinguish Italian walnut from the German or Swiss walnuts by its more lively structure and its slightly more reddish tinge. Growing in the Caucasus region, on the other hand, the walnut has a pronounced black colouring. One of the most beautiful woods for drawing on and staining comes from France.

Since walnut wood is so easy to handle, to cut, and to polish, it is commonly used to make house furniture (for bedroom furniture it is particularly the darker, burnished woods whch are used), in interior fittings, for building organs and pianos, for tableware, bread-boards, toast-racks, carvings and, by way of long tradition, for making shields and rifle-butts and stocks, the last because it is very stable and will not move or warp.

The valuable veneers, with their superbly intricate figures, are taken from the axis of the branches, the lower part of the trunk, or from the root knots. Walnut trees are therefore felled not by sawing through the trunk above the ground, but by cutting below ground level. The buttressed bases are used to make very valuable veneered furniture. One cubic metre of dried wood weighs 650–750kg. The drying process is usually fairly straightforward and there is little danger that the wood will develop fissures.

In spring the young leaves unfold, odd-pinnate and still orange-brown in colour. By summer they have grown to 20–50cm in length and are strongly aromatic when crushed. The pinnate leaflets are elongated and elliptic to ovate, 6–15cm long, with an entire margin and, with the exception of the terminal leaflet, sessile.

The leaves – known as 'folia juglandis' – contain, amongst other things, walnut tannin and ethereal oil and are used in natural medicine as an antidote to poison, intestinal worms and skin disorders. A decoction of the leaves is supposed to produce a good mouth wash, and a mixture of linseed oil and walnut leaves to be an effective laxative for cattle. Common Walnut trees usually flower for the first time after 15–20 years. The male catkins dangling from the previous year's shoot emerge from the axis where the leaves have fallen. Their flowers have a six-sided case consisting of 4 perigynous leaves, 2 sprout-leaves and 6–30 anthers. The female inflorescences lie near the tip of new twigs and bear 1–3 and sometimes 5 flowers. Each of the perigynous leaves is fused with the receptacle. Their styles possess fringed stigmas. The fruits begin to ripen in September. They are incomplete, 2 or 4 layered stone fruits, enclosed inside a green, smooth, tough and fleshy outer case which turns brown upon ripening. Underneath lies the light brown, furrowed, rock-hard nut-case, with its thick seam. Inside all this is a 2–4 layered seed with large, fleshy, folded, tasty shoots, containing a good deal of oil. Trees aged 50–100 years give the best yields. The largest plantations are to be found today in France (the Grenoble walnuts are well known), Italy, Hungary and Yugoslavia. Ripe nuts are edible and are used to make salad oil. This is done by crushing the edible part of the nut, which is bright yellow and has no smell. It is also used to make soap and oil-based paints. The leaves, rind and fruit case are dried and aloes are added to them to make brown dyes for wood, wool and hair. The name 'walnut' came from the old English 'wahlnut', literally meaning foreign nut, probably a translation of the Vulgar Latin phrase 'nux Gallica' (Gaulish, hence foreign nut). The Gauls, the people who inhabited France, were known to the Teutons in the Middle Ages as Walchen or Welsche.

The tree was originally indigenous from South-West Asia to China, and was dedicated to Jupiter. The Romans called it 'jovis glans', meaning 'the nut of the great god Jove [or Jupiter]'. From this is derived its scientific name Juglans.

Excavations in Carinthia, and of stilt buildings in northern and southern Italy, have shown that the Romans were not the first to introduce the walnut tree to central Europe. Grafted varieties were brought to Italy by the Greeks and then later taken northward by the Romans. But the Walnut did not achieve a wide distribution in Europe until the time of Charlemagne.

The Common Walnut was probably introduced to Britain by the Romans, and is now grown everywhere northwards, at least to Skye, where there is a fair tree at Armadale Castle, and to Easter Ross. Some of the best trees surviving the search by timber-scouts are in Yorkshire and the Midlands, but growth is faster where summers are hotter in the south and south-east. The best tree now, as it was in 1900, is at Gayhurst, Newport Pagnell, a near perfect stem and 21m × 195cm, but many trees collapse before reaching that size. Good growth is only likely in deep, rich soils like those found along the edges of lowland alluvial valleys, and particularly where these are in chalk country.

The old tag about women, dogs and walnut trees has a certain validity for walnut trees at least, for unhindered growth can be too lush for the production of much flower and fruit. The old scheme was to collect the fruit by beating and bending the branches, and the slight wounding acted like root-pruning in slowing down leaf-production and increasing flowering.

235 Walnut in spring

236 Male catkins on previous year's shoots

237 Male flowers; (above) from the front, (below) from behind

238 Two female flowers with feathery stigma

239 Walnut in summer

240 20–50cm long, unequally pinnate leaves

241 Superior leaf surface; leaflets unequal in size, mid green in colour

242 Inferior surface of a young leaf

243 Walnut in autumn

244 Green stone fruits on new shoots

245 Light brown 'wooden' nut inside fruit case

246 Brown-grey heartwood with dark stripes

247 Walnut in winter

248 Terminal buds and two male inflorescences

249 Side buds on a long shoot

250 Short trunk with pale grey bark, vertically ridged

# European Larch

*Larix decidua* Mill.

**Mélèze**
**Europäische Lärche**

Pages 70, 128, 129

Larch trees grow to a height of 40m and to around 1.5m in diameter. They are found in regions with warm summers and cold winters, where there is little fog. The soil should be rich in nutrients, loamy and porous, and reasonably deep. Trees are less likely to flourish as well on steep, slippery slopes, or on mountainsides in the sub-alpine zone. Even so, planted larches are often found in these regions. Where they have been planted in large towns their growth is usually very poor, as they are unable to withstand the damaging effects of toxins in the atmosphere.

Originally the larch was found only in the western and central Alps (where they formed the outer edge of the forest region), in eastern parts of the Sudetan, the Tatra mountains and on the Polish plain. However, because its wood is very valuable, its distribution has been extended far beyond these original confines. It was already well established in the European uplands by the 16th century.

The first larches in Britain were a few trees grown in the gardens of botanical enthusiasts a few years before 1629. It remained very rare until after 1700. In 1727 the Duke of Atholl had two at Dunkeld, Perthshire, and these grew remarkably well. In 1737 he had a hamper of larch plants brought up from London to plant five at Dunkeld and a dozen at his home, Blair Castle. The carrier, John Menzies, dropped off a few at some estates on his way, notably at Linley, Shropshire, and Monzie Castle, Crieff, and kept a few for his home at Meggernie Castle. Any big old larch in Scotland is now reputed to have come from that hamper, by various, sometimes devious means, and several probably did, like two each at Kinloch House, Angus, and Gordon Castle, Moray. The Atholl trees, eight of which survive, grew with remarkable vigour and soon convinced the Duke that this was the tree to plant on a large scale for the Navy. Which he did, all down the Tay Valley, which he owned, planting several million trees between 1750 and 1780.

From this example, larch became the one forest tree to rival the Scots Pine as a plantation tree in Scotland. Larch forestry quickly spread to England and Wales, and until the conifers from northwestern America arrived in adequate quantity to compete, after 1860, the larch was supreme as the exotic conifer

in forestry. It was also used much in shelterbelts and parks. It is popular again now both for financial reasons, with its very early yield of marketable timber, and for its value in amenity as a deciduous tree with fine spring and autumn colours, and its attraction for wildlife. The Scottish Crossbill moves into larch from the Scots Pine, where it nests, in September because the larch seed can be extracted and eaten then, a month before that of Scots Pine. Small finches, Bullfinches and Sparrowhawks nest and feed in larch, and tall old larches are favoured for nest sites by Buzzards.

When the needles fall in the autumn, they very quickly improve the quality of the soil, which in turn improves the survival chances of more demanding species such as the Norway Spruce and the Swiss Stone Pine. The larch is therefore acknowledged to be a particularly useful 'pioneer' tree.

The European Larch requires a good deal of light and has a narrow-conic, regular and massively branched crown, which in old age becomes somewhat flatter and more open. In between the irregularly spaced main branches grow smaller, almost horizontal, bow-like branches, tending slightly upwards. The young shoots are pale yellow and surrounded by pulvini. They usually bear numerous little twigs and droop heavily. The young tree has a smooth, greenish bark. This later turns into a 10cm thick, vertically ridged, scaly bark which is grey-brown on the outside and red-purple underneath. It encases a narrow, yellow-brown layer of sapwood and the inner red-brown heartwood, which later turns much darker.

Of all the indigenous conifers, the European Larch yields the hardest and most hard-wearing wood. Because of its high resin content it is weatherproof and is therefore unbeatable for use in building, for constructing bridges, pit-props and other kinds of equipment. It is also used for making railway sleepers, fence posts, exterior doors, staircases and floors. Many tubs and containers used in the chemical industry are made from larch (because of its resistance to acid). But it is also used to make interior fittings and furniture. The larch is industrially processed to make fretwood and veneers. This wood can present difficulties to the manufacturer when he encounters particularly stubborn

branches. The drying of the wood is usually successful, although it does occasionally have a tendency to split and warp. It is pliable, tough, easily hewn and weighs around 600–750kg/m³.

The sulphurous yellow male inflorescences are roundish, ovoid catkins, about 5–10mm in length. Even before the end of the winter they are visible in the form of enlarged buds. The numerous male flowers are disposed radially, and their anthers comprise a short stalk, a scaly tip and two pollen sacs, located on the underside.

The female inflorescences are a vivid dark red, 10–25mm long, and are usually found on 2-year-old needle-bearing shoots. They consist of surface scales arranged in a spiral pattern and the small yellowish seed- or fruit-scales, each of which contains two ovules. When the inflorescence turns into a cone, these seed scales (megasphorophyll) grow vigorously and later form the round-shaped adjacent, slightly curled, cone scales with their very fine tracery of lines. The bracts, on the other hand, have arrested growth, and in the mature cone are visible only at the base of the fruit scales.

The triangular, light brown, 3–4.5mm long seeds are equipped with a 5–6mm wide 'wing' and ripen in September or October of the first year. At any time between then and the following spring they can be shed from the cone. The gestation period of the seed is about 4–5 weeks, and it is fertile for 4–5 years. Only after about 4–5 years do the cones drop, together with the dried twigs. On 2-year-old or older branches, the needles occur in tufts, on small bunches of short shoots; in the case of the new long shoots, they are found singly and are arranged spirally. The individual needles are straight, 1.5–3cm long, soft, slightly flattened, with a blunt or shortly pointed tip. In the autumn they turn golden yellow and drop before the start of winter.

In Scotland, the best timber is used for boatskins and in the building of trawlers, where the great strength is essential for the strains of trawling. The early returns come from the use of thinnings for garden fences and pergolas when small, and pit-props and estate work, especially fence-stobs when a little larger. It is remarkably durable in the ground.

251 Larch in spring

252 Male inflorescences, spherical, yellow, projecting outwards

253 Female inflorescences (cones), dark red, erect

254 Side view of a male inflorescence with stalk

255 Larch in summer

256 Needles in clusters on short shoots; arranged singly on long shoots

257 Section showing old (brown) and new parts of twig, with clustered and single needles

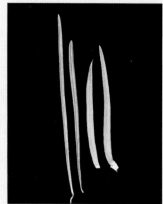

258 Needles, 1.5–3cm long, narrow-linear, soft, flattened, with rounded or slightly pointed tip

259 Larch in autumn

260 Cones 2–4cm long, broad, grey-brown in colour

261 Triangular seeds, light brown, enclosed by wing

262 Within the yellow sapwood lies the tough, resinous, brown-red heartwood

263 Larch in winter

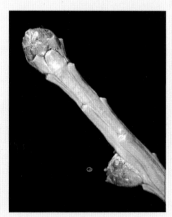

264 Half-spherical to wedge-shaped, brown, terminal and side buds

265 Young tree with medium to deeply furrowed brown-red bark

266 Old tree with thick, grey, deeply furrowed bark

# Crab Apple

*Malus sylvestris* ssp. *domestica* (Borkh.) Mansf.          **Pommier**          **Pages 112, 196, 197**
                                                             **Apfelbaum**

Large, twisting branches, thick foliage and a broad crown are the identifying features of the Crab Apple. It rarely grows above a height of 10m.

The young tree has a light grey, smooth bark. Later in its life this turns grey-brown and cracks into small, square plates. The underlying wood consists of broad, light reddish sapwood and brownish red, medium-heavy (one cubic metre of dried, sawn wood weighs 700–850kg), extremely valuable heartwood. The wood is hard, dense, difficult to cut, often with twisted fibres, contracts severely and will not withstand damp. It dries slowly and is inclined to crack and warp. The annual rings are distinctive for the wavy lines of the end-of-season wood. The wood is very hard and turns and polishes excellently but is available only in small sizes. It is used for chessmen, tool-handles and mallet-heads.

Erect umbels appear at the tips of the short shoots, known as 'spurs', together with the leaves, in May or June. Their hermaphrodite flowers possess a 1.3cm long stalk, which has a felt-like covering of hairs. Each calyx has about 5 sepal tips and is a green-brown colour, with a similar felt-like covering of hairs. Between them are found the obovate to round, acutely pointed petals. They are white, tipped with a faint pink shade at the edges and up to 25mm long. The 10–20 anthers, with their yellow pollen sacks, surround and shelter the ovary. The ovary has a fine covering of hair and slightly stunted or only half-grown styles. When the fruit develops, the ovary becomes the parchment-like casing. The flesh of the round, green, yellow or red fruit, the apple – which is in fact only a pseudocarp or 'false fruit' – is actually formed from the receptacle, not the ovary.

The alternate leaves are elliptic to ovate in outline and have stalks. The blades have a delicately notched or serrate margin and curved reticulate veins running towards the tip of the leaf.

In hilly regions, where the ground is rich in minerals and chalky, and there is plenty of sun, Crab Apples produce plentiful fruit. Areas which experience late frosts are ill-suited to the Crab Apple.

Unlike the Greeks, who knew only a few varieties of apple tree, the Romans cultivated about 29 different sorts. In central and northern Europe the cultivation of the apple tree can be traced back to the Stone Age. However, many of the varieties with which we are familiar today are not descended from the trees of the plough builder, but, like so many other types of fruit, were introduced by the Romans.

The mythological role of the apple is obscured by the fact that when the Greeks passed down their word for 'apple', the fruits of the quince and the pomegranate trees were included under the same name. Thus the interpretation of the 'golden apple' which plays an important part in the judgement of Paris can vary. In this story, Eris is said to have thrown a golden apple bearing the inscription 'to the fairest one' into the midst of three goddesses attending the wedding of Peleus and Thetis – Hera, Athene and Aphrodite. Since each of the three claimed the apple as her own, a hefty argument broke out. At first, no one could come to an agreement. In the hope of finding a solution, Paris was chosen to act as arbiter. Each of the three goddesses promised him valuable gifts. Eventually Paris chose Aphrodite, who had promised to give him Helen. Thus the fruit became the symbol of love.

The 'Golden Apples of the Hesperides', which Gaia caused to burst forth as a wedding present for Hera, must actually have been pomegranates. These fruits had the power to bestow immortality. They were watched over by the Hesperides and the dragon Ladeu. Heracles, the most popular of the Greek heroes, and prototype of all masculine strength, broke into the gardens, killed the hundred-headed dragon and seized the fruit.

Like so many symbols, the apple is ambivalent. We should not forget the story of the Fall or of Persephone, Snow White, William Tell or the Imperial apple. In the story of the Fall, the apple was the block over which Adam and Eve stumbled. After they had eaten of the forbidden fruit of the tree of knowledge they were denied access to the tree of life, and thus to immortality. Thus the apple has become the symbol of knowledge and sin. Persephone was abducted and taken down as a bride to the underworld of Hades. When Hermes came to fetch her back, Hades gave his spouse an apple to eat before she left. Through doing so she became forever bound to the underworld. In the fairy story 'Snow White', the apple conceals the deadly poison, in the tale of William Tell it becomes the symbol of hope and freedom, and in the case of the Imperial apple of the German Kaiser – the work of a goldsmith – of power and sovereignty.

The Crab Apple is native to England but uncommon, found mainly on the edge of old woodlands in the most rural areas and becoming scarce towards the north. In all parts the true native tree is less often seen than seedlings arising from domestic apples. These are most frequent beside roads and come from cores ejected from passing vehicles. The true wild tree has some thorns in its shoots and has pure white flowers. A tinge of pink in the flowers shows a tree to be a domestic seedling and it will be found to lack thorns completely.

Associated place-names include Appledore, Devon and Kent; Appledram, Sussex; Appletreewick, Yorkshire; Appleby, Cumbria; and Apley, Lincolnshire, Shropshire, Somerset and Isle of Wight.

267 Apple tree in spring

268 Several flowers in erect panicles

269 Single flower viewed from above

270 Vertical section through an apple flower: ovary, 5 styles (fused at the bottom) and anthers

271 Apple tree in summer

272 Leaves 5–9cm long, arranged alternately

273 Superior leaf-surface, often slightly wavy and glabrous

274 Inferior leaf-surface, pale, grey-green, villous at first

275 Apple tree in autumn

276 Apples

277 The fruit

278 Brown-red heartwood, very hard, heavy and valuable

279 Apple tree in winter

280 Terminal bud, ovoid to spherical, dominating the side buds

281 Side bud, narrow-ovoid, clinging to the twig

282 Older tree with grey-brown bark, flaking in thin plates

# White Poplar

*Populus alba* L.

Peuplier blanc
Weisspappel

Pages 86, 152, 153

In Britain, the average height of this rather straggly tree, with its initially dome-shaped but later broader crown, is something like 15–18m (10–30m in other parts of Europe). Under favourable conditions the trunk will grow to a circumference of around 60cm.

The White Poplar is a relatively small, bushy, suckering tree that grows rapidly when young. It is much confused with the altogether finer tree, the Grey Poplar, *Populus canescens*. It can be told apart from it by its smaller, bushier or leaning growth and, by direct comparison, the pure snowy white of the underside of the leaf. That of the Grey Poplar is less bright and tends towards pale grey. Both the White and the Grey Poplars bear lobed leaves when young but they are more marked and persist longer in the White Poplar while the Grey soon has only rounded aspen-like leaves. The White Poplar is short-lived and rarely achieves 18m before dying or being blown down. The Grey Poplar, however, can live for over 200 years and grows rapidly into an imposing tree of 35m or more with a straight, long bole and a few stout, spreading branches.

The bark of the young White Poplar is whitish grey to grey-green and turns with age into coarse, dark grey, cracked bark, which is deeply furrowed and ridged down its length. Underneath is to be found a wide layer of sapwood and an evenly constructed and stable, red to brownish yellow core of heartwood. Corresponding to the rapid growth, the annual rings are very wide. The pores are small to medium sized and, like the very fine medullary rays, are not visible to the naked eye. The very lightweight wood (one cubic metre of dry wood weighs 400–500kg) has a smooth and somewhat sandy surface. It distorts and contracts very little, and is very soft, but tough. It is elastic, but will not resist pressure or bending.

It is easy to work, to glue, to stain, but not to polish. When freshly cut this wood has a rather acidic smell. The largest user of poplar wood is the plywood industry. Plywood and joiner's boards made from this wood are very light and stable.

In addition, this wood is used for making boxes, firewood baskets, wooden tiles, drawing boards, wood-carving and for making cellulose.

Perhaps because by the time they are 30–40 years old, Grey Poplars are already 20m high, and within that short time produce a great yield, their place in folk traditions is all the more prominent.

In terms of their size, both Black and Grey Poplars, as well as the numerous other strains, outstrip all other species of indigenous tree.

Poplars thrive in soil which is rich in minerals, deep, loose, damp, sandy to loamy or sandy-humus, rich in calcium, and where the level of the water table is high. This group of trees is therefore one of those most frequently encountered in softwood meadows and riverside woodland. Where they grow in dry, deficient soil, White Poplars often have a slightly deformed, rather bush-like appearance. Of all the poplars growing in these kind of conditions, however, the White Poplar is most able to tolerate the dryness of the soil.

This tree, which first arrived from southern Europe in the Middle Ages, is a typical representative of the hilly zone. It can, on the other hand, be found growing at up to 1500m above sea level. We find it not only on the banks of the larger rivers, but more and more often as a decorative tree in parks and urban streets. Thanks to its hairy, felt-like leaves, the tree traps a lot of the dust in the atmosphere, and this helps to keep town centres clean. The dust, which sticks between the hairs, is usually washed away by heavy rainfall, so that even in heavily polluted areas the tree will not suffer any damage.

Both the White and the Grey Poplar are of southern and central European and west Asiatic origin and were brought in by early settlers long before records of such things were kept. Any tribes moving across to England very soon after the ice had retreated would have valued the White Poplar to grow for shelter in the loose sands and glacial outwash where there were no trees, and the Grey Poplar for more substantial shelterbelts in broad valleys. The best Grey Poplars today are in the wide, shallow valleys in chalklands in Hampshire and Wiltshire and on the limestones of central Ireland. Like the White Poplar, this tree can grow well on dune sand even where its roots must be in brackish water at high tide. A fine example of its resistance to sea winds, sea water, poor soil and northern extremes is a fine 30m tree on the tideline at Dunrobin Castle, Sutherland.

The White Poplar is local on farmland, by roadsides and behind sand-dunes and sometimes as an ornamental tree in town parks, in which it grows well. The Grey Poplar is much more frequent in all parts, with some big trees lining roads in the Highlands and many in farmland valleys in the chalklands of England as well as in town and city parks. It resists industrial pollution well.

Some trees have male inflorescences, others female. These emerge in March or April, before the leaves, from spherical, slightly pointed, very large buds.

The male catkins are 3–7cm long, up to 1.5cm thick, bearing innumerable flowers, at first narrowly ovoid and protruding, later narrowly cylindrical and dangling. Each flower has an irregularly dentate and villously haired bract and numerous anthers (at first crimson, later yellow).

The female flowers are also attached to long, greenish yellow catkins. The bracts are again irregularly dentate and have villous hairs.

The ovary is greenish coloured, has a short stalk, is conical and elongated. The two stigmas are also yellow-green. After the flowering season, whitish leaves with dense hairs on both surfaces unfold from pointed-ovate to conical end- and side-buds. Later they grow to 5–12cm in length, are oval or three-lobed, have a 2–4cm long stalk and at the base of the blade are either rounded or truncate. The superior surface is shiny dark green and is by now no longer hairy. The inferior surface remains thickly coated with white hairs.

In Greek mythology the tree not only receives frequent mention, but is even dedicated to a specific god – Hades, the god of the underworld. The tree owes its very existence to Hades' passion for the beautiful daughter of Okeanos, the god of the seas, whose name was Leuke. After the death of Leuke, Hades, by way of tribute to the dead woman, caused the White Poplar to grow in the Elysian fields, where the souls of the departed reside, and regarded it as a sacred tree. It was also sacred to the wife of Hades, Persephone. It was chosen to grow in the underworld on the banks of the Lake of Remembrance. Since, at that time, everyone was quite convinced of the idea that the White Poplar grew in the underworld, it was often planted in cemeteries and next to memorials.

According to another legend, the Heliades, the daughters of the sun god Zeus, froze with grief for their murdered brother Phaeton, and were turned into poplars (Virgil, Aeneid 10, 190; Ovid, Epistulae ex Ponto 1, 2, 33v). The poplar is also mentioned in connection with the cult of Dionysus. (Dionysus was the god of wine and fruitfulness and encouraged his followers to bear witness to the power of nature.) Anyone initiated into

283 White Poplar in spring

284 Many flowered, narrow-cylindrical, 3–7cm long, drooping male catkins

285 Young, still narrow-ovoid, male catkins

286 Male flowers: (above) from the front, (below) from the back

287 White Poplar in summer

288 Leaves, 5–12cm long, lobed or dentate

289 Superior leaf surface, shiny, dark green, becoming glabrous

290 Inferior leaf surface, retains dense white hair layer

291 White Poplar in autumn

292 Round shaped autumn leaf

293 Untreated wood: whitish sapwood (right) and reddish brown heartwood (left)

294 Wood treated with linseed oil: pale sapwood (right); dark reddish brown heartwood

295 White Poplar in winter

296 Broad-ovoid to spherical flower buds and pointed-ovoid leaf bud

297 Wedge-shaped side bud on short shoot

298 Originally smooth, grey-green young bark; older bark black and ridged

this cult was crowned with a ring of poplar leaves. For Dionysus, like Hades, is a chtonian god. The chtonian gods (the earth gods) rule over life and death – Hades reigns in the kingdom of the dead and Dionysus represents all the energy of the life-force. The poplar thus bears a relationship to both life and death.

In another legend we learn that Heracles (the Greeks' favourite hero) returned from the underworld with a crown of White Poplar leaves. The White Poplar was his favourite tree. The practice at Olympia of using poplar branches to weave the victor's crown has been traced back to him. It is said

that when Heracles erected an altar to Zeus, the only wood which was permitted to be burned on it was that of the White Poplar. Such traditions as the ritual burning of poplar wood and the weaving of victors' crowns from White Poplar branches obviously came about because of the silvery surface of the leaf.

# Lombardy Poplar

*Populus nigra* var. *Italica* Muenchh.

Peuplier de Lombardie
Pyramidenpappel

Pages 107, 188, 189

The Lombardy Poplar grows over 30m tall and acquires a 3m-thick trunk. Its branches grow directly upwards and its crown is narrow-columnar or extended-conical in shape. Even in trees over several hundred years old this only measures up to 2m at the most across.

The tree is a particular growth-form of the Black Poplar. Beneath the thick, cracked, ridged, ochre bark lies a whitish layer of sapwood and the grey-yellow to light brown heartwood. The annual rings are usually pretty wide and easily distinguished because of the dark end-of-season wood lines. The light-coloured wood has large fibres, is very soft, spongy, easily hewn and weighs little (mass of dry, cut wood is 400–550kg/m³). It contracts little and is not very durable when dry. It is used principally for making boxes, drying barrels, blind wood and in the match and cellulose industries.

These dioecious poplars produce female or male flowers in March or at the beginning of April out of brown, broadly conical buds.

The male inflorescences are up to 7cm long, 0.4–0.8cm across, heavy with tiny flowers and dangling. The flowers have a triangular, hairless, palmate bract and 12–30 anthers with red pollen sacks. After pollination these turn purple or black.

The female trees, have 12cm-long, many-flowered, dangling catkins. Next to the palmate bract, the flowers each have a two-carpelled ovary, at the base

of which the nectar is produced. When it ripens, the two folds of the ovary open up to release very small seeds. Being equipped with a small tuft of hair, they can be carried quite long distances away from the parent tree.

The leaves only open after the flowering season. At first they are a reddish bright green colour; later on, the superior surface turns dark green and the inferior surface grey-green. Both surfaces are hairless from the start. When fully grown they are 4–8cm long, broadly wedge-shaped at the base of the blade, with a sinuately serrate, dentate margin and a 1–3cm long stalk, slightly tinged with red.

This tree is often planted on river banks to stock up the vegetation on the water's edge, near farmhouses, as protection against lightning, on country roads, in rows to form a windbreak, and near churches and homes for decoration.

The poplar is most widespread in hilly regions, and is rarely found in the mountains. Where it does occur this high it usually does so in 'bush' form.

In ideal ground conditions – in damp, humus-rich soil – the Lombardy Poplar can grow to a height of 20–25m within the first 40–50 years. If, though, as a result of changes in the water supply, the soil loses its humidity, not only does it cease to grow, but also starts to become sickly, the first sign of which becomes apparent when the topmost branches turn dry and brittle. It is much

more sensitive to frost and cold than the Black Poplar.

This species of poplar did not find its way from Persia to the Mediterranean region until the end of the 17th century. And it is a very late arrival in central Europe. The true Lombardy Poplar is a male clone. In 1740 a male tree from Lombardy is said to have been planted in a park in Worlitz bei Dachau. Many of the trees growing in central and East Germany are thought to be descended from this tree. Female examples, of unknown origin, were found for the first time in 1859 in Karlsruhe and Vienna, and again in 1870 in Frankfurt am Oder.

The Lombardy Poplars in France, Alsace and western Switzerland are supposed to be of French origin, because Napoleon I is thought to have had a fondness for them and to have planted them along his armies' routes.

The true Lombardy Poplar was brought to England from Turin in 1758 by the Earl of Rochford and planted at his home, St Osyth Priory in Essex, where it still is, split into two trunks, each with several young stems growing to 21m. This tree is very common in all settled areas except parts of the Highlands. It is often 30m tall even in very open, exposed places, and many are now over 35m. It is remarkably windfirm, but the 1987 hurricane blew down the tallest, which was 40m tall, in Marble Hill Park, Twickenham.

299 Lombardy Poplar in spring

300 Male catkins up to 7cm long, many-flowered, drooping

301 Male flowers: (above) from behind, (below) from the front

302 Flower bract, markedly palmate

303 Lombardy Poplar in summer

304 Leaves 4–8cm long, diamond-shaped in outline, arranged alternately

305 Superior leaf surface, grey-green, glabrous

306 Lombardy Poplar in autumn

307 Lombardy Poplar in autumn

308 Diamond-shaped autumn leaf

309 Poplar wood treated with linseed

310 Young tree with ochre-coloured bark, with occasional deep furrows

311 Lombardy Poplar in winter

312 Narrow-spherical terminal buds

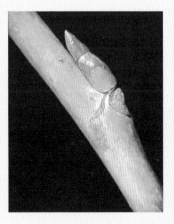

313 Narrow-ovoid, pointed side bud

314 Older tree with thick, cracked, grey bark

# Common Pear

*Pyrus communis* var. *sativa* L.

Poirier
Birnbaum

Pages 112, 196, 197

When growing singly, the pear tree can reach a height of 20m. It has a straight, slender stem with a reasonably broad, conic crown, which is largely formed of ascending branches. Its light grey to blackish bark is cracked into small squares by horizontal and vertical lines. All single trees produce small, early-ripening fruits, which are usually used for making fruit juices or wine. Certain grafted varieties of pear tree, yielding large quantities of fruit, require a protected site. An increasing preference is developing in the fruit industry for trellis and 'bush' varieties, as opposed to fully grown trees, as they are much less expensive to harvest, prune and protect from disease. Bushes, being closer to the ground, have a stronger defence against dehydration and frost than tall trees.

The Common Pear is one of the mature woods. Sapwood and heartwood are scarcely distinguishable.

The heartwood is light brown, with a reddish tinge, fairly hard, very compact, difficult to hew, not very supple, often wavy-grained, very durable in its dry state, and, compared to the wood of the apple tree, has fairly fine fibres. One cubic metre of naturally dried wood weighs 650–750kg. As it has a strong tendency to warp, it must be dried very slowly. If it has been well dried it is easy to handle, to carve, polish and cut. It readily accepts the application of varnish and staining agents. Pear wood is one of the finest indigenous woods. It is used to make furniture, musical instruments, letter-openers, rulers, casting moulds, and precision instruments. As it also reacts well to being steamed and painted black, it is used for making piano keys by way of a substitute for ebony.

The leaves are alternately spaced along the twigs, and are up to 8cm long, elliptic, ovate or orbicular, with a slender stalk. Their margin is finely serrate or entire in places. In autumn they turn yellow to dark red.

Between May and June, up to 9cm long panicles appear on the end of short, leaf-bearing shoots. The individual flowers each have 5 triangular, greenish sepals, both surfaces of which are hairy, and 5 ovate to orbicular petals, both surfaces of which are white.

The 20–30 anthers on the young flowers are dark red in colour. The inferior ovary, with its 5 free-waving styles, which are often hairy at the base, consist of 5 carpels.

During the last 2–4 days of the female flower's development, the insect pollination takes place. The first thing that happens is that the anthers, inside the flower, which up until now have been pointing inwards, turn outwards and release their pollen grains. This phenomenon (known as heterostyly) precludes the possibility of self-pollination. In rare instances, though, it does nevertheless occur. However, the resulting fruit is usually not very healthy.

Common Pear trees grow very slowly. They will only reach a height of 20m when growing in deep, damp, calcareous soil, in a position which is exposed on the south side. When the climate and soil conditions are not appropriate the tree will have stunted and often rather deformed growth.

The Common Pear is indigenous to hilly and mountain regions and can actually be sown at very high altitudes.

As early as the Stone Age, man was gathering the fruit of the pear tree. He actually began to cultivate it at a much later stage, in Persia and Armenia. From there it spread to Greece, then to Rome, and thence to northern Europe. Several varieties were already known at the time of the Romans. We can be sure that the early Greeks were familiar with the cultivated pear tree from the epic poem about Tantalos. He was one of the sons of Zeus, and at first was in good favour with the gods. But later he sinned, and was condemned to eternal atonement in Hades. He was made to stand in water, and was afflicted with an unquenchable thirst. If he bent down to drink, the source dried up. If he stretched upwards, the branches of the overhanging pear trees would shrink out of his reach. At the same time, a boulder was poised just above his head, threatening to crash down on top of him at any moment.

In ancient Greek, the word for the Common Pear was 'Apion' or 'Apies'. According to Athenaios, the archipelago of the Peloponnes was known as the Apia, that is, the land of the pear tree.

As we learn from Pliny, the ancient Romans were already familiar with 35 different varieties of pear.

In the Middle Ages, new varieties were cultivated on country estates and in monasteries.

The pear tree plays a less prominent role in cultural tradition than the apple tree. From time to time, however, it does crop up as a symbol of fertility.

In Britain, the only truly wild pear is *Pyrus cordata*, a small, spiny, bushy tree in Devon and Cornwall, where it is very rare and was discovered in 1865. The widespread, apparently wild trees frequently found in hedgerows are seedlings of introduced cultivated forms. In Gloucestershire and Herefordshire there are still many trees surviving in fields that were formerly perry orchards. They often carry large bunches of mistletoe. In the Vale of Evesham, Worcestershire, some hedges retain many trees from older orchards of eating pears, and these are a feature in autumn when the leaves turn bronze, orange and dark red.

The wood is too knotty and inferior to have any uses, and is even useless as fuel.

315   Pear tree in spring

316   Flowers with stalks up to 3cm long in panicles of 3–9

317   Young flower seen from above: anthers still red

318   Vertical section of a flower

319   Pear tree in summer

320   Leaves up to 7cm long, arranged alternately

321   Superior leaf surface, pale green and glabrous

322   Inferior leaf surface, pale green and glabrous

323   Pear tree in autumn

324   Fruit at end of September

325   Cross section through a pear with core and flesh

326   Brownish red pear wood (treated with linseed)

327   Pear tree in winter

328   Narrow- and broad-ovoid side and terminal buds

329   Projecting side buds on a long shoot

330   Grey-black bark cracked into small squares by vertical and horizontal lines

# Wild Cherry, Gean

*Prunus avium* L.

Cerisier
Kirschbaum

Pages 118, 204, 205

When growing in woodland, the Wild Cherry has a long, straight trunk with thick branching arising from its upper reaches, and will grow to a maximum height of 25m. When growing in the open, on the other hand, it has a short, almost circular bole, with ascending branches.

Its crown is whorled like that of a pine or spruce, a ring of branches at the end of each year's growth. Since young trees usually grow 0.8m or so in a year, the whorls are this much apart, making a very open crown. In later years growth slows down and the crown becomes more dense, the lower crown from lateral shoots. Trees are often over 22m tall and occasionally over 27m but their lives are usually short and 1m is a good diameter before decay sets in. One tree, however, at Studley Royal in Yorkshire was 144cm in diameter in 1966 and, when it should have been dead in 1984, it was a robust 170cm.

The outer rind is smooth, leathery, shiny and silvery grey. It peels away in horizontal strips, and is therefore known as ring bark. It later develops lengthwise ridges and turns black.

Underneath the bark is a narrow band of reddish white sapwood, enclosing the reddish yellow heartwood. Over the course of the year, the sapwood soon comes to look very similar to the heartwood, and they are therefore fairly interchangeable. As a result of exposure to light over the years, Wild Cherry wood gradually darkens in colour. It becomes increasingly attractive, to the point where it achieves its unique and unparalleled red-brown shade. It is a very valuable wood. It is hard, pliable, difficult to chop, compact, fine-fibred, supple, heavy (600–700kg/m³), not weatherproof, but very tough. The reason it is so difficult to chop is that its fibres are so fine and its composition so compact.

It is often used to make very expensive veneers for interior fittings. Also, as basic material for brush and knife handles, for arts and crafts, and musical instruments. Wood with an attractive grain is always very much sought after for use in marquetry.

Wild Cherry wood is easily combined with other woods such as fir, maple and larch. It is often used in these combinations in the furniture industry.

If the bole is not to be artificially dried, it should really be left for 2–3 years inside the bark, somewhere dry, with good air circulation. During this time the initial tendency to sharp contraction will be overcome and the wood will settle. After the first incision has been made, the bark is stripped off and stored carefully in a barn. Sometimes green stripes may appear during the drying process. As long as these are not too severe, they can be treated with hydrogen peroxide. Wild Cherry wood does have rather a tendency to crack and contract. The wood of Wild Cherry trees growing in woodlands is usually darker than that of a tree growing out in the open.

Characteristic of Wild Cherry wood are its very straight, light-coloured, medullary rays.

There is a special and very limited market for this wood in England. The best trees grow on or near the chalk downs and a group of estates on the southern slopes of the Chiltern Hills across the Buckinghamshire–Hertfordshire border are organised to supply it.

In April or May, umbellate clusters of white flowers break out from the round, chubby terminal buds left by the previous year's shoots. Their stalks are 3–5mm in length and either protrude or droop. The 5 sepals are ovate, short-acuminate, with, for the most part, entire margins. They are usually slightly bent backwards. Between them lie the 5 white, ovate to orbicular, slightly emarginate, 10–15mm long petals.

Shortly before the end of the flowering period, or immediately after it, obovate leaves with a wedge-shaped or rounded base unfold from ovate, pointed, reddish-brown buds. The leaf stalks support 2–4 large red nectar glands. Apart from at the tip of the leaf, the margin is sharply serrate. The leaves are 6–15mm long, alternate along the branch, and turn yellow or red in the autumn.

The cherry is a stoned fruit. Its flesh is yellow-red, red or black, and encloses a hard, usually one-seeded stone. The Wild Cherry does not always yield as much fruit as it might, owing to damage caused by birds, rain, hailstones and the cherry fly.

For it to be able to grow naturally and produce large quantities of fruit, the Wild Cherry tree needs warm, deep, porous, nutritious soil. Since the tree flowers early it is very susceptible to late frosts, so it is often planted on slopes at fairly high altitudes, or on upland plains, where cold air is less likely to accumulate. It is hardly ever found more than 1000 feet above sea level.

All varieties of Wild Cherry are related to the Bird Cherry which, as fossils and prehistoric discoveries have shown, has always been indigenous to central Europe. (Excavations of Neolithic or Bronze Age sites on the edges of the Alps have revealed that its wood was used to make props for early 'stilt' houses.) Grafted varieties were, however, unknown in Europe before the Roman period, but were to be found in Asia Minor.

According to Diphylos and Theophrastus, assorted varieties of Wild Cherry were familiar to the Greeks as early as 400 BC. The Romans, on the other hand, from the time of Servius until the introduction of the grafted varieties of Wild Cherry by Lucullus, only knew the wild varieties, with their bitter fruit.

An important centre for the cultivation of the cherry tree was to be found on the Pontos coast of Asia Minor, near the town of Kerasos. When this town was destroyed, Lucullus (a Roman commander, 79–37 BC) brought fruit from the grafted species back to Rome.

Cultivation of domestic cherry trees was common in the time of Lysimachos of Pella (c. 360–281 BC, a high-ranking officer under Alexander the Great).

The Romans took grafted varieties of cherry over the Alps, as is proven by discoveries in numerous Roman settlements.

This tree crossed the land-bridge to England not so long before that eroded and when it was a chalk ridge, but long enough to have spread into Scotland, where it is called the 'gean'. It spreads rapidly because thrushes, blackbirds and starlings eat the little fruit avidly and the passage through their highly acidic stomachs makes the seeds ready to germinate. The lack of place-names of Anglo-Saxon origin involving the cherry and the first mention of it as a wild tree being as late as 1634 has made it possible to dispute that it is a native and to credit the Romans with its introduction. Its early spread to all parts is easy to explain if even a very few were grown in remote gardens, but it seems likely that such a tree would come here unaided.

This tree has been much planted lately because of its value as a fast-growing ornamental tree, on chalk and clay soils, its abundance of spring flowers being followed in autumn by yellow, orange and crimson colouring, and its value to birds.

331 Cherry tree in spring

332 Flowers 3–5cm long, single or in clusters

333 Flower seen from above: petals white, obovate and emarginate

334 Vertical section through a cherry flower

335 Cherry tree in summer

336 Leaves 6–15cm long, arranged alternately

337 Superior leaf surface, dark green, glabrous, often wrinkled

338 Inferior leaf surface, pale green, slightly villous when young

339 Cherry tree in autumn

340 Red fruits

341 Black fruits

342 Reddish heartwood, turning darker on exposure to light

343 Cherry tree in winter

344 Terminal buds on a long shoot

345 Heaped leaf and flower buds on a short shoot

346 Older tree with vertical ridges and grey-black bark

47

# Common Oak, Pedunculate Oak

*Quercus robur* L.

Chêne pédonculé
Stiel-Eiche Sommer-Eiche

Pages 89, 158, 159

The English Oak has a strong, irregular, heavily branched crown, with protruding, horizontal branches. It usually has a life span of around 500 years, although 700 to 1200-year-old trees are sometimes to be found. It can grow to a height of 30–35m, or, exceptionally, even 60m. Its long, deep-reaching and very strong central root accounts for the oak's resistance in the face of storms. Young oak trees grow very quickly, but this rate slows down after about 100-200 years. They continue, however, to increase in thickness, if not in height. Numerous branches often erupt from the trunk only a few metres above the ground, and this can lend the tree an almost 'two-tiered' aspect.

The English Oak was later to arrive after the Ice Ages than the Sessile Oak and this would tend to explain the largely southern and eastern occurrence today of English Oak woods, and the northern and western preponderance of Sessile Oak woods. In the clay lowlands, the English Oak soon replaced the Small-leaved Lime as the main element in the woods and has been ever since, the commonest tree in woodlands other than those on the chalk hills.

Climate and soil also take a part in the current distribution of the two oaks common in England. The Sessile Oak prefers a humid site with high rainfall but fairly rapid drainage and therefore grows well on mountainsides from rocky ghylls to shaley slopes in the cool of the heights of Dartmoor, Exmoor, the Welsh hills, Cumbria and the Highlands. It has occasional outliers on gravels and clays in the high-lying parts of the Weald of Surrey and Sussex and throughout Enfield Chase, the area along the west side of the lower River Lee. The English Oak can tolerate warmer, drier air but needs as much moisture at the root, so it grows where the soil is retentive, in thick clays and valley bottoms. It may prefer humid air as well, as the English Oaks in the bottoms of Highland glens, especially in Perthshire and Angus, are much taller than those in eastern England, 30-35m being far from rare heights, when elsewhere trees are seldom much above 25m. Growing where it can reach moisture, the English Oak is not reported as having ever suffered from drought, even in 1976. It often spreads, through acorn-planting by jays, far on to sandy heaths but makes there only low, bushy trees.

The comparative uselessness of the narrow, brownish-white sapwood is made up for by the yellow-brown heartwood, which has a pattern of broadly spaced medullary rays and is superior in strength and durability to any other European wood. It is hard, easy to split and to work with, very heavy (670–1400kg/m³), and preserves well under water. It is used as building wood for overground structures, foundations, ship-building, for making barrels, railway sleepers and parquet as well as other kinds of floors, boat frames, window ledges and water wheels. Oak veneers are also much sought after.

The most common flaws in oak wood are frost cracks, and the holes made by the lichen bock. After felling, the trees are cut into beams and then left lying out in the open for several years to allow them to dry out. They are then brought inside to dry out completely.

From time to time we come across the name 'bog oak'. This is not a new variety of tree, but wood taken from the English Oak which has lain for many years in marshland or water. This not only makes it heavier, but also gives it a beautiful dark brown, almost black colour.

Clusters of alternate, short-stalked leaves, each 5–16cm long, are found at the tips of the new shoots. Their blades each have 4–5 elliptic, round-ended, irregularly formed lobes, each with its margin entire; the two bottom-most lobes each have small but perceptible auricles.

At the same time as the leaves, that is, in May, loosely flowered, 2–5cm long, yellow-green, narrow, dangling male catkins emerge from the previous year's shoots. Each flower bears 6–10, usually 8 anthers. Above them, several leaves appear on the new shoots shortly afterwards, after which come the female inflorescences. Their flowers are found singly or in groups of 2–5 at the end of a common stalk, each in the axil of its own scaly bract. They consist of 6 perigynous sepals and a three- layered, three-styled ovary. A small, bowl-shaped, small-scaled cupule encloses the simple flower case.

At the end of summer the egg-shaped fruits start to ripen. They have a high starch and tannin content. They used to be roasted to make a kind of coffee substitute, or to fortify spirits and, in cases of dire necessity, to make bread. In many regions they also constituted a major part of the pig's diet, and in the forest at Kew this was in fact the case until quite recently. These fruits are commonly known as acorns.

If there is a heavy fall of acorns in autumn this, according to long-standing belief, is a sign of a hard winter to come. Similar conclusions are drawn from such signs as the oak tree keeping its leaves for longer than usual, or the acorns being particularly deep-set inside their cups.

If the oak trees are heavy with fruit this is thought to indicate that the harvest will be good. This is a rural belief which can be traced right back to antique times. In those days a heavy crop of acorns on the Holm Oak also meant that the field harvest would be plentiful.

Reference to the benefits of a plentiful harvest of acorns is made in more immediately practical terms in Gilbert White's 'Journals'. In his entry for 12 October 1783 he records: 'The crop of acorns is so prodigious that the trees look quite white without them; and the poor make, as it were, a second harvest of them, by gathering them at one shilling per bushel. At the same time not one beech-mast is to be seen. This plenty of acorns has raised store-pigs to an extravagant price.'

Traditionally the oak is regarded as the king of trees. In Greece and Italy it was known as the 'first tree', to which the origin of man could be traced back. The oak acquired a special significance through its close association with the gods. Thus in Greece it was dedicated to Zeus, in Roman Italy to Jupiter and in Teutonic Germany to the god of thunder and lightning, Donar. The reason for this is no doubt that of all indigenous trees the oak is particularly frequently struck by lightning – and this has actually been confirmed by scientific tests.

Any oak within an oak wood to be found with mistletoe hanging from it was considered holy by the Gauls. They believed that when a god singled out any particular tree for attention, he would leave mistletoe hanging from its boughs.

For many Indo-Germanic peoples, the oak was the most sacred of all trees. The reason for this, apart from its powerful appearance, may have been that it served in early times as a source of human food. Perhaps even at that very early stage in its history it was looked upon as a kind of totem. An echo of this cult of the oak can be found in the numerous tales of holy oaks which are common in many parts of Europe. Presumably because of its early function of providing nourishment it is often seen as a symbol of fertility and fruitfulness.

As the English navy grew, between the 16th and 18th centuries, the oak, which had always been considered the

347 Oak in spring

348 Male catkins, 2–5cm long, drooping

349 Section of a catkin; individual flowers with 6–10 anthers

350 Female flowers, 2–5 on a common villous stalk; stigmae yellowish or red

351 Oak in summer

352 Leaves 5–16cm long, lobed, arranged alternately

353 Superior leaf surface, shiny, dark green and glabrous

354 Inferior leaf surface, blue-green, slightly villous

355 Oak in autumn

356 Fruit clusters

357 Individual fruits, stalks 3–6cm long

358 Untreated yellow-brown to dark brown, very hard wood

359 Oak in winter

360 Fat, ovoid-spherical terminal buds heaped at the tip of a twig

361 Pointed-ovoid side buds projecting from the twig

362 Older Oak with brown-black, deeply ridged bark

king of trees in this country, became something of a national symbol. So loyal, indeed, were the British people to this symbol, and its associations of strength, solidity, vigour and masculinity, that they refused to acknowledge the inferiority of its timber to that of other species, a vanity which was not altogether in the best interests of national security, considering that the English navy was largely constructed from it.

The many veteran oaks in the British Isles, some with names and legends attached, are all English Oaks except for some in Powys, the 'Capon Tree' at Jedburgh, a few more in Scotland, and the 'Michenden' or 'Chandos Oak' near Enfield. The most famous and one of only two trees marked on the standard Ordnance Survey maps, is the Major Oak near Ollerton, Nottinghamshire, 329cm diameter. It was 295cm in 1906 and this, together with other dated measurements, shows that it is unlikely to be more than 450 years old or less than about 400. Contrary to local belief, it is certainly not, by a good margin, the biggest oak in Britain, nor the oldest, and connections with Robin Hood are as mythical as he was. The biggest is at Bowthorpe, Lincolnshire, 383cm and very hollow with a large entrance, while 'Majesty' at Fredville Park, Kent, is 369cm with a good, apparently solid bole. The 'King's Oak' at Sparkford, Somerset, is also sound but has big, low branches and is 334cm. At Lydham Hall, Shropshire, one which is solid burrs all round is 374cm.

Place-names abound which are self-evidently derived from oak, like Sevenoaks, Kent; Hatfield Broad Oak, Hertfordshire; and Oakham, Rutland; and there are many less obvious, like Acton and the Yorkshire Acklam, and even Aigburth, near Liverpool.

# White Willow

*Salix alba* L.

Saule blanc
Silberweide, Weissweide

Pages 119, 208, 209

In the absence of human interference the rapidly growing White Willow will reach a height of 20-25m. Branching begins quite near to the base of the trunk. By the time the tree is 80 to 100 years old the trunk can have a diameter of up to 1m and bear an irregularly formed and billowing crown.

Advocates of this tree as the best source of beating rods very often support their case with the argument that it bears knotty protuberances along the length of its twigs. Although these knots soon become hollow, they continue to put out shoots from the thin layer of bark. These are not only used to make baskets, but also for tying up the shoots.

Inside the initially smooth, white-grey skin, which later turns into a thick brown bark with longitudinal fissures, is to be found the brownish-white sapwood and reddish heartwood.

In the process of whitening leather, the young bark is used to make 'Russian leather' and 'Danish glove leather'.

The fine vessels are numerous and dispersed and create fine delicate cracks in the lengthwise-cut wood.

The wood is very soft, with coarse fibres, and is spongy and pliable. One cubic metre of seasoned wood weighs 400-500kg. It dries quickly, is easy to work with, to stain and varnish but not to polish. It is mostly used to make boxes, baskets, wooden shoes, wood wool, in boat construction and in the matchwood and paper industries. This kind of willow wood is also very good for making drawing boards and, of course, cricket bats.

In April or May the flowers appear, at the same time as the leaves.

Male trees develop 3-6cm long, slender, stalked, slightly curved catkins. Their flowers are composed of a bract, an ovary and a gland.

As the White Willow flowers so early in the year, it is a useful source of honey. After the pollination of the ovules has taken place, the ovaries develop into oblanceolate capsule fruits, covered with a film of grey hairs. When the fruits ripen these flap open and release numerous seeds, each with a white tuft of hair. Out of the leaves unfold tiny buds, which are pressed close to the twig, at exactly the same time as the flowers. In the young tree, both surfaces are covered with a thick, silvery layer of hair. Later in the year the superior surface turns dark green and loses most of its hairs. The inferior surface retains its silvery coating. The leaves are 5-10cm long, narrowly lanceolate to lanceolate, and their margin is finely and regularly serrate. In order to reach the stately height of 25m, White Willows require damp to wet soil, and a lot of light. These requirements are most easily met along river banks, at the edges of ponds and lakes, in marshy ground and in meadow woodlands. They can also survive for a long time in water, or with part of their trunk submerged, without incurring any damage. Its roots enable it to keep the mounting deposits on the bank at bay and it is therefore useful in gradually extending the river foreshore.

We come across the willow in Greek mythology. For example, it is found in the underworld, in Persephone's grove (wife of Hades, the god of the kingdom of the dead), and at the entrance of the cave on Crete in which Zeus's child was raised. In traditional folklore the willow is associated with sinister spirits and witches. According to an old tale, love-smitten witches disappear into the hollows of willow trees, reappearing later in the form of hissing cats to frighten the village folk.

Traditional medicine recommends the administering of a decoction of leaves and pieces of young bark as a cure for fever.

This is probably a native tree except in the north and west of Scotland, but doubts have been expressed because it is found only near habitations. Since riversides, in the north at least, were the obvious centres of early settlers, this association is inevitable and probably without further significance. Nevertheless, it may well have been restricted to the south, for today all the big specimens are in the southern half of England. None of these is very old, and the big hulks noted 30 years ago have all gone. The biggest now plainly were planted, and probably within this century. One in the Home Park Private at Windsor was 148cm diameter in 1972; one in the University Parks, Oxford, is 24m × 110cm, while the biggest of many on The Fen, Cambridge, is 25m × 116cm.

The Bat Willow is the form grown commercially and seen by field ditches

363 White Willow in spring

364 Many-flowered female catkins, 3–6cm long

365 Many-flowered male catkins, 4cm long

366 Female flowers, 4mm long: ovary at the base, roundish gland, elongated bract

367 White Willow in summer

368 Leaves 5–10cm long, narrow-lanceolate, alternately arranged

369 Superior leaf surface, dark green with slight hair covering later

370 Inferior leaf surface with permanent silver-white hair covering

371 White Willow in autumn

372 Leaf margin, serrate, with fine glands

373 Lanceolate autumn leaf

374 Wood with brownish white sapwood and reddish heartwood

375 White Willow in winter

376 Narrow-ovoid villous terminal and side buds

377 Side buds lying close to twig

378 Ochre-grey old bark, deeply furrowed with distinct fluting and ridging

in Kent and East Anglia but also in some town parks. It grows remarkably fast and trees of nine years have been measured 14m × 38cm; trees of 16 years, 21m × 61cm. At Thorp Perrow, Yorkshire, one 52 years old is 25m × 108cm; and an undated tree in Marble Hill Park, Twickenham, was 31m × 127cm.

Place-names derived from willow mainly refer to the Osier *Salix viminalis* rather than the White or Crack Willow, and many come from the same root as *Salix* and Sallow, as in Salhouse, Norfolk, and Sale, Cheshire, while more derive from 'withy', the cut shoots of the Osier, as in Withington, Cheshire and other counties, and Wythburn, Cumbria.

# Rowan, Mountain Ash

*Sorbus aucuparia* L.    Sorbier des oiseleurs    Pages 78, 138, 139
Vogelbeerbaum

The bush-like Mountain Ash may grow to anything between 5m and 10m. Its maximum diameter is around 40cm, and its maximum age around 120 years. Its crown is ovoid to spherical. Because of its far-reaching and deeply embedded network of roots, it is particularly well suited to the role of holding together the sides of mountains which might otherwise be prone to avalanches. The one thing it cannot tolerate, though, is being water-logged.

It thrives best in fresh, damp, loose, fertile soil. It is, however, one of the least demanding of all trees and will also grow where the bottom soil is dry and of poor quality. It will also tolerate a good deal of shade, which means it will also willingly take root in shady exposed and windy positions.

On the edges of woodland, the Mountain Ash affords shelter for young conifers in bad weather conditions. We find it growing wild in mountainous and subalpine regions, where it is almost always found in company with the Norway Spruce. But it is also found in many places above the tree-line.

In the far north it crops up again, to the north of the enclosed coniferous forests, where it occurs together with the Aspen Poplar and dwarf species of the birch and willow.

Apart from in the areas of southern Europe where the forests have been destroyed by man, the distribution of this Euro-Siberian species is spread throughout Europe.

A very early colonist of Britain, this tree ranges to the far north, and being also hardy and rugged, it grows at up to 900m on the mountains, which is higher than any other tree. It is common on the edges of lowland woods and on sandy heaths and hills. It will grow quite well on clays and with paving over its roots, so it is frequently seen in streets and city parks. It is not long-lived, and trunks 80cm diameter are rare and have little future, but in their prime some trees are 18m tall.

The name 'Mountain Ash' arises from the compound leaf resembling slightly that of the true Ash, but the tree is in the Rose Family and the Ash is quite unrelated to it, in the Olive Family. Many people, and all with botanical leanings or an interest in keeping old words alive where appropriate, call it the Rowan, from Old English, *roan*.

Each year the soil is enriched with the leaves of the Mountain Ash. These decompose very quickly to produce an excellent humus. This tree also works as a weed controller and since wild deer are able to feast on the Mountain Ash to their hearts' content it is in a position, to a certain extent, to protect other species from such attack. The ash itself reacts by rapidly putting out numerous new shoots.

The silvery grey, shiny, young bark produces a lot of tannin and is therefore used in the tanning process to give leather its lovely brown colour. With age the bark toughens, turns grey-black in colour and develops longitudinal ridges. This is wrapped around a wide band of reddish-white sapwood, inside which is the light brown, slightly red-streaked heartwood.

The wood is fairly pliable and supple, not very durable, extremely difficult to chop, with a diffuse pattern of pores, weighing 600–700kg/m³. It is easy to carve, plane, polish and stain and it dries fairly normally. It is used by carpenters and cartwrights. Selected pieces are especially sought after for fine wood-carving and making craft objects. The annual rings are sharply defined by lovely brown end-of-season wood marks, which considerably enhance the appearance of the wood. The alternate leaves, each 10–25cm long, are odd-pinnate and bear 4–9 pairs of leaflets. These are oblong-lanceolate, 2–6cm long and, with the exception of the terminal leaflet, touch the rachis directly, or, at least, have only very short stalks.

Tea can be made from the leaves. It is not particularly pleasant tasting, because of its high tannin content, but is thought to be effective against intestinal and stomach problems.

The foliage is supposed to be particularly good fodder for goats and sheep.

In May, or, in higher regions, in June, the many-flowered cyme appear. The flowers are 4–7mm in diameter and are composed of 5 small, yellow-green, tri-angular, villous or glabrous sepals, each 1.5–1.8mm long, 5 orbicular or ovate shaped, yellow-white petals, numerous anthers and an ovary with 2–4 styles. The ovary is fused with the inner wall of the cup-shaped, hollow flower axil. Inside the berry, which is initially yellow, later turning bright red, lie the flat, narrow, pointed, reddish-coloured seeds. The berries provide food for birds and cattle, as well as being a source of vinegar, spirits and liqueurs. The dried fruit is also supposed to be effective in combating diarrhoea.

Many legends speak of so-called 'blood trees', grown from the blood of innocents who had been wrongly hanged. Along with the blood, the victim's soul also entered the tree. An old Icelandic tale has it that a rowan tree sprang from the blood of two innocents, a brother and sister falsely accused of incest. Every Christmas Eve, lights could be seen on every branch, which could not be extinguished, not even by the strongest gale.

The rowan has more folk-names than any other tree and was regarded as singularly potent against witchcraft. Miles Hadfield wrote that until the 1950s on May Day, branches were placed around farm buildings, and possibly they still are today.

379 Mountain Ash in spring

380 Flowers in erect cymes

381 Flower from above: petals white and rounded to broad-ovate

382 Vertical section of a flower: 3–5 styles

383 Mountain Ash in summer

384 Leaves 10–20cm long, unequally pinnate, alternately arranged

385 Superior leaf surface, dark green, with silver-grey hairs

386 Inferior leaf surface, felt-like grey green; later becoming glabrous

387 Mountain Ash in autumn

388 Ripening clusters of fruit

389 Pea size berries, first yellow, later coral red

390 Young trunk with yellow-white sapwood; heartwood later light brown

391 Mountain Ash in winter

392 Terminal bud, pointed-ovoid and larger than side buds

393 Side bud lying close to long shoot

394 Yellow-grey shiny bark, becoming grey-black and vertically ridged with age

# Large-leaved Lime

*Tilia platyphyllos* Scop.

Tilleul à grandes feuilles
Sommerlinde

Pages 106, 186, 187

In fresh, deep, well-aerated, calcareous soil, the Large-leaved Lime will grow to a height of 40m. Its short, straight, thick trunk bears a low-set, broadly dome-shaped, thick crown, supported by strong, gnarled branches.

Up to its 60th year, it does not grow particularly quickly. Thereafter, however, it suddenly spurts upwards, reaching its maximum height when it is around 150 years old. It continues to expand outwards even after this. It is said of the lime tree that it grows for 300 years, stands still for 300 years and takes 300 years to die.

The young bark is smooth, grey-green, with vertical wavy streaks. In between there are dark brown fissures. In old trees, the bark is coarse, ridged and dark brown, with a fine rhomboid pattern. In times gone by the young bark was often used for basketry and roof-covering.

This species of tree is one of the mature woods, and has a fairly broad layer of sapwood. Because it does not have a distinctly coloured heartwood, or pith, the wood is the same colour throughout. It can be whitish, yellowish or sometimes light brown or reddish. Between its green and its dried conditions (dried wood weighs 450–550kg/m³) it contracts moderately to severely. Once dried it is easy and clean to handle. Because it is very high in protein it is often attacked by woodworm.

Lime wood is tough, stable, pliable, but not very supple, and, cut length-ways, exposes very fine, delicate cracks. It is not very durable in harsh weather conditions or when exposed to water. It is therefore not very well suited for use in external construction. Because it is so soft, it is good for making drawing boards, toys, small boxes, barrels and chests. It also makes good wood-wool, excellent veneers and high quality charcoal. Because lime wood was so commonly used by masters of wood-carving in the Middle Ages to make figures of Christ on the cross, the Virgin Mary or the Apostles, it came to be known as 'sacrum lignum'. When the peoples of Europe first started to settle, they had no metal from which to make axes or saws. With simple stone axes they were unable to work on hardwood, and were restricted to using softwoods only. Lime, as a major softwood, was used widely to build primitive houses and shortly after that to make hunting bows. Shields made of several layers of interwoven lime phloem were also able to withstand very heavy blows. With the invention of the metal axe it became possible to peel off the bark of lime trees in strips and thus to obtain the necessary bast for housing and clothing requirements. A tree trunk with a diameter of around 35cm would yield around 45kg of phloem. This was sufficient to make, for example, 10–12 mats.

In May or June the Large-leaved Lime begins to flower. The flowers are found in clusters of 3–6 in a cyme. The first half of the stalk is fused with a wing-like, leathery bract. It later serves as a flight aid for the multiple fruit. The five sepals are ovate, yellow-white and 3–4mm long. The five petals are elongated, 5–8mm long and also yellow-white. The very hairy superior ovary is surrounded by 30–40 anthers. The flowers have pharmacological properties, and in this context are known as 'flores tiliae'. They contain a lot of mucilage, sugar, wax, tannin and traces of ethereal oil, which contains the aromatic fern oil. As early as the 16th century, herb books mentioned lime-flower tea as an antidote to fever in sufferers from cold or 'flu.

Out of the green ovary develops a spherical, 4–5-ribbed, hard, wood-like nut, with a velvety covering of hair. It falls in autumn or winter, and is a welcome source of food for small rodents, during what is otherwise a very lean period.

In Continental Europe, almost all the big, named and famous lindens or limes are trees of Large-leaved Lime or Small-leaved Lime, but in the British Isles this is not so. They are all the Common Lime, the hybrid between these two species, which may have been brought from Europe before 1600 or may have arisen in England. It is known to reach 46m tall and over 200cm diameter. The Large-leaved Lime, or Broadleaf Lime, was a late-arriving native, found now apparently only on limestone cliffs by the lower River Wye and in Yorkshire. It is widely planted in parks, gardens and streets, favoured by those who know that it is a much more shapely and cleaner tree, very rarely growing sprouts round the base and never on the stem. It flowers a week or more before the Common Lime and three or four before the Small-leaved, with fewer and bigger flowers in each cyme. The bracts from which the flowers hang are also bigger, paler, nearly white, and more prominent. In the autumn it is distinguished by retaining on the lower, outer crown, many browned bracts and their fruit. It is rarely over 30m tall, although one tree at Knightshayes, Devon, and another at Scone Palace, Perth, are 37m. Two trees at West Dean House, Sussex, are 180cm in diameter, but an extraordinary tree at Pitchford House in Shropshire is 236cm and has a house with a table and chairs over 2m up where three immense branches spring, which is reputed to have been put there in 1600.

On newly emerged foliage, the dense soft hairs on the shoots and leaf-stalks distinguish the species, and fully developed leaves retain soft fine hairs over the upper surface and longer more sparse hairs on the veins beneath. By autumn, most of the hairiness has gone from the shoot, but a little usually remains near the tip. A form seen in streets and gardens has rather smaller leaves with dense hairs on the stalk and around the base of the blade.

According to Greek legend, Philemon and his wife Baukis, despite being very poor, led a happy and contented life. When Zeus and Hermes took on the form of earthly men and visited their village it was to this couple that they came for hospitality. During the meal, the couple realised the identity of their guests when the wine in the jug failed to run dry. As a punishment to the other villagers for their hard-heartedness, Zeus sent a flood to destroy the village. Only Philemon and Baukis's hut was left standing. This he transformed into a magnificent temple. The two hosts were also allowed one wish. They asked that when the time came they should be allowed to end their lives together. After their deaths, Philemon was turned into an oak and Baukis into a lime.

This is where the lime tree acquired its feminine character. This is reinforced by another association – the use of lime leaves to weave garlands for the goddess Aphrodite – the Greek goddess of sensual love and beauty.

Place-names have been derived via linden, as in Lyndhurst, Hampshire; Lindal, Lancashire; Linsheels, Northumberland; and Lindley, Yorkshire.

395 Large-leaved Lime in spring

396 Stalked flowers in groups of 2-5 in cymes

397 Flower from above showing numerous anthers, 5 short sepals and 5 long petals

398 Vertical section through lime flower: superior ovary with many hairs

399 Large-leaved Lime in summer

400 Superior leaf surface, dark green, somewhat hairy

401 Inferior leaf surface, with pronounced veins

402 Inferior leaf surface with small, white tufts of hair in the vein axils

403 Large-leaved Lime in autumn

404 Spherical nuts, with 4-5 ribs and long stalks

405 (left) Young, still green, spherical nut; (right) older nut with 5 ribs

406 Soft, light wood, yellowish white to reddish

407 Large-leaved Lime in winter

408 Terminal buds, narrow- to broad-ovoid, tinged with red on sunny side

409 Side buds, narrow- to broad-ovoid, pointed, slightly flattened

410 Coarse, furrowed bark, grey-brown, with diamond pattern

# Wych Elm

*Ulmus glabra* Huds. emend. Moss

**Orme de montagne
Bergulme, Bergruster**

Pages 109, 192, 193

The young Wych Elm grows very quickly. Within 30 years it can grow up to as much as 90% of its maximum height. Once it is 60 years old, it more or less stops growing upwards. It is not rare to find Wych Elms around 30m high. They only grow to between 30m and 40m where there is a sufficient supply of light, warmth and little frost, and where the water in the soil is rich in nutrients. Such favourable conditions as these are most commonly found in mixed lime woods. In sycamore–ash or beech–hornbeam woods, elms are also quite able to establish themselves.

The crown is usually smoothly rounded and regular. The trunk may continue all the way up, or may branch out in the region of the crown. It reaches its maximum height after around 500 years. Elms of this great age may by this time have a circumference of 6–7m at a point 1.5m above the ground.

A strong and deeply embedded system of roots anchors the tree to the ground. On the side of the tree exposed to the wind it is often provided with lateral roots which make the tree more stable and secure.

The young bark is silvery grey to brownish and smooth. This later develops into grey to dark brown bark, with longitudinal ridges. The phloem used to be used for binding, knitting and basket weaving. Underneath the bark the sapwood is yellow-white, contrasting with the brown heartwood. In between is a layer of mature wood. It is because of this that the elm is classified as a mature heartwood.

The heartwood is very decorative, and is one of the most attractive of European woods. It is hard, resistant to pressure, but not to tension, moderately supple, tough, pliable and durable. As it has a marked tendency to crack and warp, the drying process should be carried out very carefully and slowly. Dried, sawn wood weighs between 550 and 850kg/m³. It is not difficult to work. The treatment of the surfaces should not present too many problems either. It is easily joined, using glue, screws or nails. The wood is also easy to shave, cut and plane, but very difficult to split.

It is principally used for indoor fittings and for making furniture and parquet. Decorative elm veneers are very much sought after. Wood taken from the roots, with its lovely grain, is particularly popular with the carver. It used to be a common practice to stain elm wood and use it as a substitute for walnut and mahogany.

It is almost as good a firewood as beech, but it is far less popular for this purpose, as it is so difficult to chop. The cause of the death of so many elm trees has been *Ceratocystis ulmi*, a fungus, which first came to Europe in about 1920. The beetle eats out a path underneath the rind and thus allows the spores of the fungus to penetrate through to the vascular bundles inside the trunk. The fungus causes the cell walls to form blister-like protrusions. These growths then block up the water routes and upset the water balance to such an extent that within a very short time the twigs and branches begin to wither. Very shortly after, the whole tree dies. If measures are to be taken to combat the disease they must be directed at the beetle.

In hilly and mountainous regions the Wych Elm favours nutritious, particularly damp soil, avoiding dry, stony mountainsides. When the level of the water table sinks this can actually be detected in the drying up of the tip of the tree. Like the Sycamore, this tree really belongs in the company of the beech and will either welcome the chalk in the ground or be indifferent to it. Compared to other forest trees, elms are not prolific, and self-contained stands are rare. Usually they are found scattered individually, or at most are found in thickets. They are also frequently found in hillside or valley woodlands, together with the European Ash and the Sycamore.

Spherical inflorescences unfold from spherical and many-scaled terminal and side buds in March or April. The numerous flowers are 3–6mm long and consist of 5 reddish-purple or greenish perigynous petals, 5 anthers and a superior ovary. After pollination, this develops into an ovoid, green, winged fruit. This can ripen as early as June. The oval seed lies at the foot of the elm, enclosed inside a now brown, wiry case. Only every second or third year is there a really good fruit crop.

The leaves do not sprout until after the tree has flowered. When fully grown they are 5–16cm long, elliptic, ovate or obovate in outline, usually broadest in the upper third of the leaf, often irregularly triangular, with a 3–6mm long stalk. This is often slightly hidden by one half of the blade. The tip of the leaf is sharply pointed, its base very slightly asymmetric, and the leaf margin coarsely doubly serrate. Each of the teeth curves forward. The superior surface is dark green and perceptibly rough to the touch. The inferior surface is a somewhat lighter green and on the larger veins, delicate white tufts of hair appear.

Unlike the Smooth-leaved Elm, with its 12 pairs of side veins, the Wych Elm has 14–20 pairs. The European White Elm has a similar number. The leaves of the latter two species are easily distinguished from each other in having completely different laminal bases (the two halves of the blade in the European White Elm are completely asymmetric).

In Ancient Greece the elm was dedicated to the messenger god Hermes – who watched over merchants and thieves. The winged elm fruits also accompanied the souls of those who were brought before the Lord of Judgement by Hermes. Shady elms were planted by nymphs in remembrance of fallen heroes.

In the south of France the elm takes on the role normally played by the lime. Once upon a time, under its shadow, right was meted out and God's word preached.

The Wych Elm is the only elm with undisputed claims to be native in Britain. There are grave suspicions about the English Elm, which was most likely to have been brought by Iron Age tribes, and does not set viable seed here. The Wych Elm came early and was among those trees to spread early far to the north, where it is common by streamsides deep in the Highlands of Scotland and in the Pennine Hills. It was less common in the English lowlands and has now all but disappeared south of Cumbria. Elm disease is currently spreading into Scotland where the city parks rely greatly on Wych Elm, notably in Glasgow and Edinburgh, as it was able to flourish where industrial fogs were thick and frequent. Today there are still some trees in rural Yorkshire 35m tall, but near Dundee in Angus a group with some 40m tall died in 1986. Not far from those, one 220cm diameter was in good health in 1987.

Place-names with the prefixes 'Wych-', 'Wyke-' and 'Wick-' are widespread, but there are pitfalls in what is dubbed 'folk- etymology' since such names may have derivations from quite other words than Wych Elm.

411 Wych Elm in spring

412 Flowers in spherical bundles, appearing before the leaves

413 Spherical inflorescence with numerous flowers

414 4 young, individual flowers

415 Wych Elm in summer

416 5–16cm long leaves, arranged alternately

417 Superior leaf surface, dark green and coarse

418 Inferior leaf surface, mid green, with fine hairs along larger veins

419 Wych Elm in autumn

420 Older flower with young, winged fruit

421 Young, winged fruits, with oval seed at the centre

422 Heartwood light to dark brown or reddish brown, darkening with age

423 Wych Elm in winter

424 Narrow-ovoid, pointed terminal bud (here a leaf bud)

425 Spherical flower bud at an angle to the twig

426 Bark on older tree, with long furrows and dark brown flaking plates

# Common Silver Fir

**Abies alba** Mill.

Sapin pectine
Weisstanne

Pages 66, 120, 121

Growing in a commercial forest, the Common Silver Fir will live to an age of 180–200 years, and grow to a height of 30–40m, with a diameter of 1m. But in a natural forest it can live for up to 500 years, reaching a height of 55m and a diameter of 1.5m. An elderly tree will have a central root leading down from the trunk, and a 'stork's nest', flattened crown. It is able to develop this shape only because the growth of the side branches is more rapid than the growth of the summit branches. If a summit branch breaks off, a side branch will grow upwards to replace it.

The outer bark is smooth, whitish grey, sometimes with a reddish tinge. Inside it is found the lightweight, soft, easily chopped wood. It is almost white in colour, with a yellowish or reddish tint. It is similar to the wood of the Norway Spruce, but of a slightly paler shade. The sapwood and heartwood are not sharply differentiated. It is very quickly dried, and there is only a slight danger of warping, but it is inclined to crack. One cubic metre of dried, cut wood weighs, on average, around 550kg. Nowadays it is mainly used to make furniture, wooden containers, matches and kindling.

The needles are up to 3cm long, flattened, usually rounded at the tip, narrowing towards the base, attached to the twig by a circular base. The superior surface is dark green, the inferior surface, with its 2 white, narrow bands, a paler green. After 6–11 years, the needles drop. Since the leaf-scars left after the fall are flat and not raised, the branches feel completely smooth.

Trees growing singly start to flower around their 30th year; those in stands after some 60–70 years. Male flowers grow on the lower surface of the previous year's shoots, in cylindrical, downward-pointing catkins. The female flowers are found on the top branches inside 6cm-long, light green, erect cones. By the time the seed is ripe, it is between 10cm and 18cm long. The seeds fall in October and the spindle remains on the branch. The dark brown seeds are large, triangular, with a high turpentine content and a large wing attachment. The tree will yield a large quantity of seeds only once every 2–6 years.

The Common Silver Fir is a very demanding mountain tree, found largely in central and southern Europe. It favours damp, slightly acidic, deep, loamy to clay, fertile soil, and grows best in a sheltered position. These requirements are met particularly on westerly and northern slopes in areas of high altitude. It rarely occurs as high up as the subalpine zone, but is often planted in the hill zone. This tree is seldom found in soil which has a high acidic content, is dry, or completely flat.

The first Silver Fir recorded as being planted in Britain was one in Edmonton in 1603, but the first introduction may have been a little earlier. During the 18th century there was a great deal of it planted as a forest and estate tree, especially in the mountain areas of Wales and Scotland, where it grows particularly well and seeds itself freely around, but also in England on good oakwood soil. Before 1800, the biggest trees in Britain were Common Silver Firs.

# Norway Spruce

**Picea abies** L. (**P. excelsa** Link)

Epicéa
Fichte, Rottane

Pages 67, 122, 123

The Norway Spruce grows to a height of 30–40m when standing alone and up to 60m when growing in a stand. It usually has a conical crown and a flattened, wide-reaching root system.

The branching of the spruce can vary greatly from one tree to another. The most common form is perhaps the 'comb spruce', with its curtain-like, downward sweeping twigs. In close proximity to this is often found the 'bush spruce', which has much shorter twigs, arranged in a bush-like pattern, and at a higher level, the 'leaf spruce', whose twigs are disposed more or less horizontally. Another variation is the 'hazel spruce', which is characterised by having particularly fine quality wood.

The bark of the young tree is usually red-brown, smooth, with small scales. It turns grey-brown with age, and flakes off in the form of little round scales. It encloses consistently white to bright yellow, resinous, soft, light, elastic, sturdy wood which warps only moderately and is reasonably weatherproof. The annual rings are sharply defined by the difference between the lighter spring wood and the darker end-of-season wood. It dries quickly and easily. One cubic metre of dried, cut wood usually weighs around 450kg. Planed and sanded surfaces have a beautiful shine to them. This wood can be put to many different uses.

The needles are very stout, spirally arranged, four-sided, 5–25mm long, slightly crescent-shaped, almost square in cross-section, and rather obtuse to pointed. They can last 5–7 years.

Single trees first start to flower after 30–40 years. Once the tree is sexually mature it will produce a healthy crop of seeds every 3–4 years (every 6–12 years in colder climates).

The female inflorescences, found on the tip of the previous year's shoots, are a luminous purple-red in colour, cone-shaped, 4–5cm long and erect.

The male flowers, which are found in amongst the needles of the leaves, have attached to their axil a scale-like leaf, above which are found the numerous anthers.

Each anther has a short stem and a scale-like, curved tip, underneath which are located the two pollen sacks.

At first the flowers droop downwards, but when they come into bloom they straighten up and display their reddish colouring.

Ripe cones are 10–15cm long, 3–4cm wide, and brown in colour. The topmost and bottom-most scales are sterile. The seeds are pointed-ovoid, dark brown, 4–5cm long, and equipped with a light brown, translucent wing. By the following spring they have become detached. Once this has occurred the entire cone drops off the tree.

The date of introduction to Britain cannot be known, as it was already common when first mentioned in 1548. By 1800 it was, with the Scots Pine and European Larch, a main component of plantation forestry and common in shelterbelts, shelterwoods for game birds and in gardens. It holds its own today in forestry in inland areas too liable to late frosts, by reason of altitude or being in a frost-hollow, for the normally preferred Sitka Spruce to be grown.

427 Common Silver Fir in summer

428 Fir twig with new shoots, still pale green

429 Male catkins in upper region of crown

430 Female flowers in 2–6cm long, light green, erect cones

431 Cone 10–18cm long, cylindrical, erect and light brown

432 Dark brown seed, large, triangular, fused with a broad wing

433 Heartwood reddish white, easily split, containing no resin

434 Young bark, light to dark grey and smooth; older bark with uneven vertical furrows

435 Norway Spruce in summer

436 Spruce twig with pale, green, young shoots

437 Male flowers in spherical catkins, which grow up to 2–3cm

438 Female flowers in erect cones, 2–4cm long, later drooping

439 Ripe, brown cones, 10–15cm long, drooping

440 Dark brown seed, pointed-ovoid, with light brown wing

441 Yellowish white, soft, strong wood

442 Grey-brown bark on an older tree, working loose in round flakes

# Swiss Stone Pine, Arolla Pine

*Pinus cembra* L.

Arole, Pin cember
Arve, Zirbelkiefer, Zirbel

Pages 70, 128, 129

In a favourable environment, the Swiss Stone Pine can grow up to a height of 25m, 1.5m across and can live for up to 600 years. After some 200 years its upwards growth is almost complete; however, it does not cease to expand outwards until the tree itself dies.

The crown of the young tree is conical, but as it grows older it assumes more of a cylindrical shape. As its roots are flat and deep, the pine has a good deal of resistance to severe and stormy weather conditions.

The young bark is silver-grey and smooth. This later develops into scaly bark which is grey-brown on the outside and red-brown on the inside. It darkens quickly on exposure to light and encloses the yellow-white sapwood and the light red to yellowish heartwood. Characteristic of the Swiss Stone Pine are its numerous, firm, red-brown branches. The wood is very light and

soft, with delicate fibres. It is durable, but will not bear a lot of strain. One cubic metre of cut wood weighs 400–500kg. It is used in carpentry for making furniture, floorboards, panels etc.

The stiffly erect, pointed needles are found in bundles of five on the short shoots. They are 5–12cm long, fairly straight and triangular in cross-section. They usually last for around 5 years.

The trees do not begin to flower until some time between the 60th and 80th years of growth (cultivated trees flower as early as after 25 years, but the resulting seeds are incapable of germination). The male catkins appear in June, July or August, depending on altitude, and are reddish coloured, gradually turning yellow. The flowers are 10–15mm long, sessile and ovoid. The female flowers are found in erect, violet-coloured conelets, at the tip of the new shoots. All the protective scales are more or less

greenish in colour, touched with red, with slightly toothed edges. To each of the bluish-violet, downward-curving fruit scales is attached a small, weak keel. The cones ripen after two years, by which time they are egg-shaped, 5–8cm long, and cinnamon brown in colour. The plump, brown, hard-cased, unwinged nuts are edible. They ripen in October of the second year and fall with the cones in the spring of the third year.

The Swiss Stone Pine will also grow in damp, loose soil, in areas with warm summers and high humidity.

Since it is the only species of tree capable of withstanding the extremes of temperature encountered at very high altitude it is found in the central alpine region at an altitude of up to 2250m above sea level.

*Pinus cembra*, known here more generally as the Arolla Pine, was introduced in 1746 and is now uncommon but present in parks and gardens.

# Scots Pine

*Pinus sylvestris* L.

Pin sylvestre
Waldkiefer

Pages 69, 126, 127

The Scots Pine grows to a height of up to 38m. It has a straight, woody trunk and a tall crown, which becomes dome-shaped with age, flattening out, umbrella-like, at the top.

Its strong central root is a continuation of the trunk itself, with numerous secondary roots leading off. Very old trees may have a diameter measuring as much as 1m. The young bark is rust red to grey-yellow, but as the tree ages it thickens considerably, turning grey-brown on the outside and red-brown on the inside. By the time it is 80 years old, the Scots Pine will have reached a height of 20–25m. In favourable conditions it may live for over 300 years.

Apart from requiring a good deal of light, it is a fairly undemanding tree. It will thrive on the edges of the steppes (warm, dry summers) and in Siberia (harsh, frosty winters) alike, and is found right through from the hilly zone to the subalpine zone, on sandy or rocky ground, in calcareous, gravelly or marly soil, or in wet marshland.

Next to that of the European Larch, the wood of the Scots Pine is the most resinous of any European tree. The sapwood is pink-white, the heartwood yellowish, darkening considerably after felling. The drying process should be quick and easy and the wood does not

tend to warp, although it is inclined to crack. Well-dried heartwood will not distort, is very durable, and will stand up well to outside weather conditions. It chops well and is easy to work with. One cubic metre of naturally dried wood weighs around 600kg.

Floorboards, window frames, doors and table-tops are often made out of Scots Pine. It is also used to build ships and carts, and in the paper industry.

The 3cm-long needles grow in pairs on the short shoots. According to the variety of the tree they may stay on the twigs for anything between 2 and 7 years. The tree will begin to flower at some stage after its 30th year of growth. The female flowers are found at the end of new, long shoots, which will continue to grow into the second year. They are roughly egg-shaped and may occur singly or in clusters. At the end of the flowering season they are not yet ripe. They are green in colour, slightly curved, elongated, with clearly visible stalks. They will not ripen fully until the autumn of their second year.

During March or April of the third year, the ripe scales on the conical, elongated, drooping, female cone curve outwards and downwards to release 3–5mm-long, ovoid, light brown seeds, each of which is equipped with a 15–

20mm-long wing. The seed contains a fatty oil, which is used in the preparation of varnishes.

The male flowers occur in place of needle-bundles amongst small scales at the base of one-year-old shoots.

Through a process of dry distillation, 'tar' can be extracted from the resinous wood. This may be used for coating ships' ropes or wooden fencing.

An early arrival among the native British trees, the Scots Pine moved to the far north and the population to the south mostly failed to hold its own against the invasion of various broadleaf trees. On some of the older estates, especially in Aberdeenshire and Moray, this is the predominant forest tree in plantations still, as it is south of the native range in Northumberland. When the Norfolk Brecklands were afforested after 1920, the Scots Pine was the main tree used, but growth deteriorated.

Although living for 300 years or more, growth becomes very slow and trees over 1.2m in diameter or 32m in height are scarce. Estates in Sussex and Kent have many big veterans, although most are likely to have perished in the October 1987 gale.

443 Swiss Stone Pine in summer

444 Needles 5–12cm long, found in tufts of 5, arranged spirally

445 Male flowers in 1–2cm long, ovoid, red catkins

446 Female flowers in violet, ovoid, stalked cones

447 Terminal bud, narrow-ovoid, often pointed

448 'Pine' nuts, fat, brown, edible, with hard shells

449 Yellowish red heartwood, high in resin, darkening rapidly on exposure to light

450 Flakey bark, grey-black on the outside, brown-red on the inside

451 Scots Pine in summer

452 Needles 3–7cm long, in pairs on short shoots, arranged spirally

453 Male flowers in 3–8cm long, narrow-pyramid catkins

454 Female flowers in ovoid, stalked, violet cones

455 Young cones, elongated-ovoid, green, curving backwards

456 Seeds 3–5mm long, ovoid, light brown

457 Resinous heartwood, yellowish in colour, with distinct, brown annual rings; darkening rapidly on exposure to light

458 Bark on older trees, reddish brown to violet, deeply furrowed, breaking away in flakes

61

# 3. Higher zones of vegetation

In climbing from the plain up into the mountain region where there is permanent snow and ice, it is possible to see how individual species and communities of plants occur only at certain altitudes. This is caused principally by:
1. A reduction in temperature
2. A shorter growth period
3. An increase in rainfall and wind-strength
4. A longer period under snow
5. An increase in direct, and especially short-wave, radiation

The more or less sharply defined zones are distinguished as follows:

## 1. Colline zone (hill zone)
- Up to a height of 600m hill region
      700m in Alpine foot-hills
      800 and 900m central and southern alps
- Average annual temperature between 8° and 12°C.
- Growth period more than 250 days
- Characterised by mixed deciduous woods
    - In lower regions mixed oak-hornbeam woods
    - In the warmest regions on calcareous soils downy oak woods
    - In dry regions pine woods
    - In higher regions mixed beech woods
    - At the southern foot of the alps on acid soils mixed oak woods; nowadays often replaced by chestnut woods.

## 2. Montane zone (lower mountain zone)
- Up to a height of 1200 and 1300m: On the northern side of the alps
      1300 and 1500m: central alps
      1500 and 1700m: southern alps
- Average annual temperature between 4° and 8°C.
- Growth period more than 200 days
- Characterised by
    - beech, beech-fir and fir woods
    - pine woods in the central alps
    - In more continental regions the spruce forms natural woods.

## 3. Subalpine zone (higher mountain zone)
- Up to a height of 1700 and 1900m: northern alps
      1900 and 2400m: central alps
      1800 and 2000m: southern alps
- Average annual temperature between 1° and −2°C.
- Growth period 100–200 days
- Characterised by
    - Spruce woods
    - In the inner ranges of the alps spruce woods pass into pine (Arolla) – larch woods
    - At the transition to the alpine zone dwarf shrubs such as the Alpenrose, Juniper and Green Alder (on steep, moist slopes); on calcareous soils stands of the erect or decumbent forms of the Mountain Pine

## 4. Alpine zone
- It comprises the treeless upper regions of the alps and extends from the tree-line to the natural snow-line (the line where the snow on horizontal surfaces melts in summer).
- The regions above the natural snow-line are often separated from the alpine zone and termed the nival zone.
- Climatic snow-line between 2400 and 3200m
- Characterised by
    - at the very bottom mainly stands of dwarf shrubs (e.g. Trailing Azalea)
    - above the swarf shrubs mainly grass

# 4. Identification keys

## 4.1. Guide to using keys I–V

● The key is built up from contrasting characters, and the character in question is shown by a large capital letter.

    **Example:** p. 65: **A =**     **Leaves needle-like**

    **Example:** p. 74: **B =**     **Leaves doubly pinnate**

The contrasting character for the one given above is indicated by doubling the same letter.

    **Example:** p. 72: **AA = Leaves scale-like**

In some cases, where the character has several forms, rather than merely 2, the relevant letter is used the appropriate number of times.

    **Example:** p. 65: **E =**     **Needles flattened, and emarginate, obtuse, or rounded at the end**

                p. 66: **EE =**    **Needles flattened, and pointed at the end**

                p. 67: **EEE = Needles 4-angled, pointed at the end, and attached at the base to a brownish, peg-like projection from the twig . . .**

    **Example:** p. 74: **B =**     **Leaves doubly pinnate**

                p. 74: **BB =**    **Leaves simply pinnate and leaflets . . .**

                p. 79: **BBB = Leaves simply pinnate with a terminal leaflet; the 3, 5, 7 or 9 leaflets coarsely toothed . . .**

● If the letter required for further description has already been used (e.g. for the description of a species) the same letter is followed by a small arabic numeral to avoid doubling the letter within the same key.

    **Example:** p. 65: **C =**     **Description of the Yew**

                p. 65: **$C_1$ =**   **Needles on long shoots always standing singly and arranged spirally or apparently in 2 rows; no real short shoots present**

    **Example:** p. 65  **F =**     **Needles narrowing at the base into a stalk . . .**

                p. 67: **$F_2$ =**   **Needles with narrow lines of stomata on each side . . .**

                p. 69  **$F_3$ =**   **Needles not more than 10cm long . . .**

● Letters used for the first time for a character or the description of a species do not have an arabic numeral

● Each of the keys begins again with the letter **A** and the arabic numeral **1**
(See p. 65, 74, 82, 90 and 105)

● Identification can be accomplished with the aid of the 5 keys (see p. 64)

# 4.2 Summary of the keys for identifying woody plants

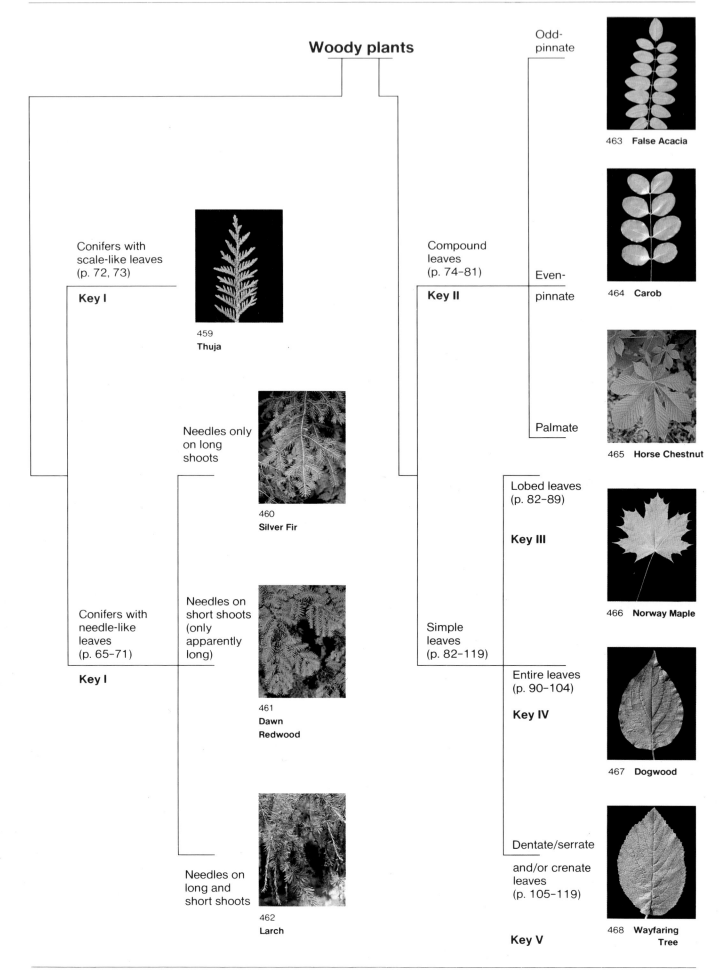

**Woody plants**

Conifers with scale-like leaves (p. 72, 73)

**Key I**

459 **Thuja**

Needles only on long shoots

460 **Silver Fir**

Conifers with needle-like leaves (p. 65–71)

**Key I**

Needles on short shoots (only apparently long)

461 **Dawn Redwood**

Needles on long and short shoots

462 **Larch**

Compound leaves (p. 74–81)

**Key II**

Odd-pinnate

463 **False Acacia**

Even-pinnate

464 **Carob**

Palmate

465 **Horse Chestnut**

Simple leaves (p. 82–119)

Lobed leaves (p. 82–89)

**Key III**

466 **Norway Maple**

Entire leaves (p. 90–104)

**Key IV**

467 **Dogwood**

Dentate/serrate and/or crenate leaves (p. 105–119)

**Key V**

468 **Wayfaring Tree**

| | | |
|---|---|---|
| **A** | Leaves needle-like (Fig. 469–519) | Correct, see **B** or **BB**<br>Wrong, see **AA** (p. 72) |

| | | |
|---|---|---|
| **B** | Needles not clearly distinguishable from the twig, but decurrent for 2–17mm, stalked or sessile (Fig. 469–471) | Correct, see **C**, **CC** or **CCC**<br>Wrong, see **BB** or **BBB** (p. 71) |

## *Taxus* – Yew

**C**

### *Taxus baccata* L.
### Yew
Fig. 469 – see p. 120/121

- Needles 1–3cm long, 2–3mm broad, linear, flattened, apiculate, entire and spirally arranged
- Stalk of needle 2–3mm long, green and decurrent
- Shiny dark green above with prominent midrib; pale or yellowish green beneath

469    Yew

## *Sequoia* – Coast Redwood

**CC**

### *Sequoia sempervirens*
(D. Don) Endl.
### Coast Redwood
Fig. 470 – see p. 120/121

- Needles 4–20mm long, 1–2.5mm broad, linear to lanceolate, flattened, straight or slightly curved, abruptly pointed, entire and spirally arranged
- Needles decurrent
- Pale to dark green above and with 2 whitish bands of stomata beneath

470    Coast Redwood

## *Araucaria* – Chile Pine

**CC**
**C**

### *Araucaria araucana* (Mol.) K. Koch
### Chile Pine, Monkey Puzzle
Fig. 471 – see p. 120/121

- Needles 2.5–5cm long, 1–2.5cm broad, triangular, stiff, ending in a sharp spiny point, entire, spirally arranged and overlapping each other
- Needles decurrent
- Both sides shiny dark green, glabrous and with parallel veins

471    Chile Pine

| | | |
|---|---|---|
| **BB** | Needles clearly distinguishable from the twig and **not** decurrent (Fig. 472–517) | Correct, see **C₁**, **C₁C₁** (p. 68) or **C₁C₁C₁** (p. 68)<br>Wrong, see **BBB** (p.71) |

| | | |
|---|---|---|
| **C₁** | Needles on long shoots always standing singly and arranged spirally or apparently in 2 rows; no real short shoots present | Correct, see **D** or **DD** (p. 68)<br>Wrong, see **C₁C₁** (p. 68) or **C₁C₁C₁** (p. 68) |

| | | |
|---|---|---|
| **D** | Needles **not** stalked (Fig. 472–494); often somewhat narrowed towards the base | Correct, see **E** or **EE** (p. 66)<br>Wrong, see **DD** (p. 68) |

472              473
**Silver Fir**      **Caucasian Fir**

| | | |
|---|---|---|
| **E** | Needles flattened and emarginate, obtuse or rounded at the end | Correct, see **F** or **FF** (p. 66)<br>Wrong, see **EE** (p. 66) or **EEE** (p. 67) |

| | | |
|---|---|---|
| **F** | Needles narrowing below into a stalk and attached to the twig by a green, enlarged, disc-shaped base | Correct, see **G** or **GG** (p. 66)<br>Wrong, see **FF** (p. 66) |

| | | |
|---|---|---|
| **G** | Midrib of the needle broad, medium or dark green and clearly visible (Fig. 474, 475) | Correct, see **H** (p. 66) or **HH** (p. 66)<br>Wrong, see **GG** (p. 66) |

474              475
**Silver Fir**      **Caucasian Fir**

## *Abies* - Fir

**H**

476   **Silver Fir**

***Abies alba*** Mill.
**Silver Fir**
Fig. 476 – see p. 120/121

- Needles to 3cm long, 2-3mm broad, flattened, linear, obtuse but usually emarginate at the end, narrowing below, and attached to the twig by a circular base
- Margin of needle: entire
- Dark green above with a slightly impressed midrib; 2 broad bands of stomata beneath

---

**HH**

477   **Caucasian Fir**

***Abies nordmanniana*** (Stev.) Spach
**Caucasian Fir**
Fig. 477 – see p. 120/121

- Needles 2-3.5cm long, 2-2.5mm broad, linear, stiff, firm, clearly furrowed, obtuse, rounded or slightly emarginate, twisted below and attached to the twig by a broadly elliptic to circular base
- Margin of needle: entire
- Dark green above with impressed midrib; the underside with a distinct green midrib and 2 broad, white bands of stomata

---

**GG**    Midrib of needles somewhat whitish and therefore appearing less distinct than that of the 2 previous species (Fig. 478)

Correct, see **H₁**
Wrong, back to **G**
(p. 65)

478   **Veitch's Fir**

---

## *Abies* - Fir

**H₁**

479   **Veitch's Fir**

***Abies veitchii*** Lindl.
**Veitch's Fir**
Fig. 479 – see p. 120/121

- Needles 1-2.5cm long, up to 2mm broad, linear, soft, often pointing diagonally forwards, brush-like, flat at the tip and distinctly emarginate, somewhat narrowed below, slightly curved and attached to the twig by an elliptic or more or less circular base
- Margin of needle: entire
- Medium to dark green above; bands of stomata on the underside chalky white

---

**FF**    Needles not attached to the twig by an enlarged, disc-shaped base (Fig. 480, 481)

Correct, see **G₁** or **G₁G₁**
Wrong, back to **F**
(p. 65)

480   **Noble Fir**      481   **Douglas Fir**

---

## *Abies* - Fir

**G₁**

482   **Noble Fir**

***Abies procera*** Rehd.
**Noble Fir**
Fig. 482 – see p. 122/123

- Needles 2.5-3.5cm long, up to 1.5mm broad, linear, firm, densely crowded, clearly curved upwards, usually obtuse at the end, and with the whole base (not enlarged) attached to the twig
- Needles abruptly curved upwards just above the base
- Margin of needle: entire
- Grey-green above, shallowly furrowed

---

## *Pseudotsuga* - Douglas Fir

**G₁**
**G₁**

483   **Douglas Fir**

***Pseudotsuga menziesii***
(Mirbel) Franco
**Douglas Fir**
Fig. 483 – see p. 122/123

- Needles 1.8-3.5cm long, 1-1.5mm broad, straight or slightly curved, flat, obtuse or somewhat pointed at the end and smelling of orange when rubbed
- Margin of needle: entire
- Medium to dark green and furrowed above; 2 silver grey bands of stomata beneath

---

**EE**    Needles flattened and pointed at the end (Fig. 484–488)

Correct, see **F₁**, **F₁F₁**, **F₁F₁F₁** or **F₁F₁F₁F₁**
(all p. 67)
Wrong, see **EEE**
(p. 67)

484   **Common Juniper**

## Juniperus – Juniper

**F₁**

485 **Common Juniper**

***Juniperus communis*** L.
*ssp.* ***communis***
**Common Juniper**
Fig. 485 – see p. 122/123

- Needles 1–2cm long, 1–2mm broad, linear, straight, sessile, sharply pointed, somewhat prickly, attached to the twig by a broad base and usually standing out at right-angles from it
- Margin of needle: entire
- Slightly grooved above and with a white central band; green and keeled beneath

**F₁F₁**

486 **Dwarf Juniper**

***Juniperus nana*** Willd.
**Dwarf Juniper**
Fig. 486 – see p. 122/123

- Needles 4–8mm long, 1–2mm broad, usually somewhat crescent-shaped, linear, sessile, shortly pointed, not prickly, and attached to the shoot by a broad base; whorls of needles close together
- Margin of needle: entire
- Dark green at the margins above with a broad band of stomata; dark green and somewhat keeled beneath

**F₁F₁**
**F₁**

487 **Savin**

***Juniperus sabina*** L.
**Savin**
Fig. 487 – see p. 130/131

- Juvenile leaves needle-like, 4–5mm long, 0.5–1mm broad, arranged in whorls of 3, sessile, obtuse or pointed and attached to the twig by a broad base
- Leaf-margin: entire

**F₁F₁**
**F₁F₁**

488 **Chinese Juniper**

***Juniperus chinensis*** L.
**Chinese Juniper**
Fig. 488 – see p. 122/123

- Juvenile leaves needle-like, 6–10mm long, 1mm broad, spreading and directed forwards, sessile, sharply pointed and arranged in whorls of 3 or opposite
- Margin of needle: entire
- 2 bluish green bands of stomata above; dark green beneath

**EE** | Needles 4-angled, pointed at the end and attached at the base to a brownish, peg-like projection from the twig, that remains as a stump after the needle has fallen (twigs rough!) | Correct, see **F₂** or **F₂F₂**
**E** | | Wrong, back to **E** (p. 65)

**F₂** | Both sides of needles with narrow lines of stomata and therefore appearing medium to dark green | Correct, see **G₂** or **G₂G₂**
| | Wrong, see **F₂F₂**

489 **Norway Spruce**    490 **Oriental Spruce**

## Picea – Spruce

**G₂**

491 **Norway Spruce**

***Picea abies*** (L.) Karst.
***P. excelsa*** (Lam.) Link
**Norway Spruce**
Fig. 491 – see p. 122/123

- Needles 0.5–2.5cm long, up to 1mm broad, stiff, somewhat crescent-shaped, almost square in cross-section, somewhat obtuse to pointed and pointing diagonally forwards above the twig
- Margin of needle: entire
- Medium to dark green and with fine lines of stomata on all 4 sides

**G₂**
**G₂**

492 **Oriental Spruce**

***Picea orientalis*** (L.) Link
**Oriental Spruce**
Fig. 492 – see p. 124/125

- Needles 5–11mm long, 1–1.3mm broad, straight or somewhat curved, shortly stalked, almost square in cross-section, obtuse, and set close together
- Margin of needle: entire
- Shiny dark green with white lines of stomata on all 4 sides

**F₂F₂** | Needles with very broad and distinct white bands of stomata and therefore appearing pale green and white (Fig. 493, 494) | Correct, see **G₃** (p. 68) or **G₃G₃** (p. 68)
| | Wrong, back to **F₂**

## *Picea* – Spruce

**G₃**

**493 Serbian Spruce**

**Picea omorika** (Panc.) Purk.
**Serbian Spruce**
Fig. 493 – see p. 124/125

- Needles 1–1.9cm long, 1.5–2mm broad, somewhat curved, distinctly flattened, closely pressed, keeled on both sides, obtuse or somewhat acute and pointing towards the end of the twig
- Margin of needle: entire
- Upper side becoming dark green: clearly visible bands of stomata on both sides of the keel below

**G₃**
**G₃**

**494 Blue Spruce**

**Picea pungens** Engelm. **'Glauca'**
**Blue Spruce**
Fig. 494 – see p. 124/125

- Needles 1.5–3cm long, up to 1.5mm thick, stiff, 4-angled, often slightly crescent-shaped, with a short, sharp point
- Margin of needle: entire
- Needles bluish white with a whitish band of stomata on each side

---

| **DD** | Needles distinctly stalked (Fig. 495) | Correct, see **E₁** |
| | | Wrong, back to **D** (p. 65) |

---

## *Tsuga* – Hemlock

**E₁**

**495 Eastern Hemlock**

**Tsuga canadensis** (L.) Carr.
**Eastern Hemlock, Canadian Hemlock**
Fig. 495 – see p. 124/125

- Needles 7–15mm long, 1.5–2.5mm broad, flattened, tapering gradually towards the tip, rounded or truncate at the end with a distinct yellowish white stalk
- Margin of needle finely serrate; teeth far apart
- Dark green above; bluish green beneath with 2 silvery bands of stomata
- Needles along centre line of shoot often twisted

---

| **C₁C₁** | Needles on short shoots (resembling long shoots) which fall together with the needles in autumn; needles pale green (Fig. 496, 497) | Correct, see **D₁** or **D₁D₁** |
| **C₁** | | Wrong, see **C₁C₁C₁** |

---

## *Metasequoia* – Dawn Redwood

**D₁**

**496 Dawn Redwood**

**Metasequoia glyptostroboides**
Hu et Cheng
**Dawn Redwood**
Fig. 496 – see p. 124/125

- Needles linear, flattened, soft, 1–4cm long and 2–3mm broad, rounded at the end or with a short point
- Needles on short shoots somewhat curved and falling in autumn with the short shoot
- Needles on long shoots falling individually in autumn
- Medium to dark green above

---

## *Taxodium* – Swamp Cypress

**D₁**
**D₁**

**497 Swamp Cypress**

**Taxodium distichum** (L.)
L.C. Rich.
**Swamp Cypress**
Fig. 497 – see p. 124/125

- Needles on short shoots 1–2cm long, 1–2mm broad, linear, flattened, somewhat pointed and falling in autumn with the green short shoot
- Arrangement of needles on short shoots alternate and in 2 rows; those on long shoots spirally arranged
- Margin of needle: entire
- At first fresh green, later pale to medium green and in autumn rusty brown

---

| **C₁C₁** | Needles on long shoots usually standing singly, those on lateral short shoots in groups of 2–5 or forming a rosette of 10–40 | Correct, see **D₂** or **D₂D₂** (p. 70) |
| **C₁** | | Wrong, back to **C₁** (p. 65) |

---

| **D₂** | Needles long, thin, flexible and in groups of 2–5 on short shoots; the latter with a membranous sheath at the base which often falls away in the 1st year | Correct, see **E₂** or **E₂E₂** (p. 69) |
| | | Wrong, see **D₂D₂** (p. 70) |

---

| **E₂** | Needles in pairs on short shoots (Fig. 498) | Correct, see **F₃** (p. 69) **F₃F₃** (p. 69) or **F₃F₃F₃** (p. 69) |
| | | Wrong, see **E₂E₂** (p. 69) |

**498 Mountain Pine**

| | | |
|---|---|---|
| **F₃** | Needles not more than 10cm long (2–8cm) and sheaths at the base of the needles on older shoots only short (Fig. 499, right) or falling early | Correct, see **G₄** Wrong, see **F₃F₃** or **F₃F₃F₃** |

## *Pinus* – Pine

| | | |
|---|---|---|
| **G₄** |  499   **Mountain Pine** | ***Pinus mugo*** Turra **Mountain Pine** Fig. 499 – see p. 126/127 <br>● Needles 2–8cm long, 1–3mm broad, stiff, straight or somewhat crescent-shaped, semicircular in cross-section and shortly pointed <br>● Sheaths short even on older shoots <br>● Margin of needle finely serrate <br>● Dark green on both sides·with numerous lines of stomata |

| | | |
|---|---|---|
| **F₃F₃** | Needles not more than 10cm long and sheaths at the base of most pairs of needles several mm long and persistent (Fig. 500, 501) | Correct, see **G₅** or **G₅G₅** Wrong, see **F₃F₃F₃** |

## *Pinus* – Pine

| | | |
|---|---|---|
| **G₅** |  500   **Scots Pine** | ***Pinus sylvestris*** L. **Scots Pine** Fig. 500 – see p. 126/127 <br>● Needles 3–7cm long, up to 2mm broad, usually distinctly twisted, semicircular in cross-section, pointed, and clustered at the end of the shoot <br>● Sheaths persistent <br>● Margin of needle finely serrate <br>● Bluish green or greyish green on both sides with very fine lines of stomata |

| | | |
|---|---|---|
| **G₅** **G₅** |  501   **Bosnian Pine** | ***Pinus leucodermis*** Ant. **Bosnian Pine** Fig. 501 – see p. 126/127 <br>● Needles 6–10cm long, 1–2mm broad, often somewhat curved, semicircular in cross-section, pointed, and clustered at the ends of the shoots <br>● Sheaths persistent <br>● Margin of needle very finely toothed <br>● Dark green on both sides; bands of stomata over the whole surface |

| | | |
|---|---|---|
| **F₃F₃** **F₃** | Needles between 10 and 25cm long and sheaths at the base of the needles persistent (Fig. 502, 503) | Correct, see **G₆** or **G₆G₆** Wrong, back to **F₃** |

## *Pinus* – Pine

| | | |
|---|---|---|
| **G₆** |  502   **Maritime Pine** | ***Pinus pinaster*** Ait. **Maritime Pine** Fig. 502 – see p. 126/127 <br>● Needles 13–25cm long, 1–2mm broad, semicircular in cross-section, and sometimes in groups of 3 on younger trees <br>● Sheaths persisting until the 3rd or 4th year <br>● Margin of needle finely serrate <br>● Upper surface dark green or greyish green; fine lines of stomata present throughout |

| | | |
|---|---|---|
| **G₆** **G₆** |  503   **Austrian Pine** | ***Pinus nigra*** Arnold **ssp.** *nigra* **Austrian Pine** Fig. 503 – see p. 126/127 <br>● Needles 10–18cm long, 1–2mm broad, usually somewhat curved, semicircular in cross-section, often somewhat flattened, pointed and fairly sharp <br>● Sheaths long and persistent <br>● Margin of needle finely toothed <br>● Whole surface dark green with lines of stomata |

| | | |
|---|---|---|
| **E₂E₂** | Needles in groups of 5 (more rarely 3 or 4) on short shoots | Correct, see **F₄** or **F₄F₄** (p. 70) Wrong, back to **E₂** (p. 68) |

| | | |
|---|---|---|
| **F₄** | Needles with large, white spots of resin (Fig. 504) | Correct, see **G₇** (p. 70) Wrong, see **F₄F₄** (p. 70) |

504   **Bristle-cone Pine**

## *Pinus* – Pine

**G₇**

*Pinus aristata* Engelm.
**Bristle-cone Pine**
Fig. 505 – see p. 126/127

● Needles 2.5–4cm long, 1mm broad, often curved, with white spots of resin, triangular in cross-section and narrowly pointed

● Sheaths persisting as reflexed lobes until the 4th year

● Margin of needle: entire

● 2 sides with lines of stomata; the 3rd side dark green without stomatic lines

505   **Bristle-cone Pine**

---

| F₄F₄ | Needles without large white spots of resin | Correct, see **G₈** or **G₈G₈** Wrong, back to **F₄** (p. 69) |
|------|---|---|

---

| G₈ | Needles 4–7cm long and distinctly curved and twisted so that the twigs appear whitish and green | Correct, see **H₂** Wrong, see **G₈G₈** |
|------|---|---|

---

## *Pinus* – Pine

**H₂**

*Pinus parviflora* Sieb. et Zucc.
**Japanese White Pine**
Fig. 506 – see p. 128/129

● Needles 4–7cm long, 0.5–1cm broad, distinctly curved and twisted, triangular in cross-section, obtuse, and clustered brush-like at the ends of the twigs

● Sheaths falling away in the 1st year

● Margin of needle finely serrate

● Dark bluish green above; the two inner surfaces with whitish lines of stomata

506   **Japanese White Pine**

---

| G₈G₈ | Needles 5–12cm long, not curved or twisted (Fig. 507, 508) | Correct, see **H₃** or **H₃H₃** Wrong, back to **G₈** |
|------|---|---|

507
**Weymouth Pine**

508
**Arolla Pine**

---

## *Pinus* – Pine

**H₃**

*Pinus strobus* L.
**Weymouth Pine**
Fig. 509 – see p. 128/129

● Needles 5–12cm long, slender and flexible, triangular in cross-section and with a pointed tip

● Sheaths falling away entirely in the 1st year

● Margin of needle very finely toothed

● 2 sides each with 2 or 3 bluish white lines of stomata; the 3rd side dark green in 2nd year

509   **Weymouth Pine**

---

**H₃**
**H₃**

*Pinus cembra* L.
**Arolla Pine, Swiss Stone Pine**
Fig. 510 – see p. 128/129

● Needles 5–12cm long, 0.8–1.5mm broad, fairly straight, triangular in cross-section, stiffly erect and pointed

● Sheaths falling away in the 1st year

● Margin of needle very finely toothed

● 2 sides each with 3–5 bluish white lines of stomata; upperside dark green

510   **Arolla Pine**

---

| D₂D₂ | Needles on lateral short shoots forming a rosette of 10–40 | Correct, see **E₃** or **E₃E₃** (p. 71) Wrong, back to **D₂** (p. 68) |
|------|---|---|

---

| E₃ | Needles soft, flattened and falling in autumn | Correct, see **F₅** or **F₅F₅** (p. 71) Wrong, see **E₃E₃** (p. 71) |
|------|---|---|

---

## *Larix* – Larch

**F₅**

*Larix decidua* Mill.
**European Larch**
Fig. 511 – see p. 128/129

● Needles 1.5–3cm long, 0.5–0.9mm broad, soft, flattened, obtuse or shortly pointed

● In groups of 30–40 on short shoots; singly, and fairly crowded on long shoots; young shoots not glaucous

● Margin of needle: entire

● Pale to dark green on both sides becoming golden yellow before falling in autumn

511   **European Larch**

**F₅**
**F₅**

### *Larix kaempferi* (Lamb.) Carr.
**Japanese Larch**
Fig. 512 – see p. 128/129

- Needles 1.5–3.5cm long, 1–1.5mm broad, soft, flattened, obtuse or acute
- In groups of 20–40 on short shoots; singly, and fairly crowded on long shoots; young shoots glaucous
- Margin of needle: entire
- Bluish green on both sides and golden yellow before leaf-fall

512   **Japanese Larch**

---

**E₃E₃** Needles stiff or rather soft (not as soft as in larches), circular, 4-angled, rhombic or triangular and lasting for several years

Correct, see **F₆** or **F₆F₆**
Wrong, back to **E₃** (p. 70)

---

**F₆** Needles 2–6.5cm long, rather soft and circular or 4-angled in cross-section

Correct, see **G₉**
Wrong, see **F₆F₆**

---

## *Cedrus* – Cedar

**G₉**

### *Cedrus deodara* (D. Don) G. Don
**Deodar**
Fig. 513 – see p. 130/131

- Needles 2–6.5cm long, up to 1mm broad, whitish, circular or 4-angled in cross-section, finely pointed and rather sharp
- Margin of needle: entire
- Dark green on all sides with fine lines of stomata

513   **Deodar**

---

**F₆F₆** Needles 1–3.5cm long, stiff, triangular to flattened rhombic or 4-angled in cross-section and sharply pointed (Fig. 514, 515)

Correct, see **G₁₀** or **G₁₀G₁₀**
Wrong, back to **F₆**

514
**Cedar of Lebanon**

515
**Atlas Cedar**

---

## *Cedrus* – Cedar

**G₁₀**

### *Cedrus libani* A. Rich.
**Cedar of Lebanon**
Fig. 516 – see p. 130/131

- Needles 1–3.5cm long, 1–1.2mm broad, stiff, sharp, triangular to rhombic in cross-section and because of the flattened surface always broader than high
- Margin of needle: entire
- Very fine lines of stomata on all sides; needles pale to dark green

516   **Cedar of Lebanon**

---

**G₁₀**
**G₁₀**

### *Cedrus atlantica*
(Endl.) Manetti ex Carr.
**Atlas Cedar**
Fig. 517 – see p. 130/131

- Needles 1–3cm long, 1–1.3mm broad, stiff, somewhat curved and very shortly pointed, irregularly 4-angled in cross-section, thicker and stiffer than in the Cedar of Lebanon
- Margin of needle: entire
- Lines of stomata on all sides; therefore appearing pale bluish green

517   **Atlas Cedar**

---

**BBB** Needles with the lower part adhering to the twig, spirally arranged (forming 3 rows), pointed, and overlapping (Fig. 518)

Correct, see **C₂**
Wrong, back to **B** (p. 65)

518   **Sierra Redwood**

---

## *Sequoiadendron* – Sierra Redwood

**C₂**

### *Sequoiadendron giganteum*
(Lindl.) Buchh.
**Sierra Redwood, Wellingtonia**
Fig. 519 – see p. 128/129

- Needles 3–6mm long (on main shoots up to 12mm), 0.8–1.2mm broad, awl-shaped to lanceolate, pointed at the tip and attached to the shoot by a broad base
- Margin of needle: entire
- Dark green and somewhat rounded above; dark green and longitudinally furrowed beneath; with fine lines of stomata over the whole surface

519   **Sierra Redwood**

| | | |
|---|---|---|
| **AA** | Leaves scale-like (Fig. 520–533) | Correct, see **B₁** or **B₁B₁** Wrong, back to **A** (p. 65) |

| | | |
|---|---|---|
| **B₁** | Branchlets cylindrical or 4-angled and scale-leaves all similar | Correct, see **C₃** or **C₃C₃** Wrong, see **B₁B₁** |

## *Cupressus* – Cypress

**C₃**

520   **Italian Cypress**

***Cupressus sempervirens*** L.
**Italian Cypress**
Fig. 520 – see p. 130/131

- Scale-leaves 1–5mm long, closely pressed and overlapping on younger shoots, later somewhat spreading, pointed, but with a blunt tip on lateral shoots
- Leaf-margin: entire
- Dark green on both sides; with an oblong, often very indistinct gland on the back

## *Juniperus* – Juniper

**C₃**
**C₃**

521   **Savin**

***Juniperus sabina*** L.
**Savin**
Fig. 521 – see p. 130/131

- Juvenile leaves needle-like; adult leaves scale-like, overlapping and blunt or pointed
- Leaf-margin: entire
- Leaves of the upper and lower ranks dark green, with a whitish waxy line and an elliptical gland; leaves of the side ranks dark green with stomatic areas at the sides

| | | |
|---|---|---|
| **B₁B₁** | Shoots flattened and lateral scale-leaves different from those of the upper and lower ranks | Correct, see **C₄** or **C₄C₄** Wrong, back to **B₁** |

| | | |
|---|---|---|
| **C₄** | Younger shoots 4–8mm broad, shiny green above, with silvery white stomatic markings beneath and leaves of the side ranks not touching (Fig. 522) | Correct, see **D₃** Wrong, see **C₄C₄** |

## *Thujopsis* – Hiba

**D₃**

522   **Hiba**

***Thujopsis dolabrata***
(L.f.) Sieb. et Zucc.
**Hiba, Hiba Arbor-vitae**
Fig. 522 – see p. 130/131

- Scale-leaves 3–8mm long, 1–4mm broad, flattened and leathery; leaves of the upper and lower ranks oblong-obovate and overlapping; leaves of the side ranks larger and keeled
- Leaves of the upper and lower ranks obtuse, those of the side ranks pointed
- Leaf-margin: entire
- Silvery white patches on the underside

| | | |
|---|---|---|
| **C₄C₄** | Younger branchlets at most 3–4mm broad and the lower to middle part of the leaves of the side ranks touching at the margins | Correct, see **D₄**, **D₄D₄** or **D₄D₄D₄** (p. 73) Wrong, back to **C₄** |

523   **Chinese Thuja**

| | | |
|---|---|---|
| **D₄** | Glands on the leaves of the upper and lower ranks inconspicuous and shoots same colour on both sides (Fig. 524) | Correct, see **E₄** Wrong, see **D₄D₄** (p. 73) or **D₄D₄D₄** (p. 73) |

## *Thuja* – Arbor-vitae

**E₄**

524   **Chinese Thuja**

***Thuja orientalis*** L.
**Chinese Thuja**
Fig. 524 – see p. 132/133

- Scale leaves 1.5–8mm long, closely oppressed to the shoots; leaves of the upper and lower ranks obtuse and overlapped on their margins by the leaves of the side ranks
- Leaf-margin: entire
- Both sides the same colour with scattered, white stomata; glands on the leaves of the upper and lower ranks inconspicuous

**D₄D₄** Glands on the leaves of the upper and lower ranks clearly visible as small, oblong raised areas, and the upper and lower sides of the shoots a different colour (Fig. 525–529)

Correct, see **E₅** or **E₅E₅**
Wrong, see **D₄D₄D₄**

525
**White Cedar**

526
**Lawson Cypress**

**E₅** Leaves of the side ranks completely appressed to the leaves of the upper and lower ranks (Fig. 527)

Correct, see **F₇**
Wrong, see **E₅E₅**

## *Thuja* – Arbor-vitae

**F₇**

527 **White Cedar**

***Thuja occidentalis*** L.
**White Cedar**
Fig. 527 – see p. 132/133

- Scale-leaves 2–7mm long; leaves of the upper and lower ranks acutely obovate, appressed to the shoot, strongly compressed and somewhat overlapped by the elliptic to triangular, keeled leaves of the side ranks
- Tip of leaf obtuse or shortly pointed
- Leaf-margin: entire
- Leaves dark green above, those of the upper and lower ranks with a clearly visible resin gland

**E₅E₅** Upper part of the leaves of the side ranks spreading away from the leaves of the upper and lower ranks

Correct, see **F₈** or **F₈F₈**
Wrong, back to **E₅**

## *Chamaecyparis* – False Cypress

**F₈**

528 **Lawson Cypress**

***Chamaecyparis lawsoniana***
(A. Murr.) Parl.
**Lawson Cypress**
Fig. 528 – see p. 132/133

- Scale-leaves 1–7mm long; visible part of the leaves of the upper and lower ranks rhombic or narrowly elliptic with a conspicuous oblong resin-gland; leaves of the side ranks pointed and with 2 inconspicuous resin glands
- Leaf-margin: entire
- Dark to greyish green above; paler green beneath

## *Thuja* – Arbor-vitae

**F₈**
**F₈**

529 **Western Red Cedar**

***Thuja plicata*** Donn ex D. Don
**Western Red Cedar**
Fig. 529 – see p. 132/133

- Scale-leaves 2–8mm long appressed to the shoot; leaves of the side ranks covering the margins of the leaves of the upper and lower ranks
- Leaf-margin: entire
- Leaves of the lateral shoots rather blunt or somewhat pointed
- Leaves rich green above and with a gland on those of the upper and lower ranks; greyish green beneath and with stomata forming an almost triangular silver grey mark

**D₄D₄**
**D₄** Leaves of the upper and lower ranks with glandular furrows (Fig. 530–533)

Correct, see **E₆** or **E₆E₆**
Wrong, back to **D₄** (p. 72)

530
**Nootka Cypress**

531
**Hinoki Cypress**

## *Chamaecyparis* – False Cypress

**E₆**

532 **Nootka Cypress**

***Chamaecyparis nootkatensis***
(D. Don) Spach
**Nootka Cypress**
Fig. 532 – see p. 132/133

- Scale-like leaves of the upper and lower ranks overlapping; leaves of the side ranks triangular, somewhat keeled and with the upper part spreading
- All leaves pointed
- Leaf-margin: entire
- Dark green on both sides; leaves of the upper and lower ranks with a glandular furrow on the back

**E₆**
**E₆** 

533 **Hinoki Cypress**

***Chamaecyparis obtusa***
(Sieb. et Zucc.) Endl.
**Hinoki Cypress**
Fig. 533 – see p. 132/133

- Scale-leaves obtuse or rounded; leaves of upper and lower ranks narrowly obovate, thickish, appressed to the shoot; leaves of side ranks crescent-shaped, closely overlapping and smaller than those of other ranks
- Leaf-margin: entire
- Shiny dark green above, those of the upper and lower ranks with a glandular furrow; greyish green beneath with white lines of stomata

**A**  Leaves pinnate (Fig. 534–565)  Correct, see **B**, **BB** or **BBB** (p. 79) Wrong, see **AA** (p. 80)

534  Upper side **Common Ash**  535  Upper side **Traveller's Joy**

---

**B**  Leaves doubly pinnate (Fig. 536)  Correct, see **C** Wrong, see **BB**

---

## *Acacia* – Wattle

**C**  *Acacia dealbata* Link **Silver Wattle, Mimosa** Fig. 536 – see p. 134/135

- Leaves 5–15cm long
- Leaf-stalk 1–3cm long
- Leaves with 15–25 pairs of leaflets, each leaflet with 20–40 pairs of smaller leaflets (leaflets of the 2nd order)
- Smaller leaflets narrowly linear, 3–5mm long, sessile, rounded or shortly pointed at the end and wedge-shaped or rounded at the base

536  Upper side **Silver Wattle**

---

**BB**  Leaves simply pinnate and leaflets entire or finely serrate to dentate  Correct, see **C₁** or **C₁C₁** Wrong, see **BBB** (p. 79)

---

**C₁**  Pairs of leaflets mostly not exactly opposite each other (Fig. 537–539); leaflets rounded at the end with a short, sometimes bristly point  Correct, see **D** or **DD** Wrong, see **C₁C₁**

---

**D**  Leaves up to 7cm long and with at most 12 leaflets, the latter with winged stalks (Fig. 537)  Correct, see **E** Wrong, see **DD**

## *Pistacia* – Mastic Tree

**E**  *Pistacia lentiscus* L. **Mastic Tree** Fig. 537 – see p. 136/137

- Leaves 3–7cm long
- Leaf-stalk 1–3cm long and winged
- Leaflets oblong to narrowly ovate, 2–4cm long, entire, usually rounded at the end with a short point and wedge-shaped at the base
- Leaves with or without a terminal leaflet

537  Upper side **Mastic Tree**

---

**DD**  Leaves with 5–18 pairs of leaflets, 30–75cm long, without a winged stalk (Fig. 538, 539)  Correct, see **E₁** or **E₁E₁** Wrong, back to **D**

---

## *Juglans* – Walnut

**E₁**  *Juglans nigra* L. **Black Walnut** Fig. 538 – see p. 134/135

- Leaves 30–60cm long
- Leaf-stalk 1–6cm long
- Leaflets lanceolate to narrowly ovate, 6–12cm long, irregularly serrate/ dentate, usually entire in the lower part, broadly wedge-shaped at the base and with a shortly pointed tip

538  Upper side **Black Walnut**

---

## *Ailanthus* – Tree of Heaven

**E₁** **E₁**  *Ailanthus altissima* (Mill.) Swingle **Tree of Heaven** Fig. 539 – see p. 134/135

- Leaves 40–75cm long
- Leaf-stalk 8–20cm long
- Leaflets oblong-ovate to obliquely elliptic, 5–15cm long, narrowing towards the pointed tip and broadly wedge-shaped or rounded at the base
- Margin of leaflets entire, except for 1–4 visually glandular teeth, and often fringed with fine hairs

539  Under side **Tree of Heaven**

---

**C₁C₁**  Pairs of leaflets mostly exactly opposite each other (Fig. 540–565)  Correct, see **D₁** (p. 75) or **D₁D₁** (p. 75) Wrong, back to **C₁**

**D₁**  Leaves without a terminal leaflet (Fig. 540)    Correct, see **E₂**  Wrong, see **D₁D₁**

**FF**  Terminal leaflet sessile or with only a short stalk (Fig. 542)    Correct, see **G₁**  Wrong, back to **F**

## *Ceratonia* – Carob

**E₂**  **Ceratonia siliqua** L.  **Carob**  Fig. 540 – see p. 134/135

- Leaves 10-20cm long
- Leaf-stalk 2-5cm long and tinged red
- Leaflets obovate or elliptic to oblong, 3-7cm long, entire, leathery, rounded and usually emarginate at the end, and rounded or broadly wedge-shaped at the base

540  Upper side  **Carob**

## *Coronilla* – Crown Vetch

**G₁**  **Coronilla emerus** L.  **Scorpion Senna**  Fig. 542 – see p. 134/135

- Leaves 2-6cm long
- Leaf-stalk up to 1cm long
- Leaflets obovate, 1-2cm long, entire, usually emarginate at the end or more rarely rounded with a bristly point, and narrowly to broadly wedge-shaped at the base

542  Upper side  **Scorpion Senna**

**D₁D₁**  Leaves with a terminal leaflet (Fig. 541–565)    Correct, see **E₃** or **E₃E₃**  Wrong, back to **D₁**

**E₃E₃**  Leaves much longer than 10cm; leaflets rounded at the end with a short or long point    Correct, see **F₁** or **F₁F₁** (p. 76)  Wrong, back to **E₃**

**E₃**  Leaves 2-10cm long; leaflets obovate and emarginate at the end (Fig. 541, 542)    Correct, see **F** or **FF**  Wrong, see **E₃E₃**

**F₁**  Leaflets entire; in the Walnut these more rarely indistinctly serrate    Correct, see **G₂** or **G₂G₂** (p. 76)  Wrong, see **F₁F₁** (p. 76)

**F**  Terminal leaflet long stalked (Fig. 541)    Correct, see **G**  Wrong, see **FF**

**G₂**  Leaves with 3-12 pairs of leaflets; the latter oblong-elliptic to ovate, 3-6cm long and obtuse, rounded or indistinctly emarginate at the end (Fig. 543)    Correct, see **H**  Wrong, see **G₂G₂** (p. 76)

## *Colutea* – Bladder Senna

**G**  **Colutea arborescens** L.  **Bladder Senna**  Fig. 541 – see p. 134/135

- Leaves 4-10cm long
- Leaf-stalk 0.5-1.5cm long
- Leaflets elliptic to obovate, 1-3.5cm long, entire, distinctly emarginate at the end and rounded or wedge-shaped at the base

541  Upper side  **Bladder Senna**

## *Robinia* – False Acacia

**H**  **Robinia pseudoacacia** L.  **False Acacia**  Fig. 543 – see p. 136/137

- Leaves 15-30cm long
- Leaf-stalk 3-4cm long and enlarged at the base
- Leaflets oblong-elliptic to ovate, 3-6cm long, entire, shortly stalked, obtuse, rounded or indistinctly emarginate at the end and rounded or broadly wedge-shaped at the base

543  Upper side  **False Acacia**

**G₂G₂** Leaves with 2–6 pairs of leaflets; the latter oblong-elliptic to oblong-ovate, 6–15cm long and distinctly pointed at the end; leaves smelling of spice when rubbed (Fig. 544)
Correct, see **H₁**
Wrong, back to **G₂** (p. 75)

## *Juglans* – Walnut

**H₁**

***Juglans regia*** L.
**Common Walnut**
Fig. 544 – see p. 136/137
- Leaves 20–50cm long
- Leaf-stalk to 20cm long and thickened at the base
- All leaflets sessile except for the terminal leaflet; all pointed at the end and wedge-shaped or rounded at the base

544    Under side **Common Walnut**

**F₁F₁** Leaflets finely to distinctly simply or doubly serrate or dentate
Correct, see **G₃** or **G₃G₃**
Wrong, back to **F₁** (p. 75)

**G₃** The 3, 5 or 7 leaflets distinctly white-felted beneath (Fig. 545)
Correct, see **H₂**
Wrong, see **G₃G₃**

## *Rubus* – Raspberry

**H₂**

***Rubus idaeus*** L.
**Raspberry**
Fig. 545 – see p. 136/137
- Leaves 5–15cm long
- Leaf-stalk 3–8cm long, hairy and often prickly
- Leaflets elliptic to broadly ovate, 6–10cm long, simply and often even doubly serrate, pointed at the end, and heart-shaped, rounded or broadly wedge-shaped at the base

545    Underside **Raspberry**

**G₃G₃** Leaflets not white-felted beneath
Correct, see **H₃** or **H₃H₃**
Wrong, back to **G₃**

**H₃** Leaf-stalks with numerous curved prickles pointing towards the base of the stalk; leaflets broadly elliptic to obovate (Fig. 546)
Correct, see **I**
Wrong, see **H₃H₃**

## *Rubus* – Blackberry

**I**

***Rubus fruticosus*** L.
**Blackberry**
Fig. 546 – see p. 136/137
- Leaves 5–15cm long
- Leaf-stalk 2–6cm long and bearing numerous curved prickles pointing towards the base of the stalk
- Leaflets broadly elliptic to obovate, 3–8cm long, simply or doubly serrate, pointed at the end and rounded or truncate at the base
- Midrib of leaflets bearing small prickles

546    Upper side **Blackberry**

**H₃H₃** Leaf-stalks without prickles or with only few (Rosa) and leaflets not broadly elliptic
Correct, see **I₁** or **I₁I₁** (p. 78)
Wrong, back to **H₃**

**I₁** Leaves without stipules at the base or, if present, stipules not like those of Roses (Fig. 547–562)
Correct, see **K** or **KK** (p. 77)
Wrong, see **I₁I₁** (p. 78)

**K** Number of leaflets 5 or 7, more rarely 9
Correct, see **L**, **LL** (p. 77) or **LLL** (p. 77)
Wrong, see **KK** (p. 77)

**L** Leaflets sessile (Fig. 547) or very shortly stalked, finely serrate or dentate and pale bluish green beneath (Fig. 548)
Correct, see **M** (p. 77)
Wrong, see **LL** (p. 77) or **LLL** (p. 77)

547    Upper side **Bladder-nut**

## *Staphylea* – Bladder-nut

**M**

*Staphylea pinnata* L.
**Bladder-nut**
Fig. 548 – see p. 136/137

- Leaves 15–25cm long
- Leaf-stalk 5–9cm long
- Lateral leaflets narrowly ovate to elliptic, 6–9cm long, sessile, shortly pointed at the end and wedge-shaped or rounded at the base
- Terminal leaflet long stalked

548   Under side **Bladder-nut**

| | | |
|---|---|---|
| **LL** | All leaflets very clearly stalked (Fig. 549) | Correct, see **M₁** Wrong, see **LLL** |

## *Fraxinus* – Ash

**M₁**

*Fraxinus ornus* L.
**Manna Ash**
Fig. 549 – see p. 138/139

- Leaves 15–30cm long
- Leaf-stalk 3–8cm long and often finely hairy
- Leaflets oblong-ovate 3–7cm long, irregularly serrate, distinctly stalked, pointed at the end and wedge-shaped or rounded at the base

549   Upper side **Manna Ash**

| | | |
|---|---|---|
| **LL** **L** | Leaflets of the same leaf shortly stalked and sessile | Correct, see **M₂** or **M₂M₂** Wrong, back to **L** (p. 76) |

| | | |
|---|---|---|
| **M₂** | Leaflets lanceolate to narrowly ovate; stalks (if present) tinged red above (Fig. 550) | Correct, see **N** Wrong, see **M₂M₂** |

550   Upper side
**Red-berried Elder, junction of leaflets with leaf-stalk**

## *Sambucus* – Elder

**N**

*Sambucus racemosa* L.
**Red-berried Elder**
Fig. 551 – see p. 138/139

- Leaves 10–25cm long
- Leaf-stalk 7–10cm long
- Leaflets lanceolate to narrowly ovate, 4–8cm long, irregularly serrate, their stalks (if present) tinged red above, tips long printed and unequally narrowly or broadly wedge-shaped or rounded at the base

551   Upper side **Red-berried Elder**

| | | |
|---|---|---|
| **M₂M₂** | Leaflets much broader (elliptic, ovate) than in the Red-berried Elder and their stalks (if present) not tinged red above (Fig. 552, 553) | Correct, see **N₁** or **N₁N₁** Wrong, back to **M₂** |

## *Sambucus* – Elder

**N₁**

*Sambucus nigra* L.
**Elder**
Fig. 552 – see p. 138/139

- Leaves 10–30cm long
- Leaf-stalk 4–10cm long and grooved above
- Leaflets elliptic, 10–15cm long, irregularly coarsely serrate, shortly stalked or sessile, shortly pointed at the end and unequally or broadly wedge-shaped or rounded at the base

552   Upper side **Elder**

## *Fraxinus* – Ash

**N₁**
**N₁**

*Fraxinus americana* L.
**White Ash**
Fig. 553 – see p. 142/143

- Leaves 15–40cm long
- Leaf-stalk 5–12cm long
- Lateral leaflets ovate, 6–12cm long, serrate or in parts entire, shortly stalked, pointed at the end and rounded at the base
- Terminal leaflet long stalked and usually wedge-shaped at the base

553   Upper side **White Ash**

| | | |
|---|---|---|
| **KK** | Number of leaflets more than 9; if only 7, then very rare and only present in the Common Ash | Correct, see **L₁** (p. 78) or **L₁L₁** (p. 78) Wrong, back to **K** (p. 76) |

| **L₁** | Leaflets elliptic or lanceolate-ovate and shortly pointed; midrib and lateral veins beneath prominent (Fig. 554); veins beneath bearing reddish brown woolly hairs, often becoming glabrous late in the year | Correct, see **M₃** Wrong, see **L₁L₁** |
|---|---|---|

| **I₁I₁** | Leaves with long, narrow and pointed stipules at their base (Fig. 557–562) | Correct, see **K₁** or **K₁K₁** Wrong, back to **I₁** (p. 76) |
|---|---|---|

| **K₁** | Leaflets tinged dark red to pale purple beneath (Fig. 557) | Correct, see **L₂** Wrong, see **K₁K₁** |
|---|---|---|

## *Fraxinus* – Ash

**M₃**

***Fraxinus excelsior*** L.
**Common Ash**
Fig. 554 – see p. 138/139

- Leaves 20–30cm long
- Leaf-stalk 3–6cm long
- Leaflets elliptic or ovate, 4–10cm long, unequally serrate and in most cases entire in the lower part, sessile or shortly stalked, shortly pointed at the end and narrowly or broadly wedge-shaped or rounded at the base
- Reddish brown woolly hairs along the veins beneath

554   Under side
**Common Ash**

## *Rosa* – Rose

**L₂**

***Rosa glauca*** Pourr.
***R. rubrifolia*** Vill.
**Red-leaved Rose**
Fig. 557 – see p. 140/141

- Leaves 4–8cm long
- Leaf-stalk 1–4cm long and covered with a bluish purple bloom
- Leaflets elliptic to oblong-ovate, 2.5–4.5cm long, usually simply serrate, pointed at the end and wedge-shaped or rounded at the base

557   Under side
**Red-leaved Rose**

| **L₁L₁** | Leaflets oblong-lanceolate or oblong-elliptic; lateral veins beneath not very prominent; white hairs along the veins beneath (the whole surface hairy in young leaves) | Correct, see **M₄** or **M₄M₄** Wrong, back to **L₁** |
|---|---|---|

## *Sorbus* – Rowan, Service Tree

**M₄**

***Sorbus aucuparia*** L.
**Rowan, Mountain Ash**
Fig. 555 – see p. 138/139

- Leaves 10–25cm long
- Leaf-stalk 2–5cm long, usually coloured alternately red and green above
- Leaflets oblong-lanceolate, 2–6cm long, simply and doubly serrate and in the lower quarter entire, pointed at the end and oblique at the broadly wedge-shaped or rounded base

555   Under side **Rowan**

| **K₁K₁** | Leaflets green or greyish green beneath | Correct, see **L₃** or **L₃L₃** (p. 79) Wrong, back to **K₁** |
|---|---|---|

| **L₃** | Leaflets oblong-elliptic and glabrous (only very rarely somewhat hairy); leaf-stalks reddish above | Correct, see **M₅** Wrong, see **L₃L₃** (p. 79) |
|---|---|---|

## *Rosa* – Rose

**M₄**
**M₄**

***Sorbus domestica*** L.
**Service Tree**
Fig. 556 – see p. 138/139

- Leaves 10–25cm long
- Leaf-stalk 3–3.5cm long, green above and especially in young leaves bearing soft white hairs
- Leaflets narrowly oblong to narrowly elliptic, 3–8cm long, more finely serrate than in the Rowan and almost entire in the lower third, shortly pointed at the end and much more regularly wedge-shaped at the base than in the Rowan

556   Under side
**Service Tree**

**M₅**

***Rosa pendulina*** L.
**Alpine Rose**
Fig. 558 – see p. 140/141

- Leaves 5–10cm long
- Leaf-stalk 1.5–3cm long, predominantly reddish above, with slender stalked glands, and long, narrow, pointed stipules which broaden towards the end and spread outwards
- Leaflets oblong-elliptic, 1–4cm long, usually doubly serrate (teeth with stalked glands), printed at the end and wedge-shaped or rounded at the base

558   Upper side
**Alpine Rose**

| | | |
|---|---|---|
| **L₃L₃** | Leaflets elliptic, ovate or roundish; leaf-stalk green (Fig. 559–562) | Correct, see **M₆** or **M₆M₆** Wrong, back to **L₃** (p. 78) |

| | | |
|---|---|---|
| **M₆** | Leaflets elliptic to ovate and glabrous on both sides, margin simply serrate and without glands (Fig. 559) | Correct, see **N₂** Wrong, see **M₆M₆** |

## *Rosa* – Rose

**N₂**

### *Rosa canina* L.
### Dog Rose
Fig. 559 – see p. 140/141

- Leaves 6–11cm long
- Leaf-stalk 2–4cm long, somewhat prickly and broadened at the base
- Leaflets elliptic to ovate, 2–4cm long, with the margin simply serrate and without glands, pointed at the end and broadly wedge-shaped or rounded at the base
- Stipules long, narrow, pointed and spreading outwards

559    Upper side
**Dog Rose**

| | | |
|---|---|---|
| **M₆M₆** | Leaflets elliptic to ovate and especially on the underside sparsely to densely covered with soft woolly hairs; margin often bearing glands | Correct, see **N₃** or **N₃N₃** Wrong, back to **M₆** |

| | | |
|---|---|---|
| **N₃** | Stipules very small and usually not reaching the middle of the leaf-stalk (Fig. 560) | Correct, see **O** Wrong, see **N₃N₃** |

## *Rosa* – Rose

**O**

### *Rosa villosa* L.
### Apple Rose
Fig. 560 – see p. 140/141

- Leaves 4–9cm long
- Leaf-stalk 1–3cm long and usually with stalked glands
- Leaflets elliptic, 1–4cm long, doubly serrate with glandular teeth, shortly pointed at the end and rounded at the base
- Stipules small and narrow

560    Upper side
**Apple Rose**

| | | |
|---|---|---|
| **N₃N₃** | Stipules reaching over half way up the leaf-stalk or to its end | Correct, see **O₁** or **O₁O₁** Wrong, back to **N₃** |

## *Rosa* – Rose

**O₁**

### *Rosa rubiginosa* L.
### Sweet Briar
Fig. 561 – see p. 140/141

- Leaves 4–7cm long
- Leaf-stalk 0.5–2.5cm long, glabrous or woolly, with stalked glands and small, slightly hooked prickles
- Leaflets elliptic or roundish, 1–2.5cm long, simply serrate/dentate, with numerous stalked glands on the margin, shortly pointed at the end and broadly wedge-shaped or rounded at the base

561    Upper side
**Sweet Briar**

**O₁**
**O₁**

### *Rosa tomentosa* Sm.
### Downy Rose
Fig. 562 – see p. 140/141

- Leaves 5–10cm long
- Leaf-stalk 1–3cm long, woolly, with stalked glands and somewhat prickly
- Leaflets broadly elliptic to roundish, 2–4cm long, simply and doubly serrate, rounded at the end with a small point and wedge-shaped or rounded at the base
- Stipules long and narrow

562    Upper side
**Downy Rose**

| | | |
|---|---|---|
| **BB** **B** | Leaves simply pinnate with a terminal leaflet; the 3, 5, 7 or 9 leaflets coarsely dentate to coarsely crenate and partly irregularly 2- or 3-lobed (in 2 or 3 sections) (Fig. 563–565) | Correct, see **C₂**, **C₂C₂** (p. 80) or **C₂C₂C₂** (p. 80) Wrong, back to **B** (p. 74) |

## *Clematis* – Clematis

**C₂**

### *Clematis alpina* (L.) Miller
### Alpine Clematis
Fig. 563 – see p. 142/143

- Leaves 10–15cm long
- Leaf-stalk 3–7cm long, green, all leaflets stalked
- Lobes of the 3 leaflets narrowly ovate, 2–4cm long, coarsely and deeply serrate, with a long point at the end and rounded or irregularly heart-shaped at the base

563    Upper side  **Alpine Clematis**

79

**C₂**
**C₂**

*Clematis vitalba* L.
**Traveller's Joy, Old Man's Beard**
Fig. 564 – see p. 142/143

- Leaves 3–10cm long
- Leaf-stalk 1–6cm long, twining and tinged wine-red to purple above
- The 3 or 5 leaflets ovate, 3–5cm long, coarsely toothed in the lower part, rounded, obtuse or shortly pointed at the end and heart-shaped at the base

564    Upper side **Traveller's Joy**

## *Acer* – Maple

**C₂**
**C₂**
**C₂**

*Acer negundo* L.
**Ash-leaved Maple, Box Elder**
Fig. 565 – see p. 142/143

- Leaves 7–15cm long
- Leaf-stalk 5–8cm long, glabrous or finely hairy and often tinged red
- Leaflets narrowly elliptic to ovate, 5–10cm long, often 2- to 3-lobed, coarsely serrate in the upper part and entire below, with a long point at the end and wedge-shaped, truncate or rounded at the base

565    Upper side
**Ash-leaved Maple**

| **AA** | Leaves palmately divided into 3, 5 or 7 leaflets (Fig. 566–577) | Correct, see **B₁** or **B₁B₁** (p. 81) Wrong, back to **A** (p. 74) |

566    Upper side
**Horse Chestnut**

| **B₁** | Leaves palmately divided into 3 leaflets (Fig. 567–572) | Correct, see **C₃** or **C₃C₃** Wrong, see **B₁B₁** (p. 81) |

| **C₃** | Margin of leaflets with more or less deep incisions and coarsely serrate, dentate or lobed; distinctly bluish grey beneath with brownish hairs on the midrib, terminal leaflet stalked (Fig. 567) | Correct, see **D₂** Wrong, see **C₃C₃** |

## *Acer* – Maple

**D₂**

*Acer griseum* (Franch.) Pax
**Paper-bark Maple**
Fig. 567 – see p. 142/143

- Leaves 6–10cm long
- Leaf-stalk 1–5cm long, often hairy and usually reddish above
- Leaflets elliptic to obovate, 3–6cm long, coarsely serrate, dentate or lobed, shortly pointed or rounded at the end and wedge-shaped or rounded at the base
- Leaflets bluish grey beneath and with brownish hairs on the midrib

567    Under side
**Paper-bark Maple**

| **C₃C₃** | Leaflets entire, pale, dark or greyish green beneath and without brownish hairs on the midrib | Correct, see **D₃** or **D₃D₃** Wrong, back to **C₃** |

| **D₃** | Leaves at most 5cm long with narrowly obovate leaflets | Correct, see **E₄** Wrong, see **D₃D₃** |

## *Cytisus* – Broom

**E₄**

*Cytisus purpureus* Scop.
**Purple Broom**
Fig. 568 – see p. 142/143

- Leaves 2–5cm long
- Leaf-stalk 1–3cm
- Leaflets narrowly obovate, 1.5–2.5cm long, rounded or obtuse at the end and narrowly wedge-shaped at the base

568    Upper side **Purple Broom**

| **D₃D₃** | Leaves 6–16cm long; leaflets narrowly ovate to narrowly elliptic (Fig. 569) or broadly elliptic to obovate (Fig. 570) | Correct, see **E₅** (p. 81) or **E₅E₅** (p. 81) Wrong, back to **D₃** |

569
Under side
**Alpine Laburnum**

570
Under side
**Common Laburnum**

## *Laburnum* – Laburnum

**E5**

**Laburnum alpinum**
(Mill.) Bercht. et J. S. Presl
**Alpine Laburnum**
Fig. 571 – see p. 144/145

- Leaves 8–16cm long
- Leaf-stalk 5–9cm long, glabrous or with spreading hairs
- Leaflets narrowly ovate to narrowly elliptic, 3–8cm long, acute or obtuse at the end; sometimes with a short, sharp point and wedge-shaped or rounded at the base

571   Upper side
**Alpine Laburnum**

**E5**
**E5**

**Laburnum anagyroides** Med.
**Common Laburnum**
Fig. 572 – see p. 144/145

- Leaves 6–12cm long
- Leaf-stalk 2–7cm long and with appressed silky hairs
- Leaflets broadly elliptic to obovate, 1.5–8cm long, rounded at the end and usually with a small sharp point and broadly wedge-shaped at the base

572   Upper side **Common Laburnum**

**B₁B₁**   Leaves palmately divided into 5 or 7 leaflets (Fig. 573–577)

Correct, see **C₄** or **C₄C₄**
Wrong, back to **B₁** (p. 80)

**C₄**   Leaf-stalk tinged red above and beneath (Fig. 573)

Correct, see **D₄**
Wrong, see **C₄C₄**

## *Aesculus* – Horse-chestnut

**D₄**

**Aesculus parviflora** Walt.
**Buckeye**
Fig. 573 – see p. 144/145

- Leaves 20–30cm long
- Leaf-stalk 10–18cm long and tinged red
- Leaflets narrowly obovate, 9–18cm long, finely pointed at the end and wedge-shaped at the base

573   Upper side **Buckeye**

**C₄C₄**   Leaf-stalks green (Fig. 574–577)

Correct, see **D₅, D₅D₅** or **D₅D₅D₅**
Wrong, back to **C₄**

574
Under side
**Horse-chestnut**

## *Aesculus* – Horse Chestnut

**D₅**

**Aesculus octandra** Marsh.
**Yellow Buckeye**
Fig. 575 – see p. 144/145

- Leaves 10–30cm long
- Leaf-stalk 5–15cm long
- Leaflets oblong-elliptic, 10–15cm long, finely serrate, usually shortly stalked, pointed at the end and narrowly wedge-shaped at the base

575   Upper side **Yellow Buckeye**

**D₅**
**D₅**

**Aesculus carnea** Hayne
**Red Horse Chestnut**
Fig. 576 – see p. 144/145

- Leaves 10–25cm long
- Leaf-stalk 5–15cm long
- Leaflets elliptic (greatest breadth always at the middle), 8–16cm long, simply and in places doubly serrate, pointed at the end and wedge-shaped at the base

576   Upper side **Red Horse Chestnut**

**D₅**
**D₅**
**D₅**

**Aesculus hippocastanum** L.
**Horse-chestnut**
Fig. 577 – see p. 144/145

- Leaves 10–30cm long
- Leaf-stalk 5–15cm long and grooved
- Leaflets oblong-obovate, the greatest breadth always in the upper third, 8–20cm long, simply and in places doubly serrate, shortly pointed at the end and wedge-shaped at the base

577   Under side **Horse Chestnut**

**A**    Leaves lobed like a maple (Fig. 578–615)

Correct, see **B** or **BB**
Wrong, see **AA** (p. 88)

578
Upper side
**Gooseberry**

579
Upper side
**Norway Maple**

---

**B**    Leaves truncate, emarginate or retuse at the end (Fig. 580)

Correct, see **C**
Wrong, see **BB**

---

## *Liriodendron* – Tulip Tree

**C**

580    Under side
**Tulip Tree**

*Liriodendron tulipifera* L.
**Tulip Tree**
Fig. 580 – see p. 146/147

● Leaves 10–25cm long and equally broad, square in outline and with 2 or 4 lobes varying in size
● Truncate, emarginate or retuse at the end
● Leaf-stalk 6–12cm long and slightly thickened at the base
● Medium to dark green and glabrous above; bluish green beneath, glabrous or with hairs arising from small depressions

---

**BB**    Leaves not truncate, emarginate or retuse at the end (Fig. 581)

Correct, see **C₁** or **C₁C₁**
Wrong, back to **B**

581
**Oriental Plane**

---

**C₁**    Leaves with small bristles on the upper side and very rough to the touch; with stiff, appressed hairs beneath or with rough spreading hairs

Correct, see **D** or **DD**
Wrong, see **C₁C₁**

---

## *Ficus* – Fig

**D**

582    Upper side
**Fig**

*Ficus carica* L.
**Fig**
Fig. 582 – see p. 146/147

● Leaves 20–30cm long, of varied outline but usually roundish and with 3, 5 or 7 lobes varying in size
● Rounded at the end
● Leaf-stalk 5–8cm long, thickish and usually with an enlarged base
● Dark green and bristly above; paler green and with soft, appressed hairs beneath

---

## *Morus* – Mulberry

**DD**

583    Upper side
**Black Mulberry**

*Morus nigra* L.
**Black Mulberry**
Fig. 583 – see p. 146/147

● Leaves 5–15cm long, broadly ovate or heart-shaped in outline, with 2 or more lobes, irregularly coarsely serrate
● Tip long and finely pointed
● Leaf-stalk 1–4cm long and often hairy
● Dark green and roughly hairy above; paler green beneath with appressed hairs

---

**C₁C₁**    Leaves not roughly hairy above

Correct, see **D₁** or **D₁D₁** (p. 83)
Wrong, back to **C₁**

---

**D₁**    Shrubs up to 5m with prickles or thorns

Correct, see **E**, **EE** (p. 83) or **EEE** (p. 83)
Wrong, see **D₁D₁** (p. 83)

---

## *Ribes* – Currant, Gooseberry

**E**

584    Under side
**Gooseberry**

*Ribes uva-crispa* L.
**Gooseberry**
Fig. 584 – see p. 146/147

● Leaves 2–6cm long, heart-shaped to roundish in outline and 3- or 5-lobed
● Rounded at the end or with a small point
● Leaf-stalk 1–2cm long and somewhat enlarged at the base
● Shiny dark green above and often slightly hairy; medium green beneath and softly hairy, later becoming glabrous

## *Crataegus* – Hawthorn

**EE**

***Crataegus laevigata*** (Poir.) DC.
**Midland Hawthorn**
Fig. 585 – see p. 146/147

● Leaves 3–5cm long, varied in outline but usually ovate, obovate or roundish

● Obtuse or flattened at the end and with small teeth

● Leaf-stalk 0.8–1.5cm long and grooved; stipules lanceolate to ovate, serrate with glandular teeth

● Shiny dark green above and pale medium green to pale bluish green beneath

585  Upper side
**Midland Hawthorn**

**EE E**

***Crataegus monogyna*** Jacq.
**Hawthorn**
Fig. 586 – see p. 146/147

● Leaves 3–6cm long, broadly ovate or rhombic in outline and deeply 3-, 5-, 7- or 9-lobed

● Often flattened at the end and often with the lobes themselves lobed about the middle

● Leaf-stalk 1–2cm long, grooved; stipules crescent-shaped and toothed

● Shiny dark green and glabrous above; bluish green beneath and often slightly hairy in the axils of the veins

586  Upper side
**Hawthorn**

| D₁D₁ | Trees or shrubs without prickles/thorns | Correct, see **E₁** or **E₁E₁** (p. 85) Wrong, back to **D₁** (p. 82) |

| **E₁** | Lobes of leaves with one or more finely printed secondary lobes (Fig. 587, 588) | Correct, see **F** or **FF** Wrong, see **E₁E₁** (p. 85) |

587
Upper side
**Silver Maple**

588
Upper side
**Norway Maple**

| **F** | Leaves conspicuously silvery to white beneath (Fig. 589, 590) | Correct, see **G** Wrong, see **FF** |

## *Acer* – Maple

**G**

***Acer saccharinum*** L.
**Silver Maple**
Fig. 589 – see p. 148/149

● Leaves 10–15cm long, broadly ovate in outline and 5-lobed

● Middle lobe with a long point at the end

● Leaf-stalk 4–7cm long, usually reddish above and without milky juice

● Medium to dark green and glabrous above; silvery grey beneath

589  Under side
**Silver Maple**

***Acer saccharinum*** L.
**f. *laciniatum*** (Carr.) Rehd. **'Wieri'**
**Silver Maple, Wier's form**
Fig. 590 – see p. 148/149

● Leaves 8–15cm long, broadly ovate to roundish in outline and deeply 5-lobed

● Middle lobe with a long point at the end

● Leaf-stalk 4–7cm long, green and without milky juice

● Dark green and glabrous above; silvery grey beneath

590  Underside
**Silver Maple, Wier's form**

| **FF** | Leaves not conspicuously silvery grey or white beneath | Correct, see **G₁** or **G₁G₁** (p. 84) Wrong, back to **F** |

| **G₁** | All lobes, or at least the middle one, completely or for the greater part finely to coarsely serrate or dentate | Correct, see **H, HH** (p. 84), **HHH** (p. 84), **HHHH** (p. 84), or **HHHHH** (p. 84) Wrong, see **G₁G₁** (p. 84) |

## *Forsythia* – Forsythia

**H**

***Forsythia europaea*** Deg. et Bald.
**European Forsythia**
Fig. 591 – see p. 148/149

● Leaves 4–8cm long, ovate to ovate-lanceolate in outline and very rarely lobed

● Pointed at the end and the tip often slightly curved to one side

● Leaf-stalk 1–3cm long

● Dark green above and pale green beneath; both sides glabrous

591  Upper side
**Balkan Forsythia**

## *Acer* – Maple

**HH**

*Acer rufinerve* Sieb. et Zucc.
**Grey-budded Snake-bark Maple**

Fig. 592 – see p. 148/149

- Leaves 5–13cm long, broadly elliptic, roundish or obliquely ovate in outline and usually distinctly 3-lobed
- Middle lobe finely pointed at the end
- Leaf-stalk 2–7cm long, pink to dark red and furrowed
- Dark green to bluish green above; paler green beneath with brownish red hairs along the veins especially on young leaves

592   Upper side **Grey-budded Snake-bark Maple**

---

**HH H**

*Acer palmatum* Thunb.
**Smooth Japanese Maple**

Fig. 593 – see p. 148/149

- Leaves 5–10cm long, circular in outline, cut more than halfway towards the centre into 3, 5, 7, 9 or 11 lobes
- Middle lobe finely pointed at the end
- Leaf-stalk 2–6cm long, glabrous or sparsely hairy, green or tinged red
- Medium green and glabrous above; pale green beneath with whitish markings in the axils of the veins

593   Upper side **Smooth Japanese Maple**

---

**HH HH**

*Acer japonicum* Thunb.
**'Aconitifolium'
Downy Japanese Maple**

Fig. 594 – see p. 148/149

- Leaves 8–15cm long, roundish in outline and divided almost to the base into 9 or 11 pinnatisect lobes
- Middle lobe finely pointed at the end
- Leaf-stalk 3–6cm long and tinged red especially above
- Medium green above, paler green beneath; silky hairy only when young

594   Upper side **Downy Japanese Maple**

---

## *Liquidambar* – Sweet Gum

**HH HH H**

*Liquidambar styraciflua* L.
**Sweet Gum**

Fig. 595 – see p. 150/151

- Leaves 10–20cm long, broadly ovate or roundish in outline, 3-lobed on young trees and 5- or 7-lobed on older trees
- Middle lobe pointed at the end
- Leaf-stalk 4–9cm long
- Shiny green and glabrous above; distinctly paler green beneath with white to brownish tufts of hairs

595   Upper side **Sweet Gum**

---

| **G₁G₁** | Middle lobe of leaves not finely serrate or dentate | Correct, see **H₁** or **H₁H₁**<br>Wrong, back to **G₁** (p. 83) |
|---|---|---|
| **H₁** | Leaves very deeply (far beyond the middle) 5- or more rarely 7-lobed; individual lobes always longer than broad (Fig. 596) | Correct, see **I**<br>Wrong, see **H₁H₁** |

## *Platanus* – Plane

**I**

*Platanus orientalis* L.
**Oriental Plane**

Fig. 596 – see p. 150/151

- Leaves 10–20cm long, broadly ovate or roundish in outline and deeply 5- or 7-lobed; only 3-lobed on younger shoots
- Middle lobe with a very long point at the end
- Leaf-stalk 3–7cm long and thickened bulb-like at the base
- Shiny medium green above and pale green beneath; finely and densely hairy when young, later becoming glabrous

596   Upper side **Oriental Plane**

---

| **H₁H₁** | The 3, 5 or 7 lobes not or only just reaching halfway towards the centre of the leaf | Correct, see **I₁** or **I₁I₁** (p. 85)<br>Wrong, Back to **H₁** |
| **I₁** | Middle lobe of leaves not or only rarely having very coarse teeth | Correct, see **K**, **KK** (p. 85) or **KKK** (p. 85)<br>Wrong, see **I₁I₁** (p. 85)<br><br>siehe **I₁I₁** (S. 85) |

## *Acer* – Maple

**K**

*Acer cappadocicum* Gled.
**Cappadocian Maple**

Fig. 597 – see p. 150/151

- Leaves 10–20cm long and equally broad, roundish or broadly heart-shaped in outline and with 5 or 7 lobes
- Middle lobe with a fine, long point at the end
- Leaf-stalk 5–15cm long
- Dark green above and paler green beneath, both sides glabrous

597   Upper side **Cappadocian Maple**

## *Platanus* - Plane

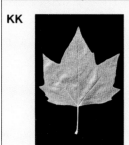

**KK**

*Platanus x acerifolia* (Ait.) Willd
*Platanus hybrida* Brot.
**London Plane**
Fig. 598 - see p. 150/151

● Leaves 10–25cm long and equally broad, very varied in outline but usually roundish and 3-, 5- or 7-lobed

● Middle lobe pointed at the end

● Leaf-stalk 3–10cm long and thickened bulb-like at the base

● Shiny green and glabrous above; paler green beneath, finely hairy, later becoming glabrous

598    Upper side
**London Plane**

## *Catalpa* - Catalpa

**KK**
**K**

*Catalpa ovata* G. Don et Zucc.
**Yellow Catalpa**
Fig. 599 - see p. 150/151

● Leaves 10–25cm long, varied in outline; usually broadly ovate or heart-shaped and often 2-, 3- or 5-lobed

● End of leaf shortly pointed

● Leaf-stalk 4–10cm long, often dark red above and green beneath

● Dark green above with very soft hairs; paler to medium green beneath and only slightly rough to the touch

599    Upper side
**Yellow Catalpa**

$I_1I_1$    Middle lobe of leaves with 2 or more clearly visible large, printed teeth (Fig. 600)    Correct, see $K_1$ or $K_1K_1$
Wrong, back to $I_1$ (p. 84)

600    Under side
**Norway Maple**

## *Acer* - Maple

**$K_1$**

*Acer platanoides* L.
**Norway Maple**
Fig. 601 - see p. 150/151

● Leaves 10–20cm long and equally broad, roundish or broadly heart-shaped in outline and with 3, 5 or 7 lobes of varying size

● Middle lobe with a long, fine point at the end

● Leaf-stalk to 15cm long, usually reddish, with milky juice and somewhat thickened at the base

● Dark green and glabrous above; pale green beneath, with tufts of hair in the axils of the veins, later glabrous

601    Upper side
**Norway Maple**

**$K_1$**
**$K_1$**

*Acer saccharum* Marsh.
**Sugar Maple**
Fig. 602 - see p. 152/153

● Leaves 8–15cm long and equally broad, broadly ovate or roundish in outline and with 3 or 5 lobes

● Middle lobe with a long fine point at the end

● Leaf-stalk 5–10cm long and often tinged red

● Medium to dark green and glabrous above; greyish green and glabrous beneath

602    Upper side
**Sugar Maple**

$E_1E_1$    Lobes of leaves without finely pointed secondary lobes (Fig. 603–615)    Correct, see $F_1$, $F_1F_1$ or $F_1F_1F_1$ (p. 86)
Wrong, back to $E_1$ (p. 83)

$F_1$    Lobes entire, without secondary lobes    Correct, see $G_2$ or $G_2G_2$
Wrong, see $F_1F_1$ or $F_1F_1F_1$ (p. 86)

## *Acer* - Maple

**$G_2$**

*Acer monspessulanum* L.
**Montpelier Maple**
Fig. 603 - see p. 152/153

● Leaves 3–6cm long, horizontally elliptic in outline with 3 lobes

● Middle lobe rounded at the end

● Leaf-stalk 1–3cm long and somewhat broadened at the base

● Shiny dark green and glabrous above; bluish grey beneath, hairy at first and later becoming glabrous

603    Upper side    **Montpelier Maple**

## *Hedera* - Ivy

**$G_2$**
**$G_2$**

*Hedera helix* L.
**Ivy**
Fig. 604 - see p. 152/153

● Leaves 4–10cm long, varied in outline; ovate to roundish on non-flowering shoots, 3- or 5-lobed, leathery and evergreen

● Middle lobe obtuse or rounded at the end

● Leaf-stalk 3–7cm long and usually brown to brownish red above

● Dark bluish green above with clearly visible pale yellow veins and glabrous; dull pale green and glabrous beneath

604    Upper side
**Ivy**

$F_1F_1$    Lobes with secondary lobes, the latter rounded and entire, more rarely undulate or coarsely crenate-sinuate (Fig. 605)    Correct, see $G_3$ (p. 86)
Wrong, see $F_1F_1F_1$ (p. 86)

## *Acer* – Maple

**G₃**

**Acer campestre** L.
**Field Maple**
Fig. 605 – see p. 152/153

- Leaves 3–10cm long, roundish to ovate in outline and with 3 or 5 lobes
- Middle lobe obtuse or rounded at the end
- Leaf-stalk 1–5 cm long and usually reddish above
- Dark green and glabrous above; paler green beneath, softly hairy and later becoming glabrous

605   Upper side
**Field Maple**

| | | |
|---|---|---|
| **F₁F₁** **F₁** | Lobes of leaves distinctly finely to coarsely serrate or dentate (Fig. 606–615) | Correct, see **G₄** or **G₄G₄** Wrong, back to **F₁** (p. 85) |

| | | |
|---|---|---|
| **G₄** | Leaves conspicuously snow-white beneath with matted woolly hairs (Fig. 606) | Correct, see **H₂** Wrong, see **G₄G₄** |

## *Populus* – Poplar

**H₂**

**Populus alba** L.
**White Poplar**
Fig. 606 – see p. 152/153

- Leaves 5–12cm long and varied in outline; elliptic to ovate on long shoots and suckers and with 3 or 5 lobes
- Middle lobe pointed or slightly rounded at the end
- Leaf-stalk 2–4cm long, flattened and white hairy
- Shiny dark green above, glabrous when mature; remaining densely white-felted beneath; at first both sides covered with matted woolly hairs

606   Under side
**White Poplar**

| | | |
|---|---|---|
| **G₄G₄** | Leaves yellow, blue, pale or dark green beneath | Correct, see **H₃**, **H₃H₃** or **H₃H₃H₃** Wrong, back to **G₄** |

| | | |
|---|---|---|
| **H₃** | Leaves less than 5cm long and the 3 or 5 lobes coarsely doubly serrate (Fig. 607) | Correct, see **I₂** Wrong, see **H₃H₃** |

## *Ribes* – Currant

**I₂**

**Ribes alpinum** L.
**Mountain Currant**
Fig. 607 – see p. 152/153

- Leaves 2–5cm long, broadly ovate to roundish in outline with 3, more rarely 5 lobes
- Middle lobe acute, obtuse or rounded at the end
- Leaf-stalk 1–2cm long with long glandular hairs
- Dark green above with scattered hairs; paler green beneath, shiny and glabrous

607   Upper side
**Mountain Currant**

| | | |
|---|---|---|
| **H₃H₃** | Leaves more than 5cm long and lobes only finely simply and doubly toothed | Correct, see **I₃** or **I₃I₃** Wrong, see **H₃H₃H₃** |

## *Ribes* – Currant

**I₃**

**Ribes nigrum** L.
**Black Currant**
Fig. 608 – see p. 154/155

- Leaves 5–10cm long, roundish in outline and with 3 or 5 lobes
- Middle lobe pointed at end
- Leaf-stalk 2–5cm long and broadened at the base
- Medium to dark green above, hairy at first, later becoming glabrous; pale green beneath with yellowish resin glands

608   Upper side
**Black Currant**

**I₃I₃**

**Ribes rubrum** L.
**Red Currant**
Fig. 609 – see p. 154/155

- Leaves 4–7cm long, roundish in outline and with 3 or 5 lobes
- Middle lobe pointed at end
- Leaf-stalk 2–3.5cm long and somewhat thickened at the base
- Dark green above, not shiny; paler green beneath and softly hairy, not dotted with glands, later becoming glabrous

609   Upper side
**Red Currant**

| | | |
|---|---|---|
| **H₃H₃** **H₃** | Leaves more strongly and coarsely serrate or dentate than in the Red and Black Currants and more than 5cm long including the leaf-stalk | Correct, see **I₄** (p. 87) or **I₄I₄** (p. 87) Wrong, back to **H₃H₃** or **H₃** |

# Key III

# Lobed leaves

**I₄** Leaves with a deep, narrow and acute basal sinus (Fig. 610)

Correct, see **K₂**
Wrong, see **I₄I₄**

## *Vitis* – Vine

**K₂**

610   Under side
**Grape-vine**

***Vitis vinifera*** L. **ssp.** *vinifera*
**Grape-vine**
Fig. 610 – see p. 154/155

● Leaves 5–15cm long, varied in outline; usually roundish and as a rule deeply 3- or 5-lobed

● Middle lobe with a short point at the end

● Leaf-stalk 4–8cm long

● Dark green above and hairy when young, later becoming glabrous; pale to greyish green beneath and often hairy

**I₄I₄** Basal sinus of leaves always shallow; base of leaf-blade truncate, heart-shaped, rounded or broadly wedge-shaped (Fig. 611–615)

Correct, see **K₃** or **K₃K₃**
Wrong, back to **I₄**

**K₃** Leaf-stalk 2–3cm long, narrowly grooved above, and with 2–4 green concave nectar-glands just below the base of the leaf-blade

Correct, see **L₂**
Wrong, see **K₃K₃**

## *Viburnum* – Viburnum

**L₂**

611   Upper side
**Guelder Rose**

***Viburnum opulus*** L.
**Guelder Rose**
Fig. 611 – see p. 154/155

● Leaves 4–12cm long, varied in outline; usualy roundish or obliquely elliptic and with 3 or 5 lobes

● Middle lobe shortly pointed or obtuse

● Leaf-stalk 2–3cm long, tinged red and with 2–4 green glands

● Dark green and glabrous above; greyish green beneath, slightly woolly and with very prominent yellowish green veins

**K₃K₃** Leaf-stalks without glands at the base of the blade and longer than 2cm

Correct, see **L₁, L₁L₁, L₁L₁L₁ or L₁L₁L₁L₁**
Wrong, back to **K₃**

## *Acer* – Maple

**L₁**

612   Upper side
**Sycamore**

***Acer pseudoplatanus*** L.
**Sycamore**
Fig. 612 – see p. 154/155

● Leaves 8–20cm long, broadly elliptic or heart-shaped in outline and 3- or 5-lobed

● Middle lobe shortly pointed, obtuse or rounded at the end

● Leaf-stalk up to 10cm long and tinged red above

● Dark green and glabrous above; pale bluish green beneath, densely hairy at first and later usually becoming glabrous; veins pale green

**L₁**
**L₁**

613   Under side
**Italian Maple**

***Acer opalus*** Mill.
**Italian Maple**
Fig. 613 – see p. 154/155

● Leaves 4–10cm long, usually a little broader, usually roundish in outline and with usually 5 lobes

● Middle lobe usually obtuse at the end

● Leaf-stalk 3–9cm long and tinged dark red above

● Dark green and glabrous above; bluish green beneath, hairy at first, later becoming glabrous; veins yellowish white

**L₁**
**L₁**
**L₁**

614   Under side
**Red Maple**

***Acer rubrum*** L.
**Red Maple**
Fig. 614 – see p. 156/157

● Leaves 5–10cm long, broadly ovate or roundish in outline and usually with 3 lobes

● Middle lobe pointed at the end

● Leaf-stalk 4–6cm long and coloured red and green above

● Dark green above and greyish green beneath; both sides glabrous or the underside hairy on the veins

## *Morus* – Mulberry

**L₁**
**L₁**
**L₁**
**L₁**

615   Upper side
**White Mulberry**

***Morus alba*** L.
**White Mulberry**
Fig. 615 – see p. 156/157

● Leaves 6–18cm long, varied in outline; without lobes but with a regularly toothed margin or with 3, 5 or 7 lobes

● Middle lobe only very shortly pointed

● Leaf-stalk 2–4cm long, grooved and woolly at first

● Shiny dark green and glabrous above; pale bluish green beneath and hairy on the larger veins; veins pale yellow to whitish

**AA** Leaves not lobed like a maple but with 3–10 lobes on each side

Correct, see **B₁** or **B₁B₁**
Wrong, back to **A** (p. 82)

**B₁** Leaves with 3–4 clearly pointed lobes on each side (Fig. 616)

Correct, see **C₂**
Wrong, see **B₁B₁**

## *Sorbus* – Service Tree, Whitebeam

**C₂**

***Sorbus torminalis*** (L.) Crantz
**Wild Service Tree**
Fig. 616 – see p. 156/157

● Leaves 6–10cm long, ovate to roundish in outline and with 3 or 4 pointed lobes on each side

● Middle lobe pointed at the end

● Leaf-stalk 2–5cm long, loosely felted, later glabrous

● Shiny dark green above and at first finely hairy; pale bluish green beneath and loosely felted, later the hairs remaining only in the axils of the veins

616   Upper side
**Wild Service Tree**

**B₁B₁** Leaves with more than 4 lobes on each side (Fig. 617–629)

Correct, see **C₃** or **C₃C₃**
Wrong, back to **B₁**

**C₃** Lobes of leaves finely serrate (Fig. 617–621)

Correct, see **D₂** or **D₂D₂**
Wrong, see **C₃C₃**

**D₂** Leaves densely white-felted beneath (Fig. 617–618)

Correct, see **E₂** or **E₂E₂**
Wrong, see **D₂D₂**

617
Under side
**Mougeot's Whitebeam**

618
Under side
**Swedish Whitebeam**

## *Sorbus* – Whitebeam

**E₂**

***Sorbus mougeotii*** Soy.-Will. et Godr.
**Mougeot's Whitebeam**
Fig. 619 – see p. 156/157

● Leaves 6–10cm long, oblong-elliptic to ovate in outline; the numerous lobes becoming smaller towards the end of the leaf

● Leaf-blade shortly pointed at the end

● Leaf-stalk 1–2cm long

● Dark green above, hairy at first, later becoming glabrous; densely white-felted beneath

619   Upper side
**Mougeot's Whitebeam**

**E₂**
**E₂**

***Sorbus intermedia*** (Ehrh.) Pers.
**Swedish Whitebeam**
Fig. 620 – see p. 156/157

● Leaves 6–12cm long, oblong-elliptic to elliptic in outline; the 5–8 lobes on each side becoming smaller towards the end of the leaf

● Leaf-blade very shortly pointed or obtuse at the end

● Leaf-stalk 1–2cm long and grey-felted

● Shiny dark green above; densely white- to grey-felted beneath

620   Upper side
**Swedish Whitebeam**

**D₂D₂** Leaves not densely white-felted beneath (Fig. 621)

Correct, see **E₃**
Wrong, back to **D₂**

## *Sorbus* – Whitebeam

**E₃**

***Sorbus latifolia*** (Lam.) Pers.
**Broad-leaved Whitebeam**
Fig. 621 – see p. 156/157

● Leaves 7–12cm long, ovate to broadly ovate in outline; the 6–9 lobes on each side becoming smaller towards the end of the leaf

● Leaf-blade shortly pointed at the end

● Leaf-stalk 1–3cm long

● Shiny dark green and glabrous above; only slightly grey-felted beneath and appearing greyish green

621   Under side
**Broad-leaved Whitebeam**

**C₃C₃** Lobes of leaves not serrate; leaves lobed like an Oak (Fig. 623–629)

Correct, see **D₃** (p. 89) or **D₃D₃** (p. 89)
Wrong, back to **C₃**

**D₃** Leaves with broad, obtuse or rounded lobes (Fig. 623–625) — Correct, see **E₄** or **E₄E₄**; Wrong, see **D₃D₃**

**E₄** An auricle (small lobe) on each side of the midrib at the base of the leaf-blade (Fig. 622) and leaf-stalk not more than 7mm long — Correct, see **F₂**; Wrong, see **E₄E₄**

622  Under side
**Auricle in Pedunculate Oak**

## *Quercus* – Oak

**F₂**

623  Upper side
**Pedunculate Oak**

*Quercus robur* L.
**Common Oak, Pedunculate Oak**
Fig. 623 – see p. 158/159

- Leaves 5–16cm long, obovate to elliptic, with the greatest breadth in the upper third and with 4 or 5 irregular, rounded lobes on each side
- Middle lobe rounded at end
- Leaf-stalk at most 7mm long
- Shiny dark green and glabrous above; pale to bluish green beneath, rarely with a few hairs

**E₄E₄** No auricles (small lobes) present at the base of the leaf-blade and leaf-stalk 7–25mm long (Fig. 624, 625) — Correct, see **F₃** or **F₃F₃**; Wrong, back to **E₄**

## *Quercus* – Oak

**F₃**

624  Upper side
**Downy Oak**

*Quercus pubescens* Willd.
**Downy Oak**
Fig. 624 – see p. 158/159

- Leaves 5–10cm long, varied in form; usually obovate, with the greatest breadth in the upper third, with 5–7 lobes on each side
- Most lobes obtuse at the end, occasionally with a very small point
- Leaf-stalk 8–12mm long
- Both sides felted at first; later the upper side dark green and glabrous; greyish green beneath because of the hairs

**F₃**
**F₃**

625  Upper side
**Sessile Oak**

*Quercus petraea* Liebl.
**Sessile Oak**
Fig. 625 – see p. 158/159

- Leaves 6–12cm long, obovate, usually broadest in the middle and with 5 to more rarely 9 rounded lobes on each side
- Middle lobe rounded at end
- Leaf-stalk 10–25mm long
- Dull dark green and glabrous above; paler green beneath with very small stellate hairs

**D₃D₃** Lobes of leaves with a short or long point — Correct, see **E₅** or **E₅E₅**; Wrong, back to **D₃**

626
Under side
**Turkey Oak**

627
Under side
**Red Oak**

## *Quercus* – Oak

**E₅**

628  Upper side
**Turkey Oak**

*Quercus cerris* L.
**Turkey Oak**
Fig. 628 – see p. 158/159

- Leaves 6–15cm long and varied in form; usually narrowly elliptic, broadest in the upper part, and with 7–9 irregular, often distinctly pointed lobes on each side
- Middle lobe usually shortly pointed at the end
- Leaf-stalk 7–15mm long
- Roughly hairy above at first, later glabrous and shiny; pale green beneath with soft woolly hairs

**E₅**
**E₅**

629  Upper side
**Red Oak**

*Quercus rubra* L.
**Red Oak**
Fig. 629 – see p. 158/159

- Leaves 10–20cm long, usually elliptic or obovate with 4–6 lobes on each side tipped by a long bristle or whisker
- Middle lobe ending in a long point
- Leaf-stalk to 5cm long
- Dull to dark green above and glabrous in older leaves; pale yellowish green beneath with stellate hairs in the angles formed by the midrib and lateral veins

A    Leaves with numerous, long, widely separated hairs on the margin (Fig. 630, 631)    Correct, see **B** or **BB**
Wrong, see **AA**

## *Rhododendron* – Rhododendron

**B**

***Rhododendron hirsutum*** L.
**Hairy Alpenrose**
Fig. 630 – see p. 160/161

- Leaves 1–3.5cm long, oblong-elliptic in outline, thick and leathery
- Obtuse or rounded at the end
- Leaf-stalk 0.3–0.8cm long
- Shiny dark green above, somewhat wrinkled and usually glabrous; pale green beneath with at first whitish and later yellowish brown glandular scales

630   Under side  **Hairy Alpenrose**

## *Erica* – Heath, Heather

**BB**

***Erica tetralix*** L.
**Cross-leaved Heath, Bog Heather**
Fig. 631 – see p. 160/161

- Leaves 3–6mm long, narrowly linear or needle-shaped in outline and with inrolled margins
- Obtuse or rounded at the end
- Leaf-stalk 1–2mm long, very broad and usually woolly hairy
- Dark green surface above under the whitish felt; white beneath with a prominent medium green midrib

631   Under side
**Cross-leaved Heath**

AA    Leaves without long hairs on the margins    Correct, see **B₁** or **B₁B₁**
Wrong, back to **A**

B₁    Under side of leaves brown because of brownish hairs or spherical glands (especially clear in older leaves) (Fig. 632–634)    Correct, see **C** or **CC**
Wrong, see **B₁B₁**

C    Under side of leaves distinctly rust-brown to brown because of crisped hairs (Fig. 632, 633)    Correct, see **D** or **DD**
Wrong, see **CC**

## *Ledum* – Ledum

**D**

***Ledum palustre*** L.
**Marsh Ledum**
Fig. 632 – see p. 160/161

- Leaves 2–5cm long, linear to lanceolate in outline and with strongly recurved margins
- Obtuse or rounded at the end and usually with a fine, short point
- Leaf-stalk 2–3mm long with rusty brown hairs
- Dark green above and distinctly felted; rust-red to brown-felted beneath

632   Under side
**Marsh Ledum**

**DD**

***Ledum groenlandicum*** Oed.
**Labrador Tea**
Fig. 633 – see p. 160/161

- Leaves 2–5cm long, oblong to oblong-ovate in outline and with the margins rolled under
- Obtuse at end
- Leaf-stalk 3–6mm long with brown hairs
- Medium to dark green above with an undulate surface; pale to dark green beneath under the dark brown, crisped hairs

633   Under side
**Labrador Tea**

CC    Under side of leaves distinctly brown because of brownish spherical glands especially in older leaves (Fig. 634)    Correct, see **D₁**
Wrong, back to **C**

## *Rhododendron* – Rhododendron

**D₁**

***Rhododendron ferrugineum*** L.
**Alpenrose**
Fig. 634 – see p. 160/161

- Leaves 2–5cm long, oblong-lanceolate to oblong-elliptic in outline, leathery and narrowing into the stalk; margins somewhat recurved
- Rounded or obtuse at the end
- Leaf-stalk up to 6mm long
- Shiny dark green and slightly wrinkled above; brown beneath because of spherical glands

634   Under side
**Alpenrose**

B₁B₁    Under side of leaves not coloured brown because of hairs or spherical glands    Correct, see **C₁** (p. 91), **C₁C₁** (p. 92) or **C₁C₁C₁** (p. 92)
Wrong, back to **B₁**

**C₁**   Margins of leaves distinctly inrolled or somewhat recurved (Fig. 635–645)

Correct, see **D₂** or **D₂D₂**
Wrong, see **C₁C₁** (p. 92) or **C₁C₁C₁** (p. 92)

**D₂**   Midrib not visible beneath (Fig. 635, 636); only a white band visible

Correct, see **E** or **EE**
Wrong, see **D₂D₂**

## Empetrum – Crowberry

**E**

### Empetrum nigrum L.
### Crowberry
Fig. 635 – see p. 160/161

- Leaves 4–7mm long, narrowly elliptic or linear in outline, leathery and with strongly inrolled margins
- Obtuse or shortly pointed at the end
- Leaf-stalk 1–2mm long, broad and appressed to the shoot
- Dark green and glabrous above; with a white keel and scattered hairs beneath

635   Under side
**Crowberry**

## Erica – Heath, Heather

**EE**

### Erica carnea L.
### Spring Heath
Fig. 636 – see p. 162/163

- Leaves 4–8mm long, needle-like or linear in outline and with inrolled margins
- Rounded at the end and usually with a prickly point
- Leaf-stalk 1–2mm long and as broad as the blade
- Medium to dark green, glabrous and shiny above; with a white longitudinal band beneath

636   Under side
**Spring Heath**

**D₂D₂**   Midrib clearly visible on the under side

Correct, see **E₁** or **E₁E₁**
Wrong, back to **D₂**

**E₁**   Leaves narrowly elliptic, needle-like or narrowly linear in outline and not longer than 10mm

Correct, see **F, FF** or **FFF**
Wrong, see **E₁E₁**

## Loiseleuria – Loiselauria

**F**

### Loiseleuria procumbens (L.)
Desv.
### Trailing Azalea
Fig. 637 – see p. 162/163

- Leaves 4–8mm long, narrowly elliptic in outline, with recurved margins and not much broader than the stalk
- Obtuse or shortly pointed at the end
- Leaf-stalk 1–3mm long
- Dark green above with shallow longitudinal furrows; bluish white beneath with very prominent midrib

637   Upper and under
**Trailing Azalea**

## Erica – Heath, Heather

**FF**

### Erica arborea L.
### Tree Heath
Fig. 638 – see p. 162/163

- Leaves 4–7mm long, needle-shaped or narrowly linear in outline with the margins strongly inrolled
- Obtuse or rounded at the end
- Leaf-stalk 1–2mm long, whitish and almost as broad as the blade
- Dark green above; whitish beneath between the inrolled margins; midrib clearly visible

638   Under and upper
**Tree Heath**

**FF
F**

### Erica vagans L.
### Cornish Heath
Fig. 639 – see p. 162/163

- Leaves 4–10mm long, narrowly linear in outline and not much broader than the stalk
- Obtuse or rounded at the end
- Leaf-stalk 1–2mm long and as broad as the blade
- Dark green above; whitish beneath with a clearly visible dark green midrib

639   Under side
**Cornish Heath**

**E₁E₁**   Leaves elliptic, ovate or oblong-ovate in outline and rarely longer than 10mm (Fig. 640)

Correct, see **F₂** (p. 92)
Wrong, see **E₁E₁E₁** (p. 92) or **E₁E₁E₁E₁** (p. 92)

640   Upper side
**Cranberry**

## *Vaccinium* – Vaccinium

**F2**

**Vaccinium oxycoccus** L.
**Cranberry**
Fig. 641 – see p. 164/165

- Leaves 5–10mm long, elliptic, ovate or oblong-ovate in outline and with recurved margins
- Obtuse or shortly pointed at the end
- Leaf-stalk at most 2mm long
- Shiny dark green above and usually with a slightly impressed midrib; with a bluish green bloom beneath

641    Under side
**Cranberry**

| | | |
|---|---|---|
| **E₁E₁** **E₁** | Leaves narrowly elliptic to obovate in outline and between 1 and 3cm long (Fig. 642, 643) | Correct, see **F₃** or **F₃F₃** Wrong, see **E₁E₁E₁E₁** |

## *Buxus* – Box

**F3**

**Buxus sempervirens** L.
**Box**
Fig. 642 – see p. 164/165

- Leaves 1–3cm long, narrowly elliptic to oblong-ovate in outline, leathery and with the margins only slightly recurved
- Usually emarginate at the end
- Leaf-stalk to 2mm long
- Shiny dark green above with an often whitish midrib; pale green beneath with prominent midrib

642    Upper side
**Box**

## *Vaccinium* – Vaccinium

**F3**
**F3**

**Vaccinium vitis-idaea** L.
**Cowberry**
Fig. 643 – see p. 164/165

- Leaves 1–3cm long, elliptic to obovate in outline, thick, leathery and with slightly recurved margins
- Usually emarginate at the end
- Leaf-stalk 2–5mm long and woolly hairy
- Dark green above with whitish veins; greyish green beneath with brownish dots

643    Under side
**Cowberry**

| | | |
|---|---|---|
| **E₁E₁** **E₁E₁** | Leaves narrowly lanceolate in outline and between 1 and 5cm long | Correct, see **F₄** or **F₄F₄** Wrong, back to **E₁** (p. 91) |

## *Andromeda* – Bog Rosemary

**F4**

**Andromeda polifolia** L.
**Bog Rosemary**
Fig. 644 – see p. 162/163

- Leaves 1–5cm long, narrowly lanceolate in outline, leathery and with strongly recurved margins
- Finely pointed at the end or with a prickly tip
- Leaf-stalk 3–7mm long and usually white
- Shiny dark green above, the surface broken up by white lateral veins; silvery, white or pale bluish green beneath with clearly visible midrib

644    Under side
**Bog Rosemary**

## *Rosmarinus* – Rosemary

**F4**
**F4**

**Rosmarinus officinalis** L.
**Rosemary**
Fig. 644 – see p. 162/163

- Leaves 3–5cm long, very narrowly lanceolate in outline, leathery and with inrolled margins
- Obtuse or rounded at the end
- Leaves sessile
- Dark green and slightly wrinkled above; densely white-felted beneath with a very prominent white midrib

645    Under side
**Rosemary**

| | | |
|---|---|---|
| **C₁C₁** | Margins of leaves curved upwards; individual leaves 1–3mm long (Fig. 646) | Correct, see **D₃** Wrong, see **C₁C₁C₁** |

## *Calluna* – Ling

**D3**

**Calluna vulgaris** (L. ) Hull
**Ling, Heather**
Fig. 646 – see p. 164/165

- Leaves 1–3mm long, needle-like or narrowly ovate in outline, scale-like and with the margins curved upwards
- Usually rounded at the end
- Leaves sessile
- Dark green above in summer, brownish red in winter and deeply grooved; keeled beneath

646    Upper side
**Ling**

| | | |
|---|---|---|
| **C₁C₁** **C₁** | Margins of leaves not inrolled or curved | Correct, see **D₄** (p. 93), **D₄D₄** (p. 93), **D₄D₄D₄** or **D₄D₄D₄D₄** (p. 94) Wrong, back to **C₁** (p. 91) |

| | | |
|---|---|---|
| **D₄** | Leaves lanceolate to obovate in outline, usually emarginate at the end and 0.3–2cm long (Fig. 647, 648) | Correct, see **E₂** or **E₂E₂** Wrong, see **D₄D₄** |

## Genista – Greenweed

**E₂**

### Genista pilosa L.
### Hairy Greenweed
Fig. 647 – see p. 164/165

● Leaves 3–12mm long, narrowly obovate to lanceolate in outline

● Emarginate or retuse at the end

● Leaves sessile or very shortly stalked

● Dark green and with short appressed hairs on both sides; later becoming glabrous

647   Under side  **Hairy Greenweed**

## Daphne – Daphne

**E₂**
**E₂**

### Daphne cneorum L.
### Garland Flower
Fig. 648 – see p. 164/165

● Leaves 5–20mm long, linear, lanceolate or spathulate in outline and rarely with a slightly recurved margin

● Emarginate or rounded at the end and then often with a small point

● Leaf-stalk very short and broad

● Medium to dark green above; bluish grey beneath with whitish veins

648   Upper side  **Garland Flower**

| | | |
|---|---|---|
| **D₄D₄** | Leaves fan-shaped in outline and with the upper margin irregularly undulate or deeply cut into several lobes (Fig. 649) | Correct, see **E₃** Wrong, see **D₄D₄D₄** |

## Ginkgo – Maidenhair Tree

**E₃**

### Ginkgo biloba L.
### Maidenhair Tree
Fig. 649 – see p. 166/167

● Leaves 6–10cm long, fan shaped in outline, with an irregularly undulate margin and fine, forked veins

● End of leaf broadened into the shape of a fan

● Leaf-stalk 2–9cm long

● Both sides glabrous and medium to dark green

649   Upper side  **Maidenhair Tree**

| | | |
|---|---|---|
| **D₄D₄** **D₄** | Leaves roundish or spathulate in outline and rounded or more rarely very slightly emarginate at the end (Fig. 650–653) | Correct, see **E₄** or **E₄E₄** Wrong, see **D₄D₄D₄D₄** (p. 94) |

| | | |
|---|---|---|
| **E₄** | Leaves 6–11cm long and base of blade deeply heart-shaped (Fig. 650) | Correct, see **F₅** Wrong, see **E₄E₄** |

## Cercis – Judas Tree

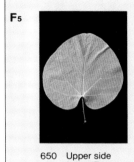

**F₅**

### Cercis siliquastrum L.
### Judas Tree
Fig. 650 – see p. 166/167

● Leaves 6–11cm long and equally broad, roundish, and occasionally slightly sinuate along the margin

● Broadly rounded or slightly emarginate at the end

● Leaf-stalk 3–4.5cm long with both sides tinged red

● Dark green above and bluish green beneath; both sides glabrous

650   Upper side
**Judas Tree**

| | | |
|---|---|---|
| **E₄E₄** | Leaves 0.4–4.5cm long and not deeply heart-shaped at the base of the blade (Fig. 651–653) | Correct, see **F₆** or **F₆F₆** Wrong, see **D₄D₄D₄D₄** |

| | | |
|---|---|---|
| **F₆** | Veins distinctly impressed on the upper side and leaf-stalk reddish on both sides (Fig. 651) | Correct, see **G** Wrong, see **F₆F₆** (p. 94) |

## Salix – Willow

**G**

### Salix reticulata L.
### Net-leaved Willow
Fig. 651 – see p. 166/167

● Leaves 1–4.5cm long and broadly elliptic to roundish in outline

● Obtuse or rounded at end

● Leaf-stalk 3–20mm long and reddish on both sides

● Dark green above with the impressed veins forming a network; grey to whitish grey beneath with very prominent veins

651   Upper side
**Net-leaved Willow**

**F₆F₆**  Veins not distinctly impressed on the upper side (Fig. 652, 653)

Correct, see **G₁** or **G₁G₁**
Wrong, back to **F₆** (p. 93)

## *Vaccinium* – Vaccinium

**G₁**

*Vaccinium uliginosum* L.
**Northern Bilberry**
Fig. 652 – see p. 166/167

● Leaves 5–20mm long, elliptic, obovate or roundish in outline and thick
● Usually rounded at the end, more rarely slightly retuse or obtuse
● Leaf-stalk 1–2mm long and slightly grooved above
● Medium green above; bluish green beneath with very prominent dark green veins

652  Under side
**Northern Bilberry**

## *Salix* – Willow

**G₁**
**G₁**

*Salix retusa* L.
**Blunt-leaved Willow**
Fig. 653 – see p. 166/167

● Leaves 4–20mm long, obovate to oblong-ovate or spathulate in outline and more rarely with small teeth at the margin
● Rounded, obtuse or emarginate at the end
● Leaf-stalk 2–5mm long
● Shiny medium to dark green and glabrous above; medium to whitish green beneath and slightly hairy when young

653  Upper side
**Blunt-leaved Willow**

**D₄D₄**  Leaves different from those in **D₄**,
**D₄D₄**  **D₄D₄** or **D₄D₄D₄** (e.g. Fig. 654, 655)

Correct, see **E₅** or **E₅E₅**
Wrong, back to **D₄** (p. 93)

654
**Butcher's Broom**

655
**Oleaster**

**E₅**  Leaves dark purple to black in colour (Fig. 656)

Correct, see **F₇**
Wrong, see **E₅E₅**

## *Fagus* – Beech

**F₇**

*Fagus sylvatica* L. **'Atropunicea'**
**Copper Beech**
Fig. 656 – see p. 168/169

● Leaves 5–10cm long, broadly elliptic to obovate in outline and with an undulate margin
● Shortly pointed at the end
● Leaf-stalk 2–5mm long and dark red to blackish in colour
● Both sides softly hairy when young and fringed at the margin; dark purple above and dark red to blackish beneath

656  Upper side
**Copper Beech**

**E₅E₅**  Leaves not dark purple in colour

Correct, see **F₈** or **F₈F₈**
Wrong, back to **E₅**

**F₈**  'Leaves' long and with a spiny tip (fig. 657)

Correct, see **G₂**
Wrong, see **F₈F₈**

## *Ruscus* – Butcher's Broom

**G₂**

*Ruscus aculeatus* L.
**Butcher's Broom**
Fig. 657 – see p. 166/167

● 'Leaves' (flattened shoots) 1–4cm long, elliptic to ovate tapering towards the end
● With a long, fine point, ending in a spine
● Leaf-stalk 1–3mm long
● Both sides medium green with dark green parallel veins

657  Upper side
**Butcher's Broom**

**F₈F₈**  Leaves not having a spiny tip

Correct, see **G₃, G₃G₃** (p. 95) or **G₃G₃G₃** (p. 95)
Wrong, back to **F₈**

**G₃**  Leaves broadly lanceolate to ovate and bluish green to greyish white beneath (Fig. 658)

Correct, see **H** (p. 95)
Wrong, see **G₃G₃** (p. 95)

## *Eucalyptus* – Gum Tree

**H**

*Eucalyptus globulus* Labill.
**Blue Gum**
Fig. 658 – see p. 168/169

- Leaves 7–15cm long and lanceolate to ovate in outline when young
- Pointed or prickly at the end
- Leaf-stalk in young leaves only very short
- Dark green above, often with a pale purple or whitish midrib; dark green or bluish green beneath

658  Under side
**Blue Gum**

---

**G₃G₃** Leaves linear to lanceolate and grey or silvery white beneath (Fig. 659, 660)

Correct, see **H₁** or **H₁H₁**
Wrong, see **G₃G₃G₃**

---

## *Hippophae* – Sea Buckthorn

**H₁**

*Hippophae rhamnoides* L.
**Sea Buckthorn**
Fig. 659 – see p. 168/169

- Leaves 5–7cm long, linear to lanceolate in outline and occasionally slightly recurved at the margin
- Obtuse or pointed at the end
- Leaf-stalk 1–3mm long and white, or leaves sessile
- With silvery scales on both sides

659  Under side **Sea Buckthorn**

---

## *Elaeagnus* – Oleaster

**H₁**
**H₁**

*Elaeagnus angustifolia* L.
**Oleaster**
Fig. 660 – see p. 168/169

- Leaves 4–8cm long and narrowly lanceolate in outline
- Slightly pointed, obtuse or rounded at the end
- Leaf-stalk 4–9mm long and white
- With silvery scales on the upper side; densely stellate hairy beneath and therefore appearing greyish white

660  Under side
**Oleaster**

---

**G₃G₃** Leaves not as in **G₃** (p. 94) and
**G₃**   **G₃G₃** (p. 95)

Correct, see **H₂** or **H₂H₂**
Wrong, back to **G₃** (p. 94)

---

**H₂** Leaves narrowly lanceolate, crescent-shaped, thick, and hanging from the twig (Fig. 661)

Correct, see **I**
Wrong, see **H₂H₂**

---

## *Eucalyptus* – Gum Tree

**I**

*Eucalyptus globulus* Labill.
**Blue Gum**
Fig. 661 – see p. 168/169

- Adult leaves 10–30cm long, somewhat crescent-shaped and narrowly lanceolate in outline
- With a long point at the end
- Leaf-stalk 1–5cm long, often slightly reddish
- Dark green above and somewhat bluish green beneath; both sides glabrous

661  Upper side
**Blue Gum**

---

**H₂H₂** Leaves narrowly lanceolate to narrowly ovate and not crescent-shaped

Correct, see **I₁, I₁I₁** (p. 96) or **I₁I₁I₁** (p. 98)
Wrong, back to **H₂**

---

**I₁** Leaves narrowly obovate and with their greatest breadth always above the middle of the blade

Correct, see **K** or **KK** (p. 96)
Wrong, see **I₁I₁** (p. 96) or **I₁I₁I₁** (p. 96)

---

**K** Leaves 3–8cm long, soft to the touch and medium to dark green beneath (Fig. 662)

Correct, see **L**
Wrong, see **KK** (p. 96)

---

## *Daphne* – Daphne

**L**

*Daphne mezereum* L.
**Mezereon**
Fig. 662 – see p. 170.171

- Leaves 3–8cm long, obovate oblong in outline and rarely with slightly recurved margins
- Shortly pointed at the end
- Leaf-stalk 3–5mm long
- Dark green above and greyish green beneath; both sides glabrous

662  Under side  **Mezereon**

| | | |
|---|---|---|
| **KK** | Leaves 6–14cm long, somewhat leathery and shiny dark green above (Fig. 663) | Correct, see **L₁** Wrong, back to **K** (p. 95) |

## *Daphne* – Daphne

**L₁**

***Daphne laureola*** L.
**Spurge Laurel**
Fig. 663 – see p. 168/169

- Leaves 6–14cm long and narrowly obovate in outline
- Shortly pointed at the end
- Leaves sessile or with a very short stalk
- Shiny dark green above and pale green beneath; both sides glabrous

663   Upper side   **Spurge Laurel**

| | | |
|---|---|---|
| **I₁I₁** | Leaves lanceolate, narrowly elliptic or narrowly obovate and with their greatest breadth at or below (rarely above) the middle of the blade (Fig. 664–676) | Correct, see **K₁** or **K₁K₁** Wrong, back to **I₁** (p. 95) |

| | | |
|---|---|---|
| **K₁** | Leaves obtuse or rounded at the end (Fig. 664–666) | Correct, see **L₂** or **L₂L₂** Wrong, see **K₁K₁** |

| | | |
|---|---|---|
| **L₂** | Globular shrubs growing on trees, their leaves with 4–8 parallel veins (Fig. 664) | Correct, see **M** Wrong, see **L₂L₂** |

## *Viscum* – Mistletoe

**M**

***Viscum album*** L.
**Mistletoe**
Fig. 664 – see p. 170/171

- Leaves 2–6.5cm long and spathulate, narrowly obovate or narrowly elliptic in outline
- Rounded at the end
- Leaves sessile
- Both sides glabrous, yellowish green and with parallel veins

664   Upper side   **Mistletoe**

| | | |
|---|---|---|
| **L₂L₂** | Shrubs not growing on trees; underside of leaves with clearly visible midrib and finer lateral veins | Correct, see **M₁** or **M₁M₁** Wrong, back to **L₂** |

## *Daphne* – Daphne

**M₁**

***Daphne alpina*** L.
**Alpine Mezereon**
Fig. 665 – see p. 170/171

- Leaves 1–5cm long, lanceolate to narrowly obovate in outline and often with their greatest breadth above the middle
- Obtuse or rounded at the end
- Leaves usually sessile
- Both sides hairy when young; dull green to dark green above and greyish green beneath

665   Upper side
**Alpine Mezereon**

## *Punica* – Pomegranate

**M₁**
**M₁**

***Punica granatum*** L.
**Pomegranate**
Fig. 666 – see p. 170/171

- Leaves 3–8cm long and oblong-elliptic in outline
- Obtuse or rounded at the end
- Leaf-stalk 1–5mm long and often reddish above
- Dark green above with an impressed midrib; pale green beneath; both sides glabrous

666   Upper side
**Pomegranate**

| | | |
|---|---|---|
| **K₁K₁** | Leaves pointed at the end | Correct, see **L₃** or **L₃L₃** (p. 97) Wrong, back to **K₁** |

| | | |
|---|---|---|
| **L₃** | Leaves 6–12cm long, oblong-lanceolate and with a dense fringe of fine hairs on the margin (Fig. 667) | Correct, see **M₂** (p. 97) Wrong, see **L₃L₃** (p. 97) |

667   Under side
**Yellow Rhododendron**

## *Rhododendron* – Rhododendron

| M₂ | *Rhododendron luteum* Sweet<br>**Yellow Rhododendron**<br>Fig. 668 – see p. 170/171<br><br>● Leaves 6–12cm long, oblong-lanceolate in outline with fine hairs on the margin<br>● Pointed at end<br>● Leaf-stalk 5–15mm long<br>● Medium green above and slightly undulate; greyish medium green beneath; both sides grey hairy when young |

668    Upper side
**Yellow Rhododendron**

| L₃L₃ | Leaves without a dense fringe of fine hairs on the margin | Correct, see **M₃**, **M₃M₃** or **M₃M₃M₃**<br>Wrong, back to **L₃** (p. 96) |

| M₃ | Leaves with very long stalks (1–4cm) and with greyish white hairs remaining on the under side; leaf-stalk green (Fig. 669) | Correct, see **N**<br>Wrong, see **M₃M₃** |

## *Pyrus* – Pear

| N | *Pyrus salicifolia* Pall.<br>**Willow-leaved Pear**<br>Fig. 669 – see p. 172/173<br><br>● Leaves 3–9cm long, narrowly elliptic in outline and occasionally with a few small teeth along the margin<br>● Obtuse or pointed at the end<br>● Leaf-stalk 1–4cm long<br>● Both sides with silvery grey hairs when young; later medium to dark green and often glabrous above; remaining greyish white and hairy beneath |

669    Under side
**Willow-leaved Pear**

| M₃M₃ | Leaves with a stalk 1–4cm long and usually with a wavy margin; leaf-stalk distinctly tinged red (Fig. 670, 671) | Correct, see **N₁**<br>Wrong, see **M₃M₃M₃** |

670    Under side
**Laurel**

## *Laurus* – Laurel

| N₁ | *Laurus nobilis* L.<br>**Laurel**<br>Fig. 671 – see p. 172/173<br><br>● Leaves 5–12cm long, oblong-lanceolate to narrowly elliptic in outline and often with a slightly wavy margin<br>● Pointed at the end<br>● Leaf-stalk 1–4cm long and usually tinged red<br>Medium to dark green above, pale green beneath, both sides glabrous; lower part of midrib beneath often reddish |

671    Upper side
**Laurel**

| M₃M₃<br>M₃ | Leaves with a stalk 0.2–3cm long and greenish beneath; leaf-stalk green | Correct, see **N₂**, **N₂N₂** (p. 98) or **N₂N₂N₂** (p. 98)<br>Wrong, back to **M₃** |

| N₂ | Leaves tapering to a short point from a broad base; lateral veins far apart (Fig. 672, 673) | Correct, see **O** or **OO**<br>Wrong, see **N₂N₂** (p. 98) or **N₂N₂N₂** (p. 98) |

## *Rhododendron* – Rhododendron

| O | *Rhododendron ponticum* L.<br>**Rhododendron**<br>Fig. 672 – see p. 172/173<br><br>● Leaves 8–15cm long, oblong-lanceolate to oblong-elliptic in outline and occasionally with slightly recurved margins<br>● Shortly pointed at the end<br>● Leaf-stalk from 1–3cm long<br>● Dark green above with a pale green midrib; pale green beneath with a prominent midrib; both sides glabrous |

672    Under side
**Rhododendron**

## *Prunus* – Cherry

| OO | *Prunus laurocerasus* L.<br>**Cherry Laurel**<br>Fig. 673 – see p. 170/171<br><br>● Leaves 10–25cm long, oblong-elliptic to oblong-obovate in outline, stiff, leathery and usually with 4 glands in the lower part of the blade<br>● With a short, narrow point at the end<br>● Leaf-stalk 5–10mm long<br>● Shiny dark green above and pale green beneath; both sides glabrous |

673    Under side
**Cherry Laurel**

**N₂N₂** Leaves tapering gradually from the middle of the blade towards the tip; lateral veins close together and almost at right angles to the midrib (Fig. 674)

Correct, see **O₁**
Wrong, see **N₂N₂N₂**

**I₁I₁** Leaves elliptic, ovate, broadly elliptic or broadly ovate

Correct, see **K₂** or **K₂K₂** (p. 99)
Wrong, back to **I₁** (p. 95)

## *Nerium* – Oleander

**K₂** Leaves distinctly heart-shaped at the base of the blade

Correct, see **L₄**, **L₄L₄** or **L₄L₄L₄**
Wrong, see **K₂K₂** (p. 99)

**O₁**

***Nerium oleander*** L.
**Oleander**
Fig. 674 – see p. 172/173

- Leaves 6–15cm long, linear-lanceolate in outline and more rarely with slightly recurved margins
- Pointed at the end
- Leaf-stalk 3–7mm long; blade narrowing into the stalk
- Medium to dark green and glabrous above; greyish or pale green beneath with prominent midrib and sparsely hairy or glabrous

674   Under side
**Oleander**

## *Syringa* – Lilac

**L₄**

***Syringa vulgaris*** L.
**Lilac**
Fig. 677 – see p. 174/175

- Leaves 5–10cm long and ovate or elliptic in outline with a pointed tip
- With a long point at the end
- Leaf-stalk 1–3cm long
- Dark green above and paler bluish green beneath; both sides glabrous

677   Upper side **Lilac**

**N₂N₂**
**N₂** Leaves tapering gradually from the middle of the blade towards the tip; lateral veins not close together (Fig. 675, 676)

Correct, see **O₂** or **O₂O₂**
Wrong, back to **N₂** (p. 97)

## *Ligustrum* – Privet

**O₂**

***Ligustrum vulgare*** L.
**Wild Privet**
Fig. 675 – see p. 172/173

- Leaves 3–7cm long and lanceolate to oblong-elliptic in outline
- Pointed at the end
- Leaf-stalk 5–15mm long
- Medium to dark green above and somewhat paler green beneath; both sides glabrous

675   Upper side **Wild Privet**

## *Catalpa* – Catalpa

**L₄**
**L₄**

***Catalpa bignonioides*** Walt.
**Indian Bean Tree**
Fig. 678 – see p. 174/175

- Leaves 10–20cm long and broadly ovate to heart-shaped in outline
- With a long, fine point at the end or with a short point
- Leaf-stalk 7–15cm long
- Medium to dark green above; paler green beneath with short, soft hairs

678   Upper side **Indian Bean Tree**

## *Olea* – Olive

**O₂**
**O₂**

***Olea europaea*** L.
**Olive**
Fig. 676 – see p. 172/173

- Leaves 4–7cm long, lanceolate in outline, thick, leathery and often with slightly wavy margins
- Pointed at the end; often with a small sharp point
- Leaf-stalk 2–6mm long
- Dull dark green to greyish green above and greyish white to silvery grey beneath

676   Under side
**Olive**

## *Catalpa ovata*

**L₄**
**L₄**
**L₄**

***Catalpa ovata*** G. Don et Zucc.
**Yellow Catalpa**
Fig. 679 – see p. 174/175

- Leaves 10–25cm long and varied in outline; usually broadly ovate or heart shaped
- With a short point at the end
- Leaf-stalk 4–10cm long, often darker on the upper side
- Medium to dark green above with very fine hairs; pale to medium green beneath and slightly rough to the touch; with dark red glandular spots in the axils of the veins beneath

679   Upper side
**Yellow Catalpa**

| | | |
|---|---|---|
| **K₂K₂** | Leaves rounded at the base of the blade or wedge-shaped | Correct, see **L₅**, **L₅L₅** or **L₅L₅L₅** Wrong, back to **K₂** (p. 98) |

| | | |
|---|---|---|
| **M₆** | Leaves densely felted beneath and so appearing greyish green | Correct, see **N₃**, **N₃N₃** or **N₃N₃N₃** Wrong, see **M₆M₆** (p. 100) |

| | | |
|---|---|---|
| **L₅** | Leaves 1–3cm long, obovate, leathery and with their greatest breadth above the middle of the blade (Fig. 680) | Correct, see **M₄** Wrong, see **L₅L₅** or **L₅L₅L₅** |

| | | |
|---|---|---|
| **N₃** | Leaves 5–10cm long, elliptic to broadly ovate in outline, with a stalk 1–2cm long covered in woolly hairs (Fig. 682) | Correct, see **O₃** Wrong, see **N₃N₃** |

## *Arctostaphylos* – Bearberry

**M₄**

***Arctostaphylos uva-ursi*** (L.) Spreng.
**Bearberry**
Fig. 680 – see p. 174/175

- Leaves 1–3cm long, obovate or obovate-oblong in outline and with dense fine hairs on the margins
- Obtuse at the end or more rarely slightly emarginate
- Leaf-stalk 1–3mm long with white hairs
- Dark green above with a clearly visible, pale green midrib; a close, dark green network of veins beneath

680    Under side
**Bearberry**

## *Cydonia* – Quince

**O₃**

***Cydonia oblonga*** Mill.
**Quince**
Fig. 682 – see p. 174/175

- Leaves 5–10cm long, elliptic to broadly ovate in outline and slightly grey-felted on the margins
- Obtuse, shortly rounded or weakly pointed at the end
- Leaf-stalk 1–2cm long covered in woolly hairs
- Dark green and usually glabrous above; grey-felted beneath

682    Under side
**Quince**

| | | |
|---|---|---|
| **L₅L₅** | Leaves 20–40cm long, obovate, and pale bluish green beneath (Fig. 681) | Correct, see **M₅** Wrong, see **L₅L₅L₅** |

| | | |
|---|---|---|
| **N₃N₃** | Leaves 6–10cm long, obovate in outline, with a white woollly stalk 1–3cm long (Fig. 683) | Correct, see **O₄** Wrong, see **N₃N₃N₃** |

## *Magnolia* – Magnolia

**M₅**

***Magnolia hypoleuca*** Sieb. et Zucc.
**Japanese Big-leaved Magnolia**
Fig. 681 – see p. 174/175

- Leaves 20–40cm long, obovate in outline and gradually narrowing towards the base
- Rounded at the end with a short point
- Leaf-stalk 3–8cm long
- Pale to medium green and glabrous above; paler bluish green and slightly hairy beneath

681    Under side
**Japanese Big-leaved Magnolia**

## *Pyrus* – Pear

**O₄**

***Pyrus nivalis*** Jacq.
**Snow Pear**
Fig. 683 – see p. 176/177

- Leaves 6–10cm long, obovate in outline and woolly hairy
- Acute at the end or rounded with a short point
- Leaf-stalk 1–3cm long covered with white woolly hairs
- Dark green above and covered with woolly hairs; densely felted beneath and so appearing greyish green

683    Under side
**Snow Pear**

| | | |
|---|---|---|
| **L₅L₅** **L₅** | Leaves 2–20cm long and elliptic, ovate or broadly ovate in outline | Correct, see **M₆**, or **M₆M₆** (p. 100) Wrong, back to **L₅** |

| | | |
|---|---|---|
| **N₃N₃** **N₃** | Leaves 2–6cm long, ovate, broadly elliptic or roundish in outline, with a hairy stalk 0.2–0.7cm long (Fig. 684, 685) | Correct, see **O₅** or **O₅O₅** (p. 100) Wrong, back to **N₃** |

## *Cotoneaster* – Cotoneaster

O5

### *Cotoneaster tomentosus* (Ait.) Lindl.
### Cotoneaster
Fig. 684 – see p. 176/177

● Leaves 3–6cm long and elliptic to broad ovate in outline

● Obtuse at the end, more rarely rounded; occasionally with a small point

● Leaf-stalk 2–7mm long and densely felted

● Dark green and loosely hairy above; densely grey-felted beneath

684   Upper side
**Cotoneaster**

---

O5
O5

### *Cotoneaster integerrimus* Medic.
### Common Cotoneaster
Fig. 684 – see p. 176/177

● Leaves 2–4cm long, broadly elliptic, ovate or roundish in outline and very finely hairy on the margins

● Obtuse or acute at the end and usually with a prickly point

● Leaf-stalk 3–6mm long and finely hairy

● Dark green and usually glabrous above; densely white or grey-felted beneath

685   Upper side
**Common Cotoneaster**

---

**M₆M₆** Leaves not woolly felted beneath; the under side whitish, green or bluish green

Correct, see **N₄**, **N₄N₄** or **N₄N₄N₄** (p. 101)
Wrong, back to **M₆** (p. 99)

---

**N₄** Leaves with the veins curving towards the tip (see Introduction!) (Fig. 686–688)

Correct, see **O₆**, **O₆O₆** or **O₆O₆O₆**
Wrong, see **N₄N₄** or **N₄N₄N₄** (p. 101)

---

## *Cornus* – Dogwood

O₆

### *Cornus sanguinea* L.
### Dogwood
Fig. 686 – see p. 176/177

● Leaves 4–10cm long, elliptic to broadly ovate in outline and with 3 or 4 pairs of lateral veins curving towards the tip

● Pointed at the end

● Leaf-stalk 5–15mm long and usually grooved and dark red above

● Both sides sparsely hairy with clearly visible veins of the 1st and 2nd order; medium to dark green above and somewhat paler green beneath

686   Upper side
**Dogwood**

---

O₆
O₆

### *Cornus mas* L.
### Cornelian Cherry
Fig. 687 – see p. 176/177

● Leaves 4–10cm long, narrowly elliptic or elliptic to ovate in outline, often with a slightly wavy margin and with 3–5 pairs of lateral veins curving towards the tip

● Usually pointed at the end

● Leaf-stalk 3–15mm long, slightly grooved, often also tinged red and with fine whitish hairs

● Both sides with scattered white appressed hairs

687   Upper side
**Cornelian Cherry**

---

O₆
O₆
O₆

### *Cornus controversa* Hemsl.
### Table Dogwood
Fig. 688 – see p. 176/177

● Leaves 7–12cm long and ovate or broadly ovate in outline

● With a short or long point at the end

● Leaf-stalk 1–3cm long

● Dark green above with clearly visible, impressed veins; bluish grey beneath and finely hairy on the veins; 6–9 pairs of lateral veins

688   Under side
**Table Dogwood**

---

**N₄N₄** Leaves with the lateral veins running parallel to each other towards the margin (Fig. 689, 690)

Correct, see **O₇** or **O₇O₇** (p. 101)
Wrong, see **N₄N₄N₄** (p. 101)

---

**O₇** Greatest breadth of leaves always above the middle (Fig. 689)

Correct, see **P**
Wrong, see **O₇O₇** (p. 101)

---

## *Fagus* – Beech

P

### *Fagus orientalis* Lipsky
### Oriental Beech
Fig. 689 – see p. 178/179

● Leaves 6–12cm long, elliptic or usually obovate in outline and with numerous fine hairs on the margin

● Acute at the end or with a small point

● Leaf-stalk 5–15mm long covered with milky hair

● Dark bluish green and glabrous above with pale yellowish green veins; medium to dark green beneath with brownish hairs on the yellowish green veins

689   Under side
**Oriental Beech**

O₇O₇ Greatest breadth of leaves always at or below the middle (Fig. 690) — Correct, see **P₁**
Wrong, back to **O₇** (p. 100)

## *Parrotia* – Persian Ironwood

**QQ**

*Parrotia persica* (DC.) C. A. Mey.
**Persian Ironwood**
Fig. 692 – see p. 178/179

● Leaves 6–10cm long, obovate or almost circular in outline, thick, leathery, and coarsely sinuate above the middle

● Obtuse or rounded at the end

● Leaf-stalk 5–8mm long

● Shiny dark green above and pale bluish green beneath and with whitish veins

692   Upper side
**Persian Ironwood**

## *Fagus* – Beech

**P₁**

*Fagus sylvatica* L.
**Common Beech**
Fig. 690 – see p. 178/179

● Leaves 5–10cm long, elliptic to broadly ovate in outline and with a wavy margin that is fringed with whitish hairs, especially when young

● Usually with a short point at the end

● Leaf-stalk 3–15mm long and often rather dark in colour

● Shiny dark green above and medium green beneath; very prominent lateral veins running parallel to each other

690   Under side
**Beech**

P₁P₁ Veins not deeply impressed on the upper side of the leaves (Fig. 693–697) — Correct, see **Q₁** or **Q₁Q₁**
Wrong, back to **P₁**

Q₁ Both sides of the leaves remaining hairy and therefore soft to the touch (Fig. 693) — Correct, see **R**
Wrong, see **Q₁Q₁**

N₄N₄
N₄ Leaves with the veins curved or forming a network — Correct, see **O₈** or **O₈O₈** (p. 102)
Wrong, back to **N₄** (p. 100)

## *Lonicera* – Honeysuckle

**R**

*Lonicera xylosteum* L.
**Fly Honeysuckle**
Fig. 693 – see p. 180/181

● Leaves 2–6cm long, elliptic, broadly ovate or obovate in outline and with the margins fringed by whitish hairs

● Obtuse or pointed at the end

● Leaf-stalk 5–10mm long with dense, appressed hairs

● Medium to dark green above and bluish green beneath; appressed hairs on both sides

693   Upper side
**Fly Honeysuckle**

O₈ Under side of leaves distinctly pale to dark bluish green — Correct, see **P₁** or **P₁P₁**
Wrong, see **O₈O₈** (p. 102)

P₁ Veins clearly deeply impressed on the upper side of the leaves (Fig. 691, 692) — Correct, see **Q** or **QQ**
Wrong, see **P₁P₁**

Q₁Q₁ Leaves glabrous or only hairy when young and later becoming glabrous (Fig. 694) — Correct, see **R₁** (p. 102), **R₁R₁** (p. 102) or **R₁R₁R₁** (p. 102)
Wrong, back to **Q₁**

## *Salix* – Willow

**Q**

*Salix hastata* L.
**Spear-leaved Willow**
Fig. 691 – see p. 178/179

● Leaves 2–8cm long, elliptic to ovate in outline and usually entire; more rarely with a few teeth wide apart

● Pointed or slightly rounded at the end

● Leaf-stalk 5–12mm long and distinctly grooved above

● Dark green and glabrous above; pale bluish green beneath and hairy at first on the prominent pale green veins

691   Upper side
**Spear-leaved Willow**

694   Under side
**Blue Honeysuckle**

## *Lonicera* – Honeysuckle

**R₁**

*Lonicera caprifolium* L.
**Perfoliate Honeysuckle**
Fig. 695 – see p. 180/181

- Leaves 2–10cm long, narrowly ovate to elliptic in outline; the uppermost leaves united to form an elliptic or circular leaf
- Obtuse or occasionally shortly pointed at the end
- Sessile or the lower leaves shortly stalked
- Dark green and glabrous above; bluish grey-green beneath and at first hairy at the base

695   Upper side
**Perfoliate Honeysu**

**R₁**
**R₁**

*Lonicera caerulea* L.
**Blue Honeysuckle**
Fig. 696 – see p. 180/181

- Leaves 2–8cm long and elliptic, oblong-elliptic or obovate in outline
- Usually obtuse or rounded at the end
- Leaf-stalk 1–4mm long, broadened at the base and slightly hairy
- Dark green above, quickly becoming glabrous; bluish green beneath and becoming glabrous except for the leaf-stalk

696   Upper side
**Blue Honeysuckle**

**R₁**
**R₁**
**R₁**

*Lonicera periclymenum* L.
**Honeysuckle**
Fig. 697 – see p. 180/181

- Leaves 4–10cm long and elliptic to obovate in outline
- Obtuse or pointed at the end
- Lower leaves with stalks up to 7mm long; the uppermost pair of leaves sessile
- Dark green above; bluish green beneath and only somewhat hairy when young

697   Upper side
**Honeysuckle**

**O₈O₈**  Under side of leaves distinctly pale to medium green, never bluish green

Correct, see **P₂** or **P₂P₂**
Wrong, back to **O₈** (p. 101)

**P₂**  Leaf-stalks distinctly winged; if only slightly winged then with a long thorn at the junction with the stem (Fig. 698, 699)

Correct, see **Q₁** or **Q₁Q₁**
Wrong, see **P₂P₂**

## *Citrus* – Orange, Lemon

**Q₁**

*Citrus sinensis* (L.) Pers.
**Orange**
Fig. 698 – see p. 178/179

- Leaves 3–7cm long, elliptic, broadly elliptic or obovate in outline, firm, leathery, and broader than in the Lemon
- Acute at the end or rounded with a small point
- Leaf-stalk 5–20mm long, green and usually distinctly winged
- Shiny dark green above and pale green beneath; both sides glabrous

698   Upper side
**Orange**

**Q₁**
**Q₁**

*Citrus limon* (L.) Burm.
**Lemon**
Fig. 699 – see p. 178/179

- Leaves 3–7cm long, narrowly elliptic to elliptic in outline, firm, leathery, very similar to the leaves of the Orange, and more rarely slightly crenate or dentate on the margin
- Pointed at the end
- Leaf-stalk 5–20mm long, often winged and usually with a thorn at its junction with the stem
- Shiny dark green above and pale green beneath; both sides glabrous

699   Upper side
**Lemon**

**P₂P₂**  Leaf-stalks not winged and without a thorn at the junction with the stem (Fig. 700–712)

Correct, see **Q₂** or **Q₂Q₂**
Wrong, back to **P₂**

**Q₂**  Leaves ovate-rhombic and shiny dark green above (Fig. 700)

Correct, see **R₂**
Wrong, see **Q₂Q₂** (p. 103)

## *Hedera* – Ivy

**R₂**

*Hedera helix* L.
**Ivy**
Fig. 700 – see p. 182/183

- Leaves 4–10cm long and varied in outline; ovate-rhombic on flowering shoots, without lobes and leathery
- Shortly pointed at the end
- Leaf-stalk 3–11cm long
- Shiny dark green above with white veins; dull pale green beneath; both sides glabrous

700   Upper side
**Ivy**

**Q₂Q₂** Leaves not ovate-rhombic (Fig. 701–712)

Correct, see **R₃** or **R₃R₃**
Wrong, back to **Q₂** (p. 102)

---

**R₃** Leaves very finely glandular serrate (appearing entire to the naked eye; teeth only clearly visible with a lens) (Fig. 701)

Correct, see **S**
Wrong, see **R₃R₃**

---

## *Euonymus* – Spindle Tree

**S**

### *Euonymus latifolius* (L.) Mill.
### Broad-leaved Spindle Tree
Fig. 701 – see p. 182/183

- Leaves 7–14cm long and elliptic to obovate in outline
- Pointed at the end
- Leaf-stalk 5–10mm long and grooved above
- Dark green above and pale green beneath; both sides glabrous

701    Upper side
**Broad-leaved Spindle Tree**

---

**R₃R₃** Leaves without small teeth

Correct, see **S₁** or **S₁S₁**
Wrong, back to **R₃**

---

**S₁** Leaves 8–20cm long

Correct, see **T** or **TT**
Wrong, see **S₁S₁** (p. 104)

---

**T** Underside of leaves with conspicuous rust-red downy hairs (Fig. 702)

Correct, see **U**
Wrong, see **TT**

702    Under side
**Evergreen Magnolia**

---

## *Magnolia* – Magnolia

**U**

### *Magnolia grandiflora* L.
### Evergreen Magnolia
Fig. 703 – see p. 182/183

- Leaves 8–20cm long, elliptic to broadly elliptic in outline, thick, leathery and falling in the 2nd year
- Obtuse to acute at the end and often with a rounded tip
- Leaf-stalk 20–25mm long and densely covered with rust-brown hairs
- Shiny dark green and glabrous above; paler green beneath with rust-red downy hairs

703    Upper side
**Evergreen Magnolia**

---

**TT** Under side of leaves without conspicuous rust-red, downy hairs (Fig. 704)

Correct, see **U₁** or **U₁U₁** (p. 104)
Wrong, back to **T**

704    Under side  **Alder Buckthorn**

---

**U₁** Veins on the underside whitish to pale yellow (Fig. 705)

Correct, see **V**
Wrong, see **U₁U₁** (p. 104)

705    Under side  **Garden Magnolia**

---

## *Magnolia* – Magnolia

**V**

### *Magnolia* x *soulangeana*
Soul.-Bod.
### Garden Magnolia
Fig. 706 – see p. 182/183

- Leaves 10–20cm long, oblong-elliptic or usually narrowly obovate in outline and broadest in the upper third
- With a short point at the end
- Leaf-stalk 1–4cm long
- Medium to dark green and glabrous above; paler green beneath and somewhat hairy

706    Upper side
**Garden Magnolia**

$U_1U_1$  Veins on the under side medium to dark green

Correct, see $V_1$
Wrong, back to $U_1$
(p. 103)

## Lonicera – Honeysuckle

$V_1$

*Lonicera alpigena* L.
**Alpine Honeysuckle**
Fig. 707 – see p. 180/181

● Leaves 8–12cm long, elliptic to obovate in outline and with a fringe of fine hairs on the margins when young

● Shortly pointed at the end

● Leaf-stalk 1–2cm long

● Dark green above; paler green and very shiny beneath with fine hairs along the midrib

707　Under side
**Alpine Honeysuckle**

$S_1S_1$  Leaves 3–8cm long

Correct, see $T_1$ or $T_1T_1$
Wrong, back to $S_1$
(p. 103)

$T_1$  Leaf stalks usually distinctly grooved above (Fig. 708)

Correct, see $U_2$ or $U_2U_2$
Wrong, see $T_1T_1$

708　Upper side **European Forsythia**

$U_2$  Midrib and lateral veins on the under side green and leaf-stalk 1–3cm long (Fig. 709)

Correct, see $V_2$
Wrong, see $U_2U_2$

709　Under side **European Forsythia**

## Forsythia – Forsythia

$V_2$

*Forsythia europaea* Deg. et Bald.
**European Forsythia**
Fig. 710 – see p. 182/183

● Leaves 4–8cm long and elliptic, ovate or ovate-lanceolate in outline

● Pointed at the end; the tip often slightly curved to one side

● Leaf-stalk 1–3cm long

● Dark green above and pale green beneath; both sides glabrous

710　Upper side
**European Forsythia**

$U_2U_2$  Midrib and lateral veins on the under side pale yellow and leaf-stalk 3–14mm long

Correct, see $V_3$
Wrong, back to $U_2$

## Lonicera – Honeysuckle

$V_3$

*Lonicera nigra* L.
**Black-berried Honeysuckle**
Fig. 711 – see p. 180/181

● Leaves 3–8cm long, elliptic, broadly elliptic to obovate in outline and often with slightly wavy margins

● Shortly pointed at the end

● Leaf-stalk 2–8mm long and grooved above

● Medium to dark green and glabrous above; medium green beneath and downy along the midrib

711　Under side
**Black-berried Honeysuckle**

$T_1T_1$  Leaf-stalks not or only slightly grooved above

Correct, see $U_3$
Wrong, back to $T_1$

## Rhamnus – Buckthorn

$U_3$

*Rhamnus frangula* L.
**Alder Buckthorn**
Fig. 712 – see p. 182/183

● Leaves 3–7cm long and elliptic to broadly elliptic in outline

● With a short point at the end

● Leaf-stalk 6–14mm long

● Dark green above and shiny pale green beneath

712　Upper side **Alder Buckthorn**

**A**　Most leaves transformed into sharp, green spines (Fig. 713) (small, very narrow leaves present only in luxuriant growth or in young plants) — Correct, see **B** / Wrong, see **AA** or **AAA**

## *Castanea* – Sweet Chestnut

**C₁**

***Castanea sativa*** Mill.
**Sweet Chestnut**
Fig. 715 – see p. 184/185

- Leaves 10–30cm long, oblong-lanceolate in outline, thick, leathery and with bristly pointed teeth
- With a short, narrow point at the end
- Leaf-stalk 2–5cm long
- Shiny dark green and glabrous above; pale green beneath and with matted woolly hairs when young; 15–20 pairs of lateral veins

715　Upper side
**Sweet Chestnut**

## *Ulex* – Gorse

**B**

***Ulex europaeus*** L.
**Gorse**
Fig. 713 – see p. 184/185

- Typical leaves often absent; most leaves and also the short shoots transformed into spines
- End of the spine sharp
- Leaf-stalks absent; spines with numerous lateral spines
- Stems grooved and often with downy hairs

713　**Gorse**

**B₁B₁**　Leaves with several coarse spiny
**B₁**　　teeth (Fig. 716, 717) — Correct, see **C₂** or **C₂C₂** / Wrong, back to **B₁**

## *Ilex* – Holly

**C₂**

***Ilex aquifolium*** L.
**Holly**
Fig. 716 – see p. 184/185

- Leaves 3–8cm long, elliptic to ovate in outline, thick, leathery and with coarse spiny teeth
- With a long, spiny point at the end
- Leaf-stalk 1cm long and grooved above
- Shiny dark green above and pale green beneath; both sides glabrous

716　Upper side **Holly**

**AA**　Margins of leaves with a fringe of sharp spines (Fig. 714), dentate with bristly teeth (Fig. 715) or with several coarse spiny teeth (Fig. 716, 717) — Correct, see **B₁, B₁B₁** or **B₁B₁B₁** / Wrong, see **AAA**

**B₁**　Leaves fringed with sharp spines (Fig. 714) — Correct, see **C** / Wrong, see **B₁B₁** or **B₁B₁B₁**

## *Quercus* – Oak

**C₂**
**C₂**

***Quercus ilex*** L.
**Evergreen Oak, Holm Oak**
Fig. 717 – see p. 184/185

- Leaves 3–8cm long and varied in form; often with 4–7 sharp teeth on each side
- With a sharp, spiny point at the end
- Leaf-stalk 7–15mm long and remaining white-felted until late in the year
- Young leaves hairy on both sides; older leaves shiny dark green and glabrous; grey to whitish beneath because of the dense covering of hair

717　Upper side
**Evergreen Oak**

## *Berberis* – Barberry

**C**

***Berberis vulgaris*** L.
**Barberry**
Fig. 714 – see p. 184/185

- Leaves 2–4cm long, narrowly obovate to obovate in outline and with the margin fringed by sharp spines
- Rounded or obtuse at the end
- Leaf-stalk 5–15mm long
- Dark green above and whitish green beneath; both sides glabrous

714　Upper side **Barberry**

**AAA**　Margins of leaves neither fringed with spines, nor dentate with bristly teeth, nor with several coarse spiny teeth, but serrate, dentate or crenate — Correct, see **B₂** (p. 106), or **B₂B₂** (p. 107) / Wrong, back to **A**

**B₁B₁**　Leaves dentate with spiny teeth (Fig. 715) — Correct, see **C₁** / Wrong, see **B₁B₁B₁**

| **B₂** | Leaves usually heart-shaped or obliquely heart-shaped (Fig. 718–725) and regularly toothed | Correct, see **C₂** or **C₂C₂**<br>Wrong, see **B₂B₂** (p. 107) |
|---|---|---|

| **C₂** | Leaves with white or pale grey matted woolly hairs beneath (Fig. 718, 719) | Correct, see **D** or **DD**<br>Wrong, see **C₂C₂** |
|---|---|---|

## *Tilia* – Lime

**D**

*Tilia tomentosa* Moench
**Silver Lime**
Fig. 718 – see p. 186/187

- Leaves 6–12cm long, roundish heart-shaped or obliquely heart-shaped in outline and with the margin fairly regularly serrate or dentate
- Shortly pointed at the end
- Leaf-stalk 2–3.5cm long and therefore shorter than in the Weeping Silver Lime
- Dark green above; with white or pale grey matted woolly hairs beneath

718   Under side
**Silver Lime**

**DD**

*Tilia petiolaris* DC.
**Weeping Silver Lime**
Fig. 719 – see p. 186/187

- Leaves 7–11cm long, obliquely heart-shaped in outline and regularly sharply serrate/dentate (leaf-teeth with a bristle-like tip)
- Shortly pointed at the end
- Leaf-stalk 3–6cm long with matted woolly hairs; leaves pendent
- Dark green above, becoming almost glabrous; felted beneath with white or greyish white stellate hairs

719   Under side
**Weeping Silver Lime**

| **C₂C₂** | Leaves green or bluish green beneath (Fig. 720–725) | Correct, see **D₁** or **D₁D₁**<br>Wrong, back to **C₂** |
|---|---|---|

| **D₁** | Leaves green beneath with whitish tufts of hair in the axils of the veins (Fig. 720) | Correct, see **E**<br>Wrong, see **D₁D₁** |
|---|---|---|

## *Tilia* – Lime

**E**

*Tilia platyphyllos* Scop.
**Large-leaved Lime**
Fig. 720 – see p. 186/187

- Leaves 7–15cm long, heart-shaped or obliquely heart-shaped in outline and with the margin regularly crenate-serrate
- With a short point at the end
- Leaf-stalk 2–5cm long and often somewhat hairy
- Dark green and somewhat hairy above; paler green beneath with whitish tufts of hair in the axils of the veins

720   Under side
**Large-leaved Lime**

| **D₁D₁** | Leaves bluish green beneath and with (Fig. 721, 724) or without (Fig. 722) brownish tufts of hair in the axils of the veins | Correct, see **E₁**, **E₁E₁** or **E₁E₁E₁** (p. 107)<br>Wrong, back to **D₁** |
|---|---|---|

721   Under side
**Small-leaved Lime**

722   Under side
**Katsura Tree**

## *Tilia* – Lime

**E₁**

*Tilia cordata* Mill.
**Small-leaved Lime**
Fig. 723 – see p. 186/187

- Leaves 4–7cm long, usually heart-shaped in outline (or obliquely heart-shaped) and with the margin finely and sharply serrate
- Shortly pointed at the end
- Leaf-stalk 2–5cm long and glabrous
- Shiny dark green to bluish green above and glabrous; pale bluish green beneath with brownish red tufts of hair in the axils of the veins

723   Upper side
**Small-leaved Lime**

**E₁E₁**

*Tilia x euchlora* K. Koch
**Caucasian Lime**
Fig. 724 – see p. 186/187

- Leaves 5–15cm long, obliquely heart-shaped in outline and irregularly toothed; teeth tipped with bristles
- With a bristle-tipped point at the end
- Leaf-stalk 3–6cm long
- Dark bluish green and glabrous above; bluish green beneath with pale yellow veins and pale brown tufts of hair in their axils

724   Under side
**Caucasian Lime**

## *Cercidiphyllum* – Katsura Tree

E₁
E₁
E₁

725   Upper side
**Katsura Tree**

**Cercidiphyllum japonicum**
Sieb. et Zucc. ex Miq.
**Katsura Tree**
Fig. 725 – see p. 186/187

- Leaves 6–12cm long, broadly ovate to roundish or heart-shaped in outline and with a crenate margin
- Very shortly pointed at the end
- Leaf-stalk 3–6cm long, green with a reddish tinge
- Dull or greyish green above; pale bluish green beneath and like the upper side glabrous

---

**B₂B₂**   Leaves not heart-shaped; but if slightly heart-shaped then the leaf-margin doubly serrate or doubly serrate/dentate (Fig. 726, 727) — Correct, see **C₃**, **C₃C₃** or **C₃C₃C₃** (p. 108) Wrong, back to **B₂** (p. 106)

---

**C₃**   Leaves oblong obovate, broadly ovate, roundish or slightly heart-shaped and doubly serrate/dentate — Correct, see **D₁** or **D₁D₁** Wrong, see **C₃C₃** or **C₃C₃C₃** (p. 108)

---

## *Corylus* – Hazel

D₁

**Corylus avellana** L.
**Hazel**
Fig. 726 – see p. 188/189

- Leaves 5–10cm long, oblong-obovate, roundish or slightly heart-shaped in outline and with the margin doubly serrate/dentate
- With a short point at the end
- Leaf-stalk 5–15mm long and glandular hairy
- Medium green above and pale to medium green beneath; both sides more or less softly hairy

726   Upper side
**Hazel**

---

D₁
D₁

**Corylus colurna** L.
**Turkish Hazel**
Fig. 727 – see p. 184/185

- Leaves 8–12cm long, broadly ovate to roundish or somewhat heart-shaped in outline, with the greatest breadth above the middle and serrate and with the margin coarsely doubly dentate
- With a fairly long point at the end
- Leaf-stalk 1.5–3cm long
- Shiny dark green above and later glabrous; medium to dark green beneath and hairy on the veins

727   Upper side
**Turkish Hazel**

---

**C₃C₃**   Leaves triangular, ovate-rhombic or rhombic in outline (Fig. 728–731) — Correct, see **D₂** or **D₂D₂** Wrong, see **C₃C₃C₃** (p. 108)

---

**D₂**   Leaf-margin regularly sinuately serrate/dentate, or crenate-serrate (Fig. 728–730) — Correct, see **E₂**, **E₂E₂** or **E₂E₂E₂** Wrong, see **D₂D₂** (p. 108)

---

## *Populus* – Poplar

E₂

728   Upper side
**Lombardy Poplar**

**Populus nigra** L.
**var. italica** Muenchh.
**Lombardy Poplar**
Fig. 728 – see p. 188/189

- Leaves 4–8cm long, lozenge-shaped or rhombic and for the most part sinuately serrate/dentate
- With a long point at the end
- Leaf-stalk 1–3cm long and often tinged with red
- Dark green above and greyish green beneath; both sides glabrous

---

E₂
E₂

**Populus x canadensis** Moench
**Hybrid Black Poplar**
Fig. 729 – see p. 188/189

- Leaves 6–10cm long, almost triangular in outline and with a wavy, crenate-serrate margin
- With a short point at the end
- Leaf-stalk 3–8cm long and occasionally somewhat reddish
- Shiny dark green above and paler green beneath; both sides glabrous

729   Under side
**Hybrid Black Poplar**

---

E₂
E₂
E₂

**Populus nigra** L.
**Black Poplar**
Fig. 730 – see p. 188/189

- Leaves 3–9cm long, triangular to rhombic in outline, reddish at first and with the margin crenate-serrate
- Pointed at the end
- Leaf-stalk 3–6cm long and laterally compressed
- Dark green above and pale bluish green beneath; lateral veins not as strongly branched as in the Hybrid Black Poplar

730   Under side
**Black Poplar**

**D₂D₂**  Leaf-margin distinctly coarsely doubly serrate/dentate (Fig. 731)

Correct, see **E₃**
Wrong, back to **D₂** (p. 107)

**E₅**  Leaves truncate at the end or in most cases emarginate (Fig. 733, 734)

Correct, see **F** or **FF**
Wrong, see **E₅E₅**

## *Betula* – Birch

**E₃**

### *Betula pendula* Roth
### Silver Birch
Fig. 731 – see p. 188/189

- Leaves 3–7cm long, triangular or ovate-rhombic in outline, often heart-shaped on suckers and usually coarsely doubly serrate/dentate (entire towards the base of the blade)
- With a long point at the end
- Leaf-stalk 2–3cm long
- Dark green above and pale greyish green beneath, both sides glabrous

731  Upper side
**Silver Birch**

## *Salix* – Willow

**F**

### *Salix herbacea* L.
### Dwarf Willow
Fig. 733 – see p. 190/191

- Leaves 8–20mm long, roundish ovate to circular in outline and with the margin crenate-serrate
- Usually emarginate at the end
- Leaf-stalk 3–6mm long and somewhat broadened at the base
- Medium to bluish green and glabrous on both sides; a clearly visible network of veins

733  Under side
**Dwarf Willow**

**C₃C₃**
**C₃**  Leaves not as in **C₃** or **C₃C₃**

Correct, see **D₃** or **D₃D₃**

## *Alnus* – Common Alder

**FF**

### *Alnus glutinosa* (L.) Gaertn.
### Alder
Fig. 734 – see p. 188/189

- Leaves 4–10cm long, broadly obovate to roundish in outline, with their greatest breadth above the middle and simply and doubly serrate/dentate
- Usually emarginate at the end, more rarely rounded
- Leaf-stalk 5–15mm long
- Medium to dark green above; paler green beneath with whitish to rust-coloured tufts of hair in the axils of the veins

734  Upper side
**Alder**

**D₃**  Leaves distinctly gland-dotted beneath (Fig. 732)

Correct, see **E₄**
Wrong, see **D₃D₃**

**E₅E₅**  Leaves obtuse or pointed at the end

Correct, see **F₁**, **F₁F₁** (p. 109), **F₁F₁F₁** (p. 109) or **F₁F₁F₁F₁** (p. 109)

## *Vaccinium* – Vaccinium

**E₄**

### *Vaccinium vitis-idaea* L.
### Cowberry
Fig. 732 – see p. 190/191

- Leaves 1–3cm long, narrowly obovate in outline, leathery, with their greatest breadth always above the middle and with the margin at times slightly crenate and dentate (some parts entire)
- Obtuse or slightly emarginate at the end
- Leaf-stalk 3–5mm and somewhat hairy
- Shiny dark green above; rather pale greyish blue-green beneath

732  Under side
**Cowberry**

**F₁**  Leaves sinuately dentate, remaining densely white-felted beneath and 5–12cm long (Fig. 735)

Correct, see **G**
Wrong, see **F₁F₁** (p. 109), **F₁F₁F₁** (p. 109) or **F₁F₁F₁F₁** (p. 109)

735  Under side  **White Poplar**

**D₃D₃**  Leaves not gland-dotted beneath

Correct, see **E₅** or **E₅E₅**
Wrong, back to **D₃**

## *Populus* – Poplar

**G**

736 Upper side
**White Poplar**

***Populus alba*** L.
**White Poplar**
Fig. 736 – see p. 190/191

- Leaves 5–12cm long and varied in outline; often triangular to ovate and sinuately dentate
- Rounded or shortly pointed at the end
- Leaf-stalk 2–4cm long, flattened and covered with white hairs
- Shiny dark green above (covered with matted woolly hairs when young) and remaining densely white-felted beneath

**F₁F₁**
**F₁F₁** Leaf-margin formed in a different way

Correct, see **G₃** or **G₃G₃** (p. 110)
Wrong, back to **F₁** (p. 108)

---

**G₃** Halves of the blade clearly differing in size and noticeably unequal at the base (Fig. 739–742)

Correct, see **H**, **HH**, **HHH** or **HHHH** (p. 110)
Wrong, see **G₃G₃** (p. 110)

---

**F₁F₁** Leaves irregularly coarsely sinuately dentate, greyish blue-green beneath (Fig. 737) and 3–10cm long

Correct, see **G₁**
Wrong, see **F₁F₁F₁** or **F₁F₁F₁F₁**

## *Populus* – Poplar

**G₁**

737 Under side
**Aspen**

***Populus tremula*** L.
**Aspen**
Fig. 737 – see p. 190/191

- Leaves 3–9cm long (up to 15cm on suckers), usually roundish in outline and irregularly sinuately dentate
- Rounded at the end or shortly pointed from a broad base
- Leaf-stalk 3–10cm long, flattened and often somewhat reddish in colour
- Brownish red at first above, later greyish blue-green; pale greyish green beneath

## *Ulmus* – Elm

**H**

739 Upper side
**Fluttering Elm**

***Ulmus laevis*** Pall.
**Fluttering Elm**
Fig. 739 – see p. 192/193

- Leaves 7–12cm long, narrowly elliptic, elliptic or roundish in outline, broadest at the middle and sharply doubly serrate/dentate
- With a short, fine point at the end
- Leaf-stalk only up to 5mm long
- Dull dark green above; greyish green and finely hairy beneath

**F₁F₁**
**F₁** Leaves regularly coarsely crenate, whitish to pale greyish green beneath with a stalk 0.2–1cm long (Fig. 738)

Correct, see **G₂**
Wrong, see **F₁F₁F₁F₁**

**HH**

740 Upper side
**Wych Elm**

***Ulmus glabra*** Huds.
**Wych Elm**
Fig. 740 – see p. 192/193

- Leaves 5–16cm long, elliptic, ovate or often obovate in outline, sometimes 3-pointed and with the margin coarsely doubly serrate
- Finely pointed at the end
- Leaf-stalk 3–6mm long, often covered by one half of the blade
- Dark green and rough above; medium green beneath and with fine white hairs on the larger veins

## *Dryas* – Mountain Avens

**G₂**

738 Under side
**Mountain Avens**

***Dryas octopetala*** L.
**Mountain Avens**
Fig. 738 – see p. 190/191

- Leaves 5–30mm long, oblong-elliptic in outline, leathery and with the margin regularly coarsely crenate and slightly recurved
- Obtuse or shortly pointed at the end
- Leaf-stalk 2–10mm long
- Shiny dark green and glabrous above; silvery white beneath with matted woolly hairs

**HH**
**H**

***Ulmus minor*** Mill.
**Smooth-leaved Elm**
Fig. 741 – see p. 192/193

- Leaves 3.5–8cm long and varied in outline; usually narrowly obovate or obovate-elliptic
- With a narrow, tapering point at the end
- Leaf-stalk 5–13mm long and usually somewhat hairy
- Dark green and usually glabrous above; paler green beneath and with conspicuous velvety tufts of hairs in the axils of the veins

741 Upper side
**Smooth-leaved Elm**

## Celtis – Nettle-tree

**HH**
**HH**

***Celtis australis*** L.
### Southern Nettle-tree
Fig. 742 – see p. 192/193

- Leaves 4–15cm long, oblong-elliptic to narrowly ovate in outline and with the margin sharply serrate
- With a slender point at the end
- Leaf-stalk 10–15mm long
- Dark green and roughly hairy above; greyish green and softly hairy beneath

742   Upper side **Southern Nettle-tree**

---

| | | |
|---|---|---|
| $G_3G_3$ | Halves of the blade more or less equal in size and attached to the stalk at about the same height | Correct, see $H_1$, $H_1H_1$, $H_1H_1H_1$ (p. 112) or $H_1H_1H_1H_1$ (p. 118) Wrong, back to $G_3$ (p. 109) |

---

| | | |
|---|---|---|
| $H_1$ | Leaves elliptic to ovate and distinctly white beneath (Fig. 743, 744) | Correct, see **I** or **II** Wrong, see $H_1H_1$, $H_1H_1H_1$ (p. 112) or $H_1H_1H_1H_1$ (p. 118) |

---

## Populus – Poplar

**I**

***Populus trichocarpa***
Torr. et A. Gray ex Hook.
### Western Balsam Poplar
Fig. 743 – see p. 192/193

- Leaves 8–14cm long, broadly ovate to somewhat rhombic in outline, thick, rather leathery and finely crenate-serrate
- Pointed at the end
- Leaf-stalk 2–5cm long and usually slightly reddish above
- Dark green and glabrous above; whitish or rust-coloured beneath and often with fairly fine downy hairs

743   Under side
**Western Balsam Poplar**

---

## Sorbus – Whitebeam

**II**

***Sorbus aria*** (L.) Crantz
### Whitebeam
Fig. 744 – see p. 192/193

- Leaves 6–12cm long, ovate, elliptic or even roundish in outline and simply or doubly serrate/dentate
- Obtuse or rounded at the end with a short point
- Leaf-stalk 1–2cm long with white hairs
- Medium green and somewhat silky-hairy above; always densely white-felted beneath

744   Under side
**Whitebeam**

---

| | | |
|---|---|---|
| $H_1H_1$ | Leaves narrowly elliptic, narrowly ovate to roundish or narrowly obovate and greyish green beneath (Fig. 745–757) | Correct, see $I_1$ or $I_1I_1$ Wrong, see $H_1H_1H_1$ (p. 112) or $H_1H_1H_1H_1$ (p. 118) |

---

| | | |
|---|---|---|
| $I_1$ | Leaves narrowly obovate or obovate (with their greatest breadth above the middle of the blade) | Correct, see **K** or **KK** Wrong, see $I_1I_1$ |

---

## Salix – Willow

**K**

***Salix aurita*** L.
### Eared Willow
Fig. 745 – see p. 190/191

- Leaves 2–5cm long, narrowly obovate to obovate in outline, with auriculate, persistent stipules and with the margin irregularly coarsely serrate, finely dentate and also wavy
- Broadly rounded at the end with a short, oblique and slightly recurved point
- Leaf-stalk 5–8mm long and hairy
- Greyish green and hairy beneath

745   Under side
**Eared Willow**

---

## Myrica – Bog Myrtle

**KK**

***Myrica gale*** L.
### Bog Myrtle, Sweet Gale
Fig. 746 – see p. 194/195

- Leaves 2–5cm long, oblong-obovate in outline, thickish and coarsely toothed in the upper half
- With a short point at the end
- Leaf-stalk 3–6mm long
- Dull dark green and rather finely hairy above; pale green beneath and finely hairy on the midrib

746   Under side
**Bog Myrtle**

---

| | | |
|---|---|---|
| $I_1I_1$ | Greatest breadth of leaves at or below the middle of the blade | Correct, see $K_1$ or $K_1K_1$ (p. 111) Wrong, back to $I_1$ |

---

| | | |
|---|---|---|
| $K_1$ | Leaves at most 3cm long (Fig. 747–750) | Correct, see **L, LL, LLL** or **LLLL** (all p. 111) Wrong, see $K_1K_1$ (p. 111) |

---

## *Betula* – Birch

**L**

### *Betula nana* L.
### Dwarf Birch
Fig. 747 – see p. 194/195

- Leaves at most 3cm long, usually roundish in outline, the margin simply toothed with broad, blunt teeth
- With a coarse tooth at the end
- Leaf-stalk 1–2mm long and dark red in colour
- Dark green above and somewhat undulate; whitish beneath with a network of dark green veins

747   Upper side
**Dwarf Birch**

---

**LL**

### *Betula x intermedia* (Hartm.)
Thomas
### Birch
Fig. 748 – see p. 194/195

- Leaves 8–25mm long, elliptic to broadly obovate in outline, and with the margin simply and coarsely serrate
- Rounded at the end with one or several teeth at the tip
- Leaf-stalk 3–7mm long
- Dark green above and greyish green beneath; both sides gland-dotted

748   Upper side
**Birch**

---

## *Nothofagus* – Southern Beech

**LL**
**L**

### *Nothofagus antarctica*
(G. Forst.) Oerst.
### Antarctic Beech
Fig. 749 – see p. 194/195

- Leaves 1–3cm long, ovate to roundish in outline and with the margin irregularly crenate, serrate and sinuate
- Rounded at the end
- Leaf-stalk 2–4mm long
- Shiny dark green above and often slightly wrinkled; greyish green beneath

749   Upper side
**Antarctic Beech**

---

## *Rhamnus* – Buckthorn

**LL**
**LL**

### *Rhamnus saxatilis* Jacq.
### Rock Buckthorn
Fig. 750 – see p. 194/195

- Leaves 1–3cm long, lanceolate to elliptic in outline, finely and regularly serrate
- Pointed at the end
- Leaf-stalk 2–5mm long
- Dark green above and whitish green beneath with dark green lateral veins; both sides glabrous

750   Upper side
**Rock Buckthorn**

---

**K₁K₁**   Leaves 3–10cm long
Correct, see **L₁** or **L₁L₁**
Wrong, back to **K₁** (p. 110)

---

**L₁**   Leaves narrowly or broadly lanceolate to ovate (or possibly even weakly obovate) (Fig. 751, 752)
Correct, see **M** or **MM**
Wrong, see **L₁L₁**

---

## *Salix* – Willow

**M**

### *Salix glabra* Scopoli
### Willow
Fig. 751 – see p. 194/195

- Leaves 3–9cm long, lanceolate to obovate in outline and with the margin regularly and finely serrate
- Tapering to the end or with a short point
- Leaf-stalk 5–15mm long and somewhat broadened at the base
- Shiny dark-green above and pale bluish-green beneath with a thick waxy bloom

751   Upper side
**Willow**

---

**MM**

### *Salix cinerea* L.
### Grey Willow
Fig. 752 – see p. 196/197

- Leaves 5–9cm long, broadly lanceolate to obovate in outline, with a wavy margin, and irregularly finely to coarsely toothed
- Shortly pointed at the end
- Leaf-stalk 5–20mm long and somewhat broadened at the base
- Dull green, without lustre, and shortly hairy above; covered beneath with greyish green velvety hairs and with prominent veins

752   Under side
**Grey Willow**

---

**L₁L₁**   Leaves different from those in **L₁**; usually elliptic to roundish (Fig. 753–757)
Correct, see **M₁**, **M₁M₁** (p. 112) or **M₁M₁M₁** (p. 112)
Wrong, back to **L₁**

---

**M₁**   Leaves with doubly serrate margin (Fig. 753)
Correct, see **N** (p. 112)
Wrong, see **M₁M₁** or **M₁M₁M₁** (p. 112)

## *Alnus* – Alder

| | |
|---|---|
| **N** | ***Alnus incana*** (L.) Moench<br>**Grey Alder**<br>Fig. 753 – see p. 196/197<br><br>• Leaves 5–10cm long, broadly ovate to broadly elliptic in outline and with the margin doubly serrate<br>• Pointed at the end<br>• Leaf-stalk 7–20mm long<br>• Dark green and glabrous above and remaining greyish green beneath; both sides softly hairy when young<br><br>753   Upper side<br>**Grey Alder** |

**M₁M₁** Leaves with a wavy or coarsely dentate to crenate margin

Correct, see **N₁**
Wrong, see **M₁M₁M₁**

## *Salix* – Willow

| | |
|---|---|
| **N₁** | ***Salix caprea*** L.<br>**Goat Willow, Pussy Willow**<br>Fig. 754 – see p. 196/197<br><br>• Leaves 4–10cm long, broadly elliptic to ovate in outline and with the margin wavy or coarsely dentate to crenate<br>• With a short, oblique point at the end<br>• Leaf-stalk 1–2cm long, somewhat broadened at the base, slightly reddish in colour and with downy hairs<br>• Brownish dark green and glabrous above; greyish green beneath because of the downy covering<br><br>754   Under side<br>**Goat Willow** |

**M₁M₁** Leaves with finely serrate or
**M₁**   serrate/dentate margin
        (Fig. 755–757)

Correct, see **N₂, N₂N₂**
or **N₂N₂N₂**
Wrong, back to **M₁**
(p. 111)

## *Malus* – Apple

| | |
|---|---|
| **N₂** | ***Malus sylvestris*** (L.) Mill.<br>**ssp.** ***domestica*** (Borkh.) Mansf.<br>**Apple**<br>Fig. 755 – see p. 196/197<br><br>• Leaves 5–9cm long, narrowly elliptic, elliptic to ovate in outline and with the margin regularly serrate<br>• With a short point at the end<br>• Leaf-stalk 2–5cm long<br>• Dark green and often somewhat undulate above; pale greyish green beneath and densely felted at first<br><br>755   Under side<br>**Apple** |

## *Salix* – Willow

| | |
|---|---|
| **N₂**<br>**N₂** | ***Salix hastata*** L.<br>**Spear-leaved Willow**<br>Fig. 756 – see p. 196/197<br><br>• Leaves 3–8cm long, elliptic to ovate in outline and with the margin finely serrate/dentate<br>• Shortly pointed at the end<br>• Leaf-stalk 3–8mm long, somewhat broadened at the base, and tinged reddish above<br>• Dark green and glabrous above; pale bluish green beneath and hairy only when young<br><br>756   Upper side<br>**Spear-leaved Willow** |

## *Pyrus* – Pear

| | |
|---|---|
| **N₂**<br>**N₂**<br>**N₂** | ***Pyrus communis*** L.<br>**Pear**<br>Fig. 757 – see p. 196/197<br><br>• Leaves 3–8cm long, elliptic, ovate or roundish in outline, thick, and with the margin finely serrate and in some parts entire<br>• With a short, narrow point at the end<br>• Leaf-stalk 1–8cm long<br>• Shiny and glabrous above; somewhat hairy beneath at first, later glabrous and slightly paler green<br><br>757   Upper side<br>**Pear** |

**H₁H₁** Leaves elliptic to roundish and
**H₁**   green to bluish green beneath

Correct, see **I₂** or
**I₂I₂** (p. 113)
Wrong, see
**H₁H₁H₁H₁** (p. 118)

**I₂**   Leaves without prominent lateral veins beneath

Correct, see **K₂, K₂K₂**
(p. 113) or **K₂K₂K₂**
(p. 113)
Wrong, see **I₂I₂**
(p. 113)

**K₂**   Leaves 1–3cm long with a 0.5–3mm long stalk (Fig. 758)

Correct, see **L₂**
Wrong, see **K₂K₂**
(p. 113) or **K₂K₂K₂**
(p. 113)

758   Upper side  **Bilberry**

## *Vaccinium* – Vaccinium

**L₂**

*Vaccinium myrtillus* L.
**Bilberry**
Fig. 758, 759 – see p. 198/199

- Leaves 1–3cm long, oblong-ovate, elliptic or ovate in outline and with the margin finely serrate, dentate or crenate
- Rounded or shortly pointed at the end
- Leaf-stalk 0.5–3mm long
- Medium to dark green above and somewhat paler green beneath

759   Upper side **Bilberry**

---

**K₂K₂**   Leaves 2–4.5cm long with an often slightly reddish stalk 1–2cm long (Fig. 760)

Correct, see **L₃**
Wrong, see **K₂K₂K₂**

---

## *Amelanchier* – Service Berry

**L₃**

*Amelanchier ovalis* Medic.
**Service Berry**
Fig. 760 – see p. 198/199

- Leaves 2–4.5cm long, ovate to roundish in outline and with the margin finely serrate or dentate; occasionally entire or crenate
- Rounded at the end
- Leaf-stalk 1–2cm long and covered with woolly hairs especially when young
- Dark green and glabrous above; somewhat paler green beneath and woolly when young

760   Upper side **Service Berry**

---

**K₂K₂**
**K₂**   Leaves always more than 5cm long

Correct, see **M₂** or **M₂M₂**
Wrong, back to **K₂** (p. 112)

---

**M₂**   Leaves pointed and usually rounded at the base of the blade (Fig. 761)

Correct, see **N₃** or **N₃N₃**
Wrong, see **M₂M₂**

761   Under side **Portugal Laurel**

---

## *Prunus* – Cherry

**N₃**

*Prunus lusitanica* L.
**Portugal Laurel**
Fig. 762 – see p. 200/201

- Leaves 6–12cm long, oblong-ovate in outline, leathery and with the margin irregularly serrate/dentate
- Pointed at the end; often with a slightly rounded top
- Leaf-stalk 10–25mm long, grooved and often tinged red above
- Dark green above and pale green beneath; both sides glabrous

762   Upper side **Portugal Laurel**

---

**N₃**
**N₃**

*Prunus armeniaca* L.
**Apricot**
Fig. 763 – see p. 198/199

- Leaves 5–10cm long, broadly ovate, roundish or slightly heart-shaped in outline and with a finely serrate margin
- Shortly pointed at the end
- Leaf-stalk 3–7cm long and dark red in colour
- Dull green above and somewhat paler green beneath; both sides glabrous

763   Upper side **Apricot**

---

**M₂M₂**   Leaves obtuse at the end, with numerous fine teeth and with the base of the blade wedge-shaped (Fig. 764)

Correct, see **N₄**
Wrong, back to **M₂**

---

## *Arbutus* – Strawberry Tree

**N₄**

*Arbutus unedo* L.
**Strawberry Tree**
Fig. 764 – see p. 198/199

- Leaves 5–10cm long, oblong-elliptic in outline and irregularly serrate with teeth of varied length
- Obtuse at the end and with several short teeth or shortly pointed
- Leaf-stalk 5–15mm long, distinctly hairy and often somewhat reddish
- Dark green and shiny above; much paler green beneath with only the midrib prominent

764   Under side **Strawberry Tree**

---

**I₂I₂**   Leaves with midrib and lateral veins prominent beneath

Correct, see **K₃** (p. 114) or **K₃K₃** (p. 115)
Wrong, back to **I₂** (p. 112)

| **K₃** | Lateral veins of leaves usually straight and not curving towards the tip; if slightly curved, then only at the end | Correct, see **L₄** or **L₄L₄** Wrong, see **K₃K₃** (p. 115) |
|---|---|---|

| **L₄** | Leaves with 4 or 5 pairs of straight lateral veins, 1–3.5cm long and with the margin irregularly coarsely serrate (Fig. 765) | Correct, see **M₃** Wrong, see **L₄L₄** |
|---|---|---|

## Betula – Birch

**M₃**

**Betula humilis** Schrank
**Shrubby Birch**
Fig. 765 – see p. 198/199

- Leaves 1–3.5cm long, elliptic, ovate to roundish in outline and with the margin simply and regularly serrate
- Rather obtuse to weakly pointed at the end
- Leaf-stalk 3–7mm long and often somewhat reddish above
- Shiny dark green and glabrous above; paler green beneath, distinctly net-veined and with 4 or 5 pairs of lateral veins

765   Under side
**Shrubby Birch**

| **L₄L₄** | Leaves with 5 or more pairs of straight lateral veins and usually longer than 3cm | Correct, see **M₄**, **M₄M₄** or **M₄M₄M₄** Wrong, back to **L₄** |
|---|---|---|

| **M₄** | Leaves unequally doubly serrate/dentate and 3–5cm long (Fig. 766) | Correct, see **N₅** Wrong, see **M₄M₄** or **M₄M₄M₄** |
|---|---|---|

## Betula – Birch

**N₅**

**Betula pubescens** Ehrh.
**Downy Birch**
Fig. 766 – see p. 198/199

- Leaves 3–5cm long, broadly ovate to rhombic in outline and with the margin unequally doubly serrate/dentate; entire at the base of the blade
- Shortly pointed at the end
- Leaf-stalk 1–2cm long and somewhat hairy
- Dark green above, becoming glabrous; finely downy beneath in the axils of the larger veins

766   Upper side
**Downy Birch**

| **M₄M₄** | Leaves very finely serrate and 5–14cm long (Fig. 767) | Correct, see **N₆** Wrong, see **M₄M₄M₄** |
|---|---|---|

## Rhamnus – Buckthorn

**N₆**

**Rhamnus alpinus** L.
**ssp. alpinus**
**Alpine Buckthorn**
Fig. 767 – see p. 202/203

- Leaves 5–14cm long, elliptic to ovate in outline and with the margin finely serrate; often crenate in the lower part
- With an abrupt short point at the end
- Leaf-stalk 8–15mm long
- Shiny dark green and glabrous above; somewhat paler green beneath and with 5–20 primary lateral veins on each side of the midrib

767   Upper side
**Alpine Buckthorn**

| **M₄M₄** **M₄** | Leaves simply and/or doubly serrate and 3–12cm long (Fig. 768–770) | Correct, see **N₇**, **N₇N₇** or **N₇N₇N₇** Wrong, back to **M₄** |
|---|---|---|

## Alnus – Alder

**N₇**

**Alnus viridis** (Chaix) DC.
**Green Alder**
Fig. 768 – see p. 200/201

- Leaves 3–6cm long, elliptic to broadly ovate in outline and with the margin simply, doubly or irregularly serrate
- Obtuse at the end with small teeth or a point
- Leaf-stalk 1–2cm long and grooved
- Dark green and glabrous above; paler green beneath; with 5–10 clearly visible lateral veins

768   Under side
**Green Alder**

## Carpinus – Hornbeam

**N₇**
**N₇**

**Carpinus betulus** L.
**Hornbeam**
Fig. 769 – see p. 200/201

- Leaves 4–12cm long, ovate to oblong-ovate in outline and with the margin finely simply and doubly serrate
- Rather obtuse or often pointed at the end
- Leaf-stalk 5–15mm long and often reddish above
- Deep rich green and glabrous above; paler green beneath and slightly hairy in the axils of the veins; folded into pleats between the lateral veins

769   Under side
**Hornbeam**

## *Ostrya* – Hop Hornbeam

**N7**
**N7**
**N7**

*Ostrya carpinifolia* Scop.
**Hop Hornbeam**
Fig. 770 – see p. 200/201

- Leaves 5–12cm long, ovate-oblong or ovate in outline and with the margin sharply simply and doubly serrate
- Pointed at the end
- Leaf-stalk 4–12mm long
- Dark green above; yellowish green beneath and somewhat hairy in the axils of the veins; not undulate between the veins

770   Under side
**Hop Hornbeam**

---

| | | |
|---|---|---|
| **K3K3** | Lateral veins of the leaves curving towards the tip | Correct, see **L5** or **L5L5** Wrong, back to **K3** (p. 114) |

---

| | | |
|---|---|---|
| **L5** | Lateral veins on the under side of the leaves appearing distinctly pale yellow to whitish yellow (Fig. 771, 772) | Correct, see **M5** or **M5M5** Wrong, see **L5L5** |

## *Morus* – Mulberry

**M5**

*Morus alba* L.
**White Mulberry**
Fig. 771 – see p. 200/201

- Leaves 7–18cm long and varied in outline; often without lobes and therefore broadly ovate
- Shortly pointed at the end or rounded and with a short terminal tooth
- Leaf-stalk 2–5cm long, grooved above and somewhat hairy
- Dark green above and smooth or slightly rough; bluish green beneath and hairy on the veins

771   Under side
**White Mulberry**

---

**M5**
**M5**

*Morus nigra* L.
**Black Mulberry**
Fig. 772 – see p. 200/201

- Leaves 6–18cm long and varied in outline; often broadly ovate to heart-shaped and with a coarsely serrate margin
- Tipped by a finer, longer point than in the White Mulberry
- Leaf-stalk 1–2cm long
- Shiny dark green above and very roughly hairy; paler bluish green and hairy beneath

772   Under side
**Black Mulberry**

---

| | | |
|---|---|---|
| **L5L5** | Lateral veins beneath not distinctly pale yellow to whitish yellow, but pale to bluish green | Correct, see **M6**, **M6M6** or **M6M6M6** (p. 117) Wrong, back to **L5** |

---

| | | |
|---|---|---|
| **M6** | Leaves elliptic to mostly roundish in outline, 2–6cm long and obtuse or with an abrupt short point at the end (Fig. 773, 774) | Correct, see **N8** or **N8N8** Wrong, see **M6M6** or **M6M6M6** (p. 117) |

## *Prunus* – Cherry

**N8**

*Prunus mahaleb* L.
**St Lucie Cherry**
Fig. 773 – see p. 202/203

- Leaves 3–6cm long, broadly ovate to roundish in outline and with a crenate-serrate margin
- Obtuse or shortly pointed at the end
- Leaf-stalk 1–2cm long and usually without glands
- Shiny dark green and glabrous above; bluish green beneath and often somewhat hairy on the midrib

773   Under side
**St Lucie Cherry**

## *Rhamnus* – Buckthorn

**N8**
**N8**

*Rhamnus pumila*
(Turra) W. Vent
**Dwarf Buckthorn**
Fig. 774 – see p. 202/203

- Leaves 2–5cm long, elliptic, obovate or roundish in outline and with the margin very finely crenate-serrate
- With a short abrupt point at the end
- Leaf-stalk 4–9mm long
- Dark green and glabrous above; paler green beneath and somewhat hairy on the veins

774   Upper side
**Dwarf Buckthorn**

---

| | | |
|---|---|---|
| **M6M6** | Leaves narrowly elliptic to broadly elliptic in outline, 2–12cm long and very shortly pointed, obtuse or rounded at the end | Correct, see **N9** or **N9N9** (P. 116) Wrong, see **M6M6M6** (p. 117) |

---

| | | |
|---|---|---|
| **N9** | Leaves narrowly wedge-shaped at the base of the blade (Fig. 775, 776) | Correct, see **O** (p. 116) or **OO** (p. 116) Wrong, see **N9N9** (p. 116) |

## *Prunus* – Cherry

**O**

***Prunus tenella*** Batsch
**Dwarf Russian Almond**
Fig. 775 – see p. 202/203

- Leaves 3–7cm long, narrowly elliptic in outline and with the margin finely and regularly serrate/dentate
- Pointed at the end
- Leaf-stalk 5–15mm long
- Shiny dark green above and pale green beneath; both sides glabrous; only the midrib really prominent

775   Upper side
**Dwarf Russian Almond**

**OO**

***Prunus domestica*** L.
**ssp. *domestica***
**Plum**
Fig. 776 – see p. 202/203

- Leaves 3–10cm long, elliptic or obovate in outline and with the margin finely serrate and crenate
- Rounded, obtuse or pointed at the end
- Leaf-stalk 10–15mm long
- Dark green above and later glabrous; pale green beneath and often remaining hairy for a long time

776   Upper side
**Plum**

| | | |
|---|---|---|
| **N₉N₉** | Leaves broadly wedge-shaped or rounded at the base of the blade | Correct, see **O₁** or **O₁O₁**<br>Wrong, back to **N₉** (p. 115) |

| | | |
|---|---|---|
| **O₁** | Leaf-stalk distinctly reddish above (Fig. 777) | Correct, see **P**<br>Wrong, see **O₁O₁** |

## *Prunus* – Cherry

**P**

***Prunus spinosa*** L.
**Blackthorn, Sloe**
Fig. 777 – see p. 204/205

- Leaves 2–5cm long, broadly lanceolate to oblong-elliptic in outline and with the margin serrate and in places crenate
- Obtuse or shortly pointed at the end
- Leaf-stalk 5–12mm long and often reddish above
- Dark green above and pale green beneath; hairy when young

777   Upper side
**Blackthorn**

| | | |
|---|---|---|
| **O₁O₁** | Leaf-stalk not or only slightly reddish above | Correct, see **P₁** or **P₁P₁**<br>Wrong, back to **O₁** |

| | | |
|---|---|---|
| **P₁** | Leaf-stalk 1–3cm long, glabrous, slightly grooved above, and with the veins very strongly curved towards the tip of the blade (Fig. 778) | Correct, see **Q**<br>Wrong, see **P₁P₁** |

## *Rhamnus* – Buckthorn

**Q**

***Rhamnus catharticus*** L.
**Buckthorn**
Fig. 778 – see p. 202/203

- Leaves 4–7cm long, elliptic to roundish in outline and with the margin finely crenate-serrate
- Usually with a short point at the end
- Leaf-stalk 1–3cm long and slightly grooved above
- Dull dark green above and medium bluish green beneath; both sides usually glabrous; with 2–4 curved lateral veins each side of the midrib

778   Upper side
**Buckthorn**

**P₁P₁**

Leaf-stalk at most 1cm long; if longer, then densely grey-felted (Fig. 779); veins not as in **P₁**

Correct, see **Q₁**, **Q₁Q₁** (p. 117) or **Q₁Q₁Q₁** (p. 117)
Wrong, back to **P₁**

779   Under side
**Wayfaring Tree**

## *Viburnum* – Viburnum

**Q₁**

***Viburnum lantara*** L.
**Wayfaring Tree**
Fig. 780 – see p. 206/207

- Leaves 5–12cm long, ovate to oblong ovate in outline and with the margin regularly and finely toothed
- Pointed at the end
- Leaf-stalk up to 15mm long and densely felted
- Medium to dark green above and somewhat wrinkled; medium green beneath and densely covered with stellate hairs

780   Upper side
**Wayfaring Tree**

## *Sorbus* – Whitebeam

**Q₁**
**Q₁**

781  Upper side
**False Medlar**

***Sorbus chamaemespilus*** (L.)
Crantz
**False Medlar**
Fig. 781 – see p. 204/205

● Leaves 3–8cm long, narrowly elliptic to elliptic in outline, with their greatest breadth usually below the middle and the margins simply and finely serrate

● Obtuse or weakly pointed at the end

● Leaf-stalk 5–10mm long

● Shiny dark green above and paler green beneath; both sides glabrous; forms with the leaves felted beneath are hybrids

## *Mespilus* – Medlar

**Q₁**
**Q₁**
**Q₁**

782  Upper side
**Medlar**

***Mespilus germanica*** L.
**Medlar**
Fig. 782 – see p. 206/207

● Leaves 5–12cm long, oblong-elliptic to obovate in outline and with the margin finely serrate/dentate; in places also entire

● Very shortly pointed at the end

● Leaf-stalk up to 10mm long or the leaf sessile

● Dull green above, somewhat downy and slightly wrinkled; pale to greyish green beneath and with whitish matted woolly hairs; veins above deeply impressed

| | | |
|---|---|---|
| **M₆M₆** **M₆** | Leaves narrowly to broadly elliptic or ovate in outline, 4–12cm long and usually with a long point at the end (Fig. 785–793) | Correct, see **N₁₀** or **N₁₀N₁₀** (p. 118) Wrong, back to **M₆** (p. 115) |

| | | |
|---|---|---|
| **N₁₀** | Most leaves with 1–4 greenish or reddish nectar-glands on the leaf-stalk (Fig. 783, 784) | Correct, see **O₂**, **O₂O₂** or **O₂O₂O₂** Wrong, see **N₁₀N₁₀** (p. 118) |

783
Nectar-glands
**Wild Cherry**

784
Nectar-glands
**Bird Cherry**

| | | |
|---|---|---|
| **O₂** | Margins of leaves very finely and regularly serrate; teeth shorter than 0.7mm (Fig. 785) | Correct, see **P₂** Wrong, see **O₂O₂** |

## *Prunus* – Cherry

**P₂**

785  Upper side
**Bird Cherry**

***Prunus padus*** L.
**Bird Cherry**
Fig. 785 – see p. 204/205

● Leaves 5–12cm long, oblong-elliptic to obovate in outline and with the margin finely and regularly serrate

● With a fine, slender point at the end

● Leaf-stalk up to 2cm long, red above and with 1–3 usually greenish nectar-glands

● Dull dark green above and pale or bluish green beneath, both sides glabrous

| | | |
|---|---|---|
| **O₂O₂** | Margins of leaves finely serrate and in places crenate (Fig. 786) | Correct, see **P₃** Wrong, see **O₂O₂O₂** |

## *Prunus* – Cherry

**P₃**

786  Upper side
**Sour Cherry**

***Prunus cerasus*** L.
**Sour Cherry**
Fig. 786 – see p. 204/205

● Leaves 4–12cm long, elliptic to ovate in outline, flat, somewhat leathery, and with the margin finely serrate and in places crenate

● Pointed at the end

● Leaf-stalk 1–3cm long and usually with green nectar-glands

● Shiny dark green above and pale green beneath; veins beneath distinctly prominent

| | | |
|---|---|---|
| **O₂O₂** **O₂** | Margins of leaves regularly or irregularly rather coarsely serrate (Fig. 787, 788) | Correct, see **P₄** or **P₄P₄** (p. 118) Wrong, back to **O₂** |

## *Prunus* – Cherry

**P₄**

787  Upper side
**Japanese Cherry**

***Prunus serrulata*** Lindl.
**Japanese Cherry**
Fig. 787 – see p. 204/205

● Leaves 8–14cm long, narrowly ovate in outline and with the margin sharply and irregularly serrate

● With a long point at the end

● Leaf-stalk 2–4cm long, reddish above and usually with 2–4 nectar-glands

● Shiny dark green above and bluish green beneath; both sides glabrous; veins distinctly prominent

**P₄**
**P₄**

788   Upper side
**Wild Cherry**

### *Prunus avium* L.
### Wild Cherry
Fig. 788 - see p. 204/205

- Leaves 6–15cm long, oblong-ovate to obovate in outline with an irregularly serrate margin
- With a slender point at the end
- Leaf-stalk 2–4cm long with 2–4 red nectar-glands
- Dark green and glabrous above; green beneath and finely hairy when young; small tufts of hair in the axils of the larger veins

---

**N₁₀**
**N₁₀**   Leaves without nectar-glands on the leaf-stalk (Fig. 789–793)

Correct, see **O₃**, **O₃O₃**, **O₃O₃O₃** or **O₃O₃O₃O₃**
Wrong, back to **N₁₀** (p. 117)

789   Under side **Spindle Tree**

---

## *Euonymus* - Spindle Tree

**O₃**

790   Upper side
**Spindle Tree**

### *Euonymus* (*Evonymus*) *europaeus* L.
### Spindle Tree
Fig. 790 - see p. 206/207

- Leaves 3–8cm long, elliptic to ovate in outline and very finely and regularly serrate
- Narrowly pointed at the end
- Leaf-stalk 5–9mm long and grooved
- Medium to dark green above and pale bluish green beneath; both sides glabrous

---

## *Forsythia* - Forsythia

**O₃**
**O₃**

791   Upper side
**Hybrid Forsythia**

### *Forsythia x intermedia* Zab.
### Hybrid Forsythia
Fig. 791 - see p. 206/207

- Leaves 6–11cm long, lanceolate to oblong-ovate in outline (sometimes also tripartite on luxuriant growth) and with the margin irregularly serrate and dentate
- Pointed at the end
- Leaf-stalk 1–2cm long and usually grooved above
- Dark green above and paler green to pale greyish green beneath; both sides glabrous

---

**O₃**
**O₃**
**O₃**

### *Forsythia europaea* Deg. et Bald.
### European Forsythia
Fig. 792 - see p. 206/207

- Leaves 5–8cm long, narrowly elliptic to narrowly ovate in outline and usually finely serrate in the upper part
- Pointed at the end
- Leaf-stalk 5–10mm long and grooved above
- Dark green above and paler green beneath; both sides glabrous

792   Upper side
**European Forsythia**

---

**O₃**
**O₃**
**O₃**
**O₃**

### *Forsythia viridissima* Lindl.
### Green Forsythia
Fig. 793 - see p. 206/207

- Leaves 4–14cm long, lanceolate to narrowly elliptic in outline and with the margin finely serrate/dentate above the middle
- Pointed at the end
- Leaf-stalk 5–30mm long and usually grooved above
- Dark green above and pale green beneath; both sides glabrous

793   Upper side
**Green Forsythia**

---

**H₁H₁**
**H₁H₁**   Leaves spathulate (1–4cm long), narrowly to broadly lanceolate and white, greyish green or greenish beneath

Correct, see **I₃** or **I₃I₃** (p. 119)
Wrong, back to **H₁** (p. 110)

---

**I₃**   Leaves 1–4cm long, very narrowly wedge-shaped at the base and with the margin fringed with spreading, white hairs 0.5–1.5mm in length (Fig. 794)

Correct, see **K₄**
Wrong, see **I₃I₃** (p. 119)

---

**K₄**

### *Arctostaphylos alpinus* (L.)
Spreng.
### Black Bearberry
Fig. 794 - see p. 208/209

- Leaves 1–4cm long, spathulate or narrowly obovate in outline and with the margin finely and closely serrate; entire towards the base
- Obtuse at the end
- Leaf-stalk only a few mm long or the leaf sessile
- Dark green and convex above; whitish green beneath with dark green veins

794   Upper side
**Black Bearberry**

| | | |
|---|---|---|
| **I₃I₃** | Leaves without long, spreading, white hairs along the margin (Fig. 795–799) | Correct, see **K₅** or **K₅K₅** Wrong, back to **I₃** (p. 118) |

| | | |
|---|---|---|
| **K₅** | Leaves green to bluish green beneath (Fig. 795, 796) | Correct, see **L₆** or **L₆L₆** Wrong, see **K₅K₅** |

| | | |
|---|---|---|
| **L₆** | Midrib on both sides very pale yellowish white and under side of leaf pale bluish green (Fig. 795) | Correct, see **M₇** Wrong, see **L₆L₆** |

## *Prunus* – Cherry

**M₇**

***Prunus dulcis*** (Mill.) D. A. Webb
**Almond**
Fig. 795 – see p. 208/209

- Leaves 4–12cm long, lanceolate to oblong-ovate and with the margin very finely serrate/dentate
- Obtuse or pointed at the end
- Leaf-stalk 10–25mm long
- Medium to dark green above and pale bluish green beneath; both sides glabrous

795   Under side
**Almond**

| | | |
|---|---|---|
| **L₆L₆** | Midrib on both sides pale green and under side of leaf medium bluish green (Fig. 796) | Correct, see **M₈** Wrong, back to **L₆** |

## *Prunus* – Cherry

**M₈**

***Prunus persica*** (L.) Batsch
**Peach**
Fig. 796 – see p. 208/209

- Leaves 5–15cm long, narrowly to broadly lanceolate in outline and with a finely serrate/dentate margin
- With a long point at the end
- Leaf-stalk 5–15mm long
- Shiny dark green above and medium green to medium bluish green beneath; both sides glabrous

796   Under side
**Peach**

| | | |
|---|---|---|
| **K₅K₅** | Leaves greyish green or white beneath | Correct, see **L₇** or **L₇L₇** Wrong, back to **K₅** |

| | | |
|---|---|---|
| **L₇** | Leaves only serrate in the upper part; entire in the lower part (Fig. 797) | Correct, see **M₉** Wrong, see **L₇L₇** |

## *Salix* – Willow

**M₉**

***Salix purpurea*** L.
**Purple Willow**
Fig. 797 – see p. 208/209

- Leaves 5–10cm long, lanceolate in outline with their greatest breadth usually in the upper third and finely serrate towards the tip; entire in the lower part
- Shortly pointed at the end
- Leaf-stalk 5–8mm long and often tinged red
- Bluish green and glabrous above; pale bluish green beneath and also glabrous

797   Under side
**Purple Willow**

| | | |
|---|---|---|
| **L₇L₇** | Leaves coarsely sinuate serrate along the whole margin (Fig. 798) or finely and regularly serrate/dentate (Fig. 799) | Correct, see **M₁₀** or **M₁₀M₁₀** Wrong, back to **L₇** |

## *Salix* – Willow

**M₁₀**

***Salix fragilis*** L.
**Crack Willow**
Fig. 798 – see p. 208/209

- Leaves 5–16cm long, oblong-lanceolate in outline, usually broadest in the lower third and coarsely sinuately serrate
- With a very long, fine point at the end
- Leaf-stalk up to 1cm long
- Dark green and slightly shiny above; with silky hairs at first beneath, later pale or bluish green

798   Under side
**Crack Willow**

**M₁₀**
**M₁₀**

***Salix alba*** L.
**White Willow**
Fig. 799 – see p. 208/209

- Leaves 5–10cm long, narrowly lanceolate to lanceolate in outline, the upper part often curved to one side and the margin finely and regularly serrate/dentate
- Narrowly and finely pointed at the end
- Leaf-stalk 5–10mm long
- Both sides with a covering of silvery hairs at first; later dark green and almost glabrous above; remaining silvery white beneath

799   Under side
**White Willow**

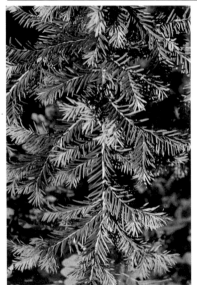

## *Taxus baccata* L.
### Yew (with many forms)
**Taxaceae - Yew family** p. 65

**Size:** 1-3cm long and 2-3cm broad

**Form of needle:** Linear, flattened, decurrent on the twig, slightly crescent-shaped and always standing singly; life-span 3-8 years

**Stalk:** 2-3mm long and green

**End of needle:** Finely pointed

**Base of needle:** Narrowed to the stalk and with the base broadly decurrent on the twig

**Margin of needle:** Entire

**Upper/under side:** Shiny dark green above with a prominent midrib; pale or yellowish green beneath, with a clearly visible midrib and on each side of it a broad, rather inconspicuous band of stomata

**Arrangement on the shoot:** Spirally arranged on long shoots

**Distribution:** From the colline to the montane zone; usually on steep slopes and in gorges in open to shady beech, fir, ash or maple woods

800    *Taxus baccata* - Yew
*Evergreen, to 20m high, very slow growing, with green shoots*

## *Sequoia sempervirens*
(D. Don) Endl.
### Coast Redwood
**Taxodiaceae - Swamp Cypress family** p. 65

**Size:** On long shoots 6-10mm long, on short shoots 4-20mm long, and 1-2.5mm broad

**Form of needle:** Linear to lanceolate, flattened, straight or slightly curved, becoming gradually smaller towards the end of the shoot and with a life-span of 2-4 years

**Stalk:** Sessile

**End of needle:** Abruptly pointed

**Base of needle:** With the whole breadth of the needle decurrent for several mm on the shoot

**Margin of needle:** Entire

**Upper/under side:** Dark green above and pale green on the younger short shoots; medium green beneath on the margins and in the middle, with 2 whitish bands of stomata in between

**Arrangement on the shoot:** Needles arranged spirally

**Distribution:** Native in the lowlands and hilly areas of the damp, misty coastal region of southern Oregon

801    *Sequoia sempervirens* - Coast Redwood *Evergreen tree, 65-100m high, with green shoots, irregularly forked*

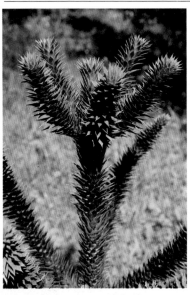

## *Araucaria araucana*
(Mol.) K. Koch
### Chile Pine, Monkey Puzzle
**Araucariaceae - Chile Pine family** p. 65

**Size:** 2.5-5cm long and 1-2.5cm broad

**Form of needle:** Needle-shaped, triangular, stiff, rather coarse, thickish, and pointing towards the end of the shoot; life-span from 10-15 years and later falling with the dead twigs

**Stalk:** Sessile

**End of needle:** Ending in a sharp, spiny point

**Base of needle:** Broadened considerably at the base and somewhat decurrent on the shoot

**Margin of needle:** Entire

**Upper/under side:** Both sides shiny dark green, glabrous and with parallel veins

**Arrangement on the shoot:** Needles spirally arranged and overlapping

**Distribution:** Native in the Andes of Chile and Argentina; frequently planted as a decorative tree in parks in the Mediterranean region; fine specimens in Ireland and England

802    *Araucaria araucana* - Chile Pine
*Evergreen conifer up to 30m high, with whorls of thick branches*

## *Abies alba* Mill.
### Common Silver Fir
**Pinaceae - Pine family** p. 58, 59, 66

**Size:** Up to 3cm long and 2-3cm broad

**Form of needle:** Flattened, linear, not prickly, without sheaths and, after falling, leaving behind broadly elliptic to circular scars; life-span 7-11 years

**Stalk:** Sessile

**End of needle:** Obtuse or distinctly emarginate

**Base of needle:** Narrowing in the lower part and attached to the twig by a circular base

**Margin of needle:** Entire

**Upper/under side:** Dark green above, the fine lines of stomata (if present) only at the tips and with a slightly impressed midrib; pale to medium green beneath with 2 distinct, silvery white bands of stomata; midrib somewhat raised

**Arrangement on the shoot:** Needles spirally arranged

**Distribution:** An important forest tree from the hill to the montane zone, forming stands in shady places where the air is very moist

803    *Abies alba* - Common Silver Fir
*Evergreen tree, up to 50m high, with greyish brown, very hairy twigs*

## *Abies nordmanniana*
(Stev.) Spach
### Caucasian Fir
**Pinaceae - Pine family** p. 66

**Size:** 2-3.5cm long and 2-2.5mm broad

**Form of needle:** Linear, stiff, coarse, pointing slightly towards the end of the short and distinctly furrowed

**Stalk:** Sessile

**End of needle:** Obtuse, rounded or slightly emarginate

**Base of needle:** Narrowing in the lower part of the needle, twisted, and attached to the twig by a broadly elliptic to circular base

**Margin of needle:** Entire

**Upper/under side:** Dark green above, without bands of stomata and grooved in the middle; striped beneath (dark green stripes) with 2 broad bands of stomata

**Arrangement on the shoot:** Needles closely set and arranged spirally

**Distribution:** In the western Caucasus and mountains of the Pontic region between 900m and 2200m, associated with the Oriental Spruce and Oriental Beech; a valuable park tree in central Europe

804    *Abies nordmanniana* - Caucasian Fir
*Evergreen conifer, 30-50m high, with olive-green shoots, grooved at first*

## *Abies veitchii* Lindl.
### Veitch's Fir
**Pinaceae - Pine family** p. 66

**Size:** 1-2.5cm long and up to 2mm broad

**Form of needle:** Linear, soft, and often pointing diagonally forwards, brush-like, so that the chalky white undersides are visible

**Stalk:** Sessile

**End of needle:** Flat and distinctly emarginate

**Base of needle:** Narrowing in the lower part of the needle, slightly curved, and attached to the twig by an elliptic or circular base

**Margin of needle:** Entire

**Upper/under side:** Medium to dark green above, without bands of stomata and slightly grooved in the middle; striped beneath (pale to medium green stripes) and with 2 broad, chalky white bands of stomata

**Arrangement on the shoot:** Needles arranged spirally

**Distribution:** Native in Japan; discovered in Japan in 1860 by J. G. Veitch and brought to England in 1861; hardy in Europe and occasionally planted in parks

805    *Abies veitchii* - Veitch's Fir
*Evergreen conifer, 15-40m high, with greyish green and very hairy young shoots*

## *Abies procera* Rehd.
### Noble Fir

**Pinaceae – Pine family** p.66

**Size:** 2.5-3.5cm long and 1.5mm broad

**Form of needle:** Linear, coarse, densely crowded and clearly curved upwards

**End of needle:** Usually obtuse

**Base of needle:** Needles with their base appressed to the twig and then curving abruptly upwards

**Margin of needle:** Entire

**Upper/under side:** Greyish green above, flattened and grooved, with lines of stomata that extend to the base as broad bands; with 2 greyish longitudinal bands beneath

**Arrangement on the shoot:** Needles densely crowded and arranged spirally

**Distribution:** Native in Pacific North America; hardy in central Europe; frequently planted in parks and gardens; brought to Europe in 1830

806   *Abies procera* – **Noble Fir**
*Evergreen conifer, up to 80m high in its native country, with olive-green to brown shoots*

## *Pseudotsuga menziesii*
(Mirbel) Franco
### Douglas Fir

**Pinaceae – Pine family** p. 66

**Size:** 1.8-3.5cm long and 1-1.5mm broad

**Form of needle:** Straight or slightly curved, flat, leathery, soft, leaving behind when it falls a raised, cushion-like scar, and smelling of orange when rubbed

**Stalk:** Small, and standing out at an angle from the twig

**End of needle:** Obtuse or somewhat pointed

**Margin of needle:** Entire

**Upper/under side:** Dull medium to dark green and furrowed above; with 2 narrow silvery grey bands of stomata beneath

**Arrangement on the shoot:** Needles densely crowded and spirally arranged

**Distribution:** Native only in the mountains near the western coast of North America; introduced into England in 1827 by D. Douglas; planted in parks and widely cultivated for afforestation

807   *Pseudotsuga menziesii* – **Douglas Fir**
*Evergreen conifer, 50-60m high, with yellowish to olive- green, hairy shoots*

## *Juniperus communis* L.
### ssp. *communis*
### Common Juniper

**Cupressaceae – Cypress family** p. 67

**Size:** 1-2cm long and 1-2mm broad

**Form of needle:** Linear, straight, not decurrent on the shoot and rather sharp

**Stalk:** Sessile

**End of needle:** Sharply pointed

**Base of needle:** Attached to the twig by a broad base and usually standing out at a right-angle

**Margin of needle:** Entire

**Upper/under side:** With a broad, white central band above and slightly grooved; shiny green and keeled beneath

**Arrangement on the shoot:** Needles arranged in whorls of 3

**Distribution:** From the hills to the montane zone; frequently on sunny, dry pastures, on rocks, and in open woods and heaths

808   *Juniperus communis* – **Common Juniper** *Evergreen, column-shaped shrub or tree up to 15m with triangular shoots*

## *Juniperus communis* L.
### ssp. *alpina* Celak
### (*J. nana* Willd.)
### Dwarf Juniper

**Cupressaceae – Cypress family** p. 67

**Size:** 4-8mm long and 1-2mm broad

**Form of needle:** Usually crescent-shaped, linear and attached to the shoot by a broad base; whorls of needles densely crowded and only about 1-3mm apart

**Stalk:** Sessile

**End of needle:** Shortly pointed; not prickly

**Margin of needle:** Entire

**Upper/under side:** Dark green on the margins above with a broad band of stomata; dark green and slightly keeled beneath

**Arrangement on the shoot:** Needles arranged in whorls

**Distribution:** In the subalpine zone; in dwarf shrub communities, screes and on sunny slopes; a strongly cold-resistant mountain plant

809   *Juniperus nana* – **Dwarf Juniper**
*Evergreen, prostrate, dwarf shrub, 20-50cm high, with short, stout branches*

## *Juniperus chinensis* L.
### Chinese Juniper 'Blaauw'

**Cupressaceae – Cypress family** p. 67

**Size:** Juvenile leaves 6-10mm long and 1mm broad; adult leaves 3-5mm long and 1-2.5mm broad

**Form of leaves:** Juvenile leaves needle-like, spreading at an acute angle; adult leaves scale-like, rhombic, densely crowded and overlapping each other

**Stalk:** Sessile

**End of needle:** Juvenile leaves spiny-pointed; adult leaves obtuse or pointed

**Margin of needle:** Entire

**Upper/under side:** Juvenile leaves with 2 separate bluish green bands of stomata above and dark green beneath; adult leaves with 2 indistinct stomatic areas at the base

**Arrangement on the shoot:** Needle-like leaves usually in whorls of 3; but also opposite

**Distribution:** Brought to England in 1767 by W. Kerr; in England up to 18m high; planted in parks and gardens

810   *Juniperus chinensis* – **Chinese Juniper**
*Evergreen conifer, 5-20m high, originating in China, Japan and Mongolia*

## *Picea abies* (L.) Karst.
### (*P. excelsa* (Lam.) Link)
### Norway Spruce

**Pinaceae – Pine family** p. 58, 59, 67

**Size:** 0.5-2.5cm long and 1mm broad

**Form of needle:** Fairly rigid, almost square in cross-section, pointing sideways and upwards from the twig and often curved, crescent-shaped; life-span 5-7 years

**Stalk:** With a very short, brownish stalk

**End of needle:** Rather obtuse to pointed

**Base of needle:** Only slightly narrowed towards the small stalk

**Margin of needle:** Entire

**Upper/under side:** Dark green on all sides with fine lines of stomata

**Arrangement on the shoot:** Needles spirally arranged

**Distribution:** Originally subalpine; planted in afforestation from the hill to the montane zone; shallow rooting, so likely to be blown down in gales

811   *Picea abies* – **Norway Spruce**
*Evergreen conifer, 30-55m high, with dull reddish brown, fairly stout shoots*

### *Picea orientalis* (L.) Link
## Oriental Spruce
**Pinaceae – Pine family** p. 67

**Size:** 5–11mm long and 1–1.3mm broad

**Form of needle:** 4-angled, almost square in cross-section, densely crowded, straight or somewhat curved and shortly stalked

**Stalk:** 0.3–0.8mm long, brownish with slightly brownish hairs

**End of needle:** Obtuse

**Base of needle:** Narrowed towards the base

**Margin of needle:** Entire

**Colour:** Shiny dark green; with white lines of stomata on all sides

**Arrangement on the shoot:** Spirally arranged

**Distribution:** Native in the Caucasus and northern Asia Minor between 600m and 2100m; occasionally planted in parks

812 **Picea orientalis – Oriental Spruce**
*Evergreen conifer, 40–50m high, with pale brown shoots, densely covered with crisped hairs*

### *Picea omorika* (Panc.) Purk.
## Serbian Spruce
**Pinaceae – Pine family** p. 68

**Size:** 1–1.9cm long and 1.5–2mm broad

**Form of needle:** Distinctly flattened, somewhat curved, densely crowded and pointing towards the end of the shoot, keeled above and beneath; life-span 10–12 years

**Stalk:** Very short and brownish in colour

**End of needle:** Obtuse or somewhat pointed but not prickly

**Base of needle:** Rounded

**Margin of needle:** Entire

**Upper/under side:** Pale green above at first, later dark green; clearly visible bands of stomata on both sides of the keel beneath

**Arrangement on the shoot:** Spirally arranged

**Distribution:** Native in S.E. Europe; seeds first reached central Europe about 1890; planted as an ornamental tree in gardens and parks

813 **Picea omorika – Serbian Spruce**
*Evergreen conifer, 30–35m high, with light brown shoots covered with brown hairs*

### *Picea pungens* Engelm.
## 'Glauca'
## Blue Spruce
**Pinaceae – Pine family** p. 68

**Size:** 1.5–3cm long and up to 1.5mm thick

**Form of needle:** Often slightly sickle-shaped, rigid and 4-angled; life-span 4–8 years

**Stalk:** Remaining as a 1mm long stump after the needle has fallen

**End of needle:** Shortly pointed and sharp

**Base of needle:** Narrowing somewhat towards the peg-like stump

**Margin of needle:** Entire

**Upper/under side:** Conspicuously bluish white, especially the young needles; underside of shoot less crowded with leaves; each side of the midrib with a band of stomata

**Arrangement on the shoot:** Needles arranged spirally

**Distribution:** Native in the Rocky Mountains, U.S.A., between 1800m and 3300m; many varieties cultivated in Europe and often planted in gardens and parks

814 **Picea pungens – Blue Spruce**
*Evergreen conifer, 25–35m high, with pale to orange-brown, glabrous shoots*

### *Tsuga canadensis* (L.) Carr.
## Eastern Hemlock,
## Canadian Hemlock
**Pinaceae – Pine family** p. 68

**Size:** 7–15mm long and 1.5–2.5mm broad

**Form of needle:** Flattened, standing out on both sides of the twig, narrowed towards the tip and of varying size; needles of the middle row frequently twisted and smaller than the needles at the side

**Stalk:** Needles with a distinctly yellowish white stalk, which is usually somewhat appressed to the twig

**End of needle:** Rounded

**Base of needle:** Rounded or truncate

**Margin of needle:** Finely serrate; teeth set far apart

**Upper/under side:** Shiny dark green above; bluish green beneath with 2 silvery bands of stomata

**Arrangement on the shoot:** Spirally arranged

**Distribution:** Native in eastern North America; reached Europe in 1730 and since then has been planted in parks and occasionally woods

815 **Tsuga canadensis – Eastern Hemlock**
*Evergreen conifer, 20–30m high, with densely brownish hairy shoots*

### *Metasequoia glyptostroboides*
Hu et Cheng
## Dawn Redwood
**Taxodiaceae – Swamp Cypress family** p. 68

**Size:** 1–4cm long and 2–3mm broad

**Form of needle:** Linear in outline, flattened, noticeably soft; needles on short shoots somewhat curved, practically opposite each other and falling in the autumn with the short shoot; needles on the long shoots falling singly in autumn

**Stalk:** 0.5–1mm long

**End of needle:** Rounded or with quite a short point

**Base of needle:** Rounded

**Margin of needle:** Entire

**Upper/under side:** Both sides pale green at first; later dark green above and somewhat paler green beneath; with an indistinct middle band beneath

**Arrangement on the shoot:** Spirally arranged on long shoots, opposite on short shoots

**Distribution:** Native in S.W. China; discovered in 1941 and in cultivation in Europe since 1948; planted in parks

816 **Metasequoia glyptostroboides – Dawn Redwood** *Deciduous conifer, 10–30m high, with slender, reddish or brownish green shoots*

### *Taxodium distichum* (L.)
L. C. Rich
## Swamp Cypress
**Taxodiaceae – Swamp Cypress family** p. 68

**Size:** 1–2cm long and 1–2mm broad

**Form of needle:** Needles on the short shoots in regular ranks, very shortly stalked or sessile, linear and flattened

**Stalk:** Sessile or shortly stalked

**End of needle:** Somewhat pointed

**Shoot:** Long shoots becoming woody, brown to reddish brown, with a slight bloom, glabrous, needles separate and falling singly in autumn; short shoots green, up to 1mm thick, not becoming woody and falling together with the needles in autumn

**Margin of needle:** Entire

**Upper/under side:** Fresh green at first, later pale to medium green and rust-brown in autumn; with fine longitudinal bands beneath

**Arrangement on the shoot:** Arranged spirally on long shoots and alternately in 2 ranks on short shoots.

**Distribution:** Native in the Florida and Mississippi region; reached Europe in 1640; has long been planted as a park tree in Europe

817 **Taxodium distichum – Swamp Cypress**
*Evergreen conifer, 20–50m high, with conspicuously slender shoots*

818  *Pinus mugo* - Mountain Pine
*An evergreen shrub with one or more stems or a tree up to 25m high*

## *Pinus mugo* Turra
## Mountain Pine
**Pinaceae - Pine family** p. 69

**Size:** 2-8cm long and 1-3mm broad

**Form of needle:** Stiff, straight or somewhat crescent-shaped, semi-circular in cross-section and densely crowded on the shoot; sheaths at the base of young needles up to 1cm long and brownish white, equally short at the base of needles on older shoots; life-span 5-10 years

**Stalk:** Sessile

**End of needle:** Shortly pointed, not prickly

**Margin of needle:** Needles finely serrate on the margin (somewhat rough to the touch if rubbed towards the base)

**Upper/under side:** Dark green on both sides with numerous fine lines of stomata

**Arrangement on the shoot:** Needles on short shoots in pairs which are arranged spirally

**Distribution:** In the subalpine zone; a species with a wide ecological distribution; on sunny slopes, in shady, north-facing localities with prolonged covering of snow, and one particular form, on raised bogs

819  *Pinus sylvestris* - Scots Pine
*Evergreen conifer up to 40m high with glabrous, light brown, grooved shoots*

## *Pinus sylvestris* L.
## Scots Pine
**Pinaceae - Pine family** p. 60, 61, 69

**Size:** 3-7cm long and up to 2mm broad

**Form of needle:** Stiff, usually distinctly twisted, in pairs on short shoots, semi-circular in cross-section, somewhat flattened and clustered at the end of the shoot; sheaths at the base 0.3-0.6cm long and persistent; life-span 2-7 years according to variety

**Stalk:** Sessile

**End of needle:** Pointed

**Margin of needle:** Needles finely serrate on the margin (somewhat rough to the touch if rubbed towards the base)

**Upper/under side:** Bluish or greyish green above and beneath with very fine lines of stomata

**Arrangement on the shoot:** Needles on short shoots in pairs which are arranged spirally

**Distribution:** From the hill to the subalpine zone; on the top of cliffs, marly screes, poor stony areas and poor, acid moorland; an important forest tree

---

820  *Pinus leucodermis* - Bosnian Pine
*Evergreen conifer, 15-20m high, with the shoots glabrous and covered with a bloom at first*

## *Pinus leucodermis* Ant.
## Bosnian Pine
**Pinaceae - Pine family** p. 69

**Size:** 6-10cm long and 1-2mm broad

**Form of needle:** Robust, often somewhat curved, semi-circular in cross-section, stiff, in pairs on short shoots, and clustered at the ends of the shoots; sheaths at the base of the short shoots 0.5-1.5cm long, dark grey and persistent; life-span 5-7 years

**Stalk:** Sessile

**End of needle:** Pointed and only slightly prickly

**Margin of needle:** Needles with very fine, small teeth on the margin (somewhat rough to the touch if rubbed towards the base)

**Upper/under side:** Dark green on both sides; bands of stomata over the whole surface

**Arrangement on the shoot:** Needles on short shoots in pairs which are arranged spirally

**Distribution:** Widely distributed in the mountain regions (800-2200m) of the Balkans; occasionally planted in central Europe; discovered in 1864 by Fr. Maly, brought to Vienna in 1865

821  *Pinus pinaster* - Maritime Pine
*Evergreen conifer, 20-30m high, with shoots dark brown at first*

## *Pinus pinaster* Ait.
## Maritime Pine
**Pinaceae - Pine family** p. 69

**Size:** 13-25cm long and 1-2mm broad

**Form of needle:** Coarse, sharp, semi-circular in cross-section and in pairs on short shoots (in threes on younger trees); life-span 3-4 years; dark brown to black sheaths retained until the 3rd or 4th year

**Stalk:** Sessile

**End of needle:** Shortly pointed and sharp

**Margin of needle:** Needles with the pale yellow margin finely serrate (somewhat rough to the touch if rubbed towards the base)

**Upper/under side:** Dark or greyish green on both sides with numerous fine lines of stomata

**Arrangement on the shoot:** Needles on short shoots in pairs which are arranged spirally

**Distribution:** Native and widely distributed in the western Mediterranean region; occasionally planted in parks in central Europe

---

822  *Pinus nigra* - Austrian Pine
*Evergreen conifer, 20-40m high, with stout, thick shoots*

## *Pinus nigra* Arnold **ssp. nigra**
## Austrian Pine
**Pinaceae - Pine family** p. 69

**Size:** 10-18cm long and 1-2mm broad

**Form of needle:** Very robust, usually somewhat curved, semi-circular in cross-section, flattened, stiff, and in pairs on short shoots; sheaths at the base of the short shoots 0.8-1.5cm long, dark grey and persistent; life-span 4-8 years

**Stalk:** Sessile

**End of needle:** Pointed, fairly sharp

**Margin of needle:** Needles with fine, small teeth on the margin (rough to the touch if rubbed)

**Upper/under side:** Dark green on both sides; lines of stomata over the whole surface

**Arrangement on the shoot:** Needles on short shoots in pairs which are arranged spirally

**Distribution:** Native in southern and eastern Europe; an important forest-forming tree in the dry parts of the limestone mountains of central and southern Europe; quite commonly found in parks

823  *Pinus aristata* - Bristle-cone Pine
*Evergreen conifer, 13-18m high, with reddish brown shoots*

## *Pinus aristata* Engelm.
## Bristle-cone Pine
**Pinaceae - Pine family** p. 70

**Size:** 2.5-4cm long and 1mm broad

**Form of needle:** In fives on short shoots, often curved, with white spots of resin, and triangular in cross-section; sheaths at the base of the short shoots becoming torn, and persisting until the 4th year as reflexed lobes; life-span 12-15 years

**Stalk:** Sessile

**End of needle:** With a fine, slender point

**Margin of needle:** Entire

**Upper/under side:** Dark green above without stomatic lines; the other two sides medium green and with lines of stomata

**Arrangement on the shoot:** Needles on short shoots in bundles of 5 (more rarely 3 or 4) which are arranged spirally

**Distribution:** Native in western North America; discovered in 1861 and later brought to Europe; occasionally planted in parks; oldest trees 4700 years old

824 **Pinus parviflora – Japanese White Pine**
*Evergreen conifer, 15–30m high (in Europe only 10m high), with pale grey shoots*

## *Pinus parviflora* Sieb. et Zucc.
## Japanese White Pine
**Pinaceae – Pine family** p. 70

**Size:** 4–7cm long and 0.5–1cm broad

**Form of needle:** Distinctly curved and twisted, triangular in cross-section, in fives on short shoots and clustered, brush-like, at the ends of the twigs; sheaths at the base of the short shoots falling in the 1st year

**Stalk:** Sessile

**End of needle:** Obtuse

**Margin of needle:** Needles with the margin finely serrate (rough to the touch if rubbed towards the base)

**Upper/under side:** Dark bluish green above; the 2 inner surfaces with lines of stomata and therefore appearing bluish white

**Arrangement on the shoot:** Needles on the short shoots in bundles of 5 which are arranged spirally

**Distribution:** Native in Japan between 1300m and 1800m; introduced into England in 1861 by J. G. Veitch, planted in parks

825 **Pinus strobus – Weymouth Pine**
*Evergreen conifer, 30–50m high, with shoots hairy at first*

## *Pinus strobus* L.
## Weymouth Pine
**Pinaceae – Pine family** p. 70

**Size:** 5–12cm long

**Form of needle:** Rather slender and flexible, triangular in cross-section and in fives on short shoots; basal sheaths filling completely in the 1st year; life-span 3 years

**Stalk:** Sessile

**End of needle:** Pointed at the tip, not prickly

**Margin of needle:** Needles with very fine, small teeth on the margin (somewhat rough to the touch if rubbed towards the base)

**Upper/under side:** Pale green at first above, dark green in the 2nd year; greyish green on the inner surfaces, each with 2 or 3 bluish white lines of stomata

**Arrangement on the shoot:** Needles on the short shoots in bundles of 5 which are arranged spirally

**Distribution:** Native only in eastern North America; this species was introduced into Europe at the end of the 16th century; since then it has been cultivated for afforestation or planted as a park tree

826 **Pinus cembra – Arolla Pine**
*Evergreen conifer, 10–25m high, with the shoots rust-red felted at first*

## *Pinus cembra* L.
## Arolla Pine,
## Swiss Stone Pine
**Pinaceae – Pine family** p. 60, 61, 70

**Size:** 5–12cm long and 0.8–1.5mm broad

**Form of needle:** Fairly straight, triangular in cross-section, stiffly upright, in fives on the short shoots and clustered at the ends of the shoots; basal sheaths falling in the 1st year; life-span 4–6 years

**Stalk:** Sessile

**End of needle:** Needles with very fine, small teeth on the margin (somewhat rough to the touch if rubbed towards the base)

**Upper/under side:** Dark green above; greyish green on the inner surfaces, each with 3–5 bluish white lines of stomata

**Arrangement on the shoot:** Needles on the short shoots in bundles of 5 which are arranged spirally

**Distribution:** Native only in the central Alps and Carpathians between 1600m and 3000m; occasionally planted in the lowlands in parks

827 **Sequoiadendron giganteum – Sierra Redwood** *Evergreen conifer, 50–100m high, with coarse, very stiff, greenish grey shoots*

## *Sequoiadendron giganteum* (Lindl.) Buchh.
## Sierra Redwood, Wellingtonia
**Taxodiaceae – Swamp Cypress family** p. 71

**Size:** 3–6mm long (on main shoots up to 12mm) and 0.8–1.2mm broad

**Form of needle:** Awl-shaped to lanceolate or scale-like, usually spreading as they grow, and smelling of aniseed when rubbed; life-span 3–4 years; needles falling with shoots

**Stalk:** Sessile

**End of needle:** Pointed

**Base of needle:** Attached to the shoot by a broad base

**Margin of needle:** Entire

**Upper/under side:** Dark green above and somewhat rounded; dark green beneath and longitudinally furrowed; with fine, white lines of stomata over the whole surface

**Arrangement on the shoot:** Needles arranged spirally (forming 3 ranks)

**Distribution:** Native on the western slopes of the Sierra Nevada, California; introduced everywhere in Europe as an ornamental and park tree

828 **Larix decidua – European Larch**
*Deciduous conifer, 25–40m high, with glabrous, straw-yellow to light brown shoots*

## *Larix decidua* Mill.
## European Larch
**Pinaceae – Pine family** p. 36, 37, 70

**Size:** 1.5–3cm long and 0.5–0.9mm broad

**Form of needle:** Narrowly linear, soft, flattened, in groups of 30–40 on short shoots, and singly but fairly densely crowded on long shoots

**Stalk:** Sessile

**End of needle:** Obtuse or shortly pointed

**Base of needle:** Attached to the shoot by a broad base

**Margin of needle:** Entire

**Upper/under side:** Needles pale to dark green and becoming golden yellow before falling in autumn; 2 paler bands of stomata beneath

**Arrangement on the shoot:** Spirally arranged on long shoots; in groups of 30–40 on short shoots

**Distribution:** Native only in the subalpine zone of central European mountains; the characteristic species of the Arolla Pine–Larch woods; also widely distributed nowadays in the lowlands by afforestation

829 **Larix kaempferi – Japanese Larch**
*Deciduous conifer, up to 30m high, with pale green young shoots covered with a bloom*

## *Larix kaempferi* (Lamb.) Carr.
## Japanese Larch
**Pinaceae – Pine family** p. 71

**Size:** 1.5–3.5cm long and 1–1.5mm broad

**Form of needle:** Flattened, soft, singly on long shoots and in groups of 20–40 on short shoots

**Stalk:** Sessile

**End of needle:** Obtuse or pointed

**Base of needle:** Attached to the shoot by a broad base

**Margin of needle:** Entire

**Upper/under side:** Needles at first pale green, later in the year bluish green and becoming golden yellow before falling in autumn; 2 clearly visible bands of stomata beneath

**Arrangement on the shoot:** Clustered on the short shoots, spirally arranged on the long shoots

**Distribution:** Native only in Japan; brought to England in 1861 by J. G. Veitch; completely hardy in central Europe and frequently planted

### Cedrus deodara
(D. Don) G. Don
## Deodar
**Pinaceae - Pine family** p. 71

**Size:** 2–6.5cm long and up to 1mm broad

**Form of needle:** Roundish or 4-angled in cross-section, soft, and with a life-span of 2–3 years

**Stalk:** Sessile

**End of needle:** Finely pointed and rather sharp

**Margin of needle:** Entire

**Upper/under side:** Dark green on all sides with fine lines of stomata

**Arrangement on the shoot:** Needles on the long shoots standing singly and arranged spirally, those on the short shoots in groups of 25–30

**Distribution:** Native in the western Himalayan region; more frequently planted in gardens and parks south of the Alps than in central Europe

830 **Cedrus deodara – Deodar**
*Evergreen tree, up to 40m high, with long shoots rounded to triangular in shape*

### Cedrus libani A. Rich
## Cedar of Lebanon
**Pinaceae - Pine family** p. 71

**Size:** 1–3.5cm long and 1–1.2mm broad

**Form of needle:** Stiff, sharp, triangular to rhombic in cross-section and, because of the flattened surface, always broader than high

**Stalk:** Sessile

**End of needle:** Pointed, sharp

**Base of needle:** Somewhat narrowed towards the base

**Margin of needle:** Entire

**Upper/under side:** With quite fine lines of stomata on all sides; needles appearing pale to dark green

**Arrangement on the shoot:** Needles on the long shoots standing singly and arranged spirally; on the short shoots in a rosette-like group of 10–20

**Distribution:** Native in Asia Minor and W. Asia (Lebanon, Syria); reached Europe in 1638; since then planted in parks and gardens in districts with a mild winter climate

831 **Cedrus libani – Cedar of Lebanon**
*Evergreen 25–30m high, with short shoots up to 2cm long and lasting for up to 10 years*

### Cedrus atlantica
(Endl.) Manetti ex Carr.
## Atlas Cedar
**Pinaceae - Pine family** p. 71

**Size:** 1–3cm long and 1–1.3mm broad

**Form of needle:** Rigid, somewhat curved at the end, irregularly 4-angled in cross-section and somewhat thicker and stiffer than those of the Cedar of Lebanon; life-span 4–7 years

**Stalk:** Sessile

**End of needle:** Very shortly pointed, not sharp

**Base of needle:** Narrowed towards the base

**Margin of needle:** Entire

**Upper/under side:** With lines of stomata on all sides, therefore appearing whitish blue-green

**Arrangement on the shoot:** On long shoots standing singly and arranged spirally; on short shoots in a rosette-like group of 10–40

**Distribution:** Native in N.W. Africa (Algeria, Atlas Mountains); reached Europe in 1839; planted in parks, especially the blue-needled form

832 **Cedrus atlantica – Atlas Cedar**
*Evergreen conifer, 30–40m high, with angular long shoots*

### Cupressus sempervirens
L.
## Italian Cypress
**Cupresssaceae - Cypress family** p. 72

**Length:** Leaves of the main shoot 2–5mm long, those of the lateral shoots 1mm long

**Form of leaves:** Scale-like, appressed and overlapping each other on the younger shoots and later spreading slightly; life-span 2–3 years and later falling with the shoot

**Stalk:** Sessile

**End of leaf:** Pointed, but with a blunt tip on the lateral shoots

**Margin of leaf:** Entire

**Upper/under side:** Dark green on both sides; with an oblong, often indistinct gland on the back

**Arrangement on the shoot:** Leaves opposite, arranged in lateral pairs

**Distribution:** Native in S.E. Europe; in the Mediterranean region a tree of gardens, avenues and cemeteries

833 **Cupressus sempervirens – Italian Cypress** *Evergreen conifer, 20–30m high, leaves forming outer surface of shoots*

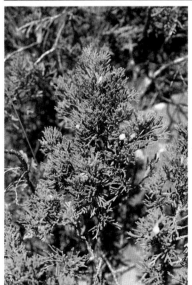

### Juniperus sabina L.
## Savin
**Cupressaceae - Cypress family** p. 72

**Size:** Juvenile leaves needle-like, 4–5mm long and 0.5–1mm broad; adult leaves up to 2.5mm long

**Form of leaves:** Juvenile leaves needle-like and in whorls of 3; adult leaves scale-like and overlapping

**Stalk:** Sessile

**End of leaf:** Obtuse or pointed

**Margin of leaf:** Entire

**Upper/under side:** Adult leaves of the upper and lower ranks dark green, with an elliptical gland and whitish waxy line; adult leaves of the side ranks dark green with stomatic areas at the sides

**Arrangement on the shoot:** Adult leaves opposite, arranged in lateral pairs

**Distribution:** From the hill to the subalpine zone; on hot, dry slopes of the continental inner Alps, in dry, grassy places under pines; often forming large colonies

834 **Juniperus sabina – Savin**
*Evergreen shrub, much-branched, the branches 1–2m long, with green shoots 1–1.5mm thick*

### Thujopsis dolabrata (L.f.)
Sieb. et Zucc.
## Hiba, Hiba Arbor-vitae
**Cupressaceae - Cypress family** p. 72

**Size:** 3–8mm long and 1–4mm broad

**Form of the scale-leaves:** Leaves of the upper and lower ranks oblong-obovate, somewhat smaller than the leaves of the side ranks, flattened, leathery and overlapping each other; leaves of the side ranks larger then those of the upper and lower ranks and keeled; life-span of the leaves 2–6 years

**End of leaf:** Leaves of the upper and lower ranks obtuse; those of the side ranks pointed

**Margin of leaf:** Scale-leaves all entire

**Upper/under side:** Both types of leaf shiny pale to dark green above; leaves of the upper and lower ranks with 2 narrow, silvery white areas of stomata beneath; leaves of the side ranks with a broad patch of stomata beneath

**Arrangement on the shoot:** Leaves opposite, arranged opposite, arranged in lateral pairs

**Distribution:** A tree native in Japan; brought to Europe in 1853 by P. F. Siebold; nowadays planted in many parks; hardy in central Europe

835 **Thujopsis dolabrata – Hiba**
*Evergreen tree, up to 35m high, with flat, fan-shaped branchlets*

## *Thuja orientalis* L.
## Chinese Thuja
**Cupressaceae – Cypress family**
p. 72

**Length:** 7–8mm long on main shoots; 1.5–2.5mm long on lateral shoots

**Form of leaves:** Scale-like, closely appressed to the shoots, dark green and with a weak resinous scent; leaves of the upper and lower ranks with their margins slightly overlapped by the leaves of the side ranks; life-span 1–3 years and later falling with the shoots

**Stalk:** Sessile

**End of leaf:** Scale-like leaves obtuse and slightly incurved at the ends

**Margin of leaf:** Entire

**Upper/under side:** Both sides the same colour with scattered white stomata; glands on the leaves of the upper and lower ranks inconspicuous

**Arrangement on the shoot:** Leaves opposite, arranged in lateral pairs

**Distribution:** Native in China and Korea; planted in Europe at the beginning of the 18th century; many varieties planted in gardens, parks and cemeteries

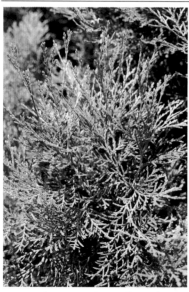

836 **Thuja orientalis – Chinese Thuja** *Evergreen shrub or tree up to 10m high with young shoots covered in scale-like leaves*

## *Thuja occidentalis* L.
## White Cedar
**Cupressaceae – Cypress family**
p. 73

**Length:** 4–7mm long on main shoots, otherwise 2–3mm

**Form of scale-leaves:** Leaves of the upper and lower ranks acutely obovate, appressed to the shoot, distinctly flattened and somewhat overlapped by the elliptic to triangular, keeled leaves of the side ranks; life-span of leaves 2–3 years and falling together with the shoot

**End of leaf:** Obtuse or shortly pointed

**Margin of leaf:** Scale-leaves entire

**Upper/under side:** Shoot dark green above, leaves of the upper and lower ranks with a clearly visible resin-gland; under side of shoot yellowish green; stomata in irregular grey lines or patches; leaves aromatically scented when rubbed

**Arrangement on the shoot:** Leaves opposite, arranged in lateral pairs

**Distribution:** Native in eastern North America; introduced into Europe by 1536; many forms planted nowadays as ornamental trees in gardens and parks

837 **Thuja occidentalis – White Cedar** *Evergreen conifer, 15–20m high, with flattened, greenish shoots*

## *Chamaecyparis lawsoniana*
(A. Murr.) Parl.
## Lawson Cypress
**Cupressaceae – Cypress family**
p. 73

**Length:** 1–2.5mm long on lateral shoots, 3–7mm long on main shoots

**Form of scale-leaves:** Visible part of the leaves of the upper and lower ranks rhombic or narrowly-elliptic and with a conspicuous, oblong resin-gland; leaves of the side ranks with 2 inconspicuous resin-glands

**Stalk:** Sessile

**End of leaf:** Obtuse to pointed

**Margin of leaf:** Entire

**Upper/under side:** Shoot dark to greyish green above and paler green beneath

**Arrangement on the shoot:** Leaves opposite, arranged in lateral pairs

**Distribution:** Originally found only in western North America; in Europe since 1854; nowadays many garden forms planted throughout the whole of Europe as ornamental trees

838 **Chamaecyparis lawsoniana – Lawson Cypress** *Evergreen tree, up to 20m high in Europe, with flattened, green shoots*

## *Thuja plicata* Donn ex D. Don
## Western Red Cedar
**Cupressaceae – Cypress family**
p. 73

**Length:** Leaves of the main shoots 6–8mm long, otherwise 2–3mm long

**Form of leaves:** Scale-like, appressed, overlapping, and aromatically scented when rubbed; leaves of the side ranks covering the margins of the leaves of the upper and lower ranks; life-span 2–3 years

**Stalk:** Sessile

**End of leaf:** Leaves of the primary shoots with long, free points; leaves of the lateral shoots rather obtuse or somewhat pointed

**Margin of leaf:** Entire

**Upper/under side:** Leaves rich green above, those of the upper and lower ranks with a gland; shoots greyish green beneath with conspicuous stomata in almost triangular silver grey patches

**Arrangement on the shoot:** Leaves opposite, arranged in lateral pairs

**Distribution:** Brought to Europe in 1854 by J. Jeffrey from the forests of the coastal mountains of the western United States; planted in parks and large gardens

839 **Thuja plicata – Western Red Cedar** *Evergreen conifer, 20–50m high, with shoots green at first*

## *Chamaecyparis nootkatensis*
(D. Don) Spach
## Nootka Cypress
**Cupressaceae – Cypress family**
p. 73

**Length:** 5–6mm long on main shoots, otherwise 2–3mm long

**Form of the scale-leaves:** Visible portion of the leaves of the upper and lower ranks acutely rhombic and overlapping; leaves of the side ranks triangular, somewhat keeled, and with the upper part spreading

**Stalk:** Sessile

**End of leaf:** All leaves sharply pointed

**Margin of leaf:** Scale-leaves entire

**Upper/under side:** Dark green on both sides; leaves of the upper and lower ranks with a more or less clearly visible glandular furrow on the back

**Arrangement on the shoot:** Leaves opposite, arranged in lateral pairs

**Distribution:** Native in Pacific North America; brought to Europe in 1851; used as an ornamental tree in parks but not so frequently as the pendulous form ('Pendula')

840 **Chamaecyparis nootkatensis – Nootka Cypress** *Evergreen tree, 20–35m high, with flattened green shoots*

## *Chamaecyparis obtusa*
(Sieb. et Zucc.) Sieb. et Zucc. ex Endl.
## Hinoki Cypress
**Cupressaceae – Cypress family**
p. 73

**Length:** 4–5mm long on main shoots, otherwise only 1.5–2.5mm

**Form of the scale-leaves:** Leaves of the upper and lower ranks narrowly obovate, thickish, and closely appressed to the shoot; leaves of the side ranks crescent-shaped, closely overlapping and somewhat smaller than those of the other ranks

**End of leaf:** All leaves obtuse or rounded

**Margin of leaf:** All leaves entire

**Upper/under side:** Shiny dark green above, and with a glandular furrow on the leaves of the upper and lower ranks; greyish green beneath with white lines of stomata

**Arrangement of the shoot:** Leaves opposite, arranged in lateral pairs

**Distribution:** Native in Japan; this species first reached Europe in 1861; many forms planted nowadays in gardens and parks

841 **Chamaecyparis obtusa – Hinoki Cypress** *Evergreen tree, up to 40m high, with flat, green shoots*

842 **Colutea arborescens - Bladder Senna**
*Unarmed, much-branched shrub with green stems,
growing 2-4m high*

## Colutea arborescens L.
## Bladder Senna

**Leguminosae - Pea family** p. 75

**Length:** 4-10cm

**Form:** Odd-pinnate, with 3-6 pairs of
leaflets; terminal leaflet long-stalked

**Stalk:** 0.5-1.5cm long

**Form of leaflets:** Elliptic to obovate,
1-3.5cm long, 0.5-2cm broad and
shortly stalked

**End of leaflets:** Distinctly
emarginate

**Base of leaflets:** Broadly wedge-
shaped

**Margin of leaflets:** Entire

**Upper/under side:** Glabrous and
medium to dark green above; white-
felted beneath (becoming glabrous
with age) and therefore greyish green

**Arrangement on the shoot:** Leaves
alternate

**Distribution:** On the edges of
Downy Oak woods, in hedges, open
woodland and on dry, rocky slopes,
especially in S. Europe and N. Africa;
centre of distribution in the Mediterranean region

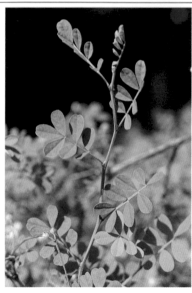

843 **Coronilla emerus - Scorpion Senna**
*Deciduous, much-branched shrub growing
30-100cm high, with angular, green stems*

## Coronilla emerus L.
## Scorpion Senna

**Leguminosae - Pea family** p. 75

**Length:** 2-6cm

**Form:** Odd-pinnate, with 7 or 9
leaflets, the terminal sessile

**Stalk:** Up to 1cm long

**Form of leaflets:** Obovate, 1-2cm
long, 0.5-1cm broad and shortly
stalked or sessile

**End of leaflets:** Usually emarginate
or more rarely rounded with a bristly
point

**Base of leaflets:** Narrowly to broadly
wedge-shaped

**Margin of leaflets:** Entire

**Upper/under side:** Dark green and
glabrous above; greyish green
beneath and with appressed hairs
when young

**Arrangement on the shoot:** Leaves
alternate

**Distribution:** On warm, dry, calcareous, rocky slopes and in open oak
and pine woods from the hill to the
montane zone

844 **Junglans nigra - Black Walnut**
*Deciduous tree, which reaches a height of 50m in
eastern North America*

## Juglans nigra L.
## Black Walnut

**Juglandaceae - Walnut family**
p. 74

**Length:** 30-60cm

**Form:** Odd-pinnate, with 5-12 pairs
of leaflets; terminal leaflet often
absent or very small, therefore also
'falsely paripinnate'

**Stalk:** 1-6cm long and often broadened at the base

**Form of leaflets:** Lanceolate to narrowly ovate, 6-12cm long, the leaflets
of each pair usually not quite opposite each other on the leaf-stalk

**End of leaflets:** Shortly pointed

**Base of leaflets:** Regularly or irregularly broadly wedge-shaped or
rounded

**Margin of leaflets:** Irregularly serrate
or dentate, usually entire towards the
base

**Upper/under side:** Dark green and
glabrous above; somewhat paler
green beneath and often hairy on the
midrib

**Distribution:** Planted in parks and
gardens

845 **Ceratonia siliqua - Carob**
*Evergreen tree, which reaches a height of 10m in
the eastern Mediterranean region*

## Ceratonia siliqua L.
## Carob

**Leguminosae - Pea family** p. 75

**Length:** 10-20cm

**Form:** Even-pinnate, with 2-6 pairs
of leaflets

**Stalk:** 2-5cm long, and tinged red
throughout its length

**Form of leaflets:** Obovate or elliptic
to roundish, 3-7cm long and 2-4cm
broad, sessile or shortly stalked and
leathery; leaflets of each pair usually
lying opposite each other

**End of leaflets:** Rounded, and often
emarginate or distinctly incised

**Base of leaflets:** Broadly wedge-
shaped

**Margin of leaflets:** Entire or slightly
undulate

**Upper/under side:** Both sides
glabrous; shiny dark green above;
greyish green beneath

**Arrangement on the shoot:** Leaves
alternate

**Distribution:** In evergreen woods, on
dry slopes and stony soils in the
Mediterranean region

846 **Acacia dealbata - Silver Wattle**
*Evergreen tree, which in its native country (Aus-
tralia) reaches a height of 30m.*

## Acacia dealbata Link
## Silver Wattle, Mimosa

**Leguminosae - Pea family** p. 74

**Length:** 7-15cm

**Form:** Doubly even-pinnate, with 15-
25 pairs of leaflets, each leaflet with
20-40 pairs of smaller leaflets (leaflets of the 2nd order); pairs of leaflets
arranged opposite each other

**Stalk:** 1-3cm long

**Form of leaflets:** Narrowly linear, 3-
5mm long and sessile

**End of leaflets:** Rounded or shortly
pointed

**Base of leaflets:** Wedge-shaped or
rounded

**Margin of leaflets:** Entire

**Upper/under side:** Leaf-axis and
leaflets silvery hairy on both sides;
more bluish green above; usually
paler green beneath

**Arrangement on the shoot:** Leaves
alternate

**Distribution:** Evergreen tree, which
was introduced into France in 1864

847 **Ailanthus altissima - Tree of Heaven**
*Deciduous tree, which reaches a height of 25m in
eastern Asia*

## Ailanthus altissima
(Mill.) Swingle
## Tree of Heaven

**Simaroubaceae - Quassia fam-
ily** p. 74

**Length:** 40-75cm

**Form:** Usually odd-pinnate, with 10-
18 pairs of leaflets

**Stalk:** 8-20cm long, broadened at
the base, and greenish or distinctly
red

**Form of leaflets:** Oblong-ovate to
obliquely elliptic, 5-15cm long and
usually shortly stalked; pairs of leaflets rarely lying exactly opposite each
other, usually slightly alternately
arranged

**End of leaflets:** Narrowed to a point

**Base of leaflets:** Broadly wedge-
shaped, rounded or more rarely
heart-shaped

**Margin of leaflets:** Entire, except for
1-4 teeth of varying size in the lower
part

**Upper/under side:** Dull dark green
above; somewhat paler green
beneath

**Arrangement on the shoot:** Leaves
alternate

**Distribution:** Planted in large gardens and parks; introduced into England from China in 1751

### *Pistacia lentiscus* L.
## Mastic Tree

**Anacardiaceae - Cashew family** p. 74

**Length:** 3-7cm

**Form:** Even-pinnate or odd-pinnate with 4-12 leaflets

**Stalk:** 1-3cm long and winged

**Form of leaflets:** Narrowly elliptic to narrowly obovate, 2-4cm long, leathery, sessile, the leaflets of each pair lying almost or exactly opposite each other on the leaf-stalk

**End of leaflets:** Usually rounded and with a short point

**Base of leaflets:** Wedge-shaped

**Margin of leaflets:** Entire

**Upper/under side:** Both sides glabrous; dark green above; pale green beneath

**Arrangement on the shoot:** Leaves alternate

**Distribution:** In open deciduous and pine woods and on rocky slopes in the Mediterranean region

848   **Pistacia lentiscus - Mastic Tree**
*Evergreen, much-branched shrub growing 4-6m high*

### *Robinia pseudoacacia* L.
## False Acacia

**Leguminosae - Pea family** p. 75

**Length:** 15-30cm

**Form:** Odd-pinnate, with 3-12 pairs of leaflets; terminal leaflet long-stalked; stipules converted into stout spines

**Stalk:** 3-4cm long and enlarged at the base

**Form of leaflets:** Oblong-elliptic to ovate, 3-6cm long, shortly but distinctly stalked

**End of leaflets:** Rounded, obtuse, or indistinctly emarginate

**Base of leaflets:** Broadly wedge-shaped or rounded

**Margin of leaflets:** Entire

**Upper/under side:** Dull pale to dark green above, becoming glabrous; greyish green beneath and only hairy at first

**Arrangement on the shoot:** Leaves alternate

**Distribution:** Planted in gardens and parks; occasionally escaping and becoming naturalised; introduced into Europe from North America about 1640 by the French botanist Jean Robin

849   **Robinia pseudoacacia - False Acacia**
*Deciduous tree, with spiny twigs, growing to a height of 25m*

### *Rubus idaeus* L.
## Raspberry

**Rosaceae - Rose family** p. 76

**Length:** 5-15cm

**Form:** Odd-pinnate, with 3 (on flowering shoots), 5 or more rarely 7 leaflets; terminal leaflet distinctly stalked

**Stalk:** 3-8cm long, hairy, and often prickly throughout its length

**Form of leaflets:** Elliptic to broadly ovate, 6-10cm long and sessile except for the terminal leaflet

**End of leaflets:** Pointed

**Base of leaflets:** Heart-shaped, rounded or even broadly wedge-shaped

**Margin of leaflets:** Simply and often also doubly serrate

**Upper/under side:** Dark green above, finely hairy, later becoming glabrous; densely silvery white-felted beneath

**Arrangement on the shoot:** Leaves alternate

**Distribution:** In open woods, undergrowth, and grassland in tall-herb communities

850   **Rubus idaeus - Raspberry**
*Deciduous shrub, growing to a height of 2m, with suckers arising from the roots*

### *Rubus fruticosus* L.
## Blackberry

(aggregate species)
**Rosaceae - Rose family** p. 76

**Length:** 5-15cm

**Form:** Odd-pinnate, with 3, 5 or 7 leaflets

**Stalk:** 2-6cm long; numerous prickles pointing towards the base

**Form of leaflets:** Broadly elliptic to obovate, 2-8cm long and 3-6cm broad, terminal leaflet long-stalked; lateral leaflets narrower and shortly stalked

**End of leaflets:** Pointed

**Base of leaflets:** Rounded or shortly truncate

**Margin of leaflets:** Simply and doubly serrate

**Upper/under side:** Dark green and somewhat shiny above; greyish green beneath and more or less densely hairy, becoming glabrous; midrib prickly beneath

**Arrangement on the shoot:** Leaves alternate

**Distribution:** In deciduous and conifer woods, hedges, and on verges

851   **Rubus fruticosus - Blackberry**
*Bushy shrub up to 2m high, with reddish stems on the side exposed to the light; numerous forms*

### *Juglans regia* L.
## Common Walnut

**Juglandaceae - Walnut family** p. 34, 35, 76

**Length:** 20-50cm

**Form:** Odd-pinnate, with 2-4 pairs of leaflets; terminal leaflet long-stalked; leaves strongly aromatic when rubbed

**Stalk:** Up to 20cm long and thickened at the base

**Form of leaflets:** Oblong-elliptic to oblong-ovate, 6-15cm long, sessile except for the terminal leaflet

**End of leaflets:** Pointed

**Base of leaflets:** Wedge-shaped or rounded

**Margin of leaflets:** Entire

**Upper/under side:** Brownish orange in colour at first; later shiny dark green above and glabrous; paler green beneath

**Arrangement on the shoot:** Leaves alternate

**Distribution:** A tree native in S. Europe and the Balkans

852   **Juglans regia - Common Walnut**
*Deciduous tree growing to 30m high with glabrous twigs*

### *Staphylea pinnata* L.
## Bladder-nut

**Staphyleaceae - Bladder-nut family** p. 77

**Length:** 15-25cm

**Form:** Odd-pinnate, with 2-3 pairs of leaflets; terminal leaflet long-stalked

**Stalk:** 5-9cm long

**Form of leaflets:** Elliptic to narrowly ovate, 6-9cm long, 3-5cm broad, and sessile except for the terminal leaflets

**End of leaflets:** Shortly pointed

**Base of leaflets:** Wedge-shaped

**Margin of leaflets:** Very finely dentate or serrate

**Upper/under side:** Dark green and glabrous above; bluish to greyish green beneath, with short, whitish hairs on the veins, later becoming glabrous

**Arrangement on the shoot:** Leaves opposite

**Distribution:** In the hill zone especially in the Föhn region; found locally on warm slopes, at the edges of woods, and amongst the herbaceous vegetation in beech, maple or oak woods

853   **Staphylea pinnata - Bladder-nut**
*Deciduous shrub or small tree growing 1.5-5m high with stems green at first*

### *Fraxinus ornus* L.
### Manna Ash
**Oleaceae - Olive family** p. 77

**Length:** 15–30cm

**Form:** Odd-pinnate, with 3–5 pairs of leaflets; terminal leaflet with a distinctly longer stalk than those of the lateral leaflets

**Stalk:** 3–8cm long and often finely hairy

**Form of leaflets:** Oblong-ovate, 3–7cm long, up to 2.5cm broad, and stalked

**End of leaflets:** Pointed

**Base of leaflets:** Wedge-shaped or rounded

**Margin of leaflets:** Irregularly serrate or dentate

**Upper/under side:** Medium green and glabrous above; paler green beneath with reddish brown or light brown hairs along the midrib

**Arrangement on the shoot:** Leaves opposite, each pair of leaves on a stem at right angles to the next

**Distribution:** Predominantly in the hill zone on dry, sunny slopes; planted as an ornamental and street tree, especially in S. Europe

854  *Fraxinus ornus* – Manna Ash
*Deciduous tree, up to 20m high, native in the eastern Mediterranean region*

### *Fraxinus excelsior* L.
### Common Ash
**Oleaceae - Olive family** p. 32, 33, 78

**Length:** 20–30cm

**Form:** Odd-pinnate, with 3–7 pairs of leaflets; terminal leaflet stalked

**Stalk:** 3–6cm long

**Form of leaflets:** Elliptic to ovate, 4–10cm long, 2–3cm broad, and sessile

**End of leaflets:** Shortly pointed

**Base of leaflets:** Narrowly or broadly wedge-shaped, the lowest leaflets often rounded

**Margin of leaflets:** Unequally serrate; mostly entire in the lowest part

**Upper/under side:** Dark green and glabrous above; paler green beneath with reddish brown woolly hairs along the veins

**Arrangement on the shoot:** Leaves opposite, each pair of leaves on a stem at right angles to the next

**Distribution:** In water-meadows, deciduous woods, valleys, by rivers and on stony slopes

855  *Fraxinus excelsior* – Common Ash
*Deciduous tree growing up to 40m high with grey twigs*

### *Sorbus aucuparia* L.
### Rowan, Mountain Ash
**Rosaceae - Rose family** p. 52, 53, 78

**Length:** 10–20cm long and 8–11cm broad

**Form:** Odd-pinnate, with 4–9 pairs of leaflets; terminal leaflet long-stalked

**Stalk:** 2–3cm long and coloured reddish and greenish above

**Form of leaflets:** Oblong-lanceolate, 2–6cm long, 1–2.5cm broad, sessile or very shortly stalked

**End of leaflets:** Pointed

**Base of leaflets:** The two halves of the leaflet ending at a different point on the midrib

**Margin of leaflets:** Coarsely serrate and entire in the lower part

**Upper/under side:** Dark green above, and at first covered with greyish silvery hairs; greyish green felted beneath

**Arrangement on the shoot:** Leaves alternate

**Distribution:** In open deciduous, Spruce and Arolla Pine woods; from the hill to the subalpine zone

856  *Sorbus aucuparia* – Rowan
*Deciduous tree or shrub, of pioneer character, growing 5–20m high*

### *Sorbus domestica* L.
### Service Tree
**Rosaceae - Rose family** p. 78

**Length:** 10–25cm

**Form:** Odd-pinnate with 5–10 pairs of leaflets

**Stalk:** 3–5.5cm long

**Form of leaflets:** Narrowly elliptic, 3–8cm long, up to 2cm broad, sessile or shortly stalked

**End of leaflets:** Shortly pointed

**Base of leaflets:** Always narrowly wedge-shaped, the two halves of the leaflet usually symmetrical and ending at the same point of the midrib

**Margin of leaflets:** Almost entire on the lower third; otherwise simply or very slightly doubly serrate

**Upper/under side:** Dark green and glabrous above; paler green beneath and softly hairy, especially along the veins

**Arrangement on the shoot:** Leaves alternate

**Distribution:** In dry Oak, Hornbeam and Downy Oak woods

857  *Sorbus domestica* – Service Tree
*Deciduous tree, native mainly in S. Europe, growing 15–20m high*

### *Sambucus racemosa* L.
### Red-berried Elder
**Caprifoliaceae - Honeysuckle family** p. 77

**Length:** 10–25cm

**Form:** Odd-pinnate, with 2–3 pairs of leaflets; terminal leaflet distinctly stalked

**Stalk:** 7–10cm long; one to several roundish glands at the base

**Form of leaflets:** Lanceolate to narrowly ovate, 4–8cm long, up to 3.5cm broad

**End of leaflets:** Long-pointed

**Base of leaflets:** Obliquely wedge-shaped or rounded

**Margin of leaflets:** Irregularly serrate

**Upper/under side:** Dark green and glabrous above; bluish grey-green beneath and hairy at first

**Arrangement on the shoot:** Leaves opposite

**Distribution:** In shady woods, on screes and rocks

858  *Sambucus racemosa* – Red-berried
**Elder** *Deciduous shrub growing to 2m high with thin, smooth stems; pith brown*

### *Sambucus nigra* L.
### Elder
**Caprifoliaceae - Honeysuckle family** p. 77

**Length:** 10–30cm

**Form:** Odd-pinnate, with usually 2, more rarely 3 pairs of leaflets; terminal leaflet distinctly stalked and much broader than in the Red-berried Elder

**Stalk:** 4–10cm long and grooved above

**Form of leaflets:** Elliptic, 10–15cm long and 3–5cm broad; upper pair of leaflets usually sessile, the lower usually stalked

**End of leaflets:** Shortly pointed

**Base of leaflets:** Wedge-shaped and rounded; the two halves of the leaflet often asymmetrical

**Margin of leaflets:** Irregularly coarsely serrate

**Upper/under side:** Dark green and glabrous above; bluish to greyish green beneath

**Arrangement on the shoot:** Leaves opposite

**Distribution:** In damp woods, on river-banks, and on waste ground; hill to montane zone

859  *Sambucus nigra* – Elder
*Deciduous shrub or tree up to 7m high with grey stems containing white pith*

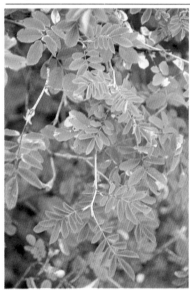

860   *Rosa pendulina* – **Alpine Rose**
*Shrub, growing 0.5–3m high, with green or reddish shoots*

## *Rosa pendulina* L.
## Alpine Rose
**Rosaceae** – Rose family  p. 78

**Length:** 5–10cm

**Form:** Odd-pinnate, with 9 or 11 leaflets; often 7 leaflets on flowering shoots

**Stalk:** 1.5–3cm long, with fine, stalked glands; often reddish above and greenish beneath; stipules long, narrow below but broadening upwards, spreading and pointed

**Form of leaflets:** Oblong-elliptic, more rarely ovate or roundish, 1–4cm long, 0.5–2.5cm broad, sessile or quite shortly stalked

**End of leaflets:** Shortly pointed

**Base of leaflets:** Usually wedge-shaped

**Margin of leaflets:** Usually doubly serrate, rarely simply serrate; teeth finely pointed and with stalked glands

**Upper/under side:** Both sides usually glabrous; dull dark green above; paler green beneath, often with stalked glands on the midrib

**Distribution:** In alpine meadows, gorges, on dwarf shrub moorland and tall-herb grassland.

861   *Rosa glauca* – **Red-leaved Rose**
*1–3m high; stems shiny reddish brown; shoots reddish or covered with a bluish bloom*

## *Rosa glauca* Pourr.
## Red-leaved Rose
**Rosaceae** – Rose family  p. 78

**Length:** 4–8cm

**Form:** Odd-pinnate, with 7 or 9 leaflets; sometimes 5 leaflets on flowering shoots

**Stalk:** 1–4cm long, glabrous, covered with a bluish purple bloom; stipules pointed and usually coloured greenish red to purple

**Form of leaflets:** Elliptic or oblong-ovate, 1.5–4.5cm long, 1–3cm broad and shortly stalked

**End of leaflets:** Narrowly pointed

**Base of leaflets:** Wedge-shaped or rounded

**Margin of leaflets:** Usually simply toothed; teeth pointing forwards; leaflets often entire in the lower part

**Upper/under side:** Both sides usually glabrous; bluish green or coppery red above; paler bluish green beneath, often purplish in places

**Distribution:** In thickets, crevasses, and clearings in the montane and subalpine zones

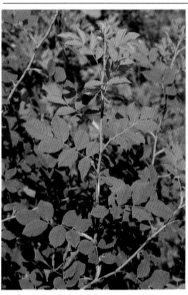

862   *Rosa canina* – **Dog Rose**
*Shrub, growing 1–3m high, with erect or arching stems*

## *Rosa canina* L.
## Dog Rose
(variable species)
**Rosaceae** – Rose family  p. 79

**Length:** 6–11cm

**Form:** Odd-pinnate, with 5 or 7 leaflets

**Stalk:** 2–4cm long, somewhat prickly, often with stalked glands and broadened at the base; stipules narrow, pointed, the tips spreading sideways

**Form of leaflets:** Ovate to elliptic, 2–4cm long, 1–2.5cm broad, sessile or very shortly stalked

**End of leaflets:** Shortly pointed

**Base of leaflets:** Broadly wedge-shaped or rounded

**Margin of leaflets:** More or less regularly simply, or sometimes doubly serrate; pointed teeth directed forwards

**Upper/under side:** Both sides usually glabrous; dull to dark greyish green above; bluish green beneath, often with fine silky hairs

**Distribution:** In hedges, glades, and neglected fields and pastures from the hill to the subalpine zone

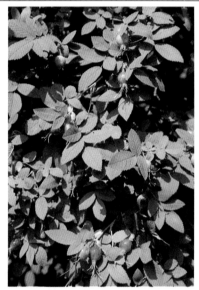

863   *Rosa villosa* – **Apple Rose**
*Dense shrub, 1.5–2m high, with shoots reddish at first and covered with a bloom*

## *Rosa villosa* L.
## Apple Rose
**Rosaceae** – Rose family  p. 79

**Length:** 4–9cm

**Form:** Odd-pinnate, with 5 or 7 leaflets; more rarely 3 or 9 leaflets

**Stalk:** 1–3cm long, green and usually with stalked glands; stipules small, narrow, broadened above and curved inwards

**Form of leaflets:** Elliptic or oblong-elliptic, 1–4cm long, 0.5–2cm broad and sessile

**End of leaflets:** Shortly pointed

**Base of leaflets:** Rounded or more rarely somewhat heart-shaped

**Margin of leaflets:** Doubly serrate; teeth broad and gland-tipped

**Upper/under side:** Greyish to dark green above with appressed hairs; paler green beneath, with densely appressed hairs, numerous stalked glands and somewhat resinous

**Distribution:** On rocky slopes and in hedges in the montane and subalpine zones

864   *Rosa rubiginosa* – **Sweet Briar**
*Shrub, growing 2–3m high, with shortly branched and prickly stems*

## *Rosa rubiginosa* L.
## Sweet Briar
**Rosaceae** – Rose family  p. 79

**Length:** 4–7cm

**Form:** Odd-pinnate, with 5, 7, or more rarely 9 leaflets

**Stalk:** 0.5–2.5cm long, glabrous or downy, with stalked glands and small, hooked prickles; stipules broad, densely fringed with glands, and with the tips pointing forwards or spreading sideways

**Form of leaflets:** Elliptic or roundish, 1–2.5cm long, 1–2cm broad and sessile

**End of leaflets:** Rounded or with a small point

**Margin of leaflets:** Doubly toothed; teeth prominent with numerous stalked glands

**Upper/under side:** Glabrous or with scattered downy hairs above, dark green, rarely glandular; slightly to densely downy beneath, paler green with numerous reddish stalked glands

**Distribution:** On moorland meadows, rocky slopes and in hedges from the hill to the subalpine zone

865   *Rosa tomentosa* – **Downy Rose**
*Shrub 0.5–2m high, with arching stems often covered with a bluish bloom*

## *Rosa tomentosa* Sm.
## Downy Rose
**Rosaceae** – Rose family  p. 79

**Length:** 5–10cm

**Form:** Odd-pinnate, with 5 or 7 leaflets

**Stalk:** 1–3cm long, with matted woolly hairs, with almost sessile glands and several hooked prickles; stipules pointed and somewhat spreading

**Form of leaflets:** Broadly ovate to elliptic, 2–4cm long, 1–2.5cm broad and sessile or shortly stalked

**End of leaflets:** Usually rounded, but with a small point

**Base of leaflets:** Broadly wedge-shaped or rounded

**Margin of leaflets:** Simply and doubly toothed; teeth very large, broad and pointed

**Upper/under side:** Dark green above and with appressed hairs; paler green beneath, softly felted, glands present or absent

**Distribution:** On the edges of woods and in open scrub from the hill to the montane zone

**866    *Acer Griseum* – Paper-bark Maple**
*Tree to 12m high, native in central China, with cinnamon brown bark*

## *Acer griseum* (Franch.) Pax
## Paper-bark Maple
**Aceraceae – Maple family** p. 80

**Length:** 6–10cm

**Form:** Trifoliolate; terminal leaflet up to 5.5cm long, lateral leaflets up to 3.5cm long

**Stalk:** 1–5cm long, often hairy and usually reddish above

**Form of leaflets:** Elliptic to obovate, 3–6cm long and sessile except for the terminal leaflet

**End of leaflets:** Obtuse or shortly pointed

**Base of leaflets:** Terminal leaflet narrowly wedge-shaped

**Margin of leaflets:** Terminal leaflet lobed in the upper half or with 3-5 coarse teeth, otherwise entire; lateral leaflets often irregularly coarsely toothed to below the middle

**Upper/under side:** Dark green and glabrous above; distinctly bluish green beneath, with brownish hairs on the midribs

**Arrangement on the shoot:** Leaves opposite

**Distribution:** Planted in gardens and parks

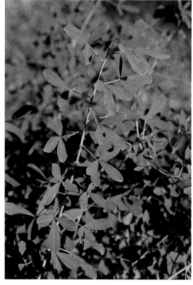

**867    *Cytisus purpureus* – Purple Broom**
*Deciduous half-shrub with stems curving upwards to a height of 30–75cm*

## *Cytisus purpureus* Scop.
## Purple Broom
**Leguminosae – Pea family** p. 80

**Length:** 2–5cm

**Form:** Trifoliolate

**Stalk:** 1–3cm long, glabrous and grooved

**Form of leaflets:** Narrowly obovate, 1.5–2.5cm long, 0.5–1cm broad and sessile

**End of leaflets:** Rounded or obtuse

**Base of leaflets:** Narrowly wedge-shaped

**Margin of leaflets:** Entire

**Upper/under side:** Both sides with scattered hairs or glabrous; somewhat darker green above than beneath

**Arrangement on the shoot:** Leaves alternate

**Distribution:** On rocky slopes and open woods in central and S. Europe from the hill to the montane zone; cultivated in rock gardens since the 18th century

**868    *Clematis vitalba* – Traveller's Joy**
*Deciduous, quick-growing climber reaching up to 10m in height*

## *Clematis vitalba* L.
## Traveller's Joy, Old Man's Beard
**Ranunculaceae – Buttercup family** p. 80

**Length:** 3–10cm

**Form:** Odd-pinnate, with 3 or 5 leaflets; the 2 lower ones may also be 3-lobed

**Stalk:** 1–6cm long, wine red to purple above and twining

**Form of leaflets:** Ovate and pointed, 3–5cm long, 2–4cm broad and stalked

**End of leaflets:** Rather obtuse or shortly pointed

**Base of leaflets:** Heart-shaped

**Margin of leaflets:** Entire in the upper third, coarsely toothed or lobed in the lower part

**Upper/under side:** Dark green above and paler green or greyish green beneath

**Arrangement on the shoot:** Leaves opposite

**Distribution:** In damp woods and the damp borders of woodland, and on shady slopes

**869    *Clematis alpina* – Alpine Clematis**
*Rather rare deciduous climber, growing up to 3m high*

## *Clematis alpina* (L.) Miller
## Alpine Clematis
**Ranunculaceae – Buttercup family** p. 79

**Length:** 10–15cm

**Form:** Odd-pinnate, with 3 leaflets, each divided into 2 or 3 parts

**Stalk:** 3–7cm long

**Form of leaflets:** Divisions of leaflets narrowly ovate, 2–4cm long and 1–2cm broad

**End of leaflets:** Divisions sometimes long-pointed

**Base of leaflets:** Rounded or irregularly heart-shaped

**Margin of leaflets:** Finely, or even coarsely and deeply serrate

**Upper/under side:** Medium green above and paler green beneath; hairy on both sides

**Arrangement on the shoot:** Leaves opposite

**Distribution:** Among herbaceous plants and shrubs in half-shady conifer woods, on shrubby grassland, in the Alpenrose–Mountain Pine region and on rocks especially in the subalpine zone

**870    *Fraxinus americana* – White Ash**
*Hardy, deciduous tree up to 15m high with always glabrous twigs*

## *Fraxinus americana* L.
## White Ash
**Oleaceae – Olive family** p. 77

**Length:** 15–40cm

**Form:** Odd-pinnate, with 2-4 pairs of leaflets; all distinctly stalked

**Stalk:** 5–12cm long

**Form of leaflets:** Elliptic to narrowly ovate, up to 8cm long; terminal leaflet with a stalk 5–12mm long

**End of leaflets:** Pointed

**Base of leaflets:** Terminal leaflet usually wedge-shaped; lateral leaflets rounded

**Margin of leaflets:** Usually entire

**Upper/under side:** Dark green and glabrous above; pale greyish green to whitish green beneath and slightly hairy, becoming glabrous

**Arrangement on the shoot:** Leaves opposite

**Distribution:** Occasionally planted in parks; growing in swamps in the U.S.A.

**871    *Acer negundo* – Ash-leaved Maple**
*Deciduous tree, often much-branched, growing 10–20m high with usually green twigs*

## *Acer negundo* L.
## Ash-leaved Maple, Box Elder
**Aceraceae – Maple family** p. 80

**Length:** 7–15cm

**Form:** Odd-pinnate, with 3, 5 or more rarely 7 or 9 leaflets; terminal leaflet with a short or long stalk

**Stalk:** 5–8cm long, glabrous or finely hairy, and often reddish above

**Form of leaflets:** Narrowly elliptic to ovate, 5–10cm long, occasionally with 2 or 3 lobes, and sessile or stalked

**End of leaflets:** Long-pointed

**Base of leaflets:** Wedge-shaped, truncate or rounded

**Margin of leaflets:** Coarsely serrate in the upper part, entire in the lower part

**Upper/under side:** Medium to dark green and glabrous above, greyish green beneath

**Arrangement on the shoot:** Leaves opposite

**Distribution:** Native in the U.S.A.; often planted in parks

872 **Laburnum alpinum – Alpine Laburnum**
*Deciduous shrub or small tree 5m high; cultivated forms up to 10m in height*

## *Laburnum alpinum* (Mill.)
Bercht et J. S. Presl
### Alpine Laburnum
**Leguminosae – Pea family** p. 81

**Length:** 8–16cm

**Form:** With 3 leaflets

**Stalk:** 5–9cm long and glabrous or with spreading hairs

**Form of leaflets:** Narrowly ovate to narrowly elliptic, 3–8cm long, 1.5–4.5cm broad and sessile

**End of leaflets:** Pointed or more rarely obtuse and sometimes with a short, bristly point

**Base of leaflets:** Wedge-shaped or rounded

**Margin of leaflets:** Entire, and with hairs 0.5–1mm long when young

**Upper/under side:** Dark green and usually glabrous above; paler green beneath, and hairy especially on the midrib

**Arrangement on the shoot:** Leaves on long shoots alternate; arranged in clusters on the lateral short shoots

**Distribution:** On rocky slopes, in clearings and open woods from the lowlands to the montane (more rarely subalpine) zone in warm but damp places

873 **Laburnum anagyroides – Common Laburnum** *Deciduous shrub or tree up to 7m high; cultivated forms up to 9m in height*

## *Laburnum anagyroides*
Med.
### Common Laburnum
**Leguminosae – Pea family** p. 81

**Length:** 6–12cm

**Form:** With 3 leaflets

**Stalk:** 2–7cm long with appressed, silky hairs

**Form of leaflets:** Broadly elliptic to obovate, 1.5–8cm long, 1.5–3cm broad and sessile

**End of leaflets:** Rounded, and usually with a short, bristly point

**Base of leaflets:** Usually broadly wedge-shaped

**Margin of leaflets:** Entire

**Upper/under side:** Dark green and glabrous above; bluish green or greyish green beneath and with appressed hairs like the leaf-stalk

**Arrangement on the shoot:** Leaves on long shoots alternate; arranged in tufts on the lateral short shoots

**Distribution:** On stony slopes, on crags, in open scrub and Pine woods from the lowlands to the montane (more rarely subalpine) zone; poisonous

874 **Aesculus parviflora – Buckeye**
*Deciduous, suckering shrub up to 4m high with light greyish brown stems*

## *Aesculus parviflora* Walt.
### Buckeye
**Hippocastanaceae – Horse Chestnut family** p. 81

**Length:** 20–30cm

**Form:** With 5 or 7 leaflets, palmately arranged

**Stalk:** 10–18cm long and coloured red

**Form of leaflets:** Narrowly obovate, 9–18cm long; the 3 middle leaflets distinctly stalked, the 2 lower ones with only short stalks

**End of leaflets:** Long-pointed

**Base of leaflets:** Narrowly wedge-shaped

**Margin of leaflets:** Crenate-serrate or finely serrate/dentate

**Upper/under side:** Medium to dark green above and bluish grey-green beneath; both sides glabrous

**Arrangement on the shoot:** Leaves alternate

**Distribution:** Occasionally planted in gardens and parks; native in south-eastern North America

875 **Aesculus octandra – Yellow Buckeye** *Deciduous, ornamental tree up to 20m high with greyish brown twigs*

## *Aesculus octandra* Marsh.
### (*A. flava* Ait., *A. lutea* Wangenh.)
### Yellow Buckeye
**Hippocastanaceae – Horse Chestnut family** p. 81

**Length:** 10–30cm

**Form:** Usually with 5 leaflets, palmately arranged

**Stalk:** 3–15cm

**Form of leaflets:** Oblong-elliptic, 10–15cm long, the 3 middle leaflets distinctly stalked, the 2 lower ones with only short stalks

**End of leaflets:** Pointed

**Base of leaflets:** Narrowly wedge-shaped

**Margin of leaflets:** Finely serrate

**Upper/under side:** Dark green and glabrous above; yellowish green beneath, hairy at first, later becoming glabrous

**Arrangement on the shoot:** Leaves opposite

**Distribution:** Ornamental tree native in eastern North America; often planted with the 2 related species to form a mixed group because of its yellow and pink flowers

876 **Aesculus hippocastanum – Horse Chestnut**
*Deciduous tree, 20–25m high, native in the mountain forests of the Balkan peninsula*

## *Aesculus hippocastanum*
L.
### Horse Chestnut
**Hippocastanaceae – Horse Chestnut family** p. 24, 25, 81

**Length:** 10–30cm long

**Form:** With 5 or 7 leaflets, palmately arranged

**Stalk:** 5–15cm long and grooved above

**Form of leaflets:** Oblong-obovate (greatest breadth always in the upper third), 5–15cm long and sessile; leaflets decreasing in size towards the leaf-base

**End of leaflets:** Shortly pointed

**Base of leaflets:** Narrowly wedge-shaped

**Margin of leaflets:** Irregularly simply and in places doubly serrate

**Upper/under side:** Dark green and glabrous above; pale to greyish green beneath with brown hairs on the veins when young

**Arrangement on the shoot:** Leaves opposite

**Distribution:** Popular shade-tree in parks, gardens, farms and hotel grounds

877 **Aesculus x carnea – Red Horse Chestnut** *Deciduous tree, 15–20m high, with greyish brown twigs*

## *Aesculus x carnea* Hayne
### (*A. hippocastanum* x *A. pavia*)
### Red Horse Chestnut
**Hippocastanaceae – Horse Chestnut family** p. 81

**Length:** 10–25cm long

**Form:** Usually with 5 leaflets, palmately arranged

**Stalk:** 5–15cm long

**Form of leaflets:** Elliptic (with the greatest breadth in the middle), 6–16cm long and usually sessile; the smallest leaflets pointing towards the leaf-base

**End of leaflets:** Pointed

**Base of leaflets:** Wedge-shaped

**Margin of leaflets:** Irregularly simply toothed and in places doubly serrate

**Upper/under side:** Dull, dark green and often wrinkled above; yellowish green beneath

**Arrangement on the shoot:** Leaves opposite

**Distribution:** The Red Horse-chestnut is a fertile hybrid between the S. European Horse Chestnut and the red-flowered Horse Chestnut native in the U.S.A.; planted as a street tree

## *Crataegus monogyna* Jacq.
### Hawthorn
**Rosaceae – Rose family** p. 83

**Length:** 3–6cm

**Form of blade:** Broadly ovate or rhombic in outline and deeply 3-, 5-, 7- or more rarely 9-lobed

**Stalk:** 1–2cm long, glabrous or hairy along the groove; stipules crescent-shaped and toothed

**Lobes:** Long, narrow and shortly pointed; the 2 lower lobes reaching almost to the midrib; sinuses acute

**End of leaf:** Terminal lobe usually flattened; a small point often present in the middle

**Base of blade:** Wedge-shaped, truncate or heart-shaped

**Margin of leaf:** Lobes entire in the lower part, otherwise finely serrate

**Upper/under side:** Shiny dark green and glabrous above; bluish green beneath and somewhat hairy in the axils of the veins

**Arrangement on the shoot:** Leaves alternate; arranged in clusters on short shoots; thorns 1–2.5cm long

**Distribution:** In hedges, deciduous woods, slopes from hill to montane

878 *Crataegus monogyna* – Hawthorn *Deciduous, densely branched and thorny shrub or small tree growing 1–8m high*

## *Crataegus laevigata*
(Poir.) DC.
### Midland Hawthorn
**Rosaceae – Rose family** p. 83

**Length:** 3–5cm

**Form of blade:** Usually ovate, obovate or oblong, and 3- or 5-lobed in the upper part

**Stalk:** 0.8–1.5cm long, glabrous or sparingly hairy and grooved; stipules lanceolate to ovate, glandular serrate and glabrous

**Lobes:** Short, broadly rounded or shortly pointed; sinuses only reaching half-way towards the midrib

**End of leaf:** Obtuse or flattened and with small teeth

**Base of blade:** Wedge-shaped

**Margin of leaf:** Lobes irregularly serrate; lowest part of leaf entire

**Upper/under side:** Shiny dark green above, whitish green beneath

**Arrangement on the shoot:** Leaves alternate; arranged in clusters on short shoots; thorns 6–15cm long

**Distribution:** In hedges, on the edges of woods, and as a pioneer tree in fields and vineyards; up to the montane zone

879 *Crataegus laevigata* – Midland Hawthorn *Deciduous, very thorny shrub or small tree 2–8m high*

## *Ribes uva-crispa* L.
### Gooseberry
**Saxifragaceae – Saxifrage family** p. 82

**Length:** 2–6cm long and equally broad

**Form of blade:** Heart-shaped to oblong in outline and 3- or 5-lobed

**Stalk:** 1–2cm long and somewhat broadened at the base

**End of leaf:** Terminal lobe rounded or with a short point

**Lobes:** Usually 3; roundish and only shortly pointed at the end; sinuses between the lobes acute

**Base of blade:** Weakly heart-shaped or truncate

**Margin of leaf:** Lobes deeply crenate and serrate above the sinuses

**Upper/under side:** Dark green, shiny, and often slightly hairy above; medium green and softly hairy beneath

**Arrangement on the shoot:** Leaves alternate on long shoots; arranged in clusters on short shoots

**Distribution:** In hedges, open woods, damp woodland and valleys and by fences

880 *Ribes uva-crispa* – Gooseberry *Deciduous shrub 60–150cm high with greyish brown stems*

## *Liriodendron tulipifera* L.
### Tulip Tree
**Magnoliaceae – Magnolia family** p. 82

**Length:** 10–25cm

**Form of blade:** Square in outline; blade with 2 or 4 lobes, unequal in size, their long sides almost parallel (the leaf-shape is unmistakable!)

**Stalk:** 6–12cm long and slightly thickened at the base

**Lobes:** 2 or 4, unequal in size, pointed; on young trees the leaves may be 4- or 6-lobed; sinuses between the lobes rounded and forming an obtuse angle

**End of leaf:** Terminal lobe truncate, emarginate or distinctly incised

**Base of blade:** Heart-shaped, rounded or truncate

**Margin of leaf:** Lobes entire

**Upper/under side:** Medium to dark green and glabrous above; bluish green beneath with hairy or glabrous depressions in the axils of the veins

**Distribution:** Cultivated in Europe since 1688; planted in parks and gardens

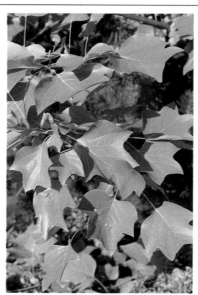

881 *Liriodendron tulipifera* – Tulip Tree *Deciduous tree, native in the eastern U.S.A., and reaching a height of 35m in Europe*

## *Morus nigra* L.
### Black Mulberry
**Moraceae – Mulberry family** p. 82

**Length:** 5–15cm

**Form of blade:** Broadly ovate or heart-shaped in outline, unequally coarsely serrate or with 2 or more irregular lobes

**Stalk:** 1–4cm long and often hairy

**Lobes:** Lateral lobes rounded and of unequal size; terminal lobe long and finely pointed, its base narrower than the middle

**End of leaf:** Terminal lobe long and finely pointed

**Base of blade:** Deeply heart-shaped

**Margin of leaf:** Lobes unequally coarsely serrate as far as the sinuses; entire in the acute or rounded sinuses

**Upper/under side:** Dark green above and rough to the touch because of the appressed hairs; paler green beneath with very prominent pale yellow veins and soft, appressed hairs

**Arrangement on the shoot:** Leaves alternate

**Distribution:** Planted in gardens in warmer districts

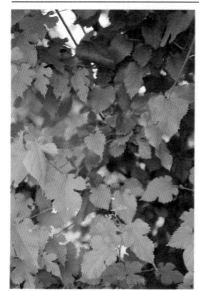

882 *Morus nigra* – Black Mulberry *Deciduous tree, growing to a height of 10–20m; cultivated especially in vine-growing regions*

## *Ficus carica* L.
### Fig
**Moraceae – Mulberry family** p. 82

**Length:** 20–30cm

**Form of blade:** With varied outline; usually roundish with 3, 5 or 7 lobes of unequal size

**Stalk:** 5–8cm long, thickish and usually with a broadened base

**Lobes:** Usually obovate, 6–12cm long, rounded or more rarely shortly pointed at the end; terminal lobe always narrower in the lower part than higher up

**End of leaf:** Terminal lobe usually rounded

**Base of blade:** Mostly heart-shaped

**Margin of leaf:** Entire, undulate, and also irregularly toothed

**Upper/under side:** Dark green above and roughly bristly; paler green beneath with pale yellow veins and soft, appressed hairs

**Arrangement on the shoot:** Leaves alternate

**Distribution:** On warm, dry, sunny slopes

883 *Ficus carica* – Fig *Small, deciduous tree up to 6m high; in plantations in warm countries*

## Forsythia europaea
Deg. et Bald.
### European Forsythia
**Oleaceae - Olive family** p. 83

**Length:** 4-8cm

**Form of blade:** Ovate to ovate-lanceolate in outline; very rarely lobed

**Stalk:** 1-3cm long and usually grooved above

**Lobes:** When present, narrow and pointed, sinuses between the lobes acute

**End of leaf:** Pointed; tip often somewhat curved to one side

**Base of blade:** Narrowly or broadly wedge-shaped

**Margin of leaf:** Entire in the lower part, otherwise distinctly serrate

**Upper/under side:** Dark green above and pale green beneath; both sides glabrous

**Arrangement on the shoot:** Leaves opposite

**Distribution:** Planted in gardens; but horticulturally unimportant

884 *Forsythia europaea* - **European Forsythia** *Deciduous shrub, growing 1.5-2.5m high; native in N. Albania and S.W. Yugoslavia*

## Acer rufinerve Sieb et Zucc.
### Grey-budded Snake-bark Maple
**Aceraceae - Maple family** p. 84

**Length:** 5-13cm

**Form of blade:** Broadly ovate in outline; often broader than long; distinctly 3-lobed

**Stalk:** 2-7cm long, pink to dark red above and furrowed

**Lobes:** Middle lobe broadly triangular or ovate and finely pointed; side lobes smaller than the middle lobe and spreading

**End of leaf:** Middle lobe finely pointed

**Base of blade:** Weakly heart-shaped or truncate

**Margin of leaf:** Lobes consistently unequally sharply serrate

**Upper/under side:** Dark to bluish green above; paler green beneath and with brownish red hairs along the veins especially when young

**Arrangement on the shoot:** Leaves opposite; each pair of leaves at right-angles to the next

**Distribution:** Often planted in gardens for autumn colour

885 *Acer rufinerve* - **Grey-budded Snake-bark Maple** *Deciduous tree, up to 10m high, native in the mountain forests of Japan*

## Acer saccharinum L.
### Silver Maple
**Aceraceae - Maple family** p. 83

**Length:** 10-15cm

**Form of blade:** Broadly ovate in outline and 5-lobed (often only obscurely 5-lobed); middle lobe often 3-lobed

**Stalk:** 4-7cm long, usually reddish above, without milky juice

**Lobes:** Of unequal size and pointed; the middle lobe only reaching half-way down the blade

**End of leaf:** Terminal lobe long-pointed

**Base of blade:** Heart-shaped or truncate

**Margin of leaf:** Lobes at the base and at the sinuses entire, otherwise coarsely serrate and dentate

**Upper/under side:** Medium to dark green and glabrous above; conspicuously silvery grey to bluish grey beneath

**Arrangement on the shoot:** Leaves opposite; each pair of leaves at right-angles to the next

**Distribution:** Cultivated in Europe since the beginning of the 18th century as a hardy ornamental tree

886 *Acer saccharinum* - **Silver Maple** *A deciduous tree, native in the river valleys of Atlantic U.S.A., and growing up to 40m high*

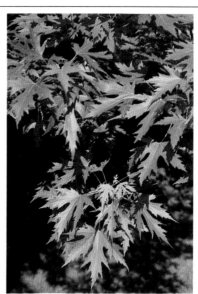

## Acer saccharinum L.
### 'laciniatum' (Carr.) Rehd. 'Wieri'
### Silver Maple, Wier's form
**Aceraceae - Maple family** p. 83

**Length:** 8-15cm

**Form of blade:** Broadly ovate to roundish in outline and deeply 5-lobed

**Stalk:** 4-7cm long, green, without milky juice

**Lobes:** Of unequal size (the 2 lowest the smallest), very narrow, deeply incised, and narrower in the lower part than in the middle; middle lobe 3-lobed; sinuses between the lobes obtuse or rounded

**End of leaf:** Terminal lobe long-pointed

**Base of blade:** Broadly arrow-shaped

**Margin of leaf:** Lobes entire in the lower quarter, otherwise with numerous smaller, pointed lobes

**Upper/under side:** Dark green and glabrous above; conspicuously silvery grey to bluish grey beneath

**Arrangement on the shoot:** Leaves opposite

**Distribution:** Found by Wier in 1873; a hardy park tree

887 *Acer saccharinum 'Wieri'* - **Silver Maple** *Tree up to 20m high with pendulous branches, native in Atlantic U.S.A.*

## Acer palmatum Thunb.
### Smooth Japanese Maple
**Aceraceae - Maple family** p. 84

**Length:** 5-10cm

**Form of blade:** Circular in outline and with 3, 5, 7, 9 or 11 lobes reaching more than halfway towards the base

**Stalk:** 4-7cm long, usually reddish above, without milky juice

**Lobes:** Ovate-lanceolate and pointed; lowermost lobe sometimes at an acute angle with the leaf-stalk and much smaller than the others; sinuses between the lobes acute

**End of leaf:** Terminal lobe finely pointed

**Base of blade:** Arrow-shaped, heart-shaped or truncate

**Margin of leaf:** Simply and doubly serrate

**Upper/under side:** Medium green and glabrous above; pale green beneath and with tufts of whitish hairs in the axils of the veins

**Arrangement on the shoot:** Leaves opposite; stems of many forms bright red; each pair of leaves at right-angles to the next

**Distribution:** Numerous forms are often planted in gardens and parks

888 *Acer palmatum* - **Smooth Japanese Maple** *Deciduous shrub or small tree, 3-8m high, native in Japan*

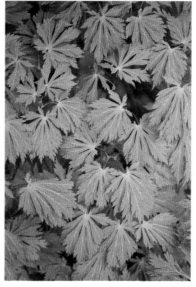

## Acer japonicum Thunb.
### 'Aconitifolium'
### Downy Japanese Maple
**Aceraceae - Maple family** p. 84

**Length:** 8-15cm

**Form of blade:** Roundish in outline and divided almost to the base into 9 or 11 pinnatisect lobes

**Stalk:** 3-6cm long and red in colour

**Lobes:** Narrowly obovate, pinnatisect, and usually long pointed; sinuses between the lobes acute

**End of leaf:** Terminal lobe finely pointed

**Base of blade:** Arrow-shaped or deeply heart-shaped

**Margin of leaf:** Lobes simply or doubly serrate

**Upper/under side:** Medium green above and paler green beneath; silky hairy only when young

**Arrangement on the shoot:** Leaves opposite; each pair of leaves at right-angles to the next

**Distribution:** Frequently planted in gardens and parks

889 *Acer japonicum* - **Downy Japanese Maple** *Small, deciduous tree, 5-7m high, native in the mountain forests of N. Japan*

148

890 **Liquidambar styraciflua – Sweet Gum**
*Conical, deciduous tree, up to 45m high, often with corky wings on the branchlets*

### *Liquidambar styraciflua* L.
### Sweet Gum
**Hamamelidaceae – Witch-hazel family** p. 84

**Length:** 10–20cm long and equally broad

**Form of blade:** Broadly ovate or roundish in outline; leaves on young trees only 3-lobed, on older trees 5- or 7-lobed

**Stalk:** 4–9cm long

**Lobes:** Narrowly triangular and pointed; sinuses between the lobes acute or obtuse

**End of leaf:** Terminal lobe pointed

**Base of blade:** Arrow-shaped, heart-shaped or truncate

**Margin of leaf:** Lobes finely serrate

**Upper/under side:** Shiny dark green above; distinctly paler green beneath with tufts of long hairs in the axils of the veins

**Arrangement on the shoot:** Leaves alternate

**Distribution:** Often dominant in the damp woods of Atlantic N. America; planted in Europe since 1688 as an ornamental tree in parks

891 **Catalpa ovata – Yellow Catalpa**
*Deciduous tree up to 10m high, native in China, with predominantly glabrous twigs*

### *Catalpa ovata*
### Yellow Catalpa
**Bignoniaceae – Bignonia family** p. 85

**Length:** 10–25cm

**Form of blade:** Varied in outline; broadly ovate or heart-shaped and often with 2, 3 or 5 lobes

**Stalk:** 4–10cm, hairy at first, later becoming glabrous, often dark red above and green beneath

**Lobes:** When present, broadly triangular, unequal in size, entire and printed; sinuses between the lobes obtuse and rounded

**End of leaf:** Shortly pointed

**Base of blade:** Rounded or heart-shaped

**Margin of leaf:** Entire and fringed with very fine hairs

**Upper/under side:** Dark green above and very soft to the touch; pale to medium green beneath and only slightly rough; veins yellowish green and distinctly prominent; reddish black glands in the axils of the veins

**Arrangement on the shoot:** Leaves opposite

**Distribution:** Planted as an ornamental tree in parks

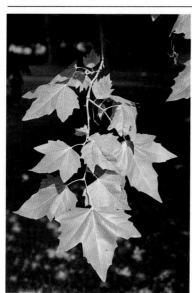

892 **Acer platanoides – Norway Maple**
*Deciduous tree, 25–30m high, with a broad crown and glabrous brown twigs*

### *Acer platanoides* L.
### Norway Maple
**Aceraceae – Maple family** p. 20, 21, 85

**Length:** 10–20cm long and broad

**Form of blade:** Roundish or broadly heart-shaped in outline and with 3, 5 or 7 lobes of unequal size

**Stalk:** Up to 15cm long, usually reddish, containing a milky juice and somewhat thickened at the base

**Lobes:** Usually 5 (more rarely 3 or 7); of unequal size and with several very long, slender teeth; sinuses between the lobes obtuse or rounded

**End of leaf:** Middle lobe with a long, fine point

**Base of blade:** Usually heart-shaped

**Margin of leaf:** Entire between the 3–5 long teeth on each lobe

**Upper/under side:** Dark green and glabrous above; pale green beneath and with tufts of hairs in the axils of the veins, later becoming glabrous

**Arrangement on the shoot:** Leaves opposite; each pair of leaves at right-angles to the next

**Distribution:** Throughout Europe in beech and mixed deciduous woods (especially damp oak, hornbeam)

893 **Acer cappadocicum – Cappadocian Maple** *Deciduous tree, 10–15m high, with distinctly smooth, green twigs*

### *Acer cappadocicum* Gled.
### Cappadocian Maple
**Aceraceae – Maple family** p. 84

**Length:** 10–20cm long and equally broad

**Form of blade:** Roundish or broadly heart-shaped in outline and with 5 or 7 lobes

**Stalk:** 5–15cm long

**Lobes:** Usually 5 lobes; broadly triangular, of unequal size, and sometimes ending in a long, fine point; sinuses between the lobes obtuse or rounded; lowest lobes pointing diagonally downwards

**End of leaf:** Middle lobe ending abruptly in a long, fine point

**Base of blade:** Heart-shaped

**Margin of leaf:** Entire; sometimes slightly undulate

**Upper/under side:** Dark green above and paler green beneath; both sides glabrous

**Arrangement on the shoot:** Leaves opposite; each pair at right-angles to the next

**Distribution:** Planted only in large gardens and parks in central Europe; native in the Caucasus and W. Asia

894 **Platanus x acerifolia – London Plane**
*Deciduous tree, up to 40m high, its pale green crown formed like a high dome*

### *Platanus* x *acerifolia*
(Ait.) Willd.
### London Plane
**Platanaceae – Plane family** p. 85

**Length:** 10–25cm long and equally broad

**Form of blade:** With a varied outline; usually roundish and with 3, 5 or 7 lobes of unequal size, which at most reach the middle of the blade

**Stalk:** 3–10cm long, thickened and bulbous at the base

**Lobes:** Usually 5 (3 on younger shoots); broadly triangular, coarsely toothed and pointed; sinuses between the lobes rounded, obtuse or acute

**End of leaf:** Middle lobe pointed

**Base of blade:** Usually truncate or weakly heart-shaped

**Margin of leaf:** Lobes entire except for the coarse teeth

**Upper/under side:** Shiny green and glabrous above; paler green beneath and becoming glabrous later

**Arrangement on the shoot:** Leaves alternate

**Distribution:** Often planted as a park or street tree in central Europe; thrives in the very dry air of towns; origin unknown

895 **Platanus orientalis – Oriental Plane** *Deciduous tree, native in W. Asia, growing to a height of over 25m*

### *Platanus orientalis* L.
### Oriental Plane
**Platanaceae – Plane family** p. 84

**Length:** 10–20cm

**Form of blade:** Broadly ovate or roundish and deeply 5- or 7-lobed; may be 3-lobed on younger shoots

**Stalk:** 3–7cm long, thickened and bulbous at the base

**Lobes:** Of unequal size, much longer than broad, often with smaller lobes and long-pointed; sinuses between the lobes rounded; middle lobe much longer than its width at the base

**End of leaf:** Terminal lobe with a very long point

**Base of blade:** Usually wedge-shaped

**Margin of leaf:** Lobes sinuately dentate and entire towards the base

**Upper/under side:** Shiny medium green above and pale green beneath; with dense, fine hairs when young, later becoming glabrous

**Arrangement on the shoot:** Leaves alternate

**Distribution:** Grows in very damp places in its native habitat; occasionally planted in parks in central Europe

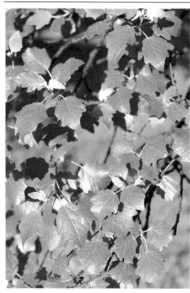

### Populus alba L.
### White Poplar

**Salicaceae - Willow family** p. 40, 41, 86

**Length:** 5-12cm

**Form of blade:** Varied in outline; on long shoots and suckers elliptic to ovate and with 3-5 large lobes

**Stalk:** 2-4cm long, flattened and with white hairs

**Lobes:** 3-5, of unequal size, triangular, pointed and often sinuately dentate; sinuses between the lobes obtuse or rounded

**End of leaf:** Middle lobe pointed or slightly rounded

**Base of blade:** Rounded, slightly heart-shaped or truncate

**Margin of leaf:** Lobes sinuately dentate

**Upper/under side:** Both sides woolly felted at first; later shiny dark green above and becoming glabrous; remaining densely white-felted beneath

**Arrangement on the shoot:** Leaves alternate

**Distribution:** On the edge of damp woods, in waste places, and by water; ascending to 1500m

**896    Populus alba – White Poplar**
*Deciduous, broad-crowned tree, 10–30m high, with long shoots white- to grey-felted*

### Ribes alpinum L.
### Mountain Currant

**Saxifragaceae - Saxifrage family** p. 86

**Length:** 2-5cm long and broad

**Form of blade:** Broadly ovate to roundish in outline, with 3 or more rarely 5 lobes

**Stalk:** 1-2cm long, fringed with long glandular hairs

**Lobes:** 3, more rarely 5, broadly triangular, with coarse, deeply cut teeth, and pointed or obtuse at end

**End of leaf:** Middle lobe pointed, obtuse or rounded

**Base of blade:** Lobes coarsely and deeply serrate; teeth only shortly pointed

**Upper/under side:** Dark green above with scattered hairs; paler green beneath, shiny and usually glabrous

**Arrangement on the shoot:** Leaves alternate

**Distribution:** Scattered amongst the luxuriant vegetation of mixed woods, in gorges, on grassland with tall-herb communities, and in open pine woods in the montane and subalpine zones; also damp woods in hill zone

**897    Ribes alpinum – Mountain Currant**
*Deciduous, much-branched, non-spiny shrub 1–2m in height*

### Acer monspessulanum L.
### Montpelier Maple

**Aceraceae - Maple family** p. 85

**Length:** 3-6cm

**Form of blade:** Horizontally elliptic in outline with 3 lobes

**Stalk:** 1-3cm long and somewhat broadened at the base

**Lobes:** 3 (more rarely 5), thick, leathery, broadly triangular, rounded, and of similar size; lateral lobes spreading more or less horizontally; sinuses between the lobes usually forming a right-angle

**End of leaf:** Middle lobe rounded

**Base of blade:** Weakly heart-shaped or rounded

**Margin of leaf:** Lobes entire; more rarely somewhat wavy

**Upper/under side:** Shiny dark green and glabrous above; bluish green beneath, softly hairy at first, later glabrous

**Arrangement on the shoot:** Leaves opposite; each pair of leaves at right-angles to the next

**Distribution:** On sunny rock slopes, in sunny oak woods; ascending to 1700m in the Caucasus

**898    Acer monspessulanum – Montpelier Maple** *Deciduous, 6–10m high, native in Mediterranean region, brownish green branchlets*

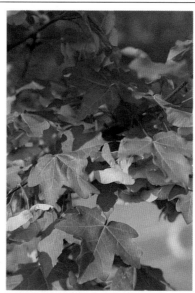

### Acer campestre L.
### Field Maple

**Aceraceae - Maple family** p. 86

**Length:** 3-10cm long and often equally broad

**Form of blade:** Roundish to ovate in outline, with 3 or 5 lobes

**Stalk:** 1-5cm long, usually reddish above and containing a milky juice

**Lobes:** 3 or 5, of unequal size, obtuse or rounded, coarsely sinuate or entire; lobes becoming smaller towards the base

**End of leaf:** Middle lobe obtuse or rounded

**Base of blade:** Heart-shaped

**Margin of leaf:** Lobes entire, except for the coarse, rounded teeth

**Upper/under side:** Dark green and glabrous above; paler green beneath and softly hairy when young, later becoming glabrous

**Arrangement on the shoot:** Leaves opposite; each pair of leaves at right-angles to the next

**Distribution:** In thickets, hedges, and in damp oak and hornbeam woods with luxuriant vegetation from the hill to the montane zone

**899    Acer campestre – Field Maple**
*Deciduous tree, 10–15m high, with a rounded crown and corky wings on the twigs*

### Hedera helix L.
### Ivy

**Araliaceae - Ivy family** p. 85

**Length:** 4-10cm

**Form of blade:** Varied in outline; on non-flowering stems ovate to roundish, 3- or 5-lobed, leathery and evergreen (lasting 3 years)

**Stalk:** 3-7cm long and usually brown to brownish red above

**Lobes:** 3 (more rarely 5), of unequal size, broadly triangular and obtuse or rounded; lateral lobes spreading horizontally; sinuses between the lobes obtuse-angled or rounded

**End of leaf:** Middle lobe obtuse or rounded

**Base of blade:** Heart-shaped

**Margin of leaf:** Lobes entire; occasionally slightly wavy

**Upper/under side:** Dark bluish green and glabrous above with prominent pale yellow veins; dull pale green and glabrous beneath

**Arrangement on the shoot:** Leaves alternate

**Distribution:** Trailing on the ground or climbing on trees and walls in deciduous mixed woods, parks and on rocks

**900    Hedera helix – Ivy**
*Evergreen climber up to 20m high with brownish green shoots rooting near the leaves*

### Acer saccharum Marsh.
### Sugar Maple

**Aceraceae - Maple family** p. 85

**Length:** 8-15cm long and equally broad

**Form of blade:** Roundish or broadly heart-shaped in outline, with 3 or 5 lobes

**Stalk:** 5-10cm long and often reddish in colour

**Lobes:** Usually 5, of unequal size, broadly triangular, long-pointed and often also with 1 or 2 large pointed teeth

**End of leaf:** Middle lobe with a long, fine point

**Base of blade:** Weakly heart-shaped

**Margin of leaf:** Lobes entire between the teeth

**Upper/under side:** Medium to dark green and glabrous above; greyish green and glabrous beneath

**Arrangement on the shoot:** Leaves opposite; each pair of leaves at right-angles to the next

**Distribution:** Planted in Europe in large gardens and parks; often cultivated in the U.S.A. for the sugar obtained from its sap; the leaf is a feature of the Canadian national flag

**901    Acer saccharum – Sugar Maple**
*Deciduous tree from U.S.A., up to 40m high in its native habitat, with brownish yellow twigs*

## *Ribes nigrum* L.
## Black Currant

**Saxifragaceae Saxifrage family** p. 86

**Length:** 5–10cm long and equally broad

**Form of blade:** Roundish in outline and 3- or 5-lobed

**Stalk:** 2–5cm long and broadened at the base

**Lobes:** 3 or 5, very broadly triangular, doubly serrate, and strongly scented; sinuses between the lobes acute

**End of leaf:** Middle lobe pointed

**Base of blade:** Heart-shaped

**Margin of leaf:** Lobes doubly serrate

**Upper/under side:** Medium to dark green above, hairy at first, later becoming glabrous; pale green beneath dotted with yellowish resin glands (magnifying glass required!)

**Arrangement on the shoot:** Leaves alternate

**Distribution:** In damp woods, thickets and alder groves; now only rarely found wild; first cultivated in 16th century; nowadays an important plant of cultivation with numerous large-fruited varieties

902 **Ribes nigrum – Black Currant**
*Deciduous shrub, 1–2m high, with young shoots finely hairy, and greyish to reddish brown*

## *Ribes rubrum* L.
## Red Currant

**Saxifragaceae - Saxifrage family** p. 86

**Length:** 4–7cm

**Form of blade:** Roundish in outline and with 3 or 5 lobes

**Stalk:** 2–3.5cm long and somewhat thickened at the base

**Lobes:** 3 or 5, moderately to broadly triangular and pointed; sinuses between the lobes acute

**End of leaf:** Middle lobe pointed

**Base of blade:** Heart-shaped or truncate

**Margin of leaf:** Lobes doubly serrate and/or crenately toothed

**Upper/under side:** Dark green and dull above; paler green and softly hairy beneath, later becoming glabrous; not gland-dotted

**Arrangement on the shoot:** Leaves alternate

**Distribution:** Cultivated in gardens, and derived from wild European species. Its parents are mainly the Wild Red Currant, R. spicatum, and the Rock Red Currant, R. petraeum.

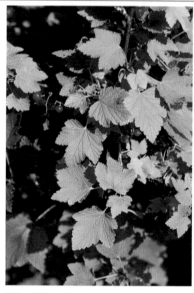

903 **Ribes rubrum – Red Currant**
*Deciduous, non-spiny shrub, 1–2m high, with red berries*

## *Vitis vinifera* L. ssp. *vinifera*
## Grape-vine

**Vitaceae - Vine family** p. 87

**Length:** 5–15cm long and broad

**Form of blade:** Varied in outline; usually roundish and as a rule moderately to deeply 3- or 5-lobed

**Stalk:** 4–8cm long

**Lobes:** 3 or 5, of varied size, triangular, pointed

**End of leaf:** Middle lobe with a short point

**Base of blade:** Deeply and narrowly heart-shaped or with a very narrow sinus where the blade joins the stalk

**Margin of leaf:** Lobes broadly toothed in the middle and upper parts; entire in the lower part and by the sinus

**Upper/under side:** Dark green above and hairy when young, later becoming glabrous; pale to greyish green beneath and often felted, more rarely becoming glabrous

**Arrangement on the shoot:** Leaves alternate

**Distribution:** Numerous varieties cultivated in the hill zone

904 **Vitis vinifera – Grape-vine**
*Deciduous climber with greyish to reddish brown fibrous bark*

## *Viburnum opulus* L.
## Guelder Rose

**Caprifoliaceae - Honeysuckle family** p. 87

**Length:** 4–12cm long and equally broad or broader

**Form of blade:** Varied in outline; usually roundish or horizontally elliptic with 3 or 5 lobes

**Stalk:** 2–3cm long with 2–6 linear, gland-tipped appendages at the base and 2–4 green, concave nectar-glands just below the blade

**Lobes:** Lateral lobes broadly triangular, pointed or obtuse; terminal lobe often rectangular

**End of leaf:** Middle lobe shortly pointed or obtuse

**Base of blade:** Heart-shaped or truncate

**Margin of leaf:** Lobes irregularly coarsely toothed except sinuses and lower parts of the lateral lobes

**Upper/under side:** Dark green and glabrous above; greyish green beneath, somewhat downy

**Arrangement on shoot:** Lvs opposite

**Distribution:** Damp woods, hedges, on wood-margins and the banks of streams; hill to montane zone

905 **Viburnum opulus – Guelder Rose**
*Quick-growing, deciduous shrub, 1–4m high, with glabrous, angular stems*

## *Acer pseudoplatanus* L.
## Sycamore

**Aceraceae - Maple family** p. 22, 23, 87

**Length:** 8–20cm long and up to 16cm broad

**Form of blade:** Broadly ovate, heart-shaped or roundish in outline and 3- or 5-lobed

**Stalk:** Up to 10cm long, red above

**Lobes:** 5, more rarely 3, of unequal size (the lowest always small), broadly triangular and pointed; sinuses between the lobes acute

**End of leaf:** Middle lobe shortly pointed, obtuse or rounded

**Base of blade:** Heart-shaped

**Margin of leaf:** Lobes irregularly coarsely serrate and dentate; entire in the sinuses and at the base of the blade

**Upper/under side:** Dark green and glabrous above; pale bluish green beneath, densely hairy at first and becoming glabrous later except between the veins; veins pale green

**Arrangement on the shoot:** Leaves opposite

**Distribution:** On the banks of streams, on waste ground, in gorges and mixed beech woods

906 **Acer pseudoplatanus – Sycamore**
*Deciduous tree, 30–40m high, developing to an impressive size, especially when free-standing*

## *Acer opalus* Mill.
## Italian Maple

**Aceraceae - Maple family** p. 87

**Length:** 4–10cm and usually a little broader

**Form of blade:** Usually roundish in outline and with 5 lobes (the 2 lower lobes often only indicated)

**Stalk:** 3–9cm long and dark red above

**Lobes:** Very broadly triangular, much shorter than in the Sycamore and usually obtuse at the end; sinuses between the lobes rounded, obtuse or acute

**End of leaf:** Middle lobe usually obtuse

**Base of blade:** Heart-shaped or truncate

**Margin of leaf:** Lobes irregularly crenate and dentate; only short sections in the sinuses entire

**Upper/under side:** Dark green and glabrous above; bluish green beneath and hairy at first, soon becoming glabrous

**Arrangement on the shoot:** Leaves opposite

**Distribution:** On south-facing slopes and, south of the Alps, in the mountains of the W. Mediterranean region

907 **Acer opalus – Italian Maple**
*Deciduous shrub or tree up to 20m high with light brown bark*

908 **Acer rubrum – Red Maple**
*Deciduous tree, up to 40m high in its native habitat, with bright red shoots in the 1st year*

### Acer rubrum L.
### Red Maple
**Aceraceae – Maple family** p. 87

**Length:** 5–10cm

**Form of blade:** Broadly ovate or roundish in outline and usually with 3 lobes (more rarely 5-lobed)

**Stalk:** 4–6cm long and dark red and green above

**Lobes:** Very broadly triangular and pointed; terminal lobe larger than the lateral lobes; sinuses between the lobes obtuse

**End of leaf:** Middle lobe pointed

**Base of blade:** Truncate or rounded

**Margin of leaf:** Lobes coarsely serrate and dentate; entire at the sinuses

**Upper/under side:** Dark green above, bluish grey beneath; both sides glabrous or hairy on the veins beneath

**Arrangement on the shoot:** Leaves opposite; each pair of leaves at right-angles to the next

**Distribution:** Native in eastern N. America; suitable for swampy areas of parks; sometimes planted for its splendid wine-red autumn colouring

909 **Morus alba – White Mulberry**
*Much-branched, deciduous tree, up to 20m high, native in China and Korea*

### Morus alba L.
### White Mulberry
**Moraceae – Mulberry family** p. 87

**Length:** 6–18cm

**Form of blade:** Varied in outline; unlobed and with an irregularly serrate margin or with 3, 5 or 7 lobes

**Stalk:** 2–4cm long, grooved and downy at first

**Lobes:** 3, 5 or 7; of unequal size, irregularly formed and rounded or shortly pointed; sinuses between the lobes acute, obtuse or rounded

**End of leaf:** Middle lobe only very shortly pointed

**Base of blade:** Equally or unequally heart-shaped or truncate

**Margin of leaf:** Irregularly serrate; entire in the lower part of the lobes and at the sinuses

**Upper/under side:** Shiny dark green and glabrous above; pale bluish green beneath, almost glabrous or hairy on the larger veins

**Arrangement on the shoot:** Leaves alternate

**Distribution:** Occasionally planted in gardens

910 **Sorbus torminalis – Wild Service Tree**
*Large, deciduous shrub or tree, 5–20m high, with shiny brown, glabrous branchlets*

### Sorbus torminalis (L.) Crantz
### Wild Service Tree
**Rosaceae – Rose family** p. 88

**Length:** 6–10cm long and almost equally broad

**Form of blade:** Ovate to roundish in outline and with 3 or 4 pointed lobes on each side

**Stalk:** 2–5cm long and loosely felted; later glabrous

**Lobes:** Narrowly to broadly triangular and pointed; lower lobes larger and usually spreading horizontally

**End of leaf:** Middle lobe pointed

**Base of blade:** Truncate or rounded

**Margin of leaf:** Simply and doubly serrate; entire or undulate at the base of the blade

**Upper/under side:** Shiny dark green above, and finely hairy for a time, but later becoming glabrous; pale bluish green and loosely felted, hairs persisting only between veins

**Arrangement on the shoot:** Leaves alternate

**Distribution:** In hornbeam, oak and beech woods; hill zone

911 **Sorbus mougeotii – Mougeot's Whitebeam** *Deciduous shrub or tree, 4–20m high, with brownish red branchlets*

### Sorbus mougeotii
Soy.-Willem. et Godr.
### Mougeot's Whitebeam
**Rosaceae – Rose family** p. 88

**Length:** 6–10cm

**Form of blade:** Oblong-elliptic to ovate in outline with a number of irregular lobes on each side, becoming smaller towards the tip

**Stalk:** 1–2cm long

**Lobes:** With about 10 lobes on each side; lobes fairly shallow, very shortly pointed and becoming smaller towards the tip

**End of leaf:** Shortly pointed

**Base of blade:** Lobes irregularly finely serrate

**Upper/under side:** Dark green above and later becoming glabrous; densely white-felted beneath and therefore appearing pale grey; veins pale greyish green; 8–12 pairs of lateral veins

**Arrangement on the shoot:** Leaves alternate

**Distribution:** On fairly dry, calcareous stony soils on warm, shady places; found here and there in deciduous mixed woods; hill to subalpine zone

912 **Sorbus intermedia – Swedish Whitebeam**
*Deciduous shrub or tree up to 15m high with olive green to brown branchlets*

### Sorbus intermedia (Ehrh.)
Pers.
### Swedish Whitebeam
**Rosaceae – Rose family** p. 88

**Length:** 6–12cm

**Form of blade:** Oblong-elliptic to elliptic in outline and with 5–8 short lobes on each side; only serrate in the upper part

**Stalk:** 1–2cm long and grey-felted

**Lobes:** 5–8 on each side, fairly shallow and only shortly pointed; sinuses between the lobes acute

**End of leaf:** Shortly pointed

**Base of blade:** Broadly wedge-shaped or rounded

**Margin of leaf:** Lobes irregularly serrate

**Upper/under side:** Shiny dark green above; remaining grey-felted beneath, but finally becoming somewhat glabrous; 6–9 pairs of lateral veins

**Arrangement on the shoot:** Leaves alternate

**Distribution:** Native in Scandinavia; often planted along streets and in parks in Sweden, Denmark and N.E. Germany because of its resistance to air pollution

913 **Sorbus latifolia – Broad-leaved Whitebeam**
*Deciduous tree up to 28m high with greyish brown to olive brown branchlets*

### Sorbus latifolia (Lam.) Pers.
### Broad-leaved Whitebeam
**Rosaceae – Rose family** p. 88

**Length:** 7–12cm long and up to 10cm broad in the lower third

**Form of blade:** Ovate to broadly ovate in outline with 6–9 lobes on each side; only serrate but no longer lobed towards the tip

**Stalk:** 1–3cm long

**Lobes:** 6–9 on each side, broadly triangular, pointed, and becoming progressively smaller towards the tip; sinuses between the lobes acute

**End of leaf:** Shortly pointed

**Base of blade:** Irregularly or regularly broadly wedge-shaped or rounded

**Margin of leaf:** Lobes irregularly finely serrate

**Upper/under side:** Shiny dark green and glabrous above; somewhat grey-felted beneath and therefore appearing pale greyish green; veins pale yellowish green

**Arrangement on the shoot:** Leaves alternate

**Distribution:** In warmer parts of the hill zone in oak-hornbeam woods; more rarely montane

914 **Quercus robur – Common Oak, Pedunculate Oak** *Deciduous tree, native in Europe, growing up to 50m high, with light brown branchlets*

## Quercus robur L.
## Common Oak, Pedunculate Oak

**Fagaceae – Beech family** p. 48, 49, 89

**Length:** 5–16cm

**Form of blade:** Obovate to elliptic in outline; the greatest breadth in the upper third; with 4 or 5 irregular lobes of unequal size on each side

**Stalk:** Usually small; at most 7mm long

**Lobes:** 4 or 5 on each side, irregular, entire, rounded, and often reaching halfway towards the midrib; sinuses between the lobes rounded

**End of leaf:** Middle lobe rounded

**Base of blade:** Usually somewhat heart-shaped and with 2 clearly visible auricles (small lobes)

**Margin of leaf:** Lobes entire

**Upper/under side:** Shiny dark green and glabrous above; dull pale to bluish green beneath; rarely slightly hairy

**Arrangement on the shoot:** Leaves alternate

**Distribution:** From the hill to the lower montane zone where winters are mild and damp

915 **Quercus pubescens – Downy Oak** *Deciduous tree, 3–20m high, with young stems densely felted at first with downy hairs*

## Quercus pubescens Willd.
## Downy Oak

**Fagaceae – beech family** p. 89

**Length:** 5–10cm

**Form of blade:** Outline varying in shape, but usually obovate with the greatest breadth in the upper third; 5–7 unequal lobes on each side

**Stalk:** 8–12cm long

**Lobes:** 5–7 on each side, obtuse or occasionally with a small point at the end; sinuses between the lobes usually rounded

**End of leaf:** Middle lobe with 2+ obtuse or shortly pointed sections

**Base of blade:** Often rounded; the 2 halves of the blade not always ending at the same point on the midrib

**Margin of leaf:** Lobes and their sections entire

**Upper/under side:** Both sides felted at first; later glabrous and dark green above; pale greyish green beneath because of the hairy covering

**Arrangement:** Leaves alternate

**Distribution:** Hill zone, more rarely montane; sunny hillsides, warm and stony slopes; deciduous and pine woods

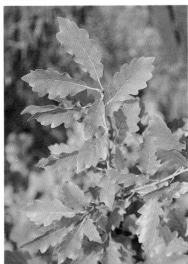

916 **Quercus petraea – Sessile Oak** *Deciduous tree, growing 20–45m high, with glabrous olive green to brown branchlets*

## Quercus petraea Liebl.
## Sessile Oak

**Fagaceae – Beech family** p. 89

**Length:** 6–12cm

**Form of blade:** Obovate in outline, broadest in the middle, and with 5–9 lobes on each side

**Stalk:** 10–25mm long

**Lobes:** 5–9 on each side, rounded, entire, and more or less equal in size; sinuses between the lobes usually acute

**End of leaf:** Middle lobe obtuse or rounded

**Base of blade:** Regularly or irregularly wedge-shaped or rounded

**Margin of leaf:** Lobes entire

**Upper/under side:** Dull dark green and glabrous above; paler green beneath with very small and scattered stellate hairs

**Arrangement on the shoot:** Leaves alternate

**Distribution:** From the hill to the lower montane zone in areas mild in winter; in beech and oak-hornbeam woods; up to 1600m in the southern Alps

917 **Quercus cerris – Turkey Oak** *Deciduous shrub or tree up to 30m high, with branchlets olive green and red at first*

## Quercus cerris L.
## Turkey Oak

**Fagaceae – Beech family** p. 89

**Length:** 6–15cm

**Form of blade:** Varied in outline; usually narrowly elliptic with the greatest breadth in the upper third; 7–9 lobes of unequal size on each side

**Stalk:** 7–15mm long

**Lobes:** 7–9 on each side, rather obtuse or more often pointed at the end; sinuses between the lobes rounded or acute

**End of leaf:** Middle lobe finely pointed, other sections also pointed

**Base of blade:** Wedge-shaped

**Margin of leaf:** Lobes and any other pointed sections entire

**Upper/under side:** Roughly hairy above at first, later glabrous and shiny dark green; pale green beneath, the very long, soft, downy hairs persistent

**Arrangement on the shoot:** Leaves alternate

**Distribution:** In hot parts of the hill zone; found here and there especially in Downy Oak woods and on stony slopes

918 **Quercus rubra – Red Oak** *Deciduous tree, 20–35m high, with reddish brown branchlets*

## Quercus rubra L.
## Red Oak

**Fagaceae – Beech family** p. 89

**Length:** 10–20cm

**Form of blade:** Usually elliptic or obovate with 4–6 lobes on each side

**Stalk:** Up to 5cm long

**Lobes:** 4–6 on each side, themselves partially lobed; lobes and additional smaller lobes with a strong point, often ending in a bristle-like tip

**End of leaf:** Middle lobe with additional smaller lobes, all sections long-pointed and usually tipped by a long bristle

**Base of blade:** Rounded or broadly wedge-shaped

**Margin of leaf:** Lobes and additional smaller lobes entire

**Upper/under side:** Dull to dark green and glabrous above; pale yellowish green beneath, with stellate hairs between the midrib and lateral veins

**Arrangement on the shoot:** Leaves alternate

**Distribution:** Native in the eastern United States; introduced into Europe a long time ago and used for afforestation; often planted in large gardens and parks as an ornamental tree

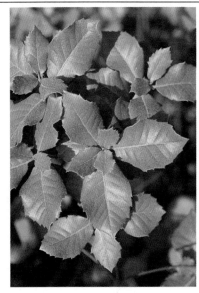

919 **Quercus ilex – Evergreen Oak** *Evergreen tree up to 25m high, with grey-felted branchlets that only gradually become glabrous*

## Quercus ilex L.
## Evergreen Oak, Holm Oak

**Fagaceae – Beech family** p. 105

**Length:** 3–8cm

**Form of blade:** Varied in outline; usually oblong-ovate to ovate with 4–7 sharp teeth on each side; often also lobed

**Stalk:** 7–15mm long and covered with long, white, matted hairs

**Lobes:** Sharply pointed, entire or undulate, leathery and thick

**End of leaf:** Sharply pointed

**Base of blade:** Broadly wedge-shaped or rounded

**Margin of leaf:** Lobes entire or undulate

**Upper/under side:** Young leaves hairy on both sides, older leaves shiny dark green and glabrous above; appearing grey to whitish beneath because of the dense covering of hairs

**Arrangement on the shoot:** Leaves alternate

**Distribution:** Widespread in the Mediterranean region; often the dominant tree in evergreen woods; planted in parks in areas with a mild winter climate as an ornamental tree

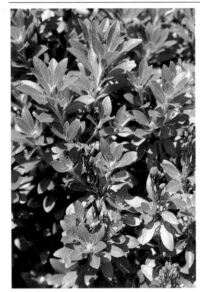

### Rhododendron hirsutum L.
### Hairy Alpenrose
Ericaceae – Heath family p. 90

**Length** 1–3.5cm

**Form of blade:** Oblong-elliptic in outline; thick and leathery

**Stalk:** 0.3–0.8cm long

**End of leaf:** Obtuse or rounded

**Base of blade:** Narrowly wedge-shaped

**Margin of leaf:** Entire, often wavy in places; with 1–2mm long, bristly, spreading hairs

**Upper/under side:** Shiny dark green above, somewhat wrinkled, glabrous, and with scattered glandular scales; pale green beneath, dotted with glands which are whitish at first, later yellowish brown

**Arrangement on the shoot:** Leaves alternate

**Distribution:** In the subalpine zone; always on calcareous subsoil in scree, clefts in rocks, and shady places covered with snow for long periods

920 **Rhododendron hirsutum – Hairy Alpenrose** Evergreen shrub up to 1m high with stems green and hairy at first

### Erica tetralix L.
### Cross-leaved Heath, Bog Heather
Ericaceae – Heath family p. 90

**Length:** 3–6mm

**Form of blade:** Narrowly linear or needle-like in outline

**Stalk:** Very short, 1–2mm long, usually felted and very broad

**End of leaf:** Obtuse or rounded

**Base of blade:** Very slightly narrowed into the broad stalk

**Margin of leaf:** Inrolled, with 0.5–1mm long, spreading, white hairs

**Upper/under side:** With a dark green surface above, but appearing whitish in places because of fine matted hairs; white beneath with a prominent medium green midrib

**Arrangement on the shoot:** Leaves arranged in whorls of 4, more rarely in whorls of 3

**Distribution:** From the lowlands to the montane zone; in peat bogs, on heaths and acid, humus-rich, sandy soils and in boggy woods

921 **Erica tetralix – Cross-leaved Heath** Prostrate, evergreen, dwarf shrub up to 50cm high with numerous branched stems

### Ledum groenlandicum Oed.
### (L. palustre ssp. groenlandicum)
### Labrador Tea
Ericaceae – Heath family p. 90

**Length:** 2–5cm

**Form of blade:** Oblong to oblong-elliptic in outline

**Stalk:** 0.3–0.6cm long with brown hairs

**End of leaf:** Obtuse

**Base of blade:** Wedge-shaped or rounded

**Margin of leaf:** Entire, the whole margin rolled under

**Upper/under side:** Medium to dark green above with an undulate surface; pale to dark green beneath, in places densely covered with medium to dark brown crisped hairs; midrib pale yellow and prominent

**Arrangement on the shoot:** Leaves alternate

**Distribution:** Abundant in N. Europe, on cold peat moors and in bogs; leaves used in time of need as a substitute for tea

922 **Ledum groenlandicum – Labrador Tea** Evergreen shrub, up to 1m high, with erect, brown-felted stems

### Rhododendron ferrugineum L.
### Alpenrose
Ericaceae – Heath family p. 90

**Length:** 2–5cm

**Form of blade:** Oblong-lanceolate to oblong-elliptic in outline, leathery, and narrowed 2–6mm stalk

**Stalk:** Very short, up to 6mm long

**End of leaf:** Rounded or obtuse

**Base of blade:** Narrowly wedge-shaped

**Margin of leaf:** Entire; margin somewhat recurved

**Upper/under side:** Shiny dark green above and slightly wrinkled; brown beneath because of the dense covering of overlapping, spherical glands; young leaves with pale yellow glands beneath; scales overlapping

**Arrangement on the shoot:** Leaves alternate

**Distribution:** In the subalpine zone; more rarely montane and alpine; on thick layers of acid raw humus amongst pines and larches above or in the forest zone

923 **Rhododendron ferrugineum – Alpenrose** Roundish, much-branched, evergreen shrub up to 1m in height

### Ledum palustre L.
### Marsh Ledum
Ericaceae – Heath family p. 90

**Length:** 2–5cm

**Form of blade:** Linear to lanceolate in outline

**Stalk:** 2–3mm long with some brownish hairs; often as broad as the blade

**End of leaf:** Obtuse or rounded and usually with a short, fine point

**Base of blade:** Slightly wedge-shaped; base of blade and stalk often as broad as each other

**Margin of leaf:** Entire; margins strongly recurved to within 1–2mm of each other

**Upper/under side:** Dark green and distinctly felted above, later often becoming glabrous; rust red to brown-felted beneath

**Arrangement on the shoot:** Leaves alternate

**Distribution:** In the hill zone; in N. Europe especially in raised bogs and transitional moorland, wooded bogs, and acid, peaty soils lacking in nutrients

924 **Ledum palustre – Marsh Ledum** Evergreen shrub, 1–1.5m high, with stems hairy at first

### Empetrum nigrum L.
### ssp. hermaphroditum
### (Hagerup) Böcher
### Crowberry
Empetraceae – Crowberry family p. 91

**Length:** 4–7mm long

**Form of blade:** Narrowly elliptic or linear in outline and leathery

**Stalk:** 1–2mm long, broad, dark green and appressed to the shoot

**End of leaf:** Obtuse or shortly pointed

**Base of blade:** Wedge-shaped, narrowing slightly to the broad base

**Margin of leaf:** Entire, margins rolled under, their fringes of white hairs touching each other, resulting in a longitudinal furrow

**Upper/under side:** Dark green and glabrous above; with a white keel beneath and sparsely hairy; margins dark green

**Arrangement on the shoot:** Leaves in irregular whorls

**Distribution:** In damp areas of the montane and subalpine zone and in the Arctic; on sunny slopes and acid soils in the Alps, in association with the Bilberry, Alpenrose, etc.

925 **Empetrum nigrum – Crowberry** Prostrate, evergreen, creeping dwarf shrub, 10–45cm high, forming tufts

### Erica carnea L.
(*E. herbacea* L.)
## Spring Heath
Ericaceae – Heath family  p. 91

**Length:** 4–8mm

**Form of blade:** Needle-like or linear in outline

**Stalk:** 1–2mm long, brownish white in colour and almost as broad as the blade

**End of leaf:** Rounded and usually with a short, sharp point

**Base of blade:** Rounded into the leaf-stalk

**Margin of leaf:** Margins rolled under; marginal glands far apart

**Upper/under side:** Medium to dark green above, glabrous and shiny; groove between the margins beneath appearing white

**Arrangement on the shoot:** Leaves in whorls of 3 or 4

**Distribution:** In the montane and subalpine zone in Pine woods, on sunny, warm hillsides, in open larch and spruce woods and on moorland

926　*Erica carnea* – **Spring Heath**
*Evergreen dwarf shrub up to 30cm high, with 4-angled stems forming dense mats*

### Erica arborea L.
## Tree Heath
Ericaceae– Heath family p. 91

**Length:** 4–7mm

**Form of blade:** Needle-like or narrowly linear in outline

**Stalk:** 1–2mm long, whitish and almost as broad as the blade

**End of leaf:** Obtuse or rounded

**Base of blade:** Abruptly narrowed

**Margin of leaf:** Entire; margins rolled under leaving only a narrow groove; glandular hairy

**Upper/under side:** Dark green above and whitish beneath between the inrolled margins; midrib pale green and clearly visible

**Arrangement on the shoot:** Leaves in whorls of 3 or 4

**Distribution:** Distributed especially throughout S. Europe, the Caucasus and N. Africa; the famous French bruyère pipes are made from the wood

927　*Erica arborea* – **Tree Heath**
*Evergreen shrub up to 5m in height with erect and hairy young stems*

### Erica vagans L.
## Cornish Heath
Ericaceae – Heath family  p. 91

**Length:** 4–10mm

**Form of blade:** Narrowly linear in outline

**Stalk:** 1–2mm, white, and almost as broad as the blade

**End of leaf:** Rounded or obtuse

**Base of blade:** Slightly narrowed at the sides

**Margin of leaf:** Entire; with glands far apart; margins rolled under

**Upper/under side:** Dark green and glabrous above; white beneath with a very prominent dark green midrib

**Arrangement on the shoot:** Leaves in whorls of 4 or 5

**Distribution:** In the hill zone; on the edges of woods and shrubby places especially in W. Europe (from Ireland to Portugal)

928　*Erica vagans* – **Cornish Heath**
*Evergreen dwarf shrub 30–80cm high, luxuriant in growth and with light brown stems*

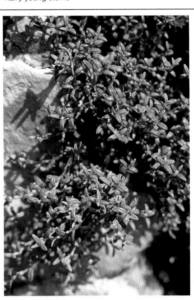

### Loiseleuria procumbens
(L.) Desv.
## Trailing Azalea
Ericaceae – Heath family  p. 91

**Length:** 4–8cm

**Form of blade:** Narrowly elliptic in outline and not much broader than the stalk

**Stalk:** 1–3mm; usually pale yellowish white in colour

**End of leaf:** Obtuse or shortly pointed

**Base of blade:** Slightly wedge-shaped

**Margin of leaf:** Entire; margins rolled under

**Upper/under side:** Dark green above, hairy at first, later glabrous, with a shallow groove along the middle; bluish white to white and glabrous beneath with a distinctly prominent, broad midrib

**Arrangement on the shoot:** Leaves opposite; each pair of leaves at right-angles to the next

**Distribution:** In the subalpine and alpine zone; on scree, rocks, ridges exposed to the wind, and on moors dominated by dwarf shrubs; a calcifuge mountain plant

929　*Loiseleuria procumbens* – **Trailing Azalea** *Prostrate, evergreen dwarf shrub forming tufts, with stems 15–40cm in length*

### Andromeda polifolia L.
## Bog Rosemary
Ericaceae – Heath family  p. 92

**Length:** 1–5cm

**Form of blade:** Narrowly lanceolate or narrowly linear in outline and leathery

**Stalk:** 0.3–0.7cm long and usually white

**End of leaf:** With a fine or sharp point

**Base of blade:** Narrowly wedge-shaped

**Margin of leaf:** Entire; margins rolled under

**Upper/under side:** Shiny dark green above, with an irregular pattern of white lateral veins; silvery white or pale bluish green beneath with a prominent white midrib

**Arrangement on the shoot:** Leaves alternate

**Distribution:** From the hill to the subalpine zone; on raised bogs and wet, acid peat moors lacking in nutrients; a plant characteristic of peat-bogs and moorland

930　*Andromeda polifolia* – **Bog Rosemary**
*Evergreen shrub, 10–20cm high, with creeping stems growing into the tussocks on raised bogs*

### Rosmarinus officinalis L.
## Rosemary
Labiatae – Mint family  p. 92

**Length:** 3–5cm

**Form of blade:** Very narrowly lanceolate or linear in outline and leathery

**Stalk:** Leaf sessile or very shortly stalked; stalk densely felted with stellate hairs

**End of leaf:** Obtuse or rounded

**Base of blade:** Narrowly wedge-shaped

**Margin of leaf:** Entire; margins rolled under

**Upper/under side:** Dark green above and slightly wrinkled; densely white-felted beneath; midrib prominent and white

**Arrangement on the shoot:** Leaves opposite, each pair at right-angles to the next

**Distribution:** In the warmer parts of the hill zone with a mild winter climate; a plant typical of the maquis and rocky steppes; particularly abundant in the Mediterranean region; Rosemary has been known since ancient times as an aromatic culinary and medicinal plant

931　*Rosmarinus officinalis* – **Rosemary**
*Evergreen, sweetly scented shrub, with grey-felted stems growing up to 1.5m high*

## Vaccinium oxycoccus L.
## Cranberry
**Ericaceae - Heath family** p. 92

**Length:** 0.5–1cm (at most 1.5cm)

**Form of blade:** Elliptic, ovate or oblong-ovate in outline

**Stalk:** At most 2mm long

**End of leaf:** Obtuse or shortly pointed

**Base of blade:** Rounded or weakly heart-shaped

**Margin of leaf:** Entire; margins recurved

**Upper/under side:** Shiny dark green above, glabrous, and usually with a pale green, slightly impressed midrib; with a bluish green bloom beneath

**Arrangement on the shoot:** Leaves alternate

**Distribution:** From the hill to the montane zone; forming the surface covering of raised bogs; particularly on the tussocks on peat-moors where it grows with Bog Rosemary and Sundew

932  **Vaccinium oxycoccus – Cranberry**
*Prostrate, evergreen half-shrub with creeping stems up to 80cm long and becoming woody*

## Calluna vulgaris (L.) Hull
## Ling, Heather
**Ericaceae - Heath family** p. 92

**Length:** 1–3mm long

**Form of blade:** Needle-like or narrowly ovate in outline, or scale-like

**Stalk:** Leaves sessile

**End of leaf:** Usually rounded

**Base of blade:** Clasping the stem, and with 2 pointed auricles, glandular on the margin and pointing downwards

**Margin of leaf:** Entire; margins curved upwards, the fringe of short hairs forming a white band

**Upper/under side:** Dark green in summer, brownish red in winter; deeply grooved above, keeled beneath and glabrous or slightly hairy

**Arrangement on the shoot:** Leaves opposite, each pair at right-angles to the next; overlapping each other and forming 4 longitudinal rows

**Distribution:** From the hill up into the alpine zone; characteristic of European heaths and moorlands; on moors and heaths, in dry and open woods and on sandy dunes

933  **Calluna vulgaris – Ling**
*Evergreen, much-branched shrub 20–60cm high, with stems 4-angled at first*

## Genista pilosa L.
## Hairy Greenweed
**Leguminosae - Pea family** p. 93

**Length:** 0.3–1.2cm long

**Form of blade:** Narrowly obovate to lanceolate in outline

**Stalk:** Leaf sessile or very shortly stalked

**End of leaf:** Emarginate or retuse

**Base of blade:** Wedge-shaped

**Margin of leaf:** Entire

**Upper/under side:** Dark green on both sides with short, appressed hairs; older leaves sometimes glabrous; midrib beneath pale green in colour

**Arrangement on the shoot:** Leaves alternate

**Distribution:** In the hill zone; on sandy, stony and sunny heaths on poor soils usually lacking in calcium, in open woods, on crags and at the edges of woods; especially in sunny, dry places, warm in summer; ascending to 1100m in the Black Forest

934  **Genista pilosa – Hairy Greenweed**
*Deciduous dwarf shrub, 10–30cm high, with finely hairy, angular stems*

## Daphne cneorum L.
## Garland Flower
**Thymelaeaceae - Daphne family** p. 93

**Length:** 0.5–2cm

**Form of blade:** Linear, lanceolate or spathulate in outline

**Stalk:** Very short and broad

**End of leaf:** Emarginate, or rounded with a small point

**Base of blade:** Wedge-shaped

**Margin of leaf:** Entire; slightly recurved

**Upper/under side:** Both sides glabrous; medium to dark green above with pale yellowish green veins; bluish grey beneath; midrib dark green and prominent, lateral veins whitish

**Arrangement on the shoot:** Leaves alternate

**Distribution:** From the hill to the montane zone, more rarely subalpine; on the edges of woods, on stony slopes, in open, dry pine woods, and in alpine meadows

935  **Daphne cneorum – Garland Flower**
*Evergreen shrub, 10–40cm high, with creeping stems and hairy young shoots*

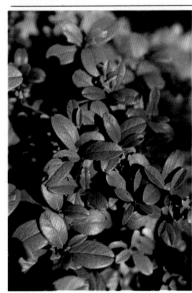

## Vaccinium vitis-idaea L.
## Cowberry
**Ericaceae - Heath family** p. 92

**Length:** 1–3cm

**Form of blade:** Elliptic to obovate in outline; leaves thick and leathery

**Stalk:** 0.2–0.5cm long, with downy hairs

**End of leaf:** Usually emarginate

**Base of blade:** Obtuse or wedge-shaped

**Margin of leaf:** Entire; margins slightly recurved; also finely dentate or crenate

**Upper/under side:** Dark green above with whitish veins; greyish green beneath with small, brown glandular hairs (therefore appearing dotted)

**Arrangement on the shoot:** Leaves alternate

**Distribution:** From the hill to the alpine zone; on raw humus in open Spruce, Pine and Larch woods, Juniper thickets, dwarf shrub communities, heaths and moors

936  **Vaccinium vitis-idaea – Cowberry**
*Evergreen, dwarf shrub, 10–30cm high, with creeping, scaly, underground stems*

## Buxus sempervirens L.
## Box
**Buxaceae - Box family** p. 92

**Length:** 1–3cm

**Form of blade:** Narrowly elliptic to oblong-ovate; broadest at or slightly below the middle; blade leathery

**Stalk:** Up to 2mm long, often slightly winged because of the narrowed base of the blade

**End of leaf:** Usually emarginate, more rarely rounded

**Base of blade:** Wedge-shaped

**Margin of leaf:** Entire; margins slightly recurved

**Upper/under side:** Shiny dark green above and the midrib often whitish and impressed; pale green beneath and midrib prominent

**Arrangement on the shoot:** Leaves opposite

**Distribution:** From the hill to the montane zone; ascending to 2000m in Greece; found here and there in warm places such as mixed deciduous woods and dry meadows; widely cultivated as a park and garden plant

937  **Buxus sempervirens – Box**
*Evergreen, densely branched shrub or tree up to 16m high with stems 4-angled at first*

### *Salix reticulata* L.
### Net-leaved Willow
Salicaceae – Willow family p. 93

**Length:** 1–4.5cm

**Form of blade:** Broadly elliptic to roundish in outline

**Stalk:** 0.3–2cm long and both sides reddish in colour

**End of leaf:** Obtuse or rounded

**Base of blade:** Broadly wedge-shaped or rounded

**Margin of leaf:** Entire

**Upper/under side:** Dark green above, hairy at first, later glabrous, with impressed veins forming a network; grey to whitish green beneath with prominent veins; margins slightly recurved

**Arrangement on the shoot:** Leaves alternate

**Distribution:** In the subalpine and alpine zone on mountain ledges and rocks, and in snow-hollows; also in the lowlands of N. Europe; a pioneer shrub

938 **Salix reticulata – Net-leaved Willow**
*Deciduous, mat-forming dwarf shrub with round stems 5–30cm long*

### *Vaccinium uliginosum* L.
### Northern Bilberry
Ericaceae – Heath family p. 94

**Length:** 0.5–2cm

**Form of blade:** Elliptic, obovate or roundish in outline, and thick

**Stalk:** 1–2mm long and often slightly grooved above

**End of leaf:** Usually rounded; more rarely weakly retuse or obtuse

**Base of blade:** Rounded or broadly wedge-shaped

**Margin of leaf:** Entire

**Upper/under side:** Both sides glabrous; medium green above and bluish green beneath, with prominent dark green veins and slightly hairy at first

**Arrangement on the shoot:** Leaves alternate

**Distribution:** From the hill to the subalpine zone, on moors together with birches, pines and heather, in open conifer woods and in dwarf shrub communities on high mountains

939 **Vaccinium uliginosum – Northern Bilberry** *Deciduous shrub, 15–90cm high, with stems creeping underground in raw humus*

### *Salix retusa* L.
### Blunt-leaved Willow
Salicaceae – Willow family p. 94

**Length:** 0.4–2cm

**Form of blade:** Obovate to oblong-ovate or spathulate in outline

**Stalk:** 2–5mm long

**End of leaf:** Rounded, obtuse or emarginate

**Base of blade:** Wedge-shaped

**Margin of leaf:** Entire; more rarely with a few small teeth

**Upper/under side:** Shiny medium to dark green above and glabrous; slightly hairy beneath when young, later glabrous and shiny medium to whitish green

**Arrangement on the shoot:** Leaves alternate

**Distribution:** In the subalpine and alpine zone, on damp rock-ledges, on boulders, alluvial land, and in north-facing places with 8–10 months' snow-cover (a characteristic plant of wetland communities)

940 **Salix retusa – Blunt-leaved Willow**
*Deciduous, low-growing shrub, with creeping stems 5–30cm long*

### *Ruscus aculeatus* L.
### Butcher's Broom
Liliaceae – Lily family p. 94

**Length:** Flattened shoot (cladode) 1–4cm long

**Form of blade:** True leaves only a few mm long, scale-like, soon withering but remaining on the plant; cladode pointed elliptic to pointed ovate in outline

**Stalk:** Base of cladode 1–3mm long

**End of leaf:** Tip of cladode long and finely pointed, ending in a spine

**Base of blade:** Base of cladode wedge-shaped

**Margin of leaf:** Entire

**Upper/under side:** Both sides medium green with dark green parallel veins; very often keeled beneath

**Arrangement on the shoot:** Leaf-like shoots alternately arranged

**Distribution:** In the hill and montane zone; on south-facing slopes in the warmest parts of the foothills of the Jura, in the southern Alps and in the Mediterranean region

941 **Ruscus aculeatus – Butcher's Broom** *Spiny, evergreen shrub, 40–80cm high, with green stems*

### *Ginkgo biloba* L.
### Maidenhair tree
Ginkgoaceae – Ginkgo family p. 93

**Length:** 6–10cm

**Form of blade:** Fan-shaped in outline, the upper edge irregularly waved or deeply divided into several lobes

**Stalk:** 2–9cm long

**End of leaf:** Fan-shaped, with an irregularly undulate margin

**Base of blade:** Obtuse or broadly wedge-shaped

**Margin of leaf:** Entire; upper edge wavy

**Upper/under side:** Both sides glabrous and medium to dark green; veins finely forked

**Arrangement on the shoot:** Rosette-like clusters of 3–6 on short shoots, alternately arranged on long shoots

**Distribution:** Decorative park and street tree, native in China; all the trees planted in Europe (since 1730) are derived from trees in E. Asian temple gardens

942 **Ginkgo biloba – Maidenhair Tree**
*Deciduous, 30–40m high, with several more or less erect branches forming acute angle with trunk*

### *Cercis siliquastrum* L.
### Judas Tree
Leguminosae – Pea family p. 93

**Length:** 6–11cm long and equally broad

**Form of blade:** Almost circular in outline

**Stalk:** 3–4.5cm long and coloured red on both sides

**End of leaf:** Rounded or weakly emarginate

**Base of blade:** Heart-shaped

**Margin of leaf:** Entire; occasionally with shallow sinuses

**Upper/under side:** Both sides glabrous; dark green above and bluish green beneath; main veins pale green beneath and prominent

**Arrangement on the shoot:** Leaves alternate

**Distribution:** In the hill zone; in Hop Hornbeam and Oriental Hornbeam woods and in wooded parts of south-facing slopes; found wild especially in the Mediterranean region; also planted there as a street tree

943 **Cercis siliquastrum – Judas Tree** *Deciduous tree up to 10m high (in gardens and parks sometimes only forming a shrub)*

## Fagus sylvatica L.
### 'Atropunicea'
### Copper Beech

**Fagaceae – Beech family** p. 94

**Length:** 5–10cm

**Form of blade:** Broadly elliptic to obovate in outline; broadest at or above the middle

**Stalk:** 0.2–0.5cm long and dark red to blackish in colour

**End of leaf:** Shortly pointed

**Base of blade:** Broadly wedge-shaped or rounded

**Margin of leaf:** Entire, often slightly undulate

**Upper/under side:** Softly hairy when young and fringed with hairs on the margin; older leaves often glabrous; dark purple to black above and dark greenish purple to blackish beneath; veins prominent; lateral veins more or less parallel to each other

**Arrangement on the shoot:** Leaves alternate (fomring 2 ranks)

**Distribution:** Planted in large gardens and parks

944   **Fagus sylvatica 'Atropunicea' – Copper Beech** Deciduous tree up to 40m high with dark brown twigs

## Eucalyptus globulus Labill.
### Blue Gum

**Myrtaceae – Myrtle family** p. 95

**Length:** 7–15cm

**Form of blade:** Juvenile leaves broadly lanceolate to ovate in outline and usually spreading

**Stalk:** Juvenile leaves sessile or very shortly stalked

**End of leaf:** Pointed, sometimes sharply

**Base of blade:** Weakly heart-shaped

**Margin of leaf:** Entire

**Upper/under side:** Juvenile leaves glabrous on both sides; dark green to bluish green above and often with a pale purple or whitish midrib; dark green to bluish grey beneath

**Arrangement on the shoot:** Juvenile leaves on young shoots opposite and spreading horizontally; adult leaves arranged alternately and hanging down

**Distribution:** Planted in the whole Mediterranean region, largely for the drainage of wet areas; grows up to 36m high in southern England

945   **Eucalyptus globulus – Blue Gum** Evergreen tree up to 45m high with slender shoots, somewhat angular in cross-section

## Hippophae rhamnoides L.
### Sea Buckthorn

**Elaeagnaceae – Oleaster family** p. 95

**Length:** 5–7cm

**Form of blade:** Linear to lanceolate in outline

**Stalk:** Leaf sessile or with a white stalk 1–3mm long

**End of leaf:** Obtuse or pointed

**Base of blade:** Wedge-shaped

**Margin of leaf:** Entire; often slightly recurved

**Upper/under side:** Shiny, silvery scales on both sides; greyish green above with scattered scales; silvery white beneath; lateral veins barely or only indistinctly visible

**Arrangement on the shoot:** Leaves alternate

**Distribution:** From the hill to the montane zone; on warm slopes, on river-banks, by pathways, in gravel-pits, open pine woods and on scree; a pioneer shrub of open places

946   **Hippophae rhamnoides – Sea Buckthorn** Deciduous, spiny, densely branched shrub or tree up to 8m in height

## Elaeagnus angustifolia L.
### Oleaster

**Elaeagnaceae – Oleaster family** p. 95

**Length:** 4–8cm

**Form of blade:** Narrowly lanceolate in outline

**Stalk:** 4–9mm long, white

**End of leaf:** Somewhat pointed, obtuse or rounded

**Base of blade:** Wedge-shaped; often slightly rounded

**Margin of leaf:** Entire

**Uper/under side:** Dull to dark green above with silvery scales; densely stellate-hairy beneath and therefore appearing greyish white

**Arrangement on the shoot:** Leaves alternate and close together

**Distribution:** In the hill zone on the banks of rivers and lakes, on coasts, stony hills, river-beds, dunes and damp woods; often in association with Sea Buckthorn and Tamarisk; an ornamental shrub in W. and central Europe

947   **Elaeagnus angustifolia – Oleaster** Deciduous, somewhat spiny shrub or small tree, 2–7m high

## Eucalyptus globulus Labill.
### Blue Gum

**Myrtaceae – Myrtle family** p. 95

**Length:** Adult leaves 10–30cm

**Form of blade:** Adult leaves narrowly lanceolate in outline, slightly crescent-shaped, thick and pendent

**Stalk:** 1–5cm long and often slightly reddish

**End of leaf:** With a long point

**Base of blade:** Broadly wedge-shaped or rounded

**Margin of leaf:** Entire

**Upper/under side:** Both sides glabrous; dark green above and often somewhat bluish green beneath

**Arrangement on the shoot:** Leaves alternate; juvenile leaves, by contrast, opposite

**Distribution:** Used for afforestation in tropical America, S. China, California, Australia and New Zealand; planted in the Mediterranean region because of its rapid growth (3–10m per year according to the climate); wood not very hard

948   **Eucalyptus globulus – Blue Gum** Evergreen tree up to 45m high (up to 65m in its native habitat) with pendent adult leaves

## Daphne laureola L.
### Spurge Laurel

**Thymelaeaceae – Daphne family** p. 96

**Length:** 6–14cm

**Form of blade:** Narrowly obovate in outline with the greatest breadth always above the middle

**Stalk:** Without a stalk, or with only a very short one

**End of leaf:** Shortly pointed

**Base of blade:** Wedge-shaped and narrowed downwards so that the stalk is often suppressed

**Margin of leaf:** Entire

**Upper/under side:** Shiny dark green above with the midrib clearly impressed; pale green beneath with the midrib distinctly prominent; both sides glabrous

**Arrangement on the shoot:** Leaves alternate

**Distribution:** From the hill to the montane zone; in fairly warm, not too dry places which are mild in winter; in beech, oak and mixed oak-hornbeam woods with luxuriant vegetation

949   **Daphne laureola – Spurge Laurel** Deciduous shrub up to 1.2m high, only slightly branched, with shoots green at first

## Daphne mezereum L.
### Mezereon

Thymelaeaceae – Daphne
family p. 95

**Length:** 3–8cm

**Form of blade:** Oblanceolate in
outline; with the greatest breadth
above the middle; leaves soft to the
touch

**Stalk:** Very small, between 0.3cm
and 0.5cm long

**End of leaf:** Shortly pointed

**Base of blade:** Wedge-shaped,
narrowing in the short stalk

**Margin of leaf:** Entire; margins level
or slightly recurved, glabrous or
slightly hairy

**Upper/under side:** Both sides
glabrous; dark green above and
greyish green beneath

**Arrangement on the shoot:** Leaves
alternate, and clustered at the ends
of the stems

**Distribution:** From the hill to the
subalpine zone; in mixed beech
woods with rich vegetation, on
grassland with tall-herb communities,
in clearings, on scree and by
watercourses

950    *Daphne mezereum* – Mezereon
*Deciduous, weakly branched shrub, 30–120cm
high; young shoots with silvery hairs*

## Daphne alpina L.
### Alpine Mezereon

Thymelaeaceae – Daphne
family p. 96

**Length:** 1–5cm

**Form of blade:** Lanceolate to
narrowly obovate in outline; with the
greatest breadth at or above the
middle

**Stalk:** Leaves usually sessile

**End of leaf:** Obtuse or rounded

**Base of blade:** Narrowly wedge-
shaped narrowing to the leaf-base

**Margin of leaf:** Entire; finely hairy

**Upper/under side:** Both sides hairy
when young and therefore soft to the
touch; later dull dark green above
with only a few appressed hairs
remaining; greyish green beneath,
remaining slightly hairy

**Arrangement on the shoot:** Leaves
clustered at the ends of the stems

**Distribution:** From the hill to the
subalpine zone; in the warmer places
on crags, rocks and walls

951    *Daphne alpina* – Alpine Mezereon
*Deciduous shrub, 15–120cm high, with twigs
finely hairy at first*

## Viscum album L.
### Mistletoe

Loranthaceae – Mistletoe family
p. 96

**Length:** 2–6.5cm

**Form of blade:** Spathulate, narrowly
obovate or narrowly elliptic in outline

**Stalk:** Leaves sessile

**End of leaf:** Rounded

**Base of blade:** Wedge-shaped

**Margin of leaf:** Entire

**Upper/under side:** Both sides
yellowish green, glabrous and
parallel-veined; leaves more
yellowish in winter

**Arrangement on the shoot:** Leaves
opposite, at the ends of the forked
stems

**Distribution:** Growing on trees; from
the hill to the montane zone

**1st form:** On deciduous trees such
as poplar, willow, birch, hornbeam,
chestnut and lime

**2nd form:** On fir

**3rd form:** On pine and spruce

952    *Viscus album* – Mistletoe
*Evergreen shrub, almost globular, up to 1m
across, with forked stems*

## Punica granatum L.
### Pomegranate

Punicaceae – Pomegranate
family p. 96

**Length:** 3–8cm

**Form of blade:** Oblong-elliptic in
outline

**Stalk:** 0.1–0.5cm long and usually
reddish above

**End of leaf:** Obtuse or rounded

**Base of blade:** Wedge-shaped

**Margin of leaf:** Entire

**Upper/under side:** Both sides
glabrous; dark green above and with
a clearly impressed midrib; pale
green beneath with the midrib
distinctly prominent

**Arrangement on the shoot:** Leaves
opposite; sometimes alternate on
young shoots

**Distribution:** On sunny, stony slopes
in mixed Oriental Beech woods in
S.E. Europe; native in Iran and
adjacent countries and cultivated
since ancient times; found today in
the whole of the Mediterranean
region north to the Valais and S. Tyrol

953    *Punica granatum* – Pomegranate
*Deciduous, spiny shrub or tree 1–5m high with
shoots 4-angled at first*

## Prunus laurocerasus L.
### Cherry Laurel

Rosaceae – Rose family p. 97

**Length:** 10–25cm

**Form of blade:** Oblong-elliptic to
oblong-obovate in outline; stiff,
leathery and thick; usually with 4
glands in the lower part of the blade

**Stalk:** 0.5–1cm long

**End of leaf:** With a short, narrow
point

**Base of blade:** Narrowly wedge-
shaped

**Margin of leaf:** Entire; margins
slightly recurved

**Upper/under side:** Both sides
glabrous dark green above and shiny
as if varnished; pale green beneath

**Arrangement on the shoot:** Leaves
alternate

**Distribution:** In the hill zone; planted
in gardens, parks and cemeteries;
cultivated in central Europe since the
15th century; as undergrowth in open
oak woods, in thickets, on stony
slopes and walls; native in S.E.
Europe

954    *Prunus laurocerasus* – Cherry Laurel
*Evergreen shrub or small tree, 2–8m high, young
shoots glabrous and green*

## Rhododendron luteum
Sweet
### Yellow Rhododendron

Ericaceae – Heath family p. 97

**Length:** 6–12cm

**Form of blade:** Oblong-lanceolate in
outline

**Stalk:** 0.5–1.5cm long

**End of leaf:** Pointed

**Base of blade:** Narrowly wedge-
shaped

**Margin of leaf:** Entire; fringed with
fine hairs

**Upper/under side:** With grey hairs
on both sides when young; medium
green above and slightly undulate;
greyish medium green beneath and
later only sparingly hairy

**Arrangement on the shoot:** Leaves
alternate

**Distribution:** Native in E. Europe;
planted in gardens and parks; a
vigorous, hardy plant of great value;
one of the parents of numerous
garden hybrids

955    *Rhododendron luteum* – Yellow
Rhododendron
*Deciduous shrub, 1–4m high and broad; young
growth sticky with matted glandular hairs*

## Ligustrum vulgare L.
### Wild Privet
**Oleaceae - Olive family** p. 98

**Length:** 3-7cm

**Form of blade:** Lanceolate to oblong-elliptic in outline

**Stalk:** 0.5-1.5cm long

**End of leaf:** Pointed

**Base of blade:** Wedge-shaped

**Margin of leaf:** Entire

**Upper/under side:** Both sides glabrous; medium to dark green above; somewhat paler green beneath with a distinctly prominent midrib

**Arrangement on the shoot:** Leaves opposite or in whorls of 3

**Distribution:** In the hill zone; in open deciduous and Pine woods, thickets, hedges, in sunny groves, on the edges of woods, banks, walls and in fields on poor soils; the genus is mainly distributed in S. and E. Asia; the only species native in Europe is the Wild Privet

**956    Ligustrum vulgare - Wild Privet**
*Deciduous shrub, 4-7m high, with the young shoots finely hairy*

## Olea europaea L.
### Olive
**Oleaceae - Olive family** p. 98

**Length:** 4-7cm

**Form of blade:** Lanceolate in outline, thick and leathery

**Stalk:** 0.2-0.6cm long

**End of leaf:** Tapering often to a small, sharp point

**Base of blade:** Wedge-shaped

**Margin of leaf:** Entire; margins often slightly wavy

**Upper/under side:** Dull dark green to greyish green above and almost glabrous; greyish white to silvery grey beneath; covered with scale-like hairs

**Arrangement on the shoot:** Leaves opposite

**Distribution:** Originally a Mediterranean plant; spread by cultivation throughout all the warmer regions of the world. Since ancient times the Olive has played an important part in religious rites. The cultivation of the Olive is thought to have originated with the Semitic-Hamitic races

**957    Olea europaea - Olive**
*Evergreen shrub or small tree, 2-10m high, with greyish green branchlets*

## Pyrus salicifolia Pall.
### Willow-leaved Pear
**Rosaceae - Rose family** p. 97

**Length:** 3-9cm

**Form of blade:** Narrowly elliptic in outline

**Stalk:** 1-4cm long

**End of leaf:** Obtuse or pointed

**Base of blade:** Narrowly wedge-shaped

**Margin of leaf:** Entire as a rule; occasionally with a few small teeth

**Upper/under side:** With silvery grey hairs on both sides when young; later medium to dark green above and more or less glabrous; greyish white hairs remaining beneath

**Arrangement on the shoot:** Leaves alternate; clustered on short shoots; short shoots often ending in a spine

**Distribution:** Native in mixed deciduous woods in the Caucasus and Asia Minor; often planted in European gardens as an ornamental tree

**958    Pyrus salicifolia - Willow-leaved Pear**
*Deciduous, 5-8m high, with pendent branches and young branchlets densely grey-felted*

## Nerium oleander L.
### Oleander
**Apocynaceae - Periwinkle family** p. 98

**Length:** 6-15cm

**Form of blade:** Linear-lanceolate in outline

**Stalk:** 0.3-0.7cm long; blade narrowed into the stalk

**End of leaf:** Pointed

**Base of blade:** Wedge-shaped

**Margin of leaf:** Entire; margins slightly recurved

**Upper/under side:** Medium to dark green and glabrous above; greyish or pale green beneath, sparsely hairy or glabrous and with a distinctly prominent midrib; lateral veins numerous, close together, and parallel to each other

**Arrangement on the shoot:** Leaves in whorls of 3 or 4; more rarely opposite

**Distribution:** Frequent in dry river-beds, on gravel soils, and on stony slopes in the Mediterranean region; cultivation of the Oleander is only possible in the mildest areas; a winter temperature of 5-8°C is necessary for proper flower-formation

**959    Nerium oleander - Oleander**
*Erect, bushy, evergreen shrub, 2-6m high, with dark green stems*

## Rhododendron ponticum L.
### Rhododendron
**Ericaceae - Heath family** p. 97

**Length:** 8-15cm

**Form of blade:** Oblong-lanceolate to oblong-elliptic in outline

**Stalk:** 1-3cm long

**End of leaf:** Shortly pointed

**Base of blade:** Narrowly wedge-shaped

**Margin of leaf:** Entire; margins often slightly recurved

**Upper/under side:** Dark green above with a pale green midrib; pale green beneath with a distinctly prominent midrib; both sides glabrous

**Arrangement on the shoot:** Leaves alternate

**Distribution:** Native from Spain and Portugal to Asia Minor; used as a rootstock in hybridisation; hardy, and therefore occasionally planted in parks and gardens in central Europe

**960    Rhododendron ponticum - Rhododendron**
*Evergreen shrub or small tree 3-5m high, with young branchlets covered with sticky hairs*

## Laurus nobilis L.
### Laurel
**Lauraceae - Laurel family** p. 97

**Length:** 5-12cm

**Form of blade:** Oblong-lanceolate to narrowly elliptic in outline

**Stalk:** 1-4cm long and usually reddish in colour

**End of leaf:** Pointed

**Base of blade:** Wedge-shaped

**Margin of leaf:** Entire, with margins slightly wavy; more rarely slightly crenate

**Upper/under side:** Both sides glabrous; medium to dark green above and pale green beneath; lower part of midrib beneath often reddish

**Arrangement on the shoot:** Leaves alternate

**Distribution:** In the hill zone; on stony slopes and in open woods; cultivated especially in the Mediterranean region; native in Asia Minor; a dominant species in evergreen woods in the Mediterranean region; cultivated in entrance halls and winter gardens since the time of Louis XIV

**961    Laurus nobilis - Laurel**
*Evergreen shrub or tree, 1-8m high, with young shoots reddish green and glabrous*

962 **Arctostaphylos ura-ursi – Bearberry**
*Evergreen, much branched dwarf shrub, forming large, dense mats*

### Arctostaphylos uva-ursi
(L.) Spreng.
## Bearberry
**Ericaceae – Heath family** p. 99

**Length:** 1–3cm

**Form of blade:** Obovate or obovate-oblong in outline, with the greatest breadth above the middle, leathery and thick

**Stalk:** 1–3mm long with white hairs

**End of leaf:** Obtuse or more rarely slightly emarginate

**Base of blade:** Wedge-shaped

**Margin of leaf:** Entire, and densely fringed with fine white hairs

**Upper/under side:** Both sides glabrous with an indistinct network of veins; dark green above with a clearly visible pale green midrib; with a dense network of dark green veins beneath

**Arrangement on the shoot:** Leaves alternate

**Distribution:** From the hill to the alpine zone; in open pine woods, on loamy soils in association with heather and above the tree-line into the dwarf shrub region

963 **Syringa vulgaris – Lilac**
*Deciduous shrub or small tree, 2–8m high, with straight, glabrous, olive green stems*

### Syringa vulgaris L.
## Lilac
**Oleaceae – Olive family** p. 98

**Length:** 5–10cm

**Form of blade:** Pointed ovate or pointed elliptic in outline

**Stalk:** 1–3cm long

**End of leaf:** With a long point

**Base of blade:** Truncate or heart-shaped

**Margin of leaf:** Entire

**Upper/under side:** Both sides glabrous; dark green above, paler bluish green beneath

**Arrangement on the shoot:** Leaves opposite

**Distribution:** From the hill to the montane zone; many forms and hybrids cultivated in Europe since the 16th century; found in S.E. Europe on rocky slopes in sun or half shade, in thickets, in open woods and on the edges of woods; the Common Lilac was brought from Constantinople to Vienna about 1560 by the ambassador Busbecq, and spread quickly throughout central Europe

964 **Catalpa bignonioides – Indian Bean Tree** *Deciduous tree up to 15m high with a short, cylindrical trunk*

### Catalpa bignonioides Walt.
## Indian Bean Tree
**Bignoniaceae – Bignonia family** p. 98

**Length:** 10–20cm long and often equally broad

**Form of blade:** Broadly ovate to heart-shaped

**Stalk:** 7–15cm long

**End of leaf:** With a long, fine point on a short, abrupt point

**Base of blade:** Weakly heart-shaped or truncate

**Margin of leaf:** Entire; more rarely with indistinct lateral lobes

**Upper/under side:** Medium to dark green above; paler green beneath and softly hairy; pleasantly scented when rubbed; veins beneath distinctly prominent

**Arrangement on the shoot:** Leaves opposite or in whorls of 3

**Distribution:** Native only in S.E. United States; frequently planted as an ornamental tree in large gardens and parks

965 **Catalpa ovata – Yellow Catalpa**
*Deciduous tree, native in China, up to 10m high, with mainly glabrous branchlets*

### Catalpa ovata G. Don et Zucc.
## Yellow catalpa
**Bignoniaceae – Bignonia family** p. 98

**Length:** 10–25cm

**Form of blade:** Varied in outline; broadly ovate or heart-shaped

**Stalk:** 4–10cm long, hairy at first, later becoming glabrous; often darker coloured above; green beneath

**End of leaf:** With a tapering point or a short, abrupt point

**Base of blade:** Usually heart-shaped

**Margin of leaf:** Entire, and usually fringed with fine hairs

**Upper/under side:** Medium to dark green above with fine, soft hairs; pale to medium green beneath and only slightly rough to the touch; veins distinctly yellowish green and prominent; reddish black glandular spots in the axils of the veins

**Arrangement on the shoot:** Leaves opposite or alternate

**Distribution:** Planted as an ornamental tree in large gardens and parks

966 **Magnolia hypoleuca – Japanese Big-leaved Magnolia**
*Deciduous tree up to 30m high with a broad crown and light to dark brown branchlets*

### Magnolia hypoleuca
Sieb. et Zucc. (*M. obovata* Thunb.)
## Japanese Big-leaved Magnolia
**Magnoliaceae – Magnolia family** p. 99

**Length:** 20–40cm

**Form of blade:** Obovate in outline gradually narrowing to the base

**Stalk:** 3–8cm long

**End of leaf:** Rounded with a short, abrupt point

**Base of blade:** Wedge-shaped, often somewhat rounded at the base

**Margin of leaf:** Entire

**Upper/under side:** Pale to medium green and glabrous above, pale bluish green and slightly hairy beneath

**Arrangement on the shoot:** Leaves alternate, but clustered at the ends of the shoots

**Distribution:** A large-leaved Magnolia, native in Japan, occasionally planted in European gardens and parks

967 **Cydonia oblonga – Quince**
*Deciduous shrub or small tree, 1–8m high; young branchlets felted*

### Cydonia oblonga Mill.
## Quince
**Rosaceae – Rose family** p. 99

**Length:** 5–10cm

**Form of blade:** Elliptic to broadly ovate in outline

**Stalk:** 1–2cm long and felted

**End of leaf:** Obtuse, shortly rounded or weakly pointed

**Base of blade:** Usually rounded, more rarely heart-shaped

**Margin of leaf:** Entire; slightly grey-felted on the margins

**Upper/under side:** Dark green and usually glabrous above; grey-felted beneath, with the hairs densely interwoven

**Arrangement on the shoot:** Leaves alternate

**Distribution:** From the hill to the montane zone; a valuable fruit-tree, numerous large-fruited forms being cultivated in gardens, parks and orchards, rarely escaping and becoming naturalised on sunny slopes, at the edges of woods and in thickets; the quince prefers deep, dry, calcareous soils

### *Cotoneaster integerrimus*
Medic.
## Common Cotoneaster
**Rosaceae - Rose family** p. 100

**Length:** 2-4cm

**Form of blade:** Broadly elliptic, ovate or roundish in outline

**Stalk:** 0.3-0.6mm long and finely hairy

**End of leaf:** Obtuse or pointed; usually with a sharp point

**Base of blade:** Wedge-shaped, obtuse or rounded

**Margin of leaf:** Entire; margins with very long, fine hairs

**Upper/under side:** Dark green and glabrous above; with dense white or yellowish grey matted hairs beneath and therefore appearing greyish green in colour

**Arrangement on the shoot:** Leaves alternate

**Distribution:** From the lowlands up into the subalpine zone; in the warmer places in rock crevices, woods, thickets, on sunny crags and in dwarf shrub communities

### *Cotoneaster tomentosus*
(Ait.) Lindl.
## Cotoneaster
**Rosaceae - Rose family** p. 100

**Length:** 3-6cm; slightly larger than the leaves of the Common Cotoneaster

**Form of blade:** Elliptic to broadly ovate in outline

**Stalk:** 0.2-0.7mm long and densely felted

**End of leaf:** Obtuse, more rarely rounded; occasionally with a small point

**Base of blade:** Weakly heart-shaped, rounded or obtuse

**Margin of leaf:** Entire

**Upper/under side:** Dark green and loosely hairy above; densely felted beneath and therefore appearing grey to white

**Arrangement on the shoot:** Leaves alternate

**Distribution:** From the lowlands up into the subalpine zone; on the edges of woods and thickets, in half shaded or sunny places in open oak and mixed woods which are warm in summer

968 *Cotoneaster integerrimus* - **Common Cotoneaster** *Deciduous, bushy, much-branched shrub, 1-2m high; shoots hairy at first*

969 *Cotoneaster tomentosus* - **Cotoneaster** *Deciduous, only moderately branched shrub with stems up to 5m long, grey-felted at first*

### *Pyrus nivalis* Jacq.
## Snow Pear
**Rosaceae - Rose family** p. 99

**Length:** 6-10cm

**Form of blade:** Obovate in outline

**Stalk:** 1-3cm long and covered in a white felt

**End of leaf:** Pointed, or rounded and with a short, abrupt point

**Base of blade:** Wedge-shaped

**Margin of leaf:** Entire and fringed with downy hairs

**Upper/under side:** Dark green above with matted hairs; veins white and clearly visible; densely felted beneath and therefore appearing greyish green

**Arrangement on the shoot:** Leaves alternate

**Distribution:** From the hill to the montane zone; in places mild in winter; distributed especially in S. Europe

### *Cornus controversa* Hemsl.
## Table Dogwood
**Cornaceae - Dogwood family** p. 100

**Length:** 7-12cm

**Form of blade:** Ovate or broadly ovate in outline

**Stalk:** 1-3cm long

**End of leaf:** With a short or long point

**Base of blade:** Wedge-shaped, truncate or rounded

**Margin of leaf:** Entire

**Upper/under side:** Dark green above with impressed, clearly visible, primary or secondary veins; bluish grey beneath and finely hairy on the distinctly prominent veins; 6-9 pairs of lateral veins

**Arrangement on the shoot:** Leaves alternate

**Distribution:** A tree native in Japan and China; planted in Europe in parks and large gardens

970 *Pyrus nivalis* - **Snow Pear** *Deciduous tree up to 10m high with young shoots white-felted*

971 *Cornus controversa* - **Table Dogwood** *Deciduous tree up to 20m high (sometimes a shrub) with shoots brownish green at first*

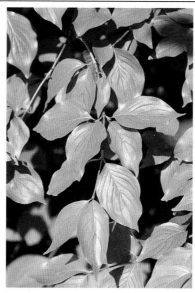

### *Cornus sanguinea* L.
## Dogwood
**Cornaceae - Dogwood family** p. 100

**Length:** 4-10cm

**Form of blade:** Elliptic to broadly ovate in outline

**Stalk:** 0.5-1.5cm long, usually dark red above and grooved

**End of leaf:** Pointed, often with a short abrupt point

**Base of blade:** Usually rounded, more rarely truncate or wedge-shaped

**Margin of leaf:** Entire; often slightly wavy; with 3 or 4 pairs of secondary veins; margins often slightly reddish in colour

**Upper/under side:** With scattered hairs on both sides; medium to dark green above and with clearly visible, pale green, primary and secondary veins; paler green beneath; hairs not in tufts but finely crisped; with distinctly prominent, pale green veins

**Arrangement on the shoot:** Leaves opposite

**Distribution:** Mainly in the hill zone, more rarely montane: in hedges, open mixed deciduous woods, damp woods, on slopes warm and dry in summer, and on the edges of woods

### *Cornus mas* L.
## Cornelian Cherry
**Cornaceae - Dogwood family** p. 100

**Length:** 4-10cm

**Form of blade:** Narrowly elliptic, elliptic to ovate in outline

**Stalk:** 0.3-1.5cm long, slightly grooved, often reddish in colour and with fine whitish hairs

**End of leaf:** Pointed, or the two halves of the leaf converging and rounded

**Base of blade:** Wedge-shaped or rounded

**Margin of leaf:** Entire; often slightly undulate; with 3-5 pairs of secondary veins

**Upper/under side:** With scattered, white, appressed hairs on both sides; medium to dark green above with only the primary lateral veins prominent; pale to medium green beneath with the midrib and lateral veins distinctly prominent; often with tufts of white hairs in the axils of the veins

**Arrangement on the shoot:** Leaves opposite

**Distribution:** In the hill zone, more rarely montane; in dry, mixed deciduous woods, in hedges, on dry slopes warm in summer, and on the edges of woods

972 *Cornus sanguinea* - **Dogwood** *Deciduous shrub, 1-5m high, stems tinged red on the side exposed to the sun*

973 *Cornus mas* - **Cornelian Cherry** *Deciduous shrub or small tree, 3-6m high; stems tinged red on the side exposed to the sun*

### *Fagus orientalis* Lipsky
### Oriental Beech

**Fagaceae – Beech family** p. 100

**Length:** 6–12cm

**Form of blade:** Elliptic or obovate in outline; always broadest above the middle

**Stalk:** 0.5–1.5cm long and covered with matted, milky hairs

**End of leaf:** With a short, abrupt point or a tapering point

**Base of blade:** Wedge-shaped or rounded

**Margin of leaf:** Entire, wavy, and densely fringed with very long, fine hairs

**Upper/under side:** Dark bluish green above, glabrous, and with pale yellowish green veins; dark green beneath with conspicuous brownish hairs on the prominent, pale yellowish green veins

**Arrangement on the shoot:** Leaves alternate

**Distribution:** Species native in Aisa Minor, the Caucasus, and N. Iran; occasionally planted in parks in central Europe

974 **Fagus orientalis – Oriental Beech**
*Deciduous tree, up to 40m high in its native habitat, with stems olive green and hairy at first*

### *Fagus sylvatica* L.
### Common Beech

**Fagaceae – Beech family**
p. 30, 31, 101

**Length:** 5–10cm

**Form of blade:** Elliptic to broadly ovate in outline; greatest breadth at or below the middle

**Stalk:** 0.3–1.5cm long and often dark in colour

**End of leaf:** With a short, tapering or abrupt point

**Base of blade:** Wedge-shaped or rounded

**Margin of leaf:** Entire and undulate; fringed with whitish hairs when young

**Upper/under side:** Softly hairy when young and fringed at the margin; older leaves usually glabrous; shiny dark green above and medium green beneath; veins prominent; lateral veins running parallel to each other

**Arrangement on the shoot:** Leaves alternate (arranged in 2 rows)

**Distribution:** From the hill to the montane zone; a constituent part of various types of wood

975 **Fagus sylvatica – Beech**
*Deciduous, much-branched tree, up to 40m high, with young shoots hairy*

### *Salix hastata* L.
### Spear-leaved Willow

**Salicaceae – Willow family** p. 101

**Length:** 2–8cm

**Form of blade:** Elliptic to ovate in outline

**Stalk:** 0.5–1.2cm long and grooved above

**End of leaf:** Pointed or slightly rounded

**Base of blade:** Rounded or weakly heart-shaped

**Margin of leaf:** Entire or with a few small teeth up to 5mm apart

**Upper/under side:** Dark green and glabrous above; pale bluish green beneath and hairy on the veins at first; veins pale green and prominent

**Arrangement on the shoot:** Leaves alternate

**Distribution:** Especially in the montane and subalpine zone; on continuously wet alluvial land by rivers and streams, in alpine alder thickets, in scrub and on scree

976 **Salix hastata – Spear-leaved Willow**
*Deciduous shrub, barely more than 1m high, with reddish brown stems hairy at first*

### *Parrotia persica* (DC.)
C. A. Mey.
### Persian Ironwood

**Hamamelidaceae – Witch-hazel family** p. 101

**Length:** 6–10cm

**Form of blade:** Obovate or almost circular in outline; leaves fairly thick and leathery

**Stalk:** 0.5–0.8cm long

**End of leaf:** Obtuse or rounded

**Base of blade:** Rounded or wedge-shaped

**Margin of leaf:** Entire; coarsely sinuate to crenate-dentate above the middle

**Upper/under side:** Shiny dark green above with clearly impressed veins of a similar colour; pale bluish green beneath with whitish green, distinctly prominent veins; with fine, brownish hairs at first

**Arrangement on the shoot:** Leaves alternate; 2 or more together on short shoots

**Distribution:** Native in N. Iran and the Caucasus; planted in large parks and botanic gardens

977 **Parrotia persica – Persian Ironwood**
*Deciduous shrub or tree up to 10m high with young twigs brownish green*

### *Citrus sinensis* (L.) Pers.
### Orange

**Rutaceae – Citrus family** p. 102

**Length:** 3–7cm

**Form of blade:** Elliptic, broadly elliptic or obovate in outline, firm and leathery; broader than that of the lemon

**Stalk:** 0.5–2cm long and with prominent green wings

**End of leaf:** Rounded at the end with a tapering or short abrupt point

**Base of blade:** Wedge-shaped

**Margin of leaf:** Entire

**Upper/under side:** Both sides glabrous; shiny dark green above and pale green beneath; the midrib particularly prominent

**Arrangement on the shoot:** Leaves alternate

**Distribution:** The orange is native in E. Asia, but is now planted widely throughout the Mediterranean region

978 **Citrus sinensis – Orange**
*Evergreen tree, 5–10m high, with twigs green and spiny at first*

### *Citrus limon* (L.) Burm.
### Lemon

**Rutaceae – Citrus family** p. 102

**Length:** 3–7cm

**Form of blade:** Narrowly elliptic to elliptic in outline, firm and leathery; very similar to the leaves of the orange

**Stalk:** 0.5–2cm long and often winged; a thorn often present where the stalk joins the shoot

**End of leaf:** Pointed

**Base of blade:** Wedge-shaped

**Margin of leaf:** Entire or very slightly crenate or dentate

**Upper/under side:** Shiny dark green above and pale green beneath; midrib and lateral veins prominent; both sides glabrous

**Arrangement on the shoot:** Leaves alternate

**Distribution:** Numerous varieties planted in the Mediterranean region and areas with a similar climate

979 **Citrus limon – Lemon**
*Evergreen tree, 5–10m high, with twigs green and spiny at first*

980 **Lonicera xylosteum – Fly Honeysuckle**
*Deciduous shrub, 1-3m high, with stems greyish brown and softly hairy at first*

## *Lonicera xylosteum* L.
### Fly Honeysuckle

**Caprifoliacae - Honeysuckle family** p. 101

**Length:** 2-6cm

**Form of blade:** Elliptic, broadly ovate or obovate in outline

**Stalk:** 0.5-1cm long, often reddish above and with densely appressed hairs

**End of leaf:** Obtuse or pointed

**Base of blade:** Wedge-shaped or rounded

**Margin of leaf:** Entire; margins sparsely fringed with whitish hairs

**Upper/under side:** With appressed hairs on both sides; medium to dark green above and bluish green beneath; veins beneath distinctly prominent

**Arrangement on the shoot:** Leaves opposite

**Distribution:** From the hill to the montane zone; amongst the luxuriant vegetation in Oak woods, in hedges, mixed Beech and conifer woods, open Pine woods, clearings, on the edges of woods and by fences; widely distributed and common in central Europe except N.W. Germany

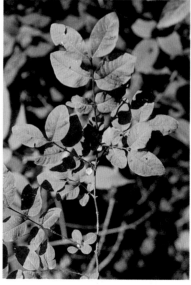

981 **Lonicera nigra – Black-berried Honeysuckle** *Deciduous shrub, 1-2m high, with yellowish brown to reddish stems*

## *Lonicera nigra* L.
### Black-berried Honeysuckle

**Caprifoliacae - Honeysuckle family** p. 104

**Length:** 3-8cm

**Form of blade:** Elliptic, broadly elliptic to obovate in outline

**Stalk:** 0.2-0.8cm long and grooved above

**End of leaf:** Shortly pointed

**Base of blade:** Rounded, truncate or wedge-shaped

**Margin of leaf:** Entire; margins often slightly undulate

**Upper/under side:** Medium to dark green and glabrous above; medium green beneath and downy along the midrib; veins pale yellowish green and distinctly prominent

**Arrangement on the shoot:** Leaves opposite

**Distribution:** In the montane and subalpine zone; in mixed woods with rich vegetation, on the edges of woods and between rocks; in the undergrowth of mountain woods and on uncultivated damp or stony soils; not very common

982 **Lonicera caprifolium – Perfoliate Honeysuckle** *Deciduous climber up to 5m, stems tinged red on side exposed to sun*

## *Lonicera caprifolium* L.
### Perfoliate Honeysuckle

**Caprifoliacae - Honeysuckle family** p. 102

**Length:** 2-10cm

**Form of blade:** Narrowly ovate to elliptic in outline and with the lower leaves shortly stalked; leaves towards the ends of the stems united in pairs by their bases; uppermost leaves united and forming an elliptic or circular structure

**Stalk:** Shortly stalked or sessile

**End of leaf:** Usually obtuse, occasionally shortly pointed

**Base of blade:** Wedge-shaped, rounded or heart-shaped

**Margin of leaf:** Entire, glabrous

**Upper/under side:** Dark green and glabrous above; bluish to greyish green beneath and hairy at the base at first, but soon becoming glabrous; midrib beneath distinctly prominent

**Arrangement on the shoot:** Leaves opposite

**Distribution:** Hill zone; often cultivated in gardens, sometimes escaping and becoming naturalised; found wild in sunny hedges and in oak woods; twines clockwise

983 **Lonicera caerulea – Blue Honeysuckle** *Deciduous shrub, up to 1.5m, stems reddish brown at first, covered with bluish bloom*

## *Lonicera caerulea* L.
### Blue Honeysuckle

**Caprifoliacae - Honeysuckle family** p. 102

**Length:** 2-8cm

**Form of blade:** Elliptic, oblong-elliptic, or obovate in outline

**Stalk:** 1-4mm long, slightly hairy, and somewhat broadened at the base

**End of leaf:** Obtuse or rounded and occasionally with a short, fine point

**Base of blade:** Rounded

**Margin of leaf:** Entire

**Upper/under side:** Both sides hairy when young; dark green above and quickly becoming glabrous; bluish green beneath, becoming glabrous except on the leaf-stalk; veins pale yellowish green and prominent

**Arrangement on the shoot:** Leaves opposite

**Distribution:** From the montane to the subalpine zone; on pine moors, in Mountain Pine woods, Alpenrose communities, and in stony places with acid raw humus

984 **Lonicera periclymenum – Honeysuckle** *Deciduous climber, turning clockwise up to 5m high with stems tinged red on the side exposed to the sun*

## *Lonicera periclymenum* L.
### Honeysuckle

**Caprifoliaceae - Honeysuckle family** p. 102

**Length:** 4-10cm

**Form of blade:** Elliptic to obovate in outline

**Stalk:** Lower leaves with a stalk up to 0.7cm long; uppermost pair of leaves sessile

**End of leaf:** Obtuse or pointed

**Base of blade:** Wedge-shaped

**Margin of leaf:** Entire

**Upper/under side:** Both sides glabrous; dark green above, bluish green beneath and only slightly hairy when young

**Arrnagement on the shoot:** Leaves opposite

**Distribution:** In the hill zone; in mixed oak and beech woods, in alder groves, hedges and clearings; prefers a climate warm in summer and mild in winter; the centre of distribution lies in atlantic Europe

985 **Lonicera alpigena – Alpine Honeysuckle** *Deciduous shrub up to 2m high with young shoots greyish brown*

## *Lonicera alpigena* L.
### Alpine Honeysuckle

**Caprifoliaceae - Honeysuckle family** p. 104

**Length:** 8-12cm

**Form of blade:** Elliptic or obovate in outline

**Stalk:** 1-2cm long

**End of leaf:** Shortly pointed

**Base of blade:** Truncate or wedge-shaped

**Margin of leaf:** Entire; younger leaves with a regular fringe of fine hairs

**Upper/under side:** Both sides glabrous; dark green above with clearly impressed veins; paler green beneath, distinctly shiny, with fine hairs along the midrib; veins pale or dark green and prominent

**Arrnagement on the shoot:** Leaves opposite

**Distribution:** In the montane and subalpine zone; amongst the rich vegetation of beech and mixed woods, in gorges, clearings, on the edges of woods and on bushy slopes

### Hedera helix L.
### Ivy
**Araliaceae - Ivy family** p. 102

**Length:** 4-10cm

**Form of blade:** Varied in outline; leaves on flowering shoots ovate-rhombic in shape and not lobed, leathery and lasting for 3 years

**Stalk:** 3-11cm long

**End of leaf:** Shortly pointed

**Base of blade:** Obtuse or truncate

**Margin of leaf:** Entire

**Upper/under side:** Shiny dark green above with white veins; dull pale green beneath; both sides glabrous

**Arrangement on the shoot:** Leaves alternate

**Distribution:** From the hill to the montane zone; creeping along the ground or climbing on trees, walls and rocks; prefers damp places mild in winter; found mainly in beech and oak woods and in damp woods

986　*Hedera helix* – Ivy
*Evergreen climber up to 20m high with stems bearing adhesive roots*

### Rhamnus frangula L.
(*Frangula alnus* Mill.)
### Alder Buckthorn
**Rhamnaceae - Buckthorn family** p. 104

**Length:** 3-7cm

**Form of blade:** Elliptic to broadly elliptic in outline

**Stalk:** 0.6-1.4cm long

**End of leaf:** With a short, abrupt point

**Base of blade:** Truncate or wedge-shaped

**Margin of leaf:** Entire

**Upper/under side:** Both sides glabrous; dark green above and shiny pale green beneath with prominent, pale yellowish green veins

**Arrangement on the shoot:** Leaves alternate

**Distribution:** From the hill to the montane zone; in damp woods, alder groves, birch moors, open woods with wet soils and boggy land; found mainly with Alder, Grey Alder, Bird Cherry and Guelder Rose

987　*Rhamnus frangula* – Alder Buckthorn
*Deciduous shrub 1-3m high, or tree up to 7m with grey to reddish brown branchlets*

### Euonymus latifolius (L.) Mill.
### Broad-leaved Spindle Tree
**Celastraceae - Spindle Tree family** p. 103

**Length:** 7-14cm

**Form of blade:** Elliptic to obovate in outline

**Stalk:** 0.5-1cm long and grooved above

**End of leaf:** Pointed

**Base of blade:** Truncate or wedge-shaped

**Margin of leaf:** Appearing entire to the naked eye; with a lens obviously finely and evenly serrate

**Upper/under side:** Both sides glabrous; dark green above and pale green beneath; veins prominent

**Arrangement on the shoot:** Leaves opposite

**Distribution:** From the hill to the montane zone; in warm, damp places amongst the rich vegetation of mixed deciduous words and on the edges of woodland

988　*Euonymus latifolius* – Broad-leaved
**Spindle Tree** *Deciduous shrub 2-5m; young branchlets 4-angled to rounded in cross-section*

### Forsythia europaea
Deg. et Bald.
### European Forsythia
**Oleaceae - Olive family** p. 104

**Length:** 4-8cm

**Form of blade:** Elliptic, ovate or ovate-lanceolate in outline

**Stalk:** 1-3cm long and usually grooved above

**End of leaf:** Pointed; tip curved to one side

**Base of blade:** Truncate or wedge-shaped

**Margin of leaf:** Entire

**Upper/under side:** Dark green above and pale green beneath; both sides glabrous; veins medium green and prominent

**Arrangement on the shoot:** Leaves opposite

**Distribution:** Planted in gardens but not of great horticultural value

989　*Forsythia europaea* – European
**Forsythia** *Deciduous shrub, 1.5-2.5m high; native in N. Albania and S.W. Yugoslavia*

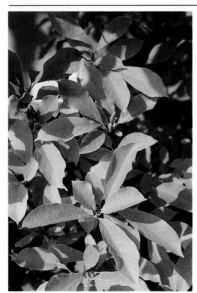

### Magnolia x sonlangeana
Sonl.-Bod.
### Garden Magnolia
**Magnoliaccae - Magnolia family** p. 103

**Length:** 10-20cm

**Form of blade:** Oblong-elliptic or usually narrowly obovate in outline; always broadest in the upper third

**Stalk:** 1-4cm long

**End of leaf:** With a short, abrupt point

**Base of blade:** Wedge-shaped

**Margin of leaf:** Entire

**Upper/under side:** Medium to dark green and glabrous above; paler green beneath, slightly hairy, and with prominent yellowish white veins

**Arrangement on the shoot:** Leaves alternate

**Distribution:** Raised by Soulange-Bodin at Fromont near Paris in 1820; first flowered in 1826; numerous forms planted nowadays in gardens and parks

990　*Magnolia x sonlangeana* - Garden
**Magnolia**
*Deciduous shrub or tree up to 5m high with greyish green young shoots*

### Magnolia grandiflora L.
### Evergreen Magnolia
**Magnoliaceae - Magnolia family** p. 103

**Length:** 8-20cm

**Form of blade:** Elliptic to broadly elliptic in outline; leaves thick, leathery, and falling in the 2nd year

**Stalk:** 2-2.5cm long, stout, and densely covered with rust brown to brownish red hairs

**End of leaf:** Obtuse to bluntly pointed

**Base of blade:** Wedge-shaped

**Margin of leaf:** Entire

**Upper/under side:** Shiny dark green and glabrous above; paler green beneath with conspicuous, rust-red, downy hairs

**Arrangement on the shoot:** Leaves alternate

**Distribution:** Native in the S.E. United States; planted nowadays as an ornamental tree especially in the Mediterranean region

991　*Magnolia grandiflora* - Evergreen
**Magnolia**
*Evergreen tree up to 25m high with young shoots densely reddish brown felted*

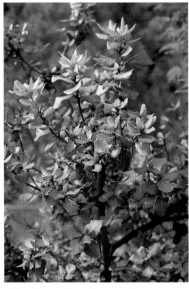

**992   Quercus ilex – Evergreen Oak**
*Evergreen tree up to 25m high with grey-felted twigs that only gradually become glabrous*

### Quercus ilex L.
## Evergreen Oak, Holm Oak
**Fagaceae – Beech family**  p. 105

**Length:** 3–8cm

**Form of blade:** Varied in outline; usually oblong-ovate to ovate and with 4–7 sharp teeth on each side; often lobed also

**Stalk:** 7–15mm long and remaining felted with long white hairs

**Lobes:** Sharply pointed, entire or undulate, leathery and thick

**End of leaf:** Sharply pointed

**Base of blade:** Broadly wedge-shaped or rounded

**Margin of leaf:** Lobes entire or undulate and spiny-toothed

**Upper/under side:** Young leaves hairy on both sides; older leaves shiny dark green and glabrous above; appearing grey or whitish beneath because of the dense covering of hairs

**Arrangement on the shoot:** Leaves alternate

**Distribution:** Widely distributed in the Mediterranean region; forms Evergreen Oak woods; planted as an ornamental tree in parks where the winters are mild

**993   Ilex aquifolium – Holly**
*Evergreen shrub or tree up to 15m high with pale or dark green twigs*

### Ilex aquifolium L.
## Holly
**Aquifoliaceae – Holly family**  p. 105

**Length:** 3–8cm

**Form of blade:** Elliptic to ovate in outline; in some forms the margin is entire and without any teeth; blade thick and leathery

**Stalk:** 1cm long and grooved above

**End of leaf:** With a long spiny point

**Base of blade:** Wedge-shaped

**Margin of leaf:** Undulate and coarsely spiny toothed; the number and kind of teeth vary according to age or garden form

**Upper/under side:** Shiny dark green above and pale green beneath; both sides glabrous

**Arrangement on the shoot:** Leaves alternate

**Distribution:** From the hill to the montane zone; especially in areas with an oceanic climate; forming the lower tree-layer in beech, beech-fir, and oak-hornbeam woods; occasionally in hedges

**994   Castanea sativa – Sweet Chestnut**
*Deciduous tree up to 35m high with angular, glabrous twigs*

### Castanea sativa Mill.
## Sweet Chestnut
**Fagaceae – Beech Family**  p. 105

**Length:** 10–30cm

**Form of blade:** Oblong-lanceolate in outline, with sharp teeth; blade thick and leathery

**Stalk:** 2–5cm long

**End of leaf:** Ending in a short, narrow point

**Base of blade:** Broadly wedge-shaped, rounded or more rarely heart-shaped

**Margin of leaf:** With very large, sharp teeth, resembling those of a saw and pointing forwards; each of the lateral veins ends in a stout pointed tooth

**Upper/under side:** Shiny dark green and glabrous above; dull pale green beneath, at first felted, later becoming glabrous; with 15–20 pairs of prominent lateral veins beneath

**Arrangement on the shoot:** Leaves alternate

**Distribution:** In the hill zone, more rarely montane; forming woods in the mountains of the S. Alps; planted in the N. Alps in wine region and valleys warmed by the Föhn wind

**995   Berberis vulgaris – Barberry**
*Deciduous shrub up to 3m high with angular, greyish brown stems*

### Berberis vulgaris L.
## Barberry
**Berberidaceae – Barberry family**
p. 105

**Length:** 2–4cm and narrowed into the stalk

**Form of blade:** Narrowly obovate to obovate in outline

**Stalk:** 0.5–1.5cm long

**End of leaf:** Rounded or obtuse

**Base of blade:** Narrowly wedge-shaped

**Margin of leaf:** Fringed with sharp spines

**Upper/under side:** Both sides glabrous; dark green above and whitish green beneath

**Arrangement on the shoot:** Leaves in clusters from the axils of 3-parted spines; clusters alternately arranged; leaves converted into single or divided spines, 1–2cm long, on long shoots

**Distribution:** From the hill to the subalpine zone; in sunny places on the edges of woods, in open oak and pine woods, hedges, and in shrub communities on dry soils

**996   Corylus colurna – Turkish Hazel**
*Deciduous tree up to 20m high occasionally planted in gardens*

### Corylus colurna L.
## Turkish Hazel
**Betulaceae – Birch family**  p. 107

**Length:** 8–12cm

**Form of blade:** Broadly ovate to roundish or heart-shaped in outline; greatest breadth usually in the upper third

**Stalk:** 1.5–3cm long

**End of leaf:** With an abrupt point of moderate size

**Base of blade:** Usually heart-shaped or obliquely heart-shaped

**Margin of leaf:** Serrate and coarsely doubly toothed

**Upper/under side:** Shiny dark green above and later glabrous; medium to dark green beneath and hairy on the veins; veins of the 2nd and 3rd order not very prominent

**Arrangement on the shoot:** Leaves alternate

**Distribution:** In the hill zone; native in S.E. Europe but naturalised in Lower Austria

**997   Ulex europaeus – Gorse**
*Very spiny shrub, 0.5–2m high, with numerous spiny short shoots up to 25mm long*

### Ulex europaeus L.
## Gorse
**Leguminosae – Pea family**  p. 105

**Form of blade:** Leaves only small and narrow, and only found occasionally on very lush growth or on young plants; often absent; all later leaves converted into sharp, green spines, 4–10mm long; short shoots also spiny. The shrub appears to consist entirely of green stems and spines

**Upper/under side:** Stems grooved and downy; spines with many lateral spines and also downy

**Arrangement on the shoot:** Spines alternately arranged

**Distribution:** A plant characteristic of Atlantic moorland; found in central Europe in mild parts of the lowlands; on shrubby slopes, on moors, and in open oak and pine woods in coastal regions

998 **Tilia tomentosa – Silver Lime**
*Deciduous tree up to 30m high with stiffly erect branches and grey-felted young shoots*

### Tilia tomentosa Moench
### Silver Lime
**Tiliaceae – Lime family** p. 106

**Length:** 6–12cm

**Form of blade:** Roundish heart-shaped or obliquely heart-shaped in outline

**Stalk:** 2–3.5cm long, much shorter than in the Weeping Silver Lime

**End of leaf:** Shortly pointed; with a slender, abrupt point

**Base of blade:** Usually heart-shaped to obliquely heart-shaped (with a deeper sinus than the Weeping Silver Lime)

**Margin of leaf:** Fairly regularly serrate/dentate; teeth not ending in a bristle, but more triangular in shape

**Upper/under side:** Dark green above with the midrib and lateral veins clearly visible; white or pale grey-felted beneath

**Arrangement on the shoot:** Leaves alternate

**Distribution:** Native in S.E. Europe and northern Asia Minor; first planted in central Europe about 1770; a favourite street-tree in towns because of its tolerance of smoke-pollution

999 **Tilia petiolaris – Weeping Silver Lime**
*Deciduous tree, reaching a height of 30m, with pendulous branches*

### Tilia petiolaris DC. *T. alba*
(K. Koch non Ait.)
### Weeping Silver Lime
**Tiliaceae – Lime family** p. 106

**Length:** 7–11cm

**Form of blade:** Obliquely heart-shaped in outline

**Stalk:** 3–6cm long and felted; leaves pendant

**End of leaf:** Shortly pointed

**Base of blade:** Obliquely heart-shaped or obliquely truncate

**Margin of leaf:** Regularly and sharply serrate/dentate; with teeth ending in a bristle

**Upper/under side:** Hairy above at first, later almost glabrous and dark green; white or greyish white beneath because of stellate hairs; midrib and lateral veins not very noticeable above

**Arrangement on the shoot:** Leaves alternate (arranged in 2 rows)

**Distribution:** Closely related to the Silver Lime, and often planted, especially in parks

1000 **Tilia platyphyllos – Large-leaved Lime**
*Deciduous tree up to 40m high with young shoots reddish brown and hairy*

### Tilia platyphyllos Scop.
### Large-leaved Lime
**Tiliaceae – Lime family**
p. 54, 55, 106

**Length:** 7–15cm

**Form of blade:** Heart-shaped or obliquely heart-shaped in outline

**Stalk:** 2–5cm long and often hairy; shorter than the blade

**End of leaf:** With a short, abrupt point

**Base of blade:** Obliquely heart-shaped or obliquely truncate

**Margin of leaf:** Regularly crenate-serrate: teeth all pointing forwards and not bristle-tipped

**Upper/under side:** Both sides hairy; dark green above and pale green beneath with tufts of whitish hairs in the axils of the veins; all veins hairy and prominent beneath

**Arrangement on the shoot:** Leaves alternate (arranged in 2 rows)

**Distribution:** In the hill zone; on steep slopes and below crags in places warm in summer; planted on hills

1001 **Tilia x euchlora – Caucasian Lime**
*Deciduous tree up to 15m high with arching branches and pendulous shoots*

### Tilia x euchlora K. Koch
(*T. cordata* x *T. dasystyla*)
### Caucasian Lime
**Tiliaceae – Lime family** p. 106

**Length:** 5–15cm

**Form of blade:** Obliquely heart-shaped in outline

**Stalk:** 3–6cm long and usually glabrous

**End of leaf:** Pointed, with a bristle at the tip

**Base of blade:** Usually obliquely heart-shaped

**Margin of leaf:** Irregularly toothed; all teeth tipped with a bristle

**Upper/under side:** Shiny dark green to bluish green above and glabrous; somewhat paler bluish green beneath with distinctly prominent veins; with tufts of usually light to medium brown, occasionally whitish hairs in the axils of the veins

**Arrangement on the shoot:** Leaves alternate

**Distribution:** Native from the Caucasus to N. Iran: planted in central Europe particularly in avenues and parks

1002 **Tilia cordata – Small-leaved Lime**
*Deciduous tree up to 30m high with young branchlets olive green and finely hairy*

### Tilia cordata Mill.
### Small-leaved Lime
**Tiliaceae – Lime family** p. 106

**Length:** 4–7cm

**Form of blade:** Heart-shaped in outline

**Stalk:** 2–5cm long and glabrous

**End of leaf:** With a short, abrupt point

**Base of blade:** Regular or obliquely heart-shaped; more rarely truncate

**Margin of leaf:** Finely and sharply serrate; teeth not tipped with a bristle

**Upper/under side:** Shiny dark green to bluish green and glabrous above; pale bluish green beneath with tufts of brownish red hairs in the axils of the veins (sometimes whitish in very young leaves); veins beneath not very prominent

**Arrangement on the shoot:** Leaves alternate (arranged in 2 rows)

**Distribution:** In the hill zone, more rarely montane; on steep slopes, below crags in mixed deciduous woods and thickets, in gorges, in mild places, warm in summer

1003 **Cercidiphyllum japonicum – Katsura Tree**
*Deciduous tree, reaching a height of up to 20m, with a high domed crown*

### Cercidiphyllum japonicum
Sieb. et Zucc. ex Miq.
### Katsura Tree
**Cercidiphylloucae – Katsura family**
p. 107

**Length:** 6–12cm

**Form of blade:** Broadly ovate to roundish or heart-shaped in outline

**Stalk:** 3–6cm long and green or tinged red

**End of leaf:** Very shortly pointed

**Base of blade:** Heart-shaped

**Margin of leaf:** Crenate

**Upper/under side:** Dull or greyish green above; pale bluish green beneath and also glabrous; leaves of long shoots with pinnate veins, those on short shoots with veins palmately arranged

**Arrangement on the shoot:** Leaves opposite (on long shoots); those on short shoots alternate

**Distribution:** Native in Japan and China; planted during the last 100 years in the parks and larger gardens of Europe as an ornamental tree

### *Populus x canadensis*
Moench
## Hybrid Black Poplar

(a cross between a European and an American species)
**Salicaceae – Willow family** p. 107

**Length:** 6–10cm, larger than the leaves of the Black Poplar

**Form of blade:** With an almost triangular outline

**Stalk:** 3–8cm long, occasionally slightly reddish

**End of leaf:** With an abrupt point

**Base of blade:** Truncate or weakly heart-shaped

**Margin of leaf:** Undulate and crenate-serrate; entire on the short point

**Upper/under side:** Shiny dark green above and paler green beneath; both sides glabrous; lateral veins more clearly branched than in the Black Poplar

**Arrangement on the shoot:** Leaves alternate

**Distribution:** Arose spontaneously in France about 1750; various forms planted throughout Europe along streets and in parks

1004　*Populus x canadensis* – Hybrid Black Poplar *Deciduous, quick-growing tree up to 30m high with light greyish brown, glabrous twigs*

### *Populus nigra* L.
### Black Poplar

**Salicaceae – Willow family** p. 107

**Length:** 4–9cm on long shoots, slightly smaller on short shoots

**Form of blade:** Rounded triangular to rhombic in outline and reddish at first

**Stalk:** 3–6cm long and laterally compressed

**End of leaf:** Pointed

**Base of blade:** Truncate or broadly wedge-shaped

**Margin of leaf:** Crenate and serrate; teeth usually rounded

**Upper/under side:** Dark green above and pale bluish green beneath; both sides glabrous; lateral veins not so strongly branched as those of the Hybrid Black Poplar

**Arrangement on the shoot:** Leaves alternate

**Distribution:** In the lowlands in damp woods and by lakes and rivers; associated especially with willows and with other species of poplar; prefers open ground

1005　*Populus nigra* – Black Poplar *Deciduous, broad-crowned tree up to 30m high with shiny yellowish brown twigs*

### *Populus nigra* L. var. *italica* Muenchh.

(*P. nigra* var. *pyramidalis* (Roz.) Spach)
## Lombardy Poplar

**Salicaceae – Willow family** p. 42, 43, 107

**Length:** 4–8cm

**Form of blade:** Lozenge-shaped or rhombic in outline

**Stalk:** 1–3cm long and often with a reddish tinge

**End of leaf:** Long pointed

**Base of blade:** Broadly wedge-shaped

**Margin of leaf:** Sinuately serrate/dentate; tip and base of blade entire

**Upper/under side:** Dark green above and greyish green beneath; both sides glabrous

**Arrangement on the shoot:** Leaves alternate

**Distribution:** From the lowlands to the montane zone; frequent on river-banks, by roads, farms and monasteries; native in Iran or Turkestan; grown in Europe since the middle of the 18th century

1006　*Populus nigra var. italica* – Lombardy Poplar *Deciduous, narrowly cone-shaped tree up to 30m high*

### *Betula pendula* Roth
### Silver Birch

**Betulaceae – Birch family** p. 28, 29, 108

**Length:** 3–7cm

**Form of blade:** Triangular, ovate-rhombic or more rarely roundish in outline; sticky when young; blades of suckers larger and often heart-shaped

**Stalk:** 2–3cm long

**End of leaf:** Usually long pointed

**Base of blade:** Wedge-shaped

**Margin of leaf:** Usually coarsely doubly serrate/dentate; entire towards the base of the blade

**Upper/under side:** Both sides glabrous; dark green above and pale greyish green beneath

**Arrangement on the shoot:** Leaves alternate

**Distribution:** From the hill to the subalpine zone; in the lowlands in oak and birch woods, at higher altitudes on moors, in alpine meadows and on heaths; valuable in providing protection for young timber-trees

1007　*Betula pendula* – Silver Birch *Deciduous tree 5–25m high; twigs with warty resin-glands.*

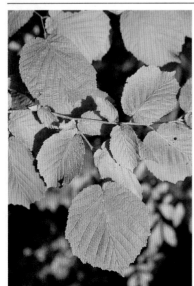

### *Corylus avellana* L.
### Hazel

**Betulaceae – Birch family** p. 107

**Length:** 5–10cm

**Form of blade:** Oblong-obovate, roundish or heart-shaped in outline

**Stalk:** 0.5–1.5cm long and glandular hairy

**End of leaf:** With a short, abrupt point

**Base of blade:** Weakly heart-shaped or rounded

**Margins of leaf:** Doubly serrate/dentate

**Upper/under side:** Both sides more or less softly hairy; medium green above and pale to medium green beneath; veins of the 2nd and 3rd order distinctly prominent

**Arrangement on the shoot:** Leaves alternate (usually in 2 rows); on strong shoots arranged all round the twig

**Distribution:** From the hill to the subalpine zone as undergrowth in woods, in hedges, meadows and pastures, on the banks of streams, the edges of woods, on steep slopes and by paths; a pioneer plant

1008　*Corylus avellana* – Hazel *Deciduous shrub, many-stemmed from the base. 2–5m high; stems glandular hairy*

### *Alnus glutinosa* (L.) Gaertn.
### Common Alder

**Betulaceae – Birch family** p. 26, 27, 108

**Length:** 4–10cm

**Form of blade:** Broadly obovate to roundish in outline and sticky when young; greatest breadth of blade above the middle

**Stalk:** 0.5–1.5cm long

**End of leaf:** Rounded or usually emarginate

**Base of blade:** Usually broadly wedge-shaped

**Margin of leaf:** Simply or doubly serrate/dentate; almost all teeth broader than long

**Upper/under side:** Medium to dark green above; paler green beneath with tufts of whitish to rust-coloured hairs in the axils of the veins; midrib and lateral veins beneath distinctly prominent

**Arrangement on the shoot:** Leaves opposite

**Distribution:** From the hill to the montane, more rarely the subalpine zone; by mountain springs, in alder groves, on river-banks and as a pioneer plant in marshes and fens

1009　*Alnus glutinosa* – Common Alder *Deciduous tree up to 20m high with shiny, olive green twigs later becoming greenish brown*

### *Vaccinium vitis-idaea* L.
### Cowberry
**Ericaceae - Heath family** p. 108

**Length:** 1–3cm

**Form of blade:** Narrowly obovate, smooth, leathery and with the greatest breadth always above the middle; life-span of leaves 3 years

**Stalk:** 0.3–0.5cm with downy hairs

**End of leaf:** Obtuse or slightly rounded

**Base of blade:** Wedge-shaped

**Margin of leaf:** Margins slightly recurved, weakly crenate and dentate, entire in places

**Upper/under side:** Shiny dark green above with prominent white veins; pale greyish or bluish green beneath and gland-dotted (important character!)

**Arrangement on the shoot:** Leaves alternate

**Distribution:** From the montane to the alpine zone usually on raw humus in open spruce and pine-larch woods, dwarf shrub communities, transitional moorland and juniper scrub

1010  *Vaccinium vitis-idaea* – Cowberry
*Dwarf, evergreen shrub, up to 30cm high, with erect shoots, and creeping rhizomes*

### *Salix herbacea* L.
### Dwarf Willow
**Salicaceae - Willow family** p. 108

**Length:** 0.8–2cm

**Form of blade:** Roundish ovate to circular in outline

**Stalk:** 0.3–0.6cm long and somewhat broadened at the base

**End of leaf:** Emarginate

**Base of blade:** Heart-shaped or truncate

**Margin of leaf:** Crenate-serrate; teeth 0.1–0.2mm long and as a rule broadly rounded

**Upper/under side:** Both sides medium to bluish green and glabrous; distinctly net-veined

**Arrangement on the shoot:** Leaves alternate

**Distribution:** In the alpine zone; more rarely extending down into the subalpine and montane zones; especially in snow-hollows; as a pioneer on grassy mountain ridges; on base-rich, usually calcareous soils or on bare rock

1011  *Salix herbacea* – Dwarf Willow
*Deciduous, dwarf shrub up to 5cm high, with creeping stems up to 15cm in length*

### *Populus alba* L.
### White Poplar
**Salicaceae - Willow family**
p. 40, 41, 109

**Length:** 5–12cm

**Form of blade:** Varied in outline; often triangular to ovate and sinuately toothed; on some twigs almost circular

**Stalk:** 2–4cm long, flattened and with white hairs

**End of leaf:** Rounded or shortly pointed

**Base of blade:** Rounded, weakly heart-shaped or truncate

**Margin of leaf:** Sinuately toothed; teeth rounded or obtuse, sinuses between them rounded

**Upper/under side:** Both sides felted at first with woolly hairs; later shiny dark green above and usually becoming glabrous; remaining densely white-felted beneath

**Arrangement on the shoot:** Leaves alternate

**Distribution:** On the edge of damp woods, on scree, in thickets on river-banks mainly in the hill zone; found in the Alps up to a height of 1500m; often planted in N. Europe

1012  *Populus alba* – White Poplar
*Deciduous, broad-crowned tree, 10–30m high, with white to grey-felted long shoots*

### *Dryas octopetala* L.
### Mountain Avens
**Rosaceae - Rose family** p. 109

**Length:** 0.5–3cm

**Form of blade:** Oblong-elliptic in outline and regularly coarsely crenate; blade leathery and wrinkled

**Stalk:** 0.2–1cm long

**End of leaf:** Obtuse or shortly pointed

**Base of blade:** Truncate or weakly heart-shaped

**Margin of leaf:** Regularly coarsely crenate and often slightly recurved

**Upper/under side:** Shiny dark green and glabrous above; felted beneath with silvery white hairs

**Arrangement on the shoot:** Leaves alternate

**Distribution:** From the montane up into the alpine zone; on calcareous scree, rocks, moraines, in strong alpine meadows and in open pine woods

1013  *Dryas octopetala* – Mountain Avens
*Evergreen, strongly creeping undershrub, with long, much-branched stems*

### *Salix aurita* L.
### Eared Willow
**Salicaceae - Willow family** p. 110

**Length:** 2–5cm

**Form of blade:** Narrowly ovate to obovate in outline; stipules auriculate, large and remaining for a long time

**Stalk:** 0.5–0.8cm long and slightly hairy

**End of leaf:** Broadly rounded, with a short, obliquely twisted tip

**Base of blade:** Wedge-shaped

**Margin of leaf:** Irregularly coarsely serrate to unevenly toothed and often also undulate

**Upper/under side:** Dull green, glabrous and slightly undulate above; greyish green and densely downy beneath; veins whitish yellow and distinctly prominent

**Arrangement on the shoot:** Leaves alternate

**Distribution:** From the hill to the subalpine zone; on wet moorland, on the banks of lakes and streams and in alder groves

1014  *Salix aurita* – Eared Willow
*Small, much-branched, deciduous shrub, 0.5–3m high with brownish twigs*

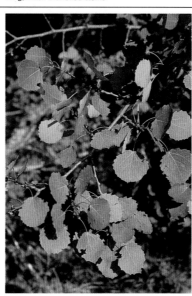

### *Populus tremula* L.
### Aspen
**Salicaceae - Willow family** p. 109

**Length:** 3–9cm; up to 15cm long on sucker growth

**Form of blade:** Ovate in outline (on suckers) or roundish; at the ends of shoots the blades are similar to those of the Black Poplar

**Stalk:** 3–10cm long, flattened, and often slightly reddish in colour

**End of leaf:** Rounded or shortly pointed from a broad base

**Base of blade:** Truncate or weakly heart-shaped

**Margin of leaf:** Irregularly sinuately dentate

**Upper/under side:** With matted silky hairs at first, later glabrous, dull, and greyish or bluish green above; pale greyish green beneath

**Arrangement on the shoot:** Leaves alternate

**Distribution:** From the hill to the subalpine zone; found in open woods, by paths, in clearings, water-meadows, on moorland and in sunny places in the mountains

1015  *Populus tremula* – Aspen
*Deciduous shrub or tree up to 10m high with roundish leaves on short shoots*

### *Ulmus glabra* Huds. emend.
Moss
(*U. scabra* Mill.)
**Wych Elm**
Ulmaceae – Elm family
p. 56, 57, 109

**Length:** 5–16cm

**Form of blade:** Elliptic, ovate or obovate in outline; broadest in the upper third; occasionally with 3 tips

**Stalk:** 3–6mm; often covered by one half of the blade

**End of leaf:** Finely pointed

**Base of blade:** Only slightly asymmetrical; the 2 halves of the blade not ending at the same point

**Margin of leaf:** Coarsely doubly serrate, simply serrate in the lower part; double teeth curving forwards

**Upper/under side:** Dark green and rough above; medium green beneath with fine white hairs on the larger veins; the 13–20 lateral veins on each side usually forked

**Arrangement on the shoot:** Leaves alternate (arranged in 2 rows)

**Distribution:** Mainly in the hill and montane zones on the edges of water-meadows, in gorges, on shady slopes and on grassland

1016   *Ulmus glabra* – Wych Elm
*Deciduous, broad-crowned tree, 30–40m high; twigs hairy and reddish brown at first*

### *Ulmus laeris* Pall.
**Fluttering Elm**
Ulmaceae – Elm family p. 109

**Length:** 7–12cm

**Form of blade:** Narrowly elliptic, elliptic or roundish in outline; broadest in the middle

**Stalk:** Only very short, up to 5mm long

**End of leaf:** With a short, fine point

**Base of blade:** Conspicuously oblique and asymmetrical

**Margin of leaf:** Sharply doubly serrate/dentate; main teeth directed forwards

**Upper/under side:** Dull dark green above; greyish green beneath with fine hairs; 12–19 primary lateral veins on each side (2 or 3 more in the longer half of the blade); lateral veins in the upper third of the leaf very rarely forked

**Arrangement on the shoot:** Leaves alternate (arranged in 2 rows)

**Distribution:** In the hill zone mainly in water-meadows, in damp mixed woods and on the edges of woodland; suitable as an avenue and street-tree

1017   *Ulmus laeris* – Fluttering Elm
*Deciduous tree up to 30m high with twigs densely covered with soft hairs at first*

### *Ulmus minor* Mill.
**U. campestris** (auct. non L.)
**Smooth-leaved Elm**
Ulmaceae – Elm family p. 109

**Length:** 3.5–8cm

**Form of blade:** Varied in outline; usually narrowly obovate or obovate-elliptic with the greatest breadth in the middle

**Stalk:** 0.5–1.3cm long and usually somewhat hairy

**End of leaf:** With a long, slender tip

**Base of blade:** Unequal; wedge-shaped or rounded

**Margin of leaf:** Simply or doubly serrate; teeth pointing towards the tip

**Upper/under side:** Dark green and glabrous above; paler green beneath with conspicuous tufts of velvety hairs in the axils of the veins; with 9–12 pairs of lateral veins, prominent, and ending in the teeth

**Arrangement on the shoot:** Leaves alternate (arranged in 2 rows)

**Distribution:** In the hill zone by water-meadows, in woods on sunny slopes and on the edges of woodland

1018   *Ulmus minor* – Smooth-leaved Elm
*Deciduous, much-branched tree up to 40m high with twigs reddish brown at first*

### *Celtis australis* L.
**Southern Nettle-tree**
Ulmaceae – Elm family p. 110

**Length:** 4–15cm

**Form of blade:** Obliquely oblong-ovate to narrowly ovate in outline

**Stalk:** 1–1.5cm long

**End of leaf:** With a slender tip

**Base of blade:** Obliquely truncate or obliquely rounded

**Margin of leaf:** Sharply serrate; teeth pointing towards the tip and ending in a slender point

**Upper/under side:** Dark green and roughly hairy above; greyish green and softly hairy beneath; on each side of the leaf a strong lateral vein extends from the base of the midrib to the middle of the blade

**Arrangement on the shoot:** Leaves alternate (arranged in 2 rows)

**Distribution:** In the hill zone; prefers warm situations; on dry and rocky slopes

1019   *Celtis australis* – Southern Nettle-tree
*Deciduous tree up to 20m high, young shoots greenish and very long*

### *Populus trichocarpa*
Torr. et A. Gray ex Hook.
**Western Balsam Poplar**
Salicaceae – Willow family p. 110

**Length:** 8–14cm; up to 25cm on strong shoots

**Form of blade:** Broadly ovate to rhombic in outline and broadest below the middle; blade thick and rather leathery

**Stalk:** 2–5cm long and usually reddish above

**End of leaf:** Pointed

**Base of blade:** Rounded or truncate; more rarely heart-shaped

**Margin of leaf:** Finely crenate-serrate

**Upper/under side:** Dark green and glabrous above; whitish or rust-coloured beneath and glabrous to finely downy

**Arrangement on the shoot:** Leaves alternate

**Distribution:** Native in N. America; often planted in parks or in areas of afforestation

1020   *Populus trichocarpa* – Western Balsam Poplar
*Deciduous tree up to 30m high with slightly angular, olive green young shoots*

### *Sorbus aria* (L.) Crantz
**Whitebeam**
Rosaceae – Rose family p. 110

**Length:** 6–12cm and up to 8cm broad

**Form of blade:** Ovate, elliptic or more rarely almost circular in outline

**Stalk:** 1–2cm long, with white woolly hairs

**End of leaf:** Obtuse or rounded and with a short point

**Base of blade:** Broadly wedge-shaped

**Margin of leaf:** Simply or doubly serrate/dentate; more rarely slightly lobed

**Upper/under side:** Medium green above and somewhat milky hairy, later becoming glabrous; densely white-felted beneath and therefore appearing pale grey to white; 10–14 pairs of prominent lateral veins beneath

**Arrangement on the shoot:** Leaves alternate (on long shoots); opposite or in whorls of 3 on short shoots

**Distribution:** On sunny, fairly dry, south-facing slopes, on crags, scree, in open deciduous and mixed deciduous woods and thickets from the hill to the subalpine zone

1021   *Sorbus aria* – Whitebeam
*Deciduous, often many-stemmed shrub or tree up to 15m high; twigs reddish on the side exposed to the sun*

### *Betula nana* L.
### Dwarf Birch

**Betulaceae - Birch family** p. 111

**Length:** Most leaves smaller than 3cm (Usually 1-1.5cm)

**Form of blade:** Usually roundish in outline and also broader than long; somewhat sticky when young

**Stalk:** 1-2mm long and dark red in colour

**End of leaf:** Ending in a coarse tooth

**Base of blade:** Truncate to weakly heart-shaped

**Margin of leaf:** Simply serrate; teeth broad and obtuse

**Upper/under side:** Dark green above, glabrous and slightly undulate; whitish beneath with a dark green network of veins

**Arrangement on the shoot:** Leaves alternate

**Distribution:** In northern, arctic, and north-eastern Europe on damp moorland and in dwarf shrub communities; on open raised bogs and pine moors

1022 **Betula nana – Dwarf Birch**
*Deciduous, much-branched, dwarf shrub, 50–100cm high, with young twigs finely felted*

### *Betula x intermedia* (Hartm.)
Thomas (*B. nana x B. pubescens*)
### Birch

**Betulaceae - Birch family** p. 111

**Length:** 0.8-2.5cm

**Form of blade:** Elliptic to broadly obovate or rhombic in outline

**Stalk:** 0.3-0.7cm long

**End of leaf:** Rounded and ending with the uppermost tooth or with 2 or more teeth

**Base of blade:** Broadly wedge-shaped

**Margin of leaf:** Coarsely simply serrate; teeth broad, rounded or shortly pointed

**Upper/under side:** Both sides dotted with glands; dark green above and greyish green beneath with dark green veins of the 2nd and subsequent orders

**Arrangement on the shoot:** Leaves alternate

**Distribution:** In N. Europe especially by lakes and rivers and on moorland

1023 **Betula x intermedia – Birch**
*Deciduous shrub 1–2m high with young shoots slightly hairy*

### *Nothofagus antarctica*
(G. Forst.) Oerst.
### Antarctic Beech

**Fagaceae - Beech family** p. 111

**Length:** 1-3cm

**Form of blade:** Ovate to roundish in outline

**Stalk:** 2-4mm long

**End of leaf:** Rounded

**Base of blade:** Regularly or irregularly truncate or heart-shaped

**Margin of leaf:** Irregularly crenate, serrate and sinuate; teeth rounded or pointed

**Upper/under side:** Shiny dark green above and often slightly wrinkled; greyish green and glabrous beneath; midrib and primary lateral veins pale brownish green; other lateral veins dark green and clearly visible

**Arrangement on the shoot:** Leaves conspicuously arranged in 2 rows

**Distribution:** Rarely taller than 6m in central Europe; occasionally planted in parks; in Britain and Ireland grown experimentally for afforestation

1024 **Nothofagus antarctica – Antarctic Beech** *Deciduous tree, up to 35m high in its native country, Chile; twigs hairy at first*

### *Rhamnus saxatilis* Jacq.
### Rock Buckthorn

**Rhamnaceae - Buckthorn family** p. 111

**Length:** 1-3cm

**Form of blade:** Lanceolate to elliptic in outline

**Stalk:** 0.2-0.5mm long

**End of leaf:** Pointed

**Base of blade:** Wedge-shaped

**Margin of leaf:** Finely and irregularly serrate

**Upper/under side:** Dark green above and whitish green beneath; dark green curved lateral veins; both sides glabrous

**Arrangement on the shoot:** Leaves opposite or almost opposite; sometimes in clusters on short shoots

**Distribution:** From the hill to the montane zone in open, sunny pine woods, thickets, on the edges of woods and rocky slopes; found wild in S. Germany, southern central Europe and in S. Europe

1025 **Rhammus saxatilis – Rock Buckthorn** *Deciduous, much-branched, very thorny shrub up to 1m high with greyish brown stems*

### *Myrica gale* L.
### Bog Myrtle, Sweet Gale

**Myricaceae - Bog Myrtle family** p. 110

**Length:** 2-5cm

**Form of blade:** Oblong obovate in outline and rather thick

**Stalk:** 0.3-0.6mm long

**End of leaf:** With a very short, abrupt point

**Base of blade:** Narrowly wedge-shaped tapering into the stalk

**Margin of leaf:** Coarsely toothed in the upper half, entire below and often undulate

**Upper/under side:** Dull dark green above with rather fine hairs; pale green beneath and finely hairy on the prominent midrib; yellowish resin-glands on both sides

**Arrangement on the shoot:** Leaves alternate

**Distribution:** From N. Germany northwards to 69° latitude, on heather moors, in peat bogs and pine woods, wet pastures and on sandy moorland

1026 **Myrica gale – Bog Myrtle**
*Deciduous, much-branched shrub, 50-125cm high; young twigs downy*

### *Salix glabra* Scopoli
### Willow

**Salicaceae - Willow family** p. 111

**Length:** 3-9cm

**Form of blade:** Lanceolate to obovate in outline

**Stalk:** 0.5-1.5cm long and somewhat broadened at the base

**End of leaf:** With a tapering or short abrupt point

**Base of blade:** Wedge-shaped

**Margin of leaf:** Regularly finely serrate

**Upper/under side:** Shiny dark green above and whitish blue-green beneath with a thick, waxy covering; both sides glabrous

**Arrangement on the shoot:** Leaves alternate

**Distribution:** In the high montane and subalpine zones on stony pastures and damp grassland; not common

1027 **Salix glabra – Willow**
*Deciduous shrub, 80-150cm high, with greyish brown, glabrous twigs*

### *Salix hastata* L.
### Spear-leaved Willow
Salicaceae – Willow family p. 112

**Length:** 3–8cm

**Form of blade:** Elliptic to ovate in outline

**Stalk:** 3–8mm long, somewhat broadened at the base and slightly reddish above

**End of leaf:** Shortly pointed

**Base of blade:** Heart-shaped

**Margin of leaf:** Finely serrate/dentate

**Upper/under side:** Dark green and glabrous above; pale greyish or bluish green beneath and hairy only at first; somewhat waxy to the touch; midrib beneath distinctly prominent

**Arrangement on the shoot:** Leaves alternate

**Distribution:** In the montane and subalpine zone; on stony and grassy slopes, on damp soils and on continuously wet alluvial ground by rivers and streams

1028 **Salix hastata – Spear-leaved Willow**
*Deciduous shrub, 0.5–1.5m high, with stems curving upwards*

### *Salix cinerea* L.
### Grey Willow
Salicaceae – Willow family p. 111

**Length:** 5–9cm

**Form of blade:** Broadly lanceolate to obovate in outline

**Stalk:** 0.5–2cm long and somewhat broadened at the base

**End of leaf:** Shortly pointed

**Base of blade:** Wedge-shaped

**Margin of leaf:** Undulate, and irregularly finely to coarsely toothed

**Upper/under side:** Dull green and shortly hairy above; greyish green and velvety beneath; veins beneath distinctly prominent

**Arrangement on the shoot:** Leaves alternate

**Distribution:** From the hill to the montane zone on moors and in wet meadows, on damp fringes of woods, by ponds and in damp, acid soils; the Grey Willow is easily recognised by its low, spreading habit

1029 **Salix cinerea – Grey Willow**
*Deciduous, erect shrub up to 5m high with stems grey at first*

### *Salix caprea* L.
### Goat Willow, Pussy Willow
Salicaceae – Willow family p. 112

**Length:** 4–10cm

**Form of blade:** Broadly elliptic to ovate in outline

**Stalk:** 1–2cm long, somewhat broadened at the base, slightly reddish tinged and downy

**End of leaf:** With a short point, bent to one side

**Base of blade:** Wedge-shaped

**Margin of leaf:** Undulate or coarsely dentate to crenate

**Upper/under side:** Brownish dark green and glabrous above; greyish green beneath because of the downy hairs; veins distinctly prominent

**Arrangement on the shoot:** Leaves alternate

**Distribution:** From the hill to the subalpine zone; one of the first colonisers in clearings, on fallow land and in gravel pits; also by lakes, on river-banks, in damp woodland, on the edges of woods, on scree and amongst rocks

1030 **Salix caprea – Goat Willow**
*Deciduous shrub or tree up to 9m high with young shoots greyish green and hairy*

### *Malus sylvestris* (L.) Mill.
### ssp. *domestica* (Borkh.)
Mansf.
### Apple
Rosaceae – Rose family
p. 38, 39, 112

**Length:** 5–9cm

**Form of blade:** Narrowly elliptic, elliptic to ovate in outline

**Stalk:** 2–5cm long

**End of leaf:** With a short, abrupt point

**Base of blade:** Wedge-shaped, rounded or truncate

**Margin of leaf:** Regularly serrate; teeth usually more than 0.5mm long and mostly pointing towards the tip; more coarsely serrate than the leaves of the pear

**Upper/under side:** Dark green above, often slightly undulate and glabrous; pale greyish green beneath and densely felted at first

**Arrangement on the shoot:** Leaves alternate

**Distribution:** Numerous varieties cultivated for their fruit from the hill to the montane zone; in gardens and orchards

1031 **Malus sylvestris ssp. domestica –**
**Apple** *Deciduous shrub or tree, up to 10m high, with reddish brown, thornless twigs*

### *Pyrus communis* L.
### Pear
Rosaceae – Rose family
p. 44, 45, 112

**Length:** 3–8cm

**Form of blade:** Elliptic, ovate or roundish in outline, and thick

**Stalk:** 1–8cm; as long as or slightly shorter than the blade

**End of leaf:** With a short, slender point

**Base of blade:** Wedge shaped or weakly rounded

**Margin of leaf:** Finely serrate, and entire in places; teeth on adult leaves 0.2–0.5mm long and not sharply pointed

**Upper/under side:** Shiny and glabrous above, somewhat hairy beneath at first, later almost or completely glabrous and somewhat paler green

**Arrangement on the shoot:** Leaves alternate

**Distribution:** From the hill to the montane zone; in gardens and orchards in regions with mild winters; numerous varieties are grown

1032 **Pyrus communis – Pear**
*Deciduous shrub (e.g. espalier Pear) or tree up to 20m with brown twigs*

### *Alnus incana* (L.) Moench
### Grey Alder
Betulaceae – Birch family p. 112

**Length:** 5–10cm

**Form of blade:** Broadly ovate to broadly elliptic in outline

**Stalk:** 0.7–2cm long

**End of leaf:** Shortly pointed

**Base of blade:** Broadly wedge-shaped

**Margin of leaf:** Doubly serrate; all teeth much broader than long

**Upper/under side:** Both sides softly hairy when young; later almost glabrous and dark green above; remaining greyish green beneath, hairy to felted; only hairy on the veins towards the end of the period of growth

**Arrangement on the shoot:** Leaves alternate

**Distribution:** From the hill to the montane zone, more rarely in the subalpine zone; used as a pioneer plant to consolidate the ground in wet woods, on river-banks and on unstable slopes; continuously wet situations are avoided but places with trickling water or occasional flooding are tolerated

1033 **Alnus incana – Grey Alder**
*Deciduous, many-stemmed shrub or a tree up to 25m high; young twigs reddish brown*

196

### Vaccinium myrtillus L.
### Bilberry
**Ericaceae – Heath family** p. 113

**Length:** 1–3cm

**Form of blade:** Oblong-ovate, elliptic or ovate in outline with the greatest breadth usually below the middle

**Stalk:** Very short, 0.5–3mm long

**End of leaf:** Rounded or shortly pointed

**Base of blade:** Broadly wedge-shaped or truncate

**Margin of leaf:** Finely serrate, dentate or crenate; teeth 0.1–0.3mm long, pointing forwards, often glandular, and shallow

**Upper/under side:** Dark green above and paler green beneath; both sides glabrous

**Arrangement on the shoot:** Leaves alternate

**Distribution:** From the hill to the subalpine zone; forming communities in deciduous and coniferous woods where only a few species are represented; also on poor pastures, acid woodland soils, moors and dwarf shrub heaths

1034  *Vaccinium myrtillus – Bilberry*
*Deciduous, stiffly erect shrub, 30–50cm high; stems green, glabrous and sharply angled*

### Betula humilis Schrank
### Shrubby Birch
**Betulaceae – Birch family** p. 114

**Length:** 1–3.5cm

**Form of blade:** Elliptic, ovate to roundish in outline

**Stalk:** 0.3–0.7cm long and often slightly reddish above

**End of leaf:** Rather obtuse to weakly pointed

**Base of blade:** Wedge-shaped

**Margin of leaf:** Simply and irregularly serrate

**Upper/under side:** Shiny dark green and glabrous above; paler green beneath with a distinct network of veins and with 4 or 5 pairs of lateral veins

**Arrangement on the shoot:** Leaves alternate

**Distribution:** From the hill to the montane zone: on open raised bogs and pine moors, acid valley bogs, in open birch woods, shrubby pastures and alder thickets

1035  *Betula humilis – Shrubby Birch*
*Deciduous shrub up to 3m high, with greyish brown stems and whitish lenticels*

### Amelanchier ovalis Medic.
### Service Berry
**Rosaceae – Rose family** p. 113

**Length:** 2–4.5cm

**Form of blade:** Ovate to roundish in outline

**Stalk:** 1–2cm long and felted, especially when young

**End of leaf:** Rounded

**Base of blade:** Rounded or weakly heart-shaped

**Margin of leaf:** Finely serrate or dentate; in places entire or crenate

**Upper/under side:** Dark green and glabrous; only slightly paler green beneath, and downy when young, later becoming glabrous

**Arrangement on the shoot:** Leaves alternate

**Distribution:** From the hill to the subalpine zone; on warm, steep slopes, in rock-crevices, oak and pine woods, open scrub, and in shrubby Mountain Pine communities in the Alps

1036  *Amelanchier ovalis – Service Berry*
*Deciduous shrub, 1–3m high, with young shoots covered with white woolly hairs*

### Betula pubescens Ehrh.
### Downy Birch
**Betulaceae – Birch family** p. 114

**Length:** 3–5cm

**Form of blade:** Broadly ovate to rhombic; with an aromatic scent when young; broadest in the middle of the blade

**Stalk:** 1–2cm long and somewhat hairy

**End of leaf:** Shortly pointed

**Base of blade:** Broadly wedge-shaped or rounded

**Margin of leaf:** Unequally doubly serrate/dentate; entire at the base of the blade

**Upper/under side:** Both sides more or less hairy; dark green above and becoming glabrous; with fine, downy hairs in the axils of the larger veins beneath

**Arrangement on the shoot:** Leaves alternate

**Distribution:** Found here and there from the hill to the subalpine zone in bogs and wet woodland, on transition moors, and in alder groves and thickets

1037  *Betula pubescens – Downy Birch*
*Large, deciduous shrub or tree up to 30m high; shoots densely downy at first*

### Prunus armeniaca L.
### Apricot
**Rosaceae – Rose family** p. 113

**Length:** 5–10cm

**Form of blade:** Broadly ovate, roundish or weakly heart-shaped in outline

**Stalk:** 3–7cm long and dark red in colour; usually with 2 glandular tubercles

**End of leaf:** Shortly pointed

**Base of blade:** Broadly wedge-shaped, rounded or truncate

**Margin of leaf:** Finely serrate

**Upper/under side:** Both sides glabrous; dull green above and slightly paler green beneath

**Arrangement on the shoot:** Leaves alternate

**Distribution:** Cultivated in vine-growing regions; prefers sunny situations protected from the cold

1038  *Prunus armeniaca – Apricot*
*Deciduous shrub or tree up to 10m high with twigs reddish brown at first*

### Arbutus unedo L.
### Strawberry Tree
**Ericaceae – Heath family** p. 113

**Length:** 5–10cm

**Form of blade:** Oblong-elliptic in outline

**Stalk:** 0.5–1.5cm long, distinctly hairy and often somewhat reddish

**End of leaf:** Obtuse and with several short teeth or shortly pointed

**Base of blade:** Wedge-shaped

**Margin of leaf:** Irregularly serrate with teeth of unequal length; teeth at the tip distinctly tinged reddish; entire towards the base of the blade

**Upper/under side:** Glabrous above, and dark green alternating with pale green areas; much paler green and glabrous beneath, with only the midrib prominent

**Arrangement on the shoot:** Leaves alternate

**Distribution:** Found especially amongst the evergreen shrubby vegetation and margins in the Mediterranean region; along the Atlantic coast (as far as Ireland); often planted as an ornamental tree in gardens and parks

1039  *Arbutus unedo – Strawberry Tree*
*Evergreen tree up to 10m high with a dense, distinctly rounded, domed crown*

### Prunus lusitanica L.
### Portugal Laurel
**Rosaceae - Rose family** p.113

**Length:** 6-12cm

**Form of blade:** Oblong-ovate in outline, thin and leathery

**Stalk:** 1-2.5cm long, often distinctly reddish and grooved above

**End of leaf:** Pointed; tip often slightly rounded

**Base of blade:** Usually rounded

**Margin of leaf:** Irregularly serrate/dentate and wavy in places

**Upper/under side:** Shiny dark green above and pale green beneath; both sides glabrous; only the midrib prominent

**Arrangement on the shoot:** Leaves alternate

**Distribution:** A native tree in Spain and Portugal; planted in gardens in the warmer parts of central Europe

1040   *Prunus lusitanica* - Portugal Laurel
*Evergreen shrub or tree up to 20m high with glabrous, red twigs*

### Alnus viridis (Chaix) DC.
### ssp. viridis
### Green Alder
**Betulaceae - Birch family** p. 114

**Length:** 3-6cm

**Form of blade:** Elliptic to broadly ovate in outline

**Stalk:** 1-2cm long and grooved, sometimes reddish tinged above in the lower part

**End of leaf:** Obtuse with small teeth or pointed

**Base of blade:** Broadly wedge-shaped, rounded or more rarely truncate or heart-shaped

**Margin of leaf:** Simply or doubly serrate or irregularly serrate; most teeth longer than broad

**Upper/under side:** Dark green and glabrous above; paler green beneath and glabrous except for possible tufts of hairs in the axils of the veins; with 10-15 pairs of distinctly prominent lateral veins

**Arrangement on the shoot:** Leaves alternate

**Distribution:** In the montane and subalpine zones, more rarely the hill zone; on damp, shady slopes, by streams, ditches, ravines, pastures

1041   *Alnus viridis* - Green Alder
*Deciduous, many-stemmed shrub, 0.5-2.5m high with reddish brown twigs*

### Carpinus betulus L.
### Hornbeam
**Betulaceae - Birch family** p. 114

**Length:** 4-12cm

**Form of blade:** Ovate to oblong-ovate in outline

**Stalk:** 0.5-1.5cm long; often reddish above

**End of leaf:** Rather obtuse or more often pointed

**Base of blade:** Regularly or obliquely rounded to heart-shaped

**Margin of leaf:** Simply or doubly serrate; individual teeth very small

**Upper/side under:** Rich green and glabrous above; paler green beneath and sparingly hairy in the axils of the veins; lateral veins running to the margin, very prominent and straight; planted between the lateral veins on both sides

**Arrangement on the shoot:** Leaves alternate; arranged in 2 distinct rows

**Distribution:** In the hill zone, more rarely montane; in oak woods, as the dominant species in hornbeam woods, on the fringes of woodland, and often planted round the edges of large gardens and parks

1042   *Carpinus betulus* - Hornbeam
*Deciduous tree up to 20m high with shoots hairy at first, later becoming glabrous*

### Ostrya carpinifolia Scop.
### Hop Hornbeam
**Betulaceae - Birch family** p. 115

**Length:** 5-12cm

**Form of blade:** Ovate-oblong or ovate in outline; leaves slightly folded in the young state

**Stalk:** 4-12mm long

**End of leaf:** Pointed

**Base of blade:** Broadly wedge-shaped or rounded

**Margin of leaf:** Sharply, and simply or doubly serrate; teeth longer and more finely pointed than in the hornbeam

**Upper/under side:** Only slightly hairy on both sides; dark green and smooth above; yellowish green beneath and slightly hairy in the axils of the veins; 11-15 pairs of lateral veins; not undulate between the veins; lower lateral veins slightly curved at the midrib

**Arrangement on the shoot:** Leaves alternate (arranged in 2 rows)

**Distribution:** In the hill and montane zone on shrubby, strong, sunny hillsides, crags, on south-facing slopes in the Downy Oakwood zone; centre in eastern Mediterranean region

1043   *Ostrya carpinifolia* - Hop Hornbeam
*Deciduous tree up to 20m high with young shoots covered with brownish hairs*

### Morus alba L.
### White Mulberry
**Moraceae - Mulberry family** p. 115

**Length:** 7-18cm

**Form of blade:** Varied in outline; often without lobes and then broadly ovate

**Stalk:** 2-5cm long, slightly hairy (later glabrous) and grooved above

**End of leaf:** Rounded and with a short tooth or shortly pointed

**Base of blade:** Truncate or weakly heart-shaped

**Margin of leaf:** Unequally serrate; teeth not so long as in the Black Mulberry and often rounded also

**Upper/under side:** Shiny dark green above and smooth or slightly rough; bluish green beneath and only hairy on the veins; veins whitish yellow and quite prominent

**Arrangement on the shoot:** Leaves alternate (usually arranged in 2 rows)

**Distribution:** Native in China and Korea and grown for 4600 years as a food-plant for silkworm and caterpillars; cultivated in S. Europe since the 11th century; naturalised here and there in the hill zone

1044   *Morus alba* - White Mulberry
*Deciduous shrub or tree up to 15m high with shoots pale brownish yellow at first*

### Morus nigra L.
### Black Mulberry
**Moraceae - Mulberry family** p. 115

**Length:** 6-18cm

**Form of blade:** Varied in outline; often broadly ovate to heart-shaped

**Stalk:** 1-2cm long

**End of leaf:** Finely pointed; the tip much more slender than in the White Mulberry

**Base of blade:** Truncate, heart-shaped to obliquely heart-shaped

**Margin of leaf:** Coarsely serrate

**Upper/under side:** Shiny dark green above and very roughly hairy; paler bluish green and hairy beneath; veins whitish yellow and distinctly prominent

**Arrangement on the shoot:** Leaves alternate

**Distribution:** Tree cultivated since ancient times; grown since the 16th century especially in the vine-growing region, and frequently found in monastery gardens; more commonly found in Tessin, Carinthia, Styria and the Tyrol; the tree was well-known to the Greeks and Romans

1045   *Morus nigra* - Black Mulberry
*Deciduous, much-branched tree 15-20m high; leaves sometimes lobed*

### Prunus mahaleb L.
### St Lucie Cherry
**Rosaceae - Rose family** p. 115

**Length:** 3–6cm

**Form of blade:** Broadly ovate to roundish in outline

**Stalk:** 1–2cm long and usually without glands

**End of leaf:** Obtuse or shortly pointed

**Base of blade:** Truncate, rounded or weakly heart-shaped

**Margin of leaf:** Crenate-serrate

**Upper/under side:** Shiny dark green and glabrous above; bluish green beneath and often somewhat hairy on the midrib; only the midrib particularly prominent beneath

**Arrangement on the shoot:** Leaves alternate

**Distribution:** In warm places in the hill and montane zones; especially on warm, dry slopes, in open oak and pine woods, in thickets and hedges

1046　**Prunus mahaleb – St Lucie Cherry**
*Deciduous tree 5–10m high with young shoots finely hairy; flowering twigs very fragrant*

### Rhamnus pumila (Turra)
W. Vent
### Dwarf Buckthorn
**Rhamnaceae - Buckthorn family** p. 115

**Length:** 2–5cm

**Form of blade:** Elliptic, obovate or roundish in outline

**Stalk:** 4–9mm long

**End of leaf:** With a short, abrupt point

**Base of blade:** Usually wedge-shaped

**Margin of leaf:** Very finely crenate-serrate

**Upper/under side:** Dark green and glabrous above; paler green beneath and somewhat hairy on the veins, later becoming glabrous; with 4–9 (12) pairs of curved and distinctly prominent lateral veins

**Arrangement on the shoot:** Leaves alternate

**Distribution:** Mainly in the subalpine and alpine zones on bare rocks and in rock-crevices; very suitable for the rock-garden; the stems spread out evenly on rocks like lattice-work

1047　**Rhamnus pumila – Dwarf Buckthorn**
*Deciduous, low-growing shrub, only 10–20cm high*

### Prunus tenella Batsch
### Dwarf Russian Almond
**Rosaceae - Rose family** p. 116

**Length:** 3–7cm

**Form of blade:** Narrowly-elliptic in outline

**Stalk:** 0.5–1.5cm long

**End of leaf:** Pointed

**Base of blade:** Wedge-shaped, narrowing into the stalk

**Margin of leaf:** Finely and regularly serrate/dentate

**Upper/under side:** Shiny dark green above and pale green beneath; both sides glabrous; midrib distinctly prominent

**Arrangement on the shoot:** Leaves alternate

**Distribution:** In the hill zone; amongst deciduous shrubs on dry soils, on dry grassland and in vineyards; distributed from E. Siberia to Hungary and Lower Austria; eating the seeds may produce symptoms of poisoning

1048　**Prunus tenella – Dwarf Russian Almond** *Deciduous, slender-stemmed, erect shrub 1–1.5m high*

### Prunus domestica L.
### ssp. domestica
### Plum
**Rosaceae - Rose family** p. 116

**Length:** 3–10cm

**Form of blade:** Elliptic in outline, or obovate, in which case the greatest breadth is above the middle

**Stalk:** 1–1.5cm long

**End of leaf:** Rounded, obtuse or pointed

**Base of blade:** Narrowly wedge-shaped or at least narrowed

**Margin of leaf:** Finely serrate and crenate

**Upper/under side:** Both sides hairy when young; dark green above and later glabrous; pale green beneath, the long hairs often persistent, and with a prominent midrib

**Arrangement on the shoot:** Alternate on long shoots and arranged in clusters on short shoots

**Distribution:** Planted in gardens in the hill zone

1049　**Prunus domestica – Plum**
*Deciduous tree, native in W. Asia, growing up to 10m high; young shoots reddish brown*

### Rhamnus catharticus L.
### Buckthorn
**Rhamnaceae - Buckthorn family** p. 116

**Length:** 4–7cm

**Form of blade:** Elliptic to roundish in outline

**Stalk:** 1–3cm long and slightly grooved above

**End of leaf:** Usually with a short, abrupt point

**Base of blade:** Broadly wedge-shaped, truncate or rounded

**Margin of leaf:** Finely crenate-serrate

**Upper/under side:** Both sides usually glabrous; dull dark green above and medium bluish green beneath; 2–4 curved lateral veins each side of the midrib

**Arrangement on the shoot:** Leaves opposite or obliquely opposite; each pair at right angles to the next

**Distribution:** From the hill to the montane zone; in sunny hedges, on dry shrubby slopes, on poor pastures and on dry boundaries of woodland

1050　**Rhamnus catharticus – Buckthorn**
*Deciduous shrub up to 3m high with grey to greyish brown stems*

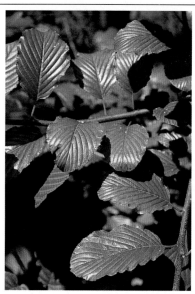

### Rhamnus alpinus L.
### ssp. alpinus
### Alpine Buckthorn
**Rhamnaceae - Buckthorn family** p. 114

**Length:** 5–14cm

**Form of blade:** Elliptic to ovate in outline

**Stalk:** 0.8–1.5cm long

**End of leaf:** With a short, abrupt point

**Base of blade:** Rounded or weakly heart-shaped

**Margin of leaf:** Finely serrate; usually crenate in the lower part; teeth in the upper part pointing towards the tip

**Upper/under side:** Shiny dark green and glabrous above; only slightly paler green beneath and usually glabrous; veins beneath distinctly prominent; with 5–20 primary lateral veins on each side of the midrib, curving upwards slightly at the end

**Arrangement on the shoot:** Leaves alternate

**Distribution:** In the montane zone; more rarely in the hill and subalpine zones; in open woods, on rocks, on scree, and in hedges in sunny places

1051　**Rhamnus alpinus – Alpine Buckthorn**
*Deciduous shrub up to 3m high with glabrous, greyish brown stems*

1052   *Prunus serrulata* – Japanese Cherry
*Deciduous tree up to 10m high, with stiffly spreading, glabrous twigs*

### *Prunus serrulata* Lindl.
## Japanese Cherry
**Rosaceae – Rose family** p. 117

**Length:** 8–14cm

**Form of blade:** Narrowly ovate in outline

**Stalk:** 2–4cm long, reddish above, with 2–4 greenish glands just below the point where it joins the blade

**End of leaf:** With a long point

**Base of blade:** Wedge-shaped

**Margin of leaf:** Sharply and regularly serrate

**Upper/under side:** Both sides glabrous; shiny dark green above and bluish green beneath; veins distinctly prominent

**Arrangement on the shoot:** Leaves alternate

**Distribution:** Tree native in China, Korea and Japan, very often planted in gardens

1053   *Prunus padus* – Bird Cherry
*Deciduous shrub or tree up to 6m high with glabrous, greyish brown twigs*

### *Prunus padus* L.
## Bird Cherry
**Rosaceae – Rose family** p. 117

**Length:** 5–12cm

**Form of blade:** Oblong-elliptic to obovate in outline

**Stalk:** Up to 2cm long, red above, and with 1–3 greenish nectar-glands

**End of leaf:** With a fine, slender tip

**Base of blade:** Usually rounded, more rarely truncate or wedge-shaped

**Margin of leaf:** Finely and regularly serrate; teeth shorter than 0.7mm

**Upper/under side:** Both sides glabrous; dull dark green above and pale or bluish green beneath

**Arrangement on the shoot:** Leaves alternate

**Distribution:** From the hill to the montane zone; in damp thickets and woods, gorges, hedges, by rivers and on marshy ground; often associated with ashes, alders and elms

1054   *Prunus cerasus* – Sour Cherry
*Deciduous tree, 5–10m high, with young shoots green, later becoming greyish brown*

### *Prunus cerasus* L.
## Sour Cherry
**Rosaceae – Rose family** p. 117

**Length:** 4–12cm

**Form of blade:** Elliptic to ovate in outline, flat and slightly leathery

**Stalk:** 1–3cm long, with or without green nectar-glands

**End of leaf:** Pointed

**Base of blade:** Broadly wedge-shaped or rounded

**Margin of leaf:** Finely serrate and in places crenate

**Upper/under side:** Shiny dark green and glabrous above; pale green beneath, somewhat hairy and later becoming glabrous; veins distinctly prominent

**Arrangement on the shoot:** Leaves alternate

**Distribution:** Brought into central Europe by the Romans; planted in gardens, often escaping and becoming naturalised; native in S.E. Asia and nowadays with many varieties in cultivation

1055   *Prunus avium* – Wild Cherry
*Deciduous tree up to 25m high; twigs brown, roundish, and with corky lenticels*

### *Prunus avium* L.
## Wild Cherry, Gean
**Rosaceae – Rose family**
p. 46, 47, 118

**Length:** 6–15cm

**Form of blade:** Oblong-elliptic to obovate in outline

**Stalk:** 2–4cm long, with 2–4 red-coloured nectar-glands just below the point where it joins the blade

**End of leaf:** Slender, abrupt point

**Base of blade:** Broadly wedge-shaped, truncate or rounded

**Margin of leaf:** Irregularly serrate

**Upper/under side:** Dark green above, usually somewhat wrinkled and glabrous; paler green beneath and finely hairy when young; with small tufts of hairs in the axils of the larger veins; veins distinctly prominent

**Arrangement on the shoot:** Leaves alternate

**Distribution:** In the hill zone; on the edges of woodland, in mixed deciduous woods, in hedges, deserted vineyards, or on uncultivated meadows and pastures; several varieties known already to the ancient Greeks

1056   *Sorbus chamaemespilus* – False Medlar
*Small, deciduous shrub, 1–3m high; stems felted at first*

### *Sorbus chamaemespilus*
(L.) Crantz
## False Medlar
**Rosaceae – Rose family** p. 117

**Length:** 3–8cm

**Form of blade:** Narrowly elliptic to elliptic in outline and with the greatest breadth usually below the middle

**Stalk:** 0.5–1cm long

**End of leaf:** Obtuse or slightly pointed

**Base of blade:** Broadly wedge-shaped or rounded

**Margin of leaf:** Simply and finely serrate; teeth about 1mm long

**Upper/under side:** Shiny dark green above; paler green beneath; both sides glabrous; forms with leaves felted beneath are hybrids; lateral veins not obviously ending in the teeth; veins distinctly prominent

**Arrangement on the shoot:** Leaves alternate

**Distribution:** In the subalpine zone, more rarely montane; a pioneer shrub; on rocks, scree, pastures, in Mountain Pine, Arolla Pine and Larch woods and in Alpenrose and Green Alder thickets

1057   *Prunus spinosa* – Blackthorn
*Deciduous, stiffly branched, very thorny shrub with young shoots softly hairy*

### *Prunus spinosa* L.
## Blackthorn, Sloe
**Rosaceae – Rose family** p. 116

**Length:** 2–5cm

**Form of blade:** Broadly lanceolate to oblong-elliptic in outline

**Stalk:** 0.5–1.2cm long and often tinged red above

**End of leaf:** Obtuse or shortly pointed

**Base of blade:** Serrate and in places crenate

**Upper/under side:** Hairy when young, later glabrous; dark green above and pale green beneath

**Arrangement on the shoot:** Leaves alternate; short shoots ending in a thorn

**Distribution:** From the hill zone ascending to the montane zone; on sunny rock and scree slopes, the edges of woods, by fences, in vineyards, meadows, hedges and as a pioneer shrub on uncultivated pastures

### Forsythia x intermedia Zab.
(F. suspensa x F. viridissima)
### Hybrid Forsythia
**Oleaceae – Olive family** p. 118

**Length:** 6–11cm

**Form of blade:** Lanceolate to oblong-ovate in outline; sometimes divided into three parts on vigorous long shoots

**Stalk:** 1–2cm long and usually grooved above

**End of leaf:** Pointed

**Base of blade:** Wedge-shaped

**Margin of leaf:** Irregularly serrate or dentate

**Upper/under side:** Dark green above and paler green to pale bluish green beneath; midrib distinctly prominent

**Arrangement on the shoot:** Leaves opposite; stems with layers of pith; solid at the nodes

**Distribution:** Found in Göttingen Botanic Garden in 1878; many forms planted in gardens and parks

1058　*Forsythia x intermedia* – **Hybrid Forsythia** *Deciduous shrub, 2–3m high, with greenish yellow stems*

### Forsythia europaea Deg. et Bald.
### European Forsythia
**Oleaceae – Olive family** p. 118

**Length:** 5–8cm

**Form of blade:** Narrowly elliptic to narrowly ovate in outline

**Stalk:** 0.5–1cm long and grooved above

**End of leaf:** Pointed

**Base of blade:** Wedge-shaped or rounded

**Margin of leaf:** Finely serrate in the upper part except for the tip; usually entire in the lower part

**Upper/under side:** Both sides glabrous; dark green above and paler green beneath

**Arrangement on the shoot:** Leaves opposite; stems with layers of pith

**Distribution:** Shrub, native in N. Albania and S.W. Yugoslavia; horticulturally unimportant and therefore only occasionally planted in gardens

1059　*Forsythia europaea* – **European Forsythia** *Deciduous shrub, 1.5–2.5m high, with stiffly erect, glabrous stems*

### Forsythia viridissima Lindl.
### Green Forsythia
**Oleaceae – Olive family** p. 118

**Length:** 4–14cm

**Form of blade:** Lanceolate to narrowly elliptic in outline

**Stalk:** 0.5–3cm long and usually grooved above

**End of leaf:** Pointed

**Base of blade:** Wedge-shaped

**Margin of leaf:** Usually finely serrate/dentate only in the upper third; otherwise entire

**Upper/under side:** Both sides glabrous; dark green above and pale green beneath

**Arrangement on the shoot:** Leaves opposite; stems with layers of pith throughout

**Distribution:** Ornamental shrub native in China; planted in gardens and parks; not common

1060　*Forsythia viridissima* – **Green Forsythia** *Erect, deciduous shrub, up to 3m high, with greenish, 4-angled stems*

### Euonymus (Evonymus) europaeus L.
### Spindle Tree
**Celastraceae – Spindle Tree family** p.118

**Length:** 3–8cm; 3.5–5cm long on flowering and fruiting stems

**Form of blade:** Elliptic to ovate in outline; greatest breadth in the middle

**Stalk:** 0.5–0.9cm long and grooved

**End of leaf:** With a narrow point

**Base of blade:** Narrowly or broadly wedge-shaped or rounded

**Margin of leaf:** Very finely and regularly serrate; teeth often rounded, therefore the margin appearing crenate in places

**Upper/under side:** Both sides glabrous; medium to dark green above and pale bluish green beneath

**Arrangement on the shoot:** Leaves opposite

**Distribution:** From the hill to the montane zone; in damp and mixed deciduous woods, on the borders of woodland, in hedges, by fences and on the verges of paths

1061　*Euonymus europaeus* – **Spindle Tree** *Deciduous shrub, 3–7m high, with green, angular stems which later become greyish brown*

### Viburnum lantana L.
### Wayfaring Tree
**Caprifoliaceae – Honeysuckle family** p. 116

**Length:** 5–12cm

**Form of blade:** Ovate to oblong-ovate in outline

**Stalk:** Up to 1.5cm long and densely grey-felted

**End of leaf:** Pointed

**Base of blade:** Rounded or weakly heart-shaped

**Margin of leaf:** Regularly and finely toothed

**Upper/under side:** Slightly wrinkled above, medium to dark green and with the veins clearly visible; medium green beneath and densely covered with stellate hairs; both sides rough to the touch; veins beneath distinctly prominent; primary veins ending in the leaf-teeth

**Arrangement on the shoot:** Leaves opposite

**Distribution:** From the hill to the montane zone; in sunny places in hedges, on the edges of woods, and in open oak and pine woods

1062　*Viburnum lantana* – **Wayfaring Tree** *Deciduous shrub, 3–5m high, with young stems densely felted*

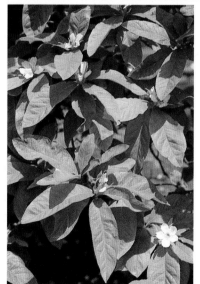

### Mespilus germanica L.
### Medlar
**Rosaceae – Rose family** p. 117

**Length:** 5–12cm

**Form of blade:** Oblong-elliptic to obovate in outline

**Stalk:** Sessile or up to 1cm long

**End of leaf:** Very shortly pointed

**Base of blade:** Usually rounded

**Margin of leaf:** Finely dentate/serrate and in places entire

**Upper/under side:** Dull green above, somewhat downy and slightly wrinkled; pale to greyish green beneath with matted whitish hairs; veins deeply impressed above

**Arrangement on the shoot:** Leaves alternate

**Distribution:** In the hill zone; escaping and becoming naturalised on sunny slopes, in hedges and open woods with Turkey Oak and Downy Oak, or in woodland communities of Hop Hornbeam and Oriental Hornbeam; a shrub with a preference for warm, moist and open situations; the Medlar was used as a fruit-tree by the Greeks

1063　*Mespilus germanica* – **Medlar** *Deciduous, thorny shrub, up to 3m high, with young branchlets loosely felted*

### Arctostaphylos alpinus (L.) Spreng.
## Black Bearberry

**Ericaceae – Heath family** p. 118

**Length:** 1–4cm

**Form of blade:** Spathulate or narrowly obovate in outline and narrowed into the stalk

**Stalk:** Only very shortly stalked

**End of leaf:** Obtuse

**Base of blade:** Very narrowly wedge-shaped

**Margin of leaf:** Finely and closely serrate, entire towards the base; fringed with spreading, white hairs, 0.5–1.5mm long

**Upper/under side:** Dark green above and undulate between the veins; whitish green beneath, with a network of dark green veins

**Arrangement on the shoot:** Leaves alternate

**Distribution:** In the subalpine and alpine zone on dwarf shrub heaths, in Mountain Pine woods, on rocks and on scree

1064 *Arctostaphylos alpinus* – Black Bearberry *Deciduous, creeping and mat-forming dwarf shrub with stems up to 60cm long*

### Salix purpurea L.
## Purple Willow

**Salicaceae – Willow family** p. 119

**Length:** 5–10cm

**Form of blade:** Lanceolate in outline; greatest breadth usually in the upper third

**Stalk:** 0.5–0.8cm long and often tinged reddish

**End of leaf:** Shortly pointed

**Base of blade:** Wedge-shaped and often also slightly rounded

**Margin of leaf:** Finely serrate towards the tip; entire in the lower part; teeth pointing towards the leaf-tip; margin not recurved

**Upper/under side:** Bluish green above, glabrous and with a clearly visible midrib; pale bluish green and glabrous beneath

**Arrangement on the shoot:** Leaves alternate; often also opposite

**Distribution:** From the hill to the subalpine zone; beside paths and on the edges of woods, in thickets, by watercourses, on sandbanks in Alpine rivers and in open pine woods; a pioneer shrub of fresh, wet ground

1065 *Salix purpurea* – Purple Willow *Deciduous shrub, up to 3m high, with young stems reddish brown*

### Salix alba L.
## White Willow

**Salicaceae – Willow family** p. 50, 51, 119

**Length:** 5–10cm

**Form of blade:** Narrowly lanceolate to lanceolate in outline and with narrow stipules at first; uppermost part of blade often curved to one side

**Stalk:** 0.5–1cm long

**End of leaf:** With a fine, slender point

**Base of blade:** Narrowly wedge-shaped

**Margin of leaf:** Finely and regularly serrate/dentate

**Upper/under side:** Both sides covered with dense, appressed, silvery hairs when young; later dark green above and usually glabrous; silvery white hairs remaining beneath; lateral veins rather inconspicuous above

**Arrangement on the shoot:** Leaves alternate

**Distribution:** In the hill zone; in association with poplars, alders and other willows by rivers, streams and lakes, and in damp woods; also on intermittently flooded ground

1066 *Salix alba* – White Willow *Deciduous tree 10–20m high; twigs at first yellowish brown and with appressed hairs*

### Salix fragilis L.
## Crack Willow

**Salicaceae – Willow family** p. 119

**Length:** 5–16cm

**Form of blade:** Oblong-lanceolate in outline; sticky when young; usually broadest in the lower third

**Stalk:** Up to 1cm long and with 2–4 glands

**End of leaf:** With a very long, fine point

**Base of blade:** Narrowly or broadly wedge-shaped

**Margin of leaf:** Coarsely sinuate-serrate; teeth curving inwards; in the typical form the glands are close against the sinuses

**Upper/under side:** Dark green and slightly shiny above; with silky hairs at first beneath, later pale or bluish green and the midrib distinctly prominent; later in the year completely glabrous

**Arrangement on the shoot:** Leaves alternate

**Distribution:** By rivers and in the water-meadows of the hill zone; avoids summer flooding

1067 *Salix fragilis* – Crack Willow *Deciduous shrub or tree up to 15m high; twigs readily breaking off*

### Prunus dulcis
(Mill.) D. A. Webb
## Almond

**Rosaceae – Rose family** p. 119

**Length:** 4–12cm

**Form of blade:** Lanceolate to oblong-elliptic in outline

**Stalk:** 1–2.5cm long

**End of leaf:** Obtuse or pointed

**Base of blade:** Wedge-shaped or rounded

**Margin of leaf:** Very finely serrate/dentate

**Upper/under side:** Medium to dark green above and pale bluish green beneath; both sides glabrous; only the midrib really prominent

**Arrangement on the shoot:** Leaves alternate

**Distribution:** In the hill zone in full sun; one of the oldest cultivated plants in the Mediterranean region; various forms and varieties were already known to the Greeks and Romans; reached China in the 11th century B.C. and Greece about 500 B.C.; main producing countries are Spain, Italy and the U.S.A.

1068 *Prunus dulcis* – Almond *Erect, deciduous shrub or tree up to 10m high with young shoots reddish on the side exposed to the sun*

### Prunus persica (L.) Batsch
## Peach

**Rosaceae – Rose family** p. 119

**Length:** 5–15cm

**Form of blade:** Narrowly to broadly lanceolate in outline

**Stalk:** 0.5–1.5cm long, occasionally with glands

**End of leaf:** With a long point

**Base of blade:** Wedge-shaped

**Margin of leaf:** Finely serrate/dentate

**Upper/under side:** Shiny dark green above and medium green beneath; both sides glabrous; only the midrib beneath distinctly prominent

**Arrangement on the shoot:** Leaves alternate

**Distribution:** Many varieties cultivated in vine-growing regions; prefers warm, dry soils in sunny, sheltered places; the wild form is presumed to have been native in China or western central Asia; grown nowadays in large plantations especially in the Mediterranean region

1069 *Prunus persica* – Peach *Deciduous shrub or small tree, 3–8m high, with shoots red on the side exposed to the sun*

# Glossary of Botanical Terms

Technical terms that cannot be replaced with more elementary language are defined in this Glossary, or interpreted in the Introduction to this book, in which case only a page-reference is given here.

**achene**: a dry, one-seeded fruit
**acuminate**: see p. 15
**acute**: see p. 15
**adult**: see p. 18
**alpine**: see p. 62
**alternate**: see p. 18
**anisophylly**: see p. 18
**anther**: the pollen-bearing organ forming at the end of a stamen
**apiculate**: see p. 15
**appressed**: lying flat and close to
**asymmetrical**: see p. 16
**attenuate**: gradually tapering
**auricle**: an ear-shaped extension at the base of a leaf
**auriculate**: see p. 16
**axil**: the angle between a shoot and a leaf, or between a midrib and a vein
**axillary tuft**: see p. 17
**axis**: see p. 17

**base**: see pp. 11, 16
**bast**: phloem
**bisexual**: hermaphrodite, having both male and female organs in the same flower
**bract**: see p. 11
**bristle-toothed**: see p. 15

**calcareous** (of soil): rich in calcium carbonate (lime)
**calyx**: the sepals collectively
**cambium**: layer of dividing cells between xylem and phloem in a stem
**capsule**: a dry fruit composed of several carpels
**carpel**: the female part of a flower: the ovary, style and stigma collectively
**catkin**: a hanging spike of small, unisexual flowers
**cellulose**: the principal component of plant cell walls
**ciliate**: see p. 15
**cladode**: see p. 11
**colline**: see p. 62
**compound** (of leaf): see p. 17
**cone**: the reproductive structure of a coniferous plant
**connate**: see p. 16
**coppice**: trees whose trunks have been cut off near ground level and which have then grown multiple stems
**corolla**: the petals collectively
**cortex**: cell tissue in a stem or root between the outer cell layer and the vascular tissue
**cotyledon**: see p. 18
**crenate**: see p. 15
**crenate-serrate**: see p. 14
**cuneate**: see p. 16
**cupule**: a cup formed by fused bracts, e.g. acorn cup
**cuspidate**: narrowing abruptly to a point
**cyme**: an often flat or convex inflorescence in which the terminal flower opens first

**deciduous**: see p. 11
**decumbent** (of stems): resting flat on the ground but with the tip rising
**decurrent**: see p. 16
**decussate**: see p. 19
**dentate**: see p. 14
**digitate**: see p. 14
**dioecious**: having male and female flowers on separate plants
**disc**: the fleshy, sometimes nectar-secreting portion of the receptacle
**doubly serrate**: see p.14

**elliptic**: see p. 12
**emarginate**: see p. 15

**entire**: see p. 14
**evergreen**: see p. 11

**fascicled**: see p. 18
**felted**: see p. 17
**fimbriate**: having a fringed margin
**foliage leaf**: see p. 11
**forked**: see p. 19

**glabrous**: without hairs
**glandular**: see p. 14

**hairy**: see p. 17
**heart-shaped**: see pp. 13, 16
**heartwood**: the central core of wood which is dead, even in the living tree
**hermaphrodite**: having both male and female organs in the same flower
**heterophylly**: see p. 18
**heterostyly**: variation in the length of stamens and styles in different flowers within a species
**hill-zone**: see p. 62
**humus**: plant and animal remains in the soil that have lost their cell structure through decomposition

**imbricate**: see p. 19
**imparipinnate**: see p. 17
**indented**: see p. 15
**indigenous**: native
**inflorescence**: flower-cluster

**juvenile**: see p. 18

**kidney-shaped**: see p. 13

**lamina**: see p. 11
**lanceolate**: see p. 12
**leaf**: see p. 11
**leaf base**: see p. 11
**leaf blade**: see p. 11
**leaf stalk**: see p. 16
**leaflet**: a leaf-like part of a compound leaf
**lenticel**: a pore in the corky covering of woody stems
**linear**: see p. 12
**loamy** (of soil): containing an even mixture of different-sized particles
**lobed**: see pp. 15, 17

**margin**: see p. 14
**medulla**: pith
**medullary ray**: the region in a stem where the outer pith meets the inner cortex
**midrib**: see p. 13
**montane**: see p. 62
**mucronate**: see p. 15

**nectary**: a nectar-secreting gland
**needle**: see p. 19
**net**: see p. 13
**node**: see p. 18
**nodule**: a swelling on a root, containing bacteria

**oblanceolate**: see p. 13
**oblique**: see p. 16
**oblong**: see p. 12
**obovate**: see p. 13
**obtuse**: see p. 15
**opposite**: see pp. 18, 19

**orbicular:** see p. 12
**ovary:** the part of the carpel of a flower that contains the ovules
**ovate:** see p. 12 (egg-shaped in 2 dimensions)
**ovoid:** egg-shaped in 3 dimensions
**ovule:** the structure which becomes the seed when fertilised

**palmate:** see pp. 14, 17
**panicle:** a much-branched inflorescence (*cf* raceme, umbel)
**parallel:** see p. 13
**paripinnate:** see p. 17
**perigon** or **perianth:** a collective term for the corolla plus the calyx
**perigynous:** having the sepals, petals and stamens inserted round the ovary on a concave structure developed from the receptacle
**petal:** one of the parts of a flower that surrounds the reproductive organs, collectively known as the corolla
**petiole:** see p. 16
**phloem:** vascular tissue which conducts nutrients made by the leaves to other parts of the plant
**pinnate:** see p. 13
**pinnatifid:** see p. 17
**pinnatipartite:** see p. 17
**pinnatisect:** see p. 17
**pith:** the central tissue of the stems of non-woody plants
**pollard:** a tree whose trunk has been cut off well above ground level (*cf* coppice), and which has then grown multiple stems
**pollen:** minute grains, produced within the anther, each of which gives rise to a male sex cell
**pollination:** the transfer of pollen from male to female reproductive organs
**pore** (in wood): a small hole
**pseudocarp:** a false fruit
**pulvinus:** a swelling on a shoot from which a leaf or its stalk arises

**quadrangular:** see p. 13

**raceme:** an unbranched inflorescence with stalked flowers opening from the base upwards (*cf* panicle, umbel)
**rachis:** the central stalk of a compound leaf, or of an inflorescence
**receptacle:** the swelling at the end of a stalk which bears the flower-parts
**recurved:** see p. 15
**reniform:** kidney-shaped
**reticulate:** marked with a network pattern
**retuse:** see p. 15
**rounded:** see pp. 15, 16

**sapwood:** young secondary xylem which after some years becomes heartwood
**scale:** see p. 11
**scale-leaf:** see p. 11
**schizocarp:** a fruit which breaks into several pieces, each usually one-seeded

**sepal:** one of the parts of a flower, collectively known as the calyx, growing outside the petals
**serrate:** see p. 14
**sessile:** see pp. 11, 16
**shoot:** see pp. 11, 18
**silky:** see p. 17
**simple:** see p. 17
**sinuate:** see pp. 14, 17
**sinuately dentate:** see p. 14
**sinus:** see p. 14
**spathulate:** spatula-shaped, with a broad rounded end and tapering gradually towards the base
**spine:** see p. 16
**spring-toothed:** see p. 15
**stamen:** one of the male organs of a flower, comprising a filament (stalk) and an anther
**staminode:** an imperfectly developed stamen, incapable of producing pollen
**stellate:** branching like a star
**stigma:** the part at the end of the style, on which the pollen alights and germinates
**stipule:** see p. 16
**stoma:** a pore on the surface of a leaf
**style:** the part of a flower which grows from the ovary and carries the stigma
**subalpine:** see p. 62
**sucker** (*verb*): to put up new and separate shoots from existing roots

**terminal leaflet:** see p. 17
**triangular:** see p. 13
**trifoliolate:** see p. 17
**truncate:** see p. 15, 16

**umbel:** an inflorescence whose flowers are borne on stalks growing from about the same point on the stem, resulting in an umbrella shape (*cf* raceme, panicle)
**undulate:** see p. 15

**vascular** (tissue): xylem plus phloem
**vascular bundles:** strands of primary vascular tissue, sandwiched with parenchyma (photosynthetic tissue)
**veining:** see p. 13
**venation:** see p. 13
**villous:** covered with long, soft hairs

**wedge-shaped:** see p. 16
**whorled:** see p. 19
**winter-green:** see p. 19
**woolly:** see p. 17

**xeromorphic:** see p. 19
**xylem:** vascular tissue conducting water and nutrients from roots to other parts of the plant

# Index of Vernacular Names of Trees

## FIELD GUIDE TO THE TREES OF BRITAIN AND NORTHERN EUROPE
**By Alan Mitchell**

40 colour plates by Preben Dahlstron and Ebbe Sunesen and 640 line drawings by Christine Darter

The definitive hardback field guide to 800 species and varieties of trees. The most thorough and respected guide available today, it allows the user to identify with accuracy and become acquainted in the greatest detail with any cultivated or wild tree growing in Europe north of the Mediterranean littoral.

ISBN 0 00 219213 6

*"Superb . . . informative, succinct, clear and magnificently illustrated."* The Times

## TREES OF BRITAIN AND NORTHERN EUROPE
**By Alan Mitchell**

Illustrated by John Wilkinson

The complete paperback pocket tree guide – 288 pages of description and colour illustration, featuring every tree – wild or planted, in woods, hedges and fields, in town streets, parks and gardens – which the reader is likely to find in Britain and Northern Europe. Over 600 species and varieties, with information on every aspect, including the finest specimens of each to be found in the British Isles.

ISBN 0 00 219857 6

## COLLINS GEM GUIDE TO TREES
**By Alistair Fitter**

Illustrated by David More

One of the many titles in the Collins *Gem Nature Guides* series. Nearly 200 trees and shrubs covered, with details of leaf, fruit and bark. Liberally illustrated accounts providing a basic botanical introduction to common species of Britain and Northern Europe. Designed to fit comfortably into even the smallest pocket!

ISBN 0 00 458803 7